The National Forgotten League

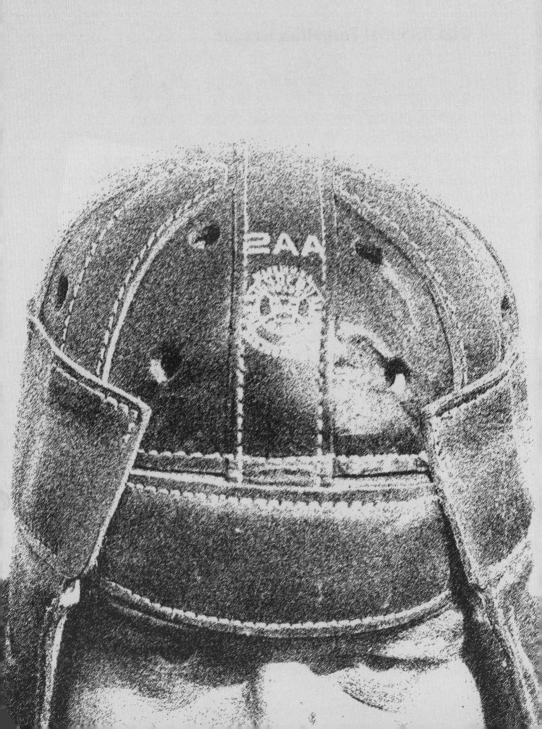

The National Forgotten League

Entertaining Stories and
Observations from Pro Football's
First Fifty Years | DAN DALY

University of Nebraska Press • Lincoln & London

Portions of this book originally appeared, in slightly different form, in the *Washington Times* as "The Unbeatable T" (August 31, 2000), "Bill Belichick's Old Man Was Pretty Amazing, Too" (August 29, 2002), "Smith after Mark with Lots of Past" (October 12, 2002), "Sing Sing Was Tough in the '30s" (May 26, 2005), and "Going Sideways into History" (October 17, 2007).

Library of Congress Cataloging-in-Publication Data

Daly, Dan.
The national forgotten league: entertaining stories and observations from pro football's first fifty years / Dan Daly.
p. cm.
Includes bibliographical references.
ISBN 978-0-8032-4343-9 (pbk.: alk. paper)
1. Football—United States—History.
2. National Football League—History. I. Title.
GV954.D35 2012
796.323'64—dc23
2012007288

Set in Scala.

For Laurel, Danny, Patrick, and Ellen Crahan

Oh, it's a fine game, football—a noble game. Originated in England in 1823. An enterprising young man named William Weber Ellis—who studied for the ministry, by the way—found his team behind in a soccer game, so he picked up the ball and ran through the amazed opponents for a thoroughly illegal touchdown. And that's how football was born—illegitimately. So it moved to America, where someone took advantage of a loophole in the rules and invented a little formation called the Flying Wedge. So many young men were maimed and killed by this clever maneuver that President Roosevelt—Theodore Roosevelt—had to call the colleges together and ask them to make the game less brutal. He was, of course, defeated in the next election.—Football coach Steve Williams (played by John Wayne) in the 1953 film *Trouble Along the Way*

Contents

Preface • xi

Acknowledgments • xv

1. The 1920s • 1
2. The 1930s • 63
3. The 1940s • 157
4. The 1950s • 247
5. The 1960s • 315

Afterword • 377

Appendix • 385

A Note about Sources • 395

Bibliography • 397

Preface

Welcome to the last twenty years of my life.

That's how long I've spent gathering material for *The National Forgotten League*—just because, well, *somebody* had to. It's always amazed me how little literary attention has been paid to pro football's early days. Baseball historians have put the game under a microscope. There's probably a book out there that'll tell you what Babe Ruth ate for breakfast on the day he swatted his 714th home run.

The story of the NFL's formative years, on the other hand, is still largely untold. Not that there isn't a good reason for this. Newspaper coverage was sparse in the first few decades; there simply wasn't much reportage beyond the games. So it's hard to get a real feel for what pro football was like in that period—and even harder to learn much about the players and personalities who helped lift the league out of the primordial swamp.

Good luck, for instance, finding an article in *any* 1930s publication about John "Bull" Doehring, the Bears quarterback who could throw a ball 60 yards behind his back. If you want to write about Doehring—or any number of other subjects in this book—you have to do it brick by brick, gathering information here (game accounts), there (interviews with teammates), and everywhere (team media guides, the odd mention in the paper). There are no shortcuts.

Which is why *The National Forgotten League* was so long in the making. In the past two decades, I've read everything I could get my hands on about the NFL's first half century—long-ago-published books, miles of newspaper microfilm, archival material at the Pro Football Hall of Fame. I've also talked to scores of players from the distant past . . . and gone to great lengths to come up with sound bites from people like Joe Carr, who served as NFL commissioner (1921–38) longer than any man except Pete Rozelle. Up to now, the game's early days have been a silent movie. I'm trying to turn them into a talkie.

To me, the first fifty years aren't just Where It All Began, they're Where It All Happened. You had football evolving from a ponderous running-and-kicking game into an explosive passing game. You had the invention of the modern T formation, which revolutionized offense (and rendered the single wing obsolete). You had the NFL surviving the Depression, the Second World War, and two pitched battles with rival leagues—the All-America Conference in the late '40s and the American Football League in the '60s. You had expansion to the west (Los Angeles, San Francisco, et al.), south (Atlanta, Miami, et al.), and in between (Dallas, Minnesota, et al.). You had blacks returning to pro football after being excluded from 1934 to '45. And you had television making the game more accessible—and profitable—than anyone could have dreamed.

It was also an era of ideas. In 1929 the Orange Tornadoes thought it would be cool to put *letters* on jerseys instead of numbers. Can you imagine that happening today? On a frigid December afternoon in 1942, Packers coach Curly Lambeau kept the Packers' subs in the locker room, all nice and warm, instead of having them freeze their butts off on the sideline. Can you imagine *that* happening today? In the first fifty years of pro football, people tried things—lots of things, just about *anything*.

The decades since have been—how shall I put this?—entertainingly anticlimactic. Once the NFL and AFL became a single entity in 1970, it all changed. When a sport ceases to have competition, it loses something—its creative edge, maybe. That's why this book ends with 1969. At that point the party, in my mind, was over. Pro football will never again be as fascinating as it was from the '20s to the '60s. It's all about *maintaining* success now, protecting everybody's investment. And that breeds conservatism. The league moves so slowly these days that it took *thirty-six years* to fix the obviously flawed overtime rules (for the playoffs, at least). If the AFL were still around, prodding the NFL into being better, the correction would have come much sooner.

Anyway, that's my story, and I'm sticking to it.

My goal in *The National Forgotten League* isn't to be encyclopedic. The format, in fact, is more like a scrapbook, one that tells the story of the game through selected events, individuals, sidelights, and statistics. The idea is to "run to daylight," to delve into areas that have been largely ignored by historians — such as the evolution of soccer-style kicking or the awful secret carried around by Sid Luckman, the Bears Hall of Fame quarterback.

Each chapter has several common elements, starting with an information box (giving you a brief snapshot of the decade) and including a Top Ten list (e.g., "Ten Great Players Who Never Played in the NFL"), a Number of the Decade, and the What I've Learned feature — inspired by the one in *Esquire* magazine — in which a player, coach, or league figure expounds on his life and the game.

Beyond that, you're liable to find just about anything between these covers (even shameless name-dropping references to Bill Murray, Errol Flynn, Eva Braun, and Dr. Sam Sheppard). I've tried to make the book as unpredictable as a game — if such a thing is possible. When you turn the page, you shouldn't have the slightest clue what's on the other side.

Let other pro football histories bill themselves, however dubiously, as "the complete story." Think of *The National Forgotten League* as all the stories "the complete story" left out. And as you'll see, there are many.

Acknowledgments

So many people were so helpful during the writing of this book. As always, Pete Fierle and Saleem Choudhry at the Pro Football Hall of Fame rolled out the red carpet and gave me the run of their archives. They were terrific, too, about digging up old game tapes so I could watch, say, the Giants' Nello Falaschi plunge his cleats into an opponent's chest to break up the wedge on a kickoff.

Special thanks, also, to the staff at the Library of Congress. The folks in the newspaper reading room were good enough to fetch me armfuls of microfilm whenever I asked. Take it from me, the library is one of the most fabulous resources this country has.

Rob Taylor, my editor at the University of Nebraska Press, believed in this book from the start and did much to make sure it got into print. I'm grateful for his efforts, and especially for giving me the leeway to write the kind of unconventional history I wanted to write. I'm also appreciative of the fine work done by the staff at the press and of the feedback given by the two (mystery) peer reviewers who read the manuscript.

I came to Rob at the encouragement of John Schulian, who sang his praises and thought the University of Nebraska Press might be more receptive to my idea than other publishers. John's the hidden hero in all this. If he hadn't pointed the way, this project might still be on the drawing board.

I'm indebted as well to my volunteer copy editors — my son Danny,

Mark Vershbow, Bob Cohn, and Dick Heller—for poring over these pages and helping to make them better.

And God bless Dave Kindred for trying his darnedest to set me up with an agent. (Alas, I flew solo on this one.)

A wide range of football folk, from front-office officials to fans, generously opened their doors to a total stranger—or spent hours on the phone—and shared their football memories. All are listed in the bibliography, but I wanted to single out a handful for going above and beyond: Sammy Baugh, Steve Belichick, Jim Black, Tom Keane, Ray Kemp, Emmett Mortell, Derrell Palmer, Joe Perry, Ede Prendergast, and Hal Van Every. Few of them were still living by the time I finished the book, and that pains me, because they added so much to it.

Finally, my family—Laurel, my infinitely tolerant wife, and Danny and Patrick, who make their dad so proud—gave me my space and were a constant source of support. I do this for me, but I do it for them, too. I hope they know that.

1.
The
1920s

1920s

NFL	1920	1929
Champion	Akron Pros	Green Bay Packers
Franchises	14	12
Roster size	At least 11	18
Teams with a player-coach	11	9
Games per season	Anywhere from 1 to 13	Anywhere from 6 to 19
Points per game	15.7	19.2
Shutouts	36 (40 games)	47 (71 games)
Ties	7	10
0–0 ties	5	6
Run/pass TD ratio	46 run, 19 pass	102 run, 80 pass
Hall of Fame players	8	10
Hall of Fame coaches	1	3

Hall of Famers who played in 1920 (8): E Guy Chamberlin, HB Paddy Driscoll, HB Joe Guyon, T Ed Healey, T Fats Henry, HB Fritz Pollard, HB Jim Thorpe, C George Trafton.

Hall of Fame coaches in 1920 (1): George Halas (Bears).

Hall of Famers who played in 1929 (10): Driscoll, QB Benny Friedman, T Cal Hubbard, G Walt Kiesling, T Link Lyman, HB Johnny (Blood) McNally, G Mike Michalske, FB Ernie Nevers, HB Ken Strong, Trafton.

Hall of Fame coaches in 1929 (3): Jimmy Conzelman (Providence Steam Roller), Halas, Curly Lambeau (Packers).

Talking Points

• As you can see, this was the, uh, Fun Decade. Shutouts were epidemic, scoreless ties far too common, and touchdown passes . . . well, put it this way: In 1920, the year the NFL was launched (as the American Professional Football Association), there were nineteen thrown in forty games—about one every other game. Thrilling.

Of course, there was a reason for that: The game was screwed up—or rather, the rules were. Passes had to be thrown from at least 5 yards behind the line of scrimmage, which made them easier to diagnose, and you got *penalized* if a pass was unsuccessful. An incompletion resulted in the loss of a down, and an incompletion in the end zone cost you possession of the ball.

• On top of that, the ball was fatter—designed more for kicking than for throwing. And since this was the single-platoon era, with many players playing sixty minutes, energy conservation was a major concern. Nobody was too anxious to wear himself out running pass routes all day.

As the decade progressed, though, the forward pass became more prominent. It was still a low-scoring, grind-it-out game, sure, but in 1929 there were more TD passes (eighty) than games played (seventy-one), so things were beginning to loosen up a bit.

• All this makes the 1929 New York Giants pretty miraculous. The Giants scored 312 points that season, an average of 20.8 per game. The other eleven clubs averaged 8.3.

Here's something that's even more amazing, though: the Giants were responsible for *23.2 percent* of the league's scoring output (1,344); one out of every four points, roughly, was the work of Benny Friedman and company. To put this in perspective, when the 1950 Rams averaged an all-time record 38.8 points, their total (466) represented only 13 percent of the league's scoring. When the 2007 Patriots put up an all-time record 589 points, their total represented only 5.3 percent of the league's scoring.

How did the Giants do it, you ask? For starters, Friedman threw twenty touchdown passes, an outrageous number for that period. He also had an all-NFL fullback in Tony Plansky, who rushed for eight TDs and scored more points (sixty-two) than four teams. It helped, too, that the Giants played fifteen games, several more than most clubs. (Back then you could play as many as you could squeeze in.) Still, you could make the argument that—relative to their time—the Giants had the greatest offense in NFL history. The 1929 New York Giants. Think about that.

OK, that's enough thinking. On with the show . . .

Game Day in the 1920s

Jim Black grew up on Staten Island and followed the NFL's Stapletons in the 1920s and '30s, before and during their years in the league. I was lucky enough to bump into him later in life, when he was living just up the road from me in Bethesda, Maryland. We talked many times about pro football's early days, and Jim even typed up some recollections for me once. What it was like to be a Stapes fan:

> I was the visiting clubhouse boy. Actually, "clubhouse" doesn't accurately describe it. A bungalow is what it was—a little bungalow that didn't have any heat. There were two dressing rooms, separated by a plasterboard partition. You couldn't talk in a normal voice because everything you said could be heard on the other side of the wall. So everybody whispered or used gestures. It didn't matter much, though, because coaches never had much to say in those days. Teams used maybe a half-dozen basic plays with variations.
>
> Long wooden benches lined each wall. A potbellied coal stove was used to heat the water for the single shower stall. Half the guys didn't even bother to take a shower after the game because they didn't want

to wait. Before one game, Verne Lewellen of the Packers gave me fifty cents to buy him two packs of cigarettes. I'm still waiting for the tip.

Thompson Stadium, the Stapes' home field, was built, owned and operated by the man who owned the lumber yard next door. A narrow dead-end street led up to the stadium, which consisted of unpainted plank stands and was enclosed by a high wooden fence. A little, roped-off walkway ran between the stands and the field and served as a re-straining area. That was all that separated the fans from the players.

The Stapletons sold season tickets for three dollars a pop. It was just a ticket with numbers printed on it. As you went through the gate the ticket was punched. Not many season tickets were sold, though, because none of the seats were reserved. Besides, general admission was only a dollar, and there was never a sellout. Anybody who came to the game with a buck got in. There was always room for one more.

The ticket sellers stood in booths the size of telephone booths in the middle of the street approaching the stadium. The two entrances were manned by two ticket takers facing each other. They were usu-ally the roughest-looking characters in town. There were no turnstiles, and as the patrons would present their tickets they would get stared at in a suspicious manner. You couldn't blame the ticket takers. They were probably still mad from the last game, which had been seen by eight thousand fans even though only six thousand or seven thousand had paid to get in.

It wasn't too tough to crash the gate. Climbing the fence was the hard way. It was much easier to wait until the takers were overwhelmed by the crush of the crowd, and just squeeze your way in. Of course, an-other way was to get a friend with a ticket to start an argument with the taker and distract him.

It was common back then for male fans, who made up the vast ma-jority of the crowd, to stop off at a speakeasy on the way to the stadium and buy a bottle. That was about all a fan took to a game — himself and his bottle. There was no team paraphernalia to wear or wave. Af-ter they emptied their bottles, fans would drop them down through the stands, and there would be the continual sound of broken glass.

As the game progressed, the effects of bathtub gin would become plainly noticeable. Drunks would drift out of the stands and wander aimlessly up and down the narrow aisles, and now and then a well-plastered fan would attempt to stagger across the field.

The Stapleton scoreboard was quite a thing for its day. It was one of the first to tell you what yard line the ball was on, what down it was and how many yards were needed for the first down. Here's how it worked: Bugs Avery, a local mailman, would position himself along the sideline wherever the action was. As soon as a play was over, Bugs would signal to someone standing in front of the scoreboard in the end zone — either by tapping his head or chest or otherwise wigwagging. The man running the scoreboard would then post the information by hanging up numbers. There was also a scoreboard clock that was operated by moving the hand on the clock face. Fans didn't pay much attention to it, though, because it was so unreliable, especially when the visiting team was knocking on the door with very little time remaining.

One day the Duluth Eskimos came to Staten Island. Their uniforms were all white. Eskimos — snow — see? Anyway, they'd put leather strips on either side of their jerseys so it looked like everybody had a football tucked under their arm. The Stapes made 'em turn the jerseys around. It held the game up for about an hour.

There was no full-time grounds crew. When they needed to get the field in shape, they'd bring over some workers from the lumber yard next door. Getting a wet field in shape basically involved dumping loads of sand in the puddles. And there were plenty of wet fields, because there was no tarpaulin. But only once was a game ever called on account of the weather, and that was when — after a week of snow — a blizzard hit on the day of the game. Even so, many fans showed up and thought the game should be played, the snow drifts notwithstanding.

Beany Bramhall was the Stapleton cheerleader. The team had one cheer, which consisted of spelling out S-T-A-P-E-S. Helping Beany were six men wearing black sweaters with a single letter on the front. If they lined up properly — which wasn't always the case — they would spell out "Stapes." Beany would take the guys to a section of the grandstand, point to each letter, and the crowd would shout out the letter.

Rarely would a team have an experienced trainer. Sometimes the assistant coach would double as the trainer, but if not . . . anyone given custody of the first-aid kit was the trainer-of-the-day. A severely injured player would be dragged to the sideline—no stretchers were used—and laid out in front of the bench or taken to the hospital. Players on visiting teams were hardly ever held over for observation, though. They usually went home with their teammates, even if they had to be carried.

After the game, the players would play craps in the bungalow. I once saw [the Stapes'] Doug Wycoff lose his entire salary—eighty dollars—on one roll.

Officiating, 1920

In the first game between the Decatur Staleys and the Chicago Tigers in 1920, Decatur's opening kickoff caromed off the crossbar and back onto the field, where one of the Staleys grabbed it and ran into the end zone. According to the *Decatur Review*, "Referee Thomas first called it a touchdown, but was soon convinced by the Tigers that it was a touchback."

Going Topless

Pudge Heffelfinger, the original pro football player, thought helmets were "sissy stuff." Duke Osborn, the ol' Canton Bulldog, was similarly scornful—and donned his lucky baseball cap instead.

Were these guys nuts or what?

They weren't alone, either. All kinds of players went bareheaded in the early years—for all kinds of reasons.

Bert Shurtleff, a lineman with Providence and Boston in the '20s, said he just plain "didn't like those helmets. In those days they barked the signals [rather than huddling], and I couldn't hear a thing with that darn thing over my ears."

Swede Johnston, a back with the Packers (among others) in the '30s, was convinced "I could run better" without a headgear. And

Dick Plasman, an end with the Bears and Cardinals in the '40s, ditched his helmet because whenever he looked up to catch a pass, "the flap always fell down over my eyes so that I couldn't follow the flight of the ball. . . . One day, after a pass bounced off my chest, [George] Halas said I wouldn't have to wear a helmet anymore."

Other players were what you might call selectively helmetless. Kickers like the Giants' Jack McBride and the Redskins' Bo Russell, for instance, would remove their headgear before booting the ball. (They did this, I'm guessing, for the same reason Plasman did: Leather helmets didn't always fit snugly, and they didn't want them to slide over their eyes when they looked down.)

Then there's this description of Frankford Yellow Jackets back Jack Finn in 1924: "Finn . . . always rushes into the game with a headgear and the best intentions in the world of keeping it on. But as soon as he gets one real hard bump, off comes the head piece and Finn settles down to playing football furiously."

Finally, a player might rid himself of his helmet because the weather was so blasted hot. That's what Fritz Pollard did during Akron's 1926 opener against Frankford.

Red Corzine, a teammate of Johnston's in St. Louis, once told me, "These guys who didn't wear helmets, they just wanted to show people they were he-men. You showed your manhood in those days." And there's some truth to that, no doubt. But clearly there were other factors involved. It wasn't just a macho thing.

And anyway, if Plasman hadn't been driving with the top down, as it were, he might not have been knocked cold when he ran into the Wrigley Field wall while chasing a pass in 1938. And if he hadn't been knocked cold, he wouldn't have met the woman of his dreams in the hospital—the nurse who kept him supplied with aspirin.

"We got married a few years after that," he later said. "It took her a while to make up her mind."

(Worse, from that day forward, according to Plasman, whenever they disagreed, his wife would be sure to say, "You know something? You never did recover from that head injury.")

Frankford's Mike Gulian might have come up with the best excuse of all for playing without a helmet. One day in 1924, after a teammate caught a punt against the Cleveland Bulldogs, Gulian took off his headgear, tucked it under his arm, and pretended *he* had the ball. Some of the Bulldogs were so confused they began chasing him—and the real returner got far downfield before he was finally tackled.

Plasman is generally credited with being the last bareheaded player in the NFL—in 1941. After that he went into the service for two years, and while he was gone the league made helmets mandatory. But he wasn't the only player that season, I've discovered, who was running around without a headgear. So were Redskins guard Vic Carroll and back Andy Farkas (as the tape of their November 23 game against the Giants, stored away at the Hall of Fame, shows). Plasman might be the "last" simply because the Bears played in the '41 title game and the Redskins didn't.

No discussion of the last helmetless pro football player would be complete without mentioning CFL legend Annis Stukus. In 1951, a decade after Plasman played, Stukus kicked for the Edmonton Eskimos without wearing headgear or shoulder pads. It's quite a tale.

Stukus, you see, had been retired for several years and was the Eskimos' coach and general manager. But then the regular kicker got hurt, and Annis was pressed into service. He waved off padding of any kind, though, "because it was my intention," he said, "to get the hell out of there once I kicked the ball."

But in the playoffs against Winnipeg, Stukus had a field goal try blocked, and the ball bounced past him toward the Edmonton goal. The *Canadian Press* described the action thusly: "The bareheaded, padless Stukus was a valiant figure as he pitted his 37-year-old legs against young Tommy Lumsden in the race for the ball. No one else was near it. Stukus was about to drop on the ball at the Edmonton 40 when Lumsden pushed him from behind and was penalized for interference. Lumsden was a cinch for a touchdown if he had reached the ball first."

It was the biggest play of the game. The Eskimos won the low-scoring battle by just three points (their margin being a 10-yard Stukus field goal).

Stukus, by the way, was also known for wearing a wristwatch while kicking—a wristwatch, but no helmet or shoulder pads. Go figure.

Practically Neighbors

One of pro football's lovelier coincidences is that Red Smith, the celebrated sports columnist, was born and raised in Green Bay, Wisconsin. It's a shame Red didn't hang around and chronicle Curly Lambeau's Packers—or at the very least, produce a nostalgic masterpiece like Bill Gildea's *When the Colts Belonged to Baltimore*. Because he didn't, an early history of the franchise, *The Green Bay Packers*, wound up being written by Arch Ward, sports editor of the *Chicago Tribune*. Sacrilege.

Smith lived only a few blocks from Hagemeister Park, where the Packers played their first games. He and Lambeau both graduated from East High School—as did future Four Horseman Jim Crowley, who was just a grade ahead of Red (or "Brick," as he was called in those days).

Growing up in such a heroic environment, how could Smith not have been a sportswriter?

Just out of curiosity, I decided to find out how far Red's house was from Lambeau's. If MapQuest is to be believed, it was about a mile—0.97 mile to be exact—from 1535 Morrow Street (the Smith manse) to 1173 East Walnut Street (Curly's home in 1918).

After Red's career had taken him to New York—to the *Herald Tribune* and then the *Times*—he would occasionally do a column on his Olde Towne Team. Here are a few lines from one that ran before the 1960 championship game, lines that only a Green Bay native could have written:

For a city of modest size, Green Bay is ordinarily a lively place. Drop into Honey's Tavern any night for a beer and a plate of fried perch, or maybe bay crabs boiled in dill, and you can depend on finding a gay and knowledgeable crowd. Right now, though, it's the dullest spot west of Singapore — with 52,000 people in town and only one topic of conversation.

A pretty sure way for a stranger to get himself slugged is to mention to the gang in Cropsey's Bar that he comes from New York. The boys in Cropsey's do not care deeply for New York at the moment. They've heard the Giants want to steal Vince Lombardi, their coach. Nothing has roused Green Bay so much since the night they cracked the Farmers' Exchange Bank.

Funny thing is, the Packers actually had a player named Red Smith in the late '20s — a squatty back who later coached under Lambeau for several seasons. In fact, Red Smith the football player went to Notre Dame with Red Smith the writer.

The football-playing Red Smith knew how to handle himself. A 1928 story in the *Sheboygan Press* refers to his "slam bang tactics" in one game. He also played Major League Baseball briefly and, as a coach with the Chicago Cubs, once got himself fined $150 and suspended for five days for "using his bulk to keep other players and policemen from stopping [a] fight" (in the words of the *United Press*).

The sportswriting Red Smith, not as physically blessed, was content to let his typewriter do his talking. You just wish he'd done more of it about the Packers, the team of his youth.

Chase Scene

In the climactic game of the 1921 season between the Chicago Staleys and Buffalo All-Americans, Dutch Sternaman kicked a field goal late in the third quarter to break a 7–7 tie and give George Halas his first NFL championship.

What happened next, though, was almost better.

Play was held up for "three or four minutes" after Sternaman's boot, the *Decatur Review* reported—and no, it wasn't because fans spilled onto the field and started celebrating.

"Dutch drove the ball over the [Wrigley Field] wall, and some kid made away with it," the newspaper said. "Five minutes later a big copper came in at the bleacher gate with the kid and the ball. The ball was put in use while John Law marched the kid up to headquarters. They are sure there when it comes to catching boys."

New Letterhead

The National Football League wasn't always called the National Football League. In the first two years of its existence it was known as the American Professional Football Association. The reason for the change?

"The other name stunk," Bears boss George Halas explained.

Best Touchdown Celebration

The 1922–23 Oorang Indians were exactly that—a team made up of Native Americans, the most famous being Jim Thorpe. They had a fullback named Eagle Feather and a left tackle named Lone Wolf.

A *Chicago Tribune* sportswriter once had great fun at the expense of Long Time Sleep, the Indians' center. "Long Time Sleep . . . then dozed off and made a bad pass," he wrote. And later: "[The Bears'] Sternaman and Knop carried the ball to the visitors' 20-yard line, where Sternaman fumbled and Long Time Sleep awakened in time to recover."

The Bears licked the Indians pretty soundly both years, 33–6 and 26–0. In the fourth quarter of the '22 game, though, Thorpe managed to spoil the shutout by crashing over for a touchdown. The *Decatur Review* described the spectacle that followed: "Six Dakota braves, garbed in war bonnets and paint, who had put on some dances before the [game], ran on the field and gloatingly went through an original snake dance."

Best of all, there was no penalty flag. The term "excessive celebration" hadn't found its way into the NFL rulebook yet.

Before Michael Vick

According to Andy Lotshaw, the Bears' longtime trainer, end Duke Hanny and tackle Ed Healey "both had a bulldog. They would tie them to the radiator in the clubhouse and bet which could whip the other. Invariably, before the dogfight was decided, Healey and Hanny would be fighting, and I mean battling."

Ten Sportswriters Who Officiated NFL Games

Stan Baumgartner, *Philadelphia Inquirer*

Ed Cochrane, *Chicago American*

Walter Eckersall, *Chicago Tribune*

Irv Kupcinet, *Chicago Times*

Tiny Maxwell, *Philadelphia Evening Public Ledger*

Paul Menton, *Baltimore Evening Sun*

John B. Old, *Los Angeles Herald Express*

Jack Reardon, *New York Times*

Gus Rooney, *Boston Traveler*

Wilfrid Smith, *Chicago Tribune*

Notes

Smith (1920–25, mostly with the Cardinals) and Kupcinet ('35 Eagles) played in the NFL. . . . College football's Maxwell Trophy is named for Tiny, who weighed in at three hundred pounds. Ring Lardner once wrote of him, "Any trouble arises, Tiny just falls on it and irons it out." . . . Cochrane was the umpire in the 1937 and '39 NFL title games, and Kupcinet was the linesman in the '40 game. They often worked on the same crew during the regular season. . . . Early in his career, when he was with the *Kansas City Journal*, Cochrane was assaulted by a Minor League Baseball player who took exception to some of his columns. The case went to court, and the judge hit the player with a whopping ten-dollar fine. . . . Baumgartner pitched in the Major League at the age of nineteen. His best season was 1924, when he won thirteen games for Connie Mack's

Philadelphia A's and had an ERA of 2.88, fourth best in the American League. . . . Menton's whistle blowing wasn't confined to football. He also refereed the title game of the 1944 NCAA basketball tournament (won by Utah over Dartmouth in overtime, 42–40). . . . Rooney made a bit of radio history in 1926 when he did the play-by-play for the first Boston Red Sox game to go out over the airwaves. . . . Old, near as can be determined, was the last sportswriter-official. He was still doing games in the All-America Conference in 1946. The next time you watch *Pride of the Yankees*, keep an eye out for him. He has a cameo as a reporter.

Headline of the Decade

"Grid Player Chokes to Death on Wad [of] Tobacco."

The unfortunate player was Chester Mares, a twenty-three-year-old fullback for a semipro team in Willoughby, Ohio, in 1923. According to the *Associated Press* Mares had just released a pass when a defender drilled him. As he fell to the turf "a wad of tobacco became lodged in his throat. Efforts of physicians on the field to prevent death failed."

Of course, football players, being football players, went right on chewing tobacco during games. Luckily, nobody else, as far as I know, ever suffered the same fate.

• • •

The first forward pass ever thrown must have been tossed by a broken-down back too tired to run. — Steve Van Buren, Eagles Hall of Fame running back

• • •

Sports Medicine, 1920s-Style

The summer before the 1921 season George Halas, the Chicago Staleys' (soon to be Bears) legendary player-coach, started having trouble with his knee. So off he went to Youngstown, Ohio, to "spend a few days with Bonesetter Reese," the *Decatur Daily Review* reported.

Doc Reese was the Dr. James Andrews of his time . . . except for one thing: He didn't have a medical degree—just the know-how he'd picked up observing lay healers in the steel mills of his native Wales. But he was such a miracle worker that the Ohio legislature granted him special permission to do, well, whatever it was he did.

John D. Reese functioned much as a chiropractor or physical therapist might today, manipulating bones and muscles until he achieved the desired effect. Countless athletes sought him out to cure what ailed them—nonathletes, too. Indeed, traveling to Youngstown could be like making a pilgrimage to Lourdes. There was something almost mystical about the man with the "million-dollar hands," as newspapers described them.

"Large, sinewy and knotty, they are the sort you'd expect to see upon a steel worker," Bill Jones wrote in the *Syracuse Herald*.

The very sight of them created the impression of power, but gives no hint of the wonderful delicacy of touch that enables him to locate instantly a displaced muscle or a tiny broken bone.

A callus on the knuckle of each middle finger is [indicative] of the great number of cases Reese has treated. These calluses, about the size of a five-cent piece, and as hard as a stone, are the result of his bone-setting practice. It is with the knuckles of his middle finger that Reese forces broken bones together. These calluses, his sensitive fingers, and powerful arms and shoulders are his only instruments.

Halas went to Bonesetter several times over the years to fix various hurts—of both the football and baseball kind. (George was a good enough outfielder to get a brief trial with the New York Yankees.) The Doc was renowned for his ability to revive pitching arms; Cy Young, Ed Walsh, and Smoky Joe Wood all sought out his services, as did boxers, jockeys, and circus acrobats.

Once, David Lloyd George, the British prime minister (and a fellow Welshman), showed up at Reese's door, complaining of strain caused by shaking so many hands on his U.S. tour. Bonesetter cured him with a "gentle handshake and quick wrench," according to *Time* magazine. (Another of the Doc's patients was the daughter of Charles W. Fairbanks, Teddy Roosevelt's vice president.)

Reese generally avoided publicity, though, despite his occasional mention in *Time*. In a rare interview in 1913 he said, "I despise notoriety, and I don't know what I can say that will be of interest. I know very few ballplayers. While it is true enough that I have treated hundreds of them, I rarely ask a player's name. In fact, I haven't asked a man his name since 1908."

But then, there was little about Reese that was orthodox. He didn't, for instance, charge his patients set fees. "If you feel like giving me something," he would tell them, "whatever you like will be all right." Thus payment could range from a ten-cent cigar to a luxury car. No one was ever turned away from 219 Park Avenue. At his peak, he saw eighty patients a day.

Among the healed was a young girl named Elma H. Wilkins, who wrote about the experience years later in the *Washington Post*. The picture she painted: "My father and I boarded the Youngstown train. We found ourselves members of a little army of cripples. Some hobbled and leaned heavily on canes; others slumped still more heavily between crutches. There seemed a sort of 'misery-loves-company' spirit among us. Before long we became acquainted, and spent the time telling stories about the different accidents which had brought us together on that particular train."

Sitting in the waiting room outside Reese's office gave you the willies, Wilkins reminisced. "Nerve-racking shrieks" were intermittently heard through the door, and patients wondered what on earth was going on in there. But then a girl, on crutches not long before, walked happily out with her mother — the first of a "succession of miracles" performed by the Doc.

In 1921, when Halas paid him a visit, Bonesetter was sixty-six years old. His hair — what was left of it — had turned white, and his bushy moustache, round features, and ruddy complexion gave him an avuncular look. His wife, Sarah, had passed away in 1914, but he had five daughters to dote on him. The youngest, Gertrude, was said to have inherited his gift for healing.

Reese never entirely understood athletes. He and his daughter attended to them "night and day, getting the ballplayers' muscles and bones fixed up," he said in 1927. "Then we turn them back to the leagues in perfect condition and go off to recuperate from our strenuous efforts while they are getting themselves smashed up again."

It particularly vexed him that he would prescribe rest for a player and "the next day I would pick up the paper and see his name in the box score." By the end of his life he had stopped treating athletes, he claimed—though some, no doubt, still sneaked unannounced into his office. His celebrity had raised expectations so high, he said, that players would "feel that I should guarantee a sure cure. I have enough work to keep me busy without treating [them]."

When Bonesetter died in 1931, testimonials poured forth. Nobody "could unkink snarled muscles and joints and break and reset broken fingers" quite like Reese, said syndicated columnist Westbrook Pegler. The Doc "contributed to the fame of Youngstown . . . almost as Schlitz contributed to the renown of Milwaukee."

Believe It or Not!

For athletes in the early twentieth century, being featured in a *Ripley's Believe It or Not!* cartoon—a hugely popular newspaper feature—was like making *Sports Illustrated*'s "Faces in the Crowd" today . . . or maybe the *SportsCenter* Top 10. A number of NFL players (and future NFLers) got the Ripley nod for various feats on and off the field. The ones I've come across:

• October 22, 1923—HOGE WORKMAN of Ohio State (1924, 1931 Cleveland Bulldogs/Indians, 1932 New York Giants) "made a 100-yard punt against [the University of] Chicago" in 1922. (How did he manage *that*, you ask? Well, according to one account, he boomed one "from his own goal line" that "roll[ed] across the Chicago goal, a distance of 100 yards.")

• October 30, 1925—RED GRANGE (1925, 1928–34 Chicago Bears, 1926–27 New York Yankees) "averaged 10 yards gain each time that he carried the ball in 1924" for Illinois. Stats: 244 touches, 2,444 yards.

• December 9, 1925—HARLAN CARR (1927 Buffalo Bisons/Pottsville Maroons) "scored a touchdown, a field goal, a safety and kicked a goal after touchdown" in Syracuse's 16–5 win over Columbia in 1925. (Turns out he scored the safety for the *other* team. Rather than punt from the end zone in the late going, he took the snap and "grounded the ball intentionally," the *New York Times* reported.)

• December 9, 1925—GRATTAN O'CONNELL (1926 Hartford Blues, 1927 Providence Steam Roller) "played 35 consecutive games of football" at Boston College. "He asked for time out twice." (The date, by the way, is not a misprint. Carr and O'Connell were actually included in the same cartoon.)

• November 20, 1926—HOUSTON STOCKTON (1925–26, 1928 Frankford Yellow Jackets, 1929 Boston Bulldogs/Providence Steam Roller) "threw forward passes for average gains of 136 yards a game" as Gonzaga's quarterback in 1923.

• March 16, 1927—BRICK MULLER (1926 Los Angeles Buccaneers) "caught a football dropped from the top of a 25-story building" in San Francisco.

• October 29, 1929—SWEDE HANSON of Temple (1931 Brooklyn Dodgers, 1932 Staten Island Stapletons, 1933–37 Philadelphia Eagles, 1938 Pittsburgh Pirates) "kicked a football 175 yards—with the wind" on April 15, 1929.

• October 20, 1930—BUSTER MOTT (1933 Green Bay Packers, 1934 Cincinnati Reds/Pittsburgh Pirates) ran 56 yards for a Georgia touchdown "the first time he touched the ball in a college game. The next time—he ran 65 yards."

• October 29, 1930—DUTCH SPECK (1920–23, 1925–26 Canton Bulldogs, 1924 Akron Pros) "played professional football 25 years."

• December 9, 1931 — TOMMY DOWLER (1931 Brooklyn Dodgers) scored a touchdown for Colgate "in the first five minutes of every game he played in 1929 (eight games)."

• December 12, 1931 — BUTCH GIBSON (1930–34 New York Giants) "can tear a deck of cards into SIXTEENTHS with his BARE HANDS!" (Glenn Presnell, the old Portsmouth Spartan, told me something else interesting about Gibson. Butch didn't wear a conventional leather helmet, Presnell said, "He wore one of these boxer's headgears." It probably gave him better protection against cauliflower ears, being a lineman and all.)

• December 28, 1936 — BYRON HAINES (1937 Pittsburgh Pirates) "scored all the points for both teams" in Washington's 6–2 win over Southern California in 1935. (Haines fumbled the opening kickoff near his goal line, the *United Press* said, and "in the scramble for possession, [he] nudged the ball over the goal and USC automatically took a pair of points.")

• November 20, 1937 — ED LYNCH of Catholic University (1925 Rochester Jeffersons, 1926 Detroit Panthers/Hartford Blues, 1927 Providence Steam Roller, 1929 Orange Tornadoes) "made 98 tackles in one game." (Jimmy Conzelman, who coached and played with Lynch in Detroit and Providence, said Ed was "one of the finest ends I ever saw. He thought that only sissies wore pads. So he played without any protective equipment except the muscles he was born with. Brother, that was plenty.")

• November 1, 1939 — VERNE MILLER (1930 Minneapolis Red Jackets) "scored nine touchdowns and kicked three [PATs] — a total of 57 points in 18 minutes" for St. Mary's College (Winona, Minnesota) vs. Dubuque in 1929.

• December 3, 1945 — WARD CUFF (1937–45 New York Giants, 1946 Chicago Cardinals, 1947 Green Bay Packers) is an "ambidextrous athlete [who] kicks with either foot, throws with either hand, bats right-handed and left-handed."

Misdirection Plays

Jim Marshall—he of the wrong-way run for the Vikings in 1962—isn't the only pro football player to commit such a blunder. He's just the only one unfortunate enough to do it on television. Heck, the Bears' Oscar Knop got similarly turned around against the Columbus Tigers in 1924. It happened like this:

With the score tied 6–6 in the second quarter, Knop intercepted a pass at the Columbus 39. But he "lost his sense of direction," the *Chicago Tribune* reported, "and started for his own goal. . . . [T]he frantic yells of his mates caused him to stop four yards away from the goal post, thus avoiding a safety. . . . Few of the Columbus players gave chase, for most of them were stretched out on the ground, laughing hysterically."

Knop, a 191-pound back, redeemed himself almost immediately. Later in the quarter he picked off another pass and ran the *right* way, to the Columbus 30, after which Joey Sternaman drop-kicked a field goal for the go-ahead points. The Bears went on to win 12–6.

Which brings us to Harry Buffington, a guard for the 1947 Brooklyn Dodgers of the All-America Conference. Talk about bad timing. Buffington's screwup took place on the *first play of the season.*

Harry was blocking a Baltimore Colt on the kickoff when a fumble suddenly appeared at his feet. He alertly scooped up the ball at the 25-yard line but then took off toward the Brooklyn end zone.

"I threw a good block and was spun around," he said, "and when I stopped spinning there was a loose ball in front of me."

It wasn't until he was two steps from the goal line that he realized his mistake, Buffington said. By the time he stopped, he was in the end zone. Not wanting to get tackled for a safety, he tried to throw a pass to teammate Mickey Colmer, but the ball was batted down and the Colts' Jim Castiglia recovered for a touchdown. (The officials ruled the play a fumble rather than an illegal pass, which would have cost the Dodgers two points instead of six.)

The score jump-started Baltimore, playing its first game in the

AAC, to a 16–7 victory, one of only two it enjoyed that season. Still, Colts coach Cecil Isbell, while grateful for the gift, might have been even more grateful that one of *his* guys hadn't committed the gaffe.

"It can happen in a sandlot, college or pro game," he said, "when players are excited and hard-pressed."

So, yes, the Vikings' Marshall made the *longest* wrong-way run in the NFL — 66 yards against the 49ers (to Knop's 35 and Buffington's 25). But it resulted in a safety, not a touchdown like Harry's. And let's not forget, the Vikes still won 27–22.

So why don't we cut the poor man just a little slack?

• • •

When I started with the Bears we had fifteen [players on the roster]. You were hired to play a football game and you played it — all sixty minutes of it, brother. [Coach George] Halas used to come into the dressing room and say, "Now boys, this half Trafton will replace Trafton, Hunk Anderson will replace Hunk Anderson, and Healey, you'd better replace Healey." — Hall of Fame center George Trafton

• • •

All's Fair

Even in the anything-goes '20s, the game between the Akron Pros and Detroit Panthers on October 25, 1925, stands out for its ferocity. So great was the carnage that twelve substitutions had to be made (Akron nine, Detroit three) — this in an era of sixteen-man rosters and sixty-minute men. Every few plays, it seems, fists would fly and a player (or two) would seek refuge on the sideline.

Did something happen that day to heighten the hostilities? The newspaper accounts don't say. What they do say is that "neither team was very solicitous about the other's welfare" (*Detroit News*) and that "football at its best is a rough game, [but] when players get personal it is something more" (*Detroit Free Press*).

Boy, was this game ever "something more."

On the Detroit side, all-pro tackle Gus Sonnenberg was knocked out of action for the first time in his career when he took a knee in the left eye and the eye swelled shut. Quarterback Jimmy Conzelman, meanwhile, was discombobulated by a blow to the head.

"The jolt robbed him of the knowledge there were three other men with him in the backfield," the *Free Press* reported. "Conzelman tried to do all the passing, running and field goal kicking. And on each play he had to ask [halfback Dutch] Laurer what the signals were. The Panthers first noticed his condition when he asked, 'Who are we playing?'"

And that was just the first quarter.

In the second, Fritz Pollard, Akron's star back, got roughed up and had to take a breather. And in the second half it only got worse. Player after player left the game "either from injury or exhaustion," the *Free Press* said. In the fourth quarter "both teams had taken time out four times before the period was 10 minutes old," according to the *News*—to clear casualties off the field, no doubt.

The *News* lambasted referee Fred Lambert for letting things get out of hand—and then having the audacity to slow up the game with "his extended and needless lectures to the players." (To which I say: needless—or fruitless?)

When the final whistle blew, some of the Pros tried to claim the football as a souvenir, and the teams almost started brawling again. Fortunately, order was restored and the players—and the crowd of fifty-four hundred—went their various ways.

Final score: Detroit 0, Akron 0.

How to Protect a Lead, 1925

An intentional safety could be a team's best friend in the first part of the '20s—even more so than today. Allow me to illustrate:

In 1925 the Giants were leading the Providence Steam Roller 13–10 with time running out, but they were backed up deep in their own end and faced a fourth down. If they chose to punt, Providence figured to get great field position—and a chance to tie or win the game. So Hinkey Haines took the snap and touched the ball down in the end zone, handing the Steam Roller two points.

Under modern rules, of course, the Giants would be required to kick the ball to Providence from the New York 20 and sweat out the final seconds. The rules in 1925 were much different, though. The Giants were allowed to keep possession and were given a fresh set of downs at the 30. They ran three more plays to kill the clock and secure a 13–12 win.

After the season the rule was changed to the one we have now. As David M. Nelson notes in *Anatomy of a Game*, it was simply too ripe for abuse: "Teams leading their opponents by a score of 7–0, with the ball in their possession, could run out the clock with as many as 15 plays by taking intentional safeties and win the game 7–6."

Thankfully, that never happened in the NFL. (Can you imagine a club with a seven-point lead playing keep-away like that for the last half of the fourth quarter?) But it easily *might* have happened if the rule makers hadn't seen the light.

Still Standing

There aren't too many plays from the 1920s that still resonate eighty-odd years later. But when the Lions' Louis Delmas picked off a Cardinals pass in 2009 and ran 101 yards for a touchdown, the Elias Sports Bureau was nice enough to note it was only the *second*-longest interception return by a rookie in NFL history.

The longest: a 103-yarder by Pete Barnum of the Columbus Tigers in a 14–2 win over the Canton Bulldogs in 1926.

Barnum's TD gave Columbus a 7–0 lead in what turned out to be the Tigers' last victory in the NFL. The famous franchise—founded by future NFL commissioner Joe Carr and at one time featuring seven Nesser brothers—dropped out of the league after that season. By then, only one Nesser, 245-pound Frank, was still on the roster.

Barnum, who'd starred in college at West Virginia, eventually gravitated to Maryland, where he got a job at a Bethlehem Steel plant and played on the company football team. In 1929, less than three years after his historic touchdown, a horrible accident cost him his life. He "stumbled and fell" into "a vat of molten metal," the *Associated Press* reported, "saving himself from instant death and cremation in the metal by grasping a ledge until pulled out by fellow workers." The burns were too severe, though. He died four days later.

His kid brother followed him to the NFL and, in *his* rookie season, won a championship with the 1938 Giants. Len Barnum—"Feets," they called him—was one of the league's better punters and kickers in that period.

(You pull a thread in the early days of pro football, there's no telling what will turn up . . .)

Look Out Below!

Promoting games in the early years required a certain creativity—pro football being so desperate for attention. When the Kansas City Cowboys went on the road, for instance, they'd arrive in town wearing ten-gallon hats and cowboy boots. The Cleveland Bulldogs, meanwhile, would send star quarterback Benny Friedman and publicist Ed Bang ahead a few days early to drum up interest.

"Ed would buy two bottles of whiskey and walk into a newspaper office," Friedman said. "He'd hand one bottle to the sports editor and the other to the sports columnist, he'd introduce me and then we'd kibitz. That was the way we got our publicity."

But that's nothing compared to the stunt the Giants pulled in 1926. Two days before their battle with the Los Angeles Buccaneers, they sent end Lynn Bomar to the top of the American Radiator Building on West Fortieth Street and stationed his teammate, halfback Hinkey Haines, 324 feet below in Bryant Park. The idea was for Bomar to complete a pass to Haines, "the longest 'forward pass' on record," the *New York Times* reported—though the pass was more downward than forward.

It was, as much as anything, a playful jab at Brick Muller, the Buccaneers' celebrated end. The year before, to advertise the East-West Shrine Game, Muller had caught a pass thrown from the roof of the Telephone Building in San Francisco. But that building was a mere 320 feet tall — 4 less than the one in New York.

"On Bomar's first heave from his lofty perch," the *Times* said, "the ball hit the sidewalk and burst." The next pass also failed to connect, and the third hit Haines with such force that it knocked him over. Hinkey then took off his coat — and no doubt licked his fingers, too — and managed to hang on to attempt number five. A crowd of "several hundred onlookers," according to another account, gave him a nice round of applause.

The Giants may have won the preliminaries — and supplanted Muller in the "record" book — but they lost the game 6–0. In fact, their passing was so futile against the Buccaneers that you would have thought their quarterbacks were throwing from the top of a tall building. They completed only two passes all day and had five picked off. One of the interceptions, tossed by Haines, was returned 22 yards for the game's only score.

Just to Clarify

Every now and then, when John Stockton was still dribbling for the Utah Jazz, a TV announcer would mention that Stockton's grandfather had played pro football. And that was that. You wouldn't get any more information. So why don't I flesh things out a bit?

John Stockton's grandfather didn't just play pro football, he was very good at it. In fact, when the Frankford Yellow Jackets won the NFL championship in 1926, it was Grandpa Stockton — *Houston Stockton* — who threw the winning touchdown pass late in the deciding game, a 7–6 win over the previously unbeaten Chicago Bears.

Stockton, a fullback/passer in Frankford's single wing, took the Yellow Jackets down the field in the closing minutes with a "series of thrilling forward passes," the *Chicago Tribune* reported. "With Stockton heaving the ball to [Rae] Crowther, former Colgate star, the ball was carried from Frankford's 25-yard line to the Bears' 27-yard line. Only a minute-and-a-half remained to play when Stockton hurled the ball over the goal line where [Two Bits] Homan, the smallest man on the field, caught it for a touchdown."

In truth, it was even more exciting than that. Stockton, according to the *Philadelphia Inquirer*, was chased back 15 yards by the Chicago rush. He unloaded the ball just as a Bear dove at him—which suggests he may have, yes, *thrown it off his back foot*. The pass, the *Inquirer* said, "looked more like a punt, it had been thrown so high."

Is this the stuff of legends or what? (Especially since the receiver was five foot five, 145 pounds.)

The victory left Frankford with a 13-1-1 record and the Bears at 11-1-2 (ties didn't count). The Jackets wrapped up the title the next two Sundays with a 24–0 win over the Providence Steam Roller—thanks to more heroics by John Stockton's grandfather—and a 0–0 tie against the Pottsville Maroons.

John's middle name, by the way, is Houston. He also named his son—who played safety at the University of Montana—Houston. Grandad, for the record, was usually called Hust. He played four years in the NFL, finishing up with Providence and the Boston Bulldogs in 1929. Those four years were pretty eventful, too. After the '25 season, for instance, when Red Grange was making his famous tour with the Bears, Hust played against him in a game in San Francisco. It was Grange's only loss on the tour (San Francisco Tigers 14, Bears 9).

But that's not why I mention it. I mention it because at one point in the proceedings, Chicago's "Ed Healey was booed when he kicked Houston Stockton," the *Oakland Tribune* reported. "The fans demanded he be thrown out of the game."

So Hust got kicked by a Hall of Fame lineman—and got even with him eleven months later by throwing the touchdown pass that cost the Bears the title. Sweet.

John Stockton's grandfather played a little pro football, all right. And in college, he helped put Gonzaga—John's alma mater—on the map. His coach was Gus Dorais, whose passes to Knute Rockne enabled tiny Notre Dame to upset Army in 1913. So it figures Dorais would let Hust put the ball in the air a time or two. Indeed, Hust was a passer of such renown that he was featured in a *Ripley's Believe It or Not!* cartoon.

(FYI: The sketch of Hust in the cartoon was right next to one of a French butler who "identified eight different kinds of white wines by tasting from unmarked bottles." The butler had a discriminating palate, you have to admit, but his feat would be a lot more impressive if he'd ever been kicked by Ed Healey.)

Of Miners and Men

Pro football was a very big deal in the 1920s in the anthracite coal region of Pennsylvania. The team in Pottsville, the Maroons, was the only one that actually joined the NFL (1925–28), but the nearby towns of Coaldale, Shenandoah, Gilberton, and Mt. Carmel—located just off Interstate 81 today—all fielded clubs that enjoyed beating up on one another.

A game between Shenandoah and Coaldale in November 1922 gives you a glimpse of what the environment was like. Here's the account that ran in newspapers across the country:

> POTTSVILLE, Pa.—Ten thousand people at a football game at Coaldale near here Sunday afternoon refused to desert the game to fight a fire when the alarm was turned in and, as a result, a house which was located on Railroad Street, a sparsely settled section of the borough, burned to the ground.
>
> Appeals were made at the game for firemen to respond, but no one budged.
>
> Coaldale tied Shenandoah 6–6.

They took their football seriously in the Coal League. Teams would sign NFL ringers—at salaries as high as $500 a game—to fortify their rosters, and miners would bet large sums on the outcome.

In *Fritz Pollard: Pioneer in Racial Advancement,* John M. Carroll writes, "Until the 1920s, many games in the coal region were never completed because fans on the losing side would start a riot in the final period so they would not lose their wagers. All this changed when Robert 'Tiny' Maxwell, a prominent referee and former Swarthmore College player, was brought in to officiate along with two other nationally known officials, Wilmer Crowell and Charles McCarthy."

But even Maxwell, a six-foot-four, three-hundred-pound mountain of persuasion, couldn't put a stop to *all* mischief. Don Thompson, a guard with the Los Angeles Buccaneers, had this memory of a visit to Pottsville's Minersville Field in 1926: "I guess our toughest defeat was [there]. There was a quarter of an inch of ice on the puddles in the playing field that had to be broken before the game. The spectators stood on the sidelines and threw chunks of coal at us through the entire contest. We scored four touchdowns that were not allowed."

Makes you wonder if the Maroons' home-field advantage might have been the biggest in NFL history. It certainly has to rank somewhere near the top.

"Those miners were great fans," Pottsville Hall of Famer Fats Henry once said. "They'd approach you on the street, the coal dust on their faces, and talk football with you. If they liked you they'd die for you. But if they didn't you'd die for them."

Nobody had better Coal League stories than Mike Palm, a back for the New York Giants who later coached in the NFL. When he wasn't otherwise occupied in those years, Palm would sneak off to Shenandoah for a weekend of well-paid bleeding on a coal slag–strewn field. "There wasn't a blade of grass in the league," he told Joe King of the *New York World-Telegram,*

> and fans wouldn't hesitate to participate in the game with rocks, sticks, stones, fists and abuse.
>
> The teams got the biggest guys they could find in the mines, regardless of football experience, and imported enough collegiate players to

rig up an attack. Coaldale had two old fighters, Honeyboy Evans and Blue Bonner, who never forgot their old trade on the gridiron.

When I played at Shenandoah, we had Frank Kutzko, who looked like [wrestler] Bull Montana and was three times as big. Once against Pottsville, Kutzko picked up Harry Robb, gave him the airplane spin and slammed him down. I rushed up objecting: "Don't do that, Frank. Do you want them to take it out on us little fellows?" Kutzko replied: "Mike, this is football. If I can kill him, I will kill him."

That was the way they played. If one of us collegians threw a pass, someone would surely yell, 'Cut out that basketball.'"

Which seems as good a place to end as any. This was the Coal League: *If I can kill him, I will kill him.*

Batter Up!

During his vaudeville travels after the 1926 World Series, Babe Ruth spent a week in Spokane, Washington. One day he stopped by Gonzaga University and — in between posing for pictures — goofed around with the football team.

The school outfitted him with a uniform — the biggest it had available — and Ruth went down to the stadium and took batting practice using footballs. There he was, leather helmet and all, knocking them "all over the lot," newspapers reported. (After the Cardinals had walked him eleven times in the Series, he must have been thrilled to get a few pitches to hit.)

One of the footballs even landed in the stands, after which the Bambino proclaimed, "That's one over the fence like I never hit before!"

Joe Williams, the syndicated columnist for the *Cleveland Press*, was greatly amused by the slugger's antics. "He must have imagined one of the Red Sox pitchers was in there chucking," he wrote.

This doesn't have anything to do with the National Forgotten League, of course — except in a tangential way. The Gonzaga coach at the time was Clipper Smith, who later coached the NFL's Boston Yanks (1947–48).

Communal Living

Nowadays NFL teammates might live in the same subdivision. Before that, they might have rented in the same apartment building. In the '20s, though, teams sometimes shared the same house.

The Frankford Yellow Jackets, 1926 league champions, were one such team. Guard Bill Hoffman's memories of those times:

> Frankford was an athletic association owned by the citizens of Frankford. And they had a nice, big Victorian home that was right down the street from our stadium. We could walk to the games. A few players—like Tex Hamer, who was married—lived someplace else, but most of us lived there together, almost like a fraternity house.
>
> You didn't have to hunt amusement. We amused ourselves. You know what my greatest amusement was in those days? Playing bridge. Lucille Chamberlin, [player-coach] Guy Chamberlin's wife, would play, too. They lived with us for a while.
>
> We had players from all over. Guy and Ed Weir were from Nebraska. Bob Fitzke was from Idaho. We had a fella from Gonzaga by the name of [Hust] Stockton. Johnny Budd was from Lafayette. I was from Lehigh. Tex Hamer and George Sullivan were from the University of Pennsylvania. We had somebody from Dartmouth [Swede Youngstrom], from Colgate [the Crowther brothers, Rae and Saville] and from a little school here named Lebanon Valley, a little back by the name of [Henry] Homan. He was only about 5-5, 145 pounds, but he was very, very good. Clever. And probably our fastest player. He could go, and he could dodge and duck. Guy nicknamed him Two Bits. That was the nickname of the bulldog Guy brought with him. Guy gave him the dog's nickname.
>
> In Frankford they gave you ten dollars every day you practiced. It was in your contract. So you'd come out to practice. And you know, ten dollars meant a lot in those days. You could eat for two or three days on that. As far as salaries, the linemen would average, I would say, two hundred to two hundred fifty dollars a game. I don't think the backs got a whole lot more. They'd pay in cash after the game.
>
> We did a lot of our eating at the YWCA. They had a nice, big cafeteria. Otherwise you had to eat in restaurants, like Bookbinders. Of

course, once in a while, we had a little feast at the house we stayed in. One of the members of the association would bring up a lot of turtle meat from around Baltimore. And maybe on a Friday night, they'd boil up a big pot of turtle soup. Was that ever good.

In Providence, the Steam Roller, the 1928 champs, didn't have a whole house to themselves, but a bunch of the players lodged with Assistant General Manager Pearce Johnson and his parents at 97 High Service Avenue, not far from Providence College. Most of the others—the good-time guys like Gus Sonnenberg, the future pro wrestling star, and Wildcat Wilson—lived at a hotel, the Crown. Johnson, who was still living in the house when I talked to him in the mid-'90s, said,

> There are three upstairs bedrooms here. We put three beds in the front room and two in each of the other rooms. That's where the players stayed. My family lived downstairs. One year we had eight players with us. Jimmy Conzelman, our player-coach, broke his leg, and he called my mother [Carolina] and asked if he could come here and live. He'd lived with us before, and he wanted mother's home cooking and home attention. So mother bought a bed and put it in the sun room.
>
> My mother was from Sweden, so her cooking was the best. She was like their mother away from home. We had Pop Williams, a fullback, with us, and Clyde Smith, the [all-pro] center. [Guard] Milt Rehnquist lived here four years. Our piano was in the sun room, where Jimmy slept, and he'd play it while he was recovering. Popular songs. He was a good singer. He also wrote songs.
>
> I was never, ever at the [Crown] hotel after hours, so all I know about life there is what the boys here would tell me. One time, they told me, Gus got drunk and pulled his steam radiator right off the wall and threw it out the window.

(Which is as good an argument for quiet communal living as any.)

The year the Steam Roller won the title, they played in Pottsville on Thanksgiving and beat the Maroons 7–0. The next day Carolina Johnson went to the store to stock up on food for the returning heroes. Pearce arrived home around 6:00 p.m. and, to his surprise, found all the lights turned out.

"He called for his mother," the *Providence Journal* reported. "She did not answer. He called again, but got no response."

A short time later his father, Conrad, an electrician, got in from work. The two searched the area and talked to neighbors, but no one had seen Carolina.

When Pearce returned to the house, the *Journal* said, he glanced at the afternoon newspaper and noticed a story about "an unidentified woman having been fatally injured when an electric [trolley] car struck her at 7:28 o'clock yesterday morning. . . . The woman was Pearce's mother."

A Lasting Moment

December 19, 1926, was no day for football at Soldier Field. But despite the wretched conditions — snow, sleet, rain, ice, and a fierce southwest wind — the Bears and Packers dutifully wrapped up the season before ten thousand frosted fans.

Green Bay led 3–0 with five minutes left when Chicago's Paddy Driscoll stepped back to try a 20-yard field goal. Since there were no hash marks in 1926, the ball was marked where the previous play had ended — "on the extreme right side of the field," according to the *Chicago Tribune.*

The *Decatur Review* went into greater detail: "He kicked from approximately 10 yards from the sideline on about a 45-degree angle into the southwest wind. It took him almost a minute to make up his mind whether to kick from placement or to drop[-kick], but he finally elected the latter. The ball barely cleared the bar, but it was directly between the uprights."

Driscoll's kick enabled the Bears to escape with a 3–3 tie, but more importantly, it was his twelfth field goal of the season, an NFL record. It would be twenty-four years before anyone booted more (the Browns' Lou Groza, to be specific). That's right, a mark set by a dropkicker was still standing as late as 1950.

Just thought you might want to know.

Daddy, I Forgot to Duck

During a Minor League Baseball game in 1927, Portland Beavers third baseman Doc Prothro hit a foul ball into the stands that struck his seven-year-old son "just below the eye," *Time* magazine reported. (Yes, it was such a one-in-a-billion thing, even *Time* had an item on it.)

I mention this for only one reason: The kid in question, Tommy Prothro, grew up to be the coach of the Los Angeles Rams (1971–72) and San Diego Chargers (1974–78).

Immovable Object

For most of pro football's first half century, the goalposts were the twelfth and thirteenth men on the field. They stood resolutely on the goal line—or maybe a step behind it—and woe to any player who came into contact with them.

That's why, from 1927 through '32, they were moved to the back of the end zone—or one of the reasons, at least. Too many guys were crashing into them. But they were returned to the goal line in the decades that followed to increase scoring (only to be moved back again in '74 because field goals were becoming too plentiful).

The goalposts could come into play in a variety of ways. A sampling of some of the things that could—and did—happen:

• November 19, 1939—After catching a pass from Tuffy Leemans in the second quarter, Giants end Chuck Gelatka plows into the goalpost and careens backward. Not only does his team fail to score a touchdown, it eventually loses the ball on downs. (A subhead in the next day's *New York Times* reads: "Goal Post Prevents Score.") The Giants beat Pittsburgh anyway, 23–7.

• September 22, 1940—Trailing 19–13 with time running out, the Eagles' Davey O'Brien fades back near his goal line and, when chased out of the pocket, collides with the goalpost. "Bewildered by this sudden obstacle," the *Cleveland Press* reports, "and before he could regain his bearings, the slippery little O'Brien was caught like a mouse in a trap. He was engulfed in the mighty embrace of tackle

[Boyd] Clay, who pinned Davey and the goal post and the football in one comprehensive hug." Safety. Game over.

• December 16, 1945 — Early in the NFL title game, the Redskins' Sammy Baugh tries to throw out of his end zone and — thanks to a gust of wind — the ball hits the crossbar for a safety. (Note: The rule was changed the next year to make it an incomplete pass.) Later, an extra point attempt by the Rams' Bob Waterfield strikes the crossbar and crawls over. Final score: Cleveland 15, Washington 14.

• November 21, 1954 — Going for the clinching touchdown in the fourth quarter against the Giants, Rams fullback Deacon Dan Towler smashes headfirst into the goalpost and fumbles. Luckily for him, center Leon McLaughlin recovers, and Los Angeles hangs on to win, 17–16. (When Towler came to his senses, Giants cornerback Dick Nolan — who obviously had a sense of humor — supposedly told him, "The next time you come this way, you get the same damn thing.")

• December 12, 1954 — Punting from behind his goal line, the Giants' Tom Landry hits the upright — and watches helplessly as the ball bounces back through the end zone for a safety. It's a fitting end to a 29–14 loss to the Eagles that drops New York to third in the final standings.

• November 20, 1960 — On the last play of the game, Steelers defensive back Junior Wren gets knocked unconscious by the goalpost while trying to cover Browns end Leon Clarke. Clarke makes a diving grab for the apparent winning score, but the officials rule it a trap, enabling Pittsburgh to escape with a 14–10 victory.

• December 10, 1961 — While pulling in his second TD pass of the day against San Francisco, Packers Pro Bowler Max McGee rams into the goalpost and fractures his rib. He misses the season finale but makes it back for the Pack's 37–0 wipeout of the Giants in the championship game.

• November 17, 1968 — Lions cornerback Lem Barney picks off a pass by the Vikings' Joe Kapp, bounces off the goalpost and — after being "momentarily staggered," according to one account—returns the ball 62 yards to the Minnesota 38. Which raises the (perfectly unanswerable) question: Is this the longest run ever made by an NFL player after smacking into a goalpost?

• • •

The language of football reporting has become so exalted in the past few years that the only thing left will be to have the noble words which sports-writers have written set to music and chanted by a male choir in white vestments from the top of Bald Mountain at dusk.—Robert Benchley in *The New Yorker*, 1927

• • •

Do Not Overinflate

What Benchley was talking about was purple prose like this, taken from a 1924 game account:

CLEVELAND, Oct. 13—His flippant forward flings flashing the tortuous trail to conquest, his punts of power and rare precision carrying a message of consternation into the camp of the erstwhile victory-bound foe, Hoge, master Workman of the gridiron—he whose deft right foot booted the Cleveland Bulldogs from out the gruesome shadows of defeat at Philadelphia only the day before—rose again to heroic heights at Dunn Field yesterday, turned the fickle tide of battle once more and supervised the annihilation of the Akron Pros, 29 to 14.

— *Evening Independent*, Massillon, Ohio

Stats, 1927

In the '20s, when newspapers were still figuring what a football box score should look like, you'd sometimes see some interesting stuff. After the Providence Steam Roller's 9–0 win over the New York Yankees in Syracuse in 1927, the *Syracuse Herald* broke down the receiving statistics thusly:

FORWARD PASSES COMPLETED

Yankees	Dist.	Ran	Tot.	Steamrollers	Dist.	Ran	Tot.
Lewellen to Grange	20	0	20	Wilson to Conzelman	5	37	42
Lewellen to Grange	4	0	4	Wilson to Conzelman	9	0	9
Lewellen to Tryon	20	9	29	Wilson to Cronin	13	0	13
				Wilson to Cronin	11	0	11
				Wilson to Conzelman	5	6	11
Totals	44	9	53		43	43	86

Note: "Dist.," obviously, is the distance the pass traveled beyond the line of scrimmage, "Ran" is how far the receiver ran with the ball after he caught it, and "Tot." is the total gain.

So in 1927 the *Herald* was giving its readers not just a log of every completed pass — all eight of 'em — but also the number of *yards gained after the catch*, a stat nobody paid much attention to until the last decade or so.

Stunning.

Of course, Red Grange played in the game. When the Galloping Ghost was in town, papers tended to jazz up their coverage with all kinds of extras.

A Real Game-Changer

The Duluth Eskimos were about to take the lead over the Chicago Bears in their 1927 season-ender when a fight broke out — between *two Bears*, center George Trafton and tackle Link Lyman. George Halas, "playing end at the time, had to intercede," the *Decatur Review* reported.

The newspaper didn't say what caused the two Hall of Famers to square off, but it did say the incident was a turning point and "spurred [Chicago] on to greater things." After the Eskimos went ahead 14–7 on a lateral from Ernie Nevers to Cobb Rooney, the Bears exploded for three touchdowns to win 27–14.

(I'm guessing Trafton, motormouth that he was, probably was giving Lyman grief for something, maybe a missed tackle.)

In the *Chicago Tribune*, Wilfrid Smith didn't even mention the bout, which suggests one of two things:

1. being a staunch league man, Smith didn't want to make the NFL look bad; or
2. the Bears did this sort of thing all the time.

• • •

The important thing to remember about the early days is that the pros brought the game to people who had no chance to see the college game. . . . It was not easy to get to a college game. Our early barnstorm teams filled the gap, and in doing so, they improved from year to year and created a great mass of fans who became rooters for all football, whether high school, college or pro. — Giants coach Steve Owen in *My Kind of Football*

• • •

Alpha(bet) Males

One of the best parts about the early NFL is that teams would try just about anything. Case in point: the 1929 Orange Tornadoes.

The Tornadoes didn't wear numbers on their jerseys, they wore *letters*. Here's their lineup for the first of two games against the Frankford Yellow Jackets:

A — Phil Scott, E, No college

B — Felix McCormick, B, Bucknell

C — Heinie Benkert, B, Rutgers

D — Leon Johnson, E, Columbia

E — George Pease, QB, Columbia

F — Ernie Cuneo, G, Penn State/Columbia

G — Frank Kirkleski, B, Lafayette

H — Ted Mitchell, C, Bucknell

J — Ernie Hambacker, B, Bucknell

L — Ralph Barkman, B, Schuylkill

M — Bob Beattie, T, Princeton

M — Steve Hamas, FB, Penn State

N — Paul Longua, E, Villanova

O — Jack McArthur, G, St. Mary's (California)

P — Bill Feaster, T, Fordham

Q — Bill Clarkin, T, No college

R — Andy Salata, G, Pittsburgh

S — Carl Waite, B, Rutgers/Georgetown

T — Jack Depler, player (C-T)-coach, Illinois

X — Johnny Tomaini, E, Georgetown

Nice touch on that last one. Tomaini's name sounds like ptomaine, so, naturally, he wore the letter *X* — for poison.

Notice anything else about the roster that's interesting (aside from the two *M*'s, which means there was probably a typographical error in the game program)?

Answer: Just as there is no *I* in team, there was no *I* on the 1929 Orange Tornadoes. (In fact, for all we know, this might have been where the saying originated.)

Last in the Line

Pro football was down to one Nesser as the 1920s drew to a close. In the game's early years as many as seven of Theodore and Katherine Nesser's famous sons had suited up for the Columbus Panhandles and other clubs. But by 1929 only Al, a balding six-foot, 195-pound guard, was still slugging it out — for the minor-league Akron (Ohio) Awnings. "Old Pig Iron," they called him.

Al was the second youngest in the brood. (The birth order went like this: John, Phil, Ted, Fred, Frank, Al, Raymond.) And while he wasn't the most talented of the Nessers — it's generally agreed that Ted, a 230-pound defensive terror, was — he was darn good. He started for two NFL championship teams, the 1920 Akron Pros and '27 New York Giants, and made all-pro in 1921. He was rough, tough enough not to wear a helmet or any padding, and still a handful in 1929 at the age of thirty-six.

In November of that year Al played the whole game — sixty furious minutes — against the NFL's Portsmouth Spartans. His team lost 15–6, but the *Portsmouth Times* called him the "best lineman" the Awnings had. "He was in on every play," the *Times* said, "making beautiful tackles and at times tearing through the line and throwing the Spartan backfield men for losses."

After the season, Al went back to being a plumber in Akron — his real job. He also decided to resume his boxing career. He'd done a little fighting earlier in the decade but hadn't been in the ring in eight years.

Around the same time, Bears center George Trafton had a much publicized bout with Art "the Great" Shires, the Chicago White Sox first baseman, and won a five-round decision. Seeing a chance for a big payday, Al immediately challenged Trafton to a fight for the "professional football championship of the world."

"Give me 24 hours' notice and I'll fight Trafton," he said. "I don't need two weeks or even two days to train. I had a battle with Trafton once before. It was in a Chicago hotel, though, and I ran him around plenty."

Trafton had a substantial size advantage over Al at six foot two, 230 pounds. But he wanted no part of The Last Nesser. As he explained years later, "Eleven of us Bears ganged up on that Nesser [one time]. We used everything but an ice pick. After 60 minutes of it he walked off the Polo Grounds into a hospital. It wasn't that I was afraid of him, but I began to wonder what I could possibly accomplish against him in there alone in five rounds if 11 of us couldn't get him down in an entire afternoon. So I retired to think it over."

With Trafton ducking him, Al took on the likes of Roughhouse Ritz and K. O. Fidler and disposed of them quickly — too quickly for some. After he knocked out Jack Dear in the first round, one newspaper said, "We still maintain the Nessers should stick to football. Dear might have been knocked cold by Nesser's right, but the ease with which he picked a soft spot on the ring floor to fall down makes one wonder just how hard he was hit."

(Westbrook Pegler had expressed a similar sentiment after the Trafton-Shires travesty: "I still believe that, given a shave, a haircut and a planked steak by way of training, Romero Rojas, the most knocked-out pro of recent years, could step into a ring with any football player in the country today, including Trafton, and win by a knockout inside of three rounds.")

In his fifth and possibly last comeback fight — these things can be hard to determine — Al finally got exposed, losing on a sixth-round TKO to Jack Sharkey. He also lost a tooth, according to Massillon's *Evening Independent.* This wasn't the Jack Sharkey who later won the heavyweight title; it was *another* Jack Sharkey, a journeyman from Cleveland. Still, Sharkey was "knocked down or wrestled to the canvas by Nesser 10 times in the first four stanzas," the paper reported.

Al spent the rest of his football days with semipro clubs for the most part. (Because he hadn't gone to college, his alma mater would be listed in the game program as the "School of Hard Knocks.") He did return to the NFL in 1931, though, with the Cleveland Indians. The next year he was playing for a team in Grand Rapids, Michigan, when he wired Portsmouth coach Potsy Clark, looking to get back in the big time.

"I understand there is no drinking on your club and all the boys go to bed early," the telegram read. "I'll do the same if you will give me a chance."

But Al was thirty-nine by then, and the Spartans were doing just fine without him.

All that's left of Al now are the stories — like the one the Packers' Jug Earp enjoyed telling. It goes like this:

One afternoon in the late '20s as they were walking off the field, Jug said to him, "That was a pretty tough game today."

"I'll say it was," Al replied. "I remember one I played in 1907 that was plenty tough, but that baby today was no slouch, either."

Maybe Jug got the year wrong — or moved it back a bit for comic effect. After all, in 1907 Al would have been fourteen. But with the Nessers, you can never be sure.

Not So Little

A nickname like "Wee Willie" in the early years could be attached to a five-foot-six, 148-pound scatback (the Giants' Willis Smith) or a six-four, 261-pound tackle (the Redskins' Wilbur Wilkin). It's called irony.

It was the same with "Babe." Henry Homan, Frankford's five-foot-five, 145-pound sparkplug, was a "Babe" (as well as a "Two Bits"). So was Harry Aloysius Connaughton, the Yellow Jackets' six-two, 285-pound roadblock. Then there's Buford Ray, the six-six, 249-pound monster for the Packers. He was a "Baby."

Let's face it, it doesn't take much imagination to call five-foot-eleven, 245-pound Pete Henry, the Canton Bulldogs Hall of Famer, "Fats"—or Ed Sauer, the Dayton Triangles' five-ten, 246-pounder, "Tubby." But to dub a huge guy "Tiny" . . .

And there were quite a few oversized fellows nicknamed "Tiny" in pro football's salad days. Here's a sampling, along with their vital statistics:

Player, Years	Team*	Height	Weight	Given name
Tiny Burdick, 1932–34	Bears	6-4	248	Lloyd Sumner
Tiny Cahoon, 1926–29	Packers	6-2	235	Ivan Wells
Tiny Croft, 1942–47	Packers	6-3	287	Milburn Russell
Tiny Engebretsen, 1932–41	Packers	6-1	238	Paul J.
Tiny Ladson, 1922	Evansville Crimson Giants	NA	254	Glessie Merritt
Tiny Mulbarger, 1920–26	Columbus Tigers	5-9	221	Joseph Griffin
Tiny Nordstrom, 1925–26	Giants	6-2	238	Harry William
Tiny Thompson, 1922	Rochester Jeffersons	5-10	233	George Bryant

Average height: 6-1. Average weight: 244.3.
*Team he's most commonly associated with.

Something else about this list that's interesting: From 1926 through 1947, a period of twenty-two years, there were only four seasons (1930–33) when the Packers didn't have a "Tiny." It was almost like a roster spot—the Team Tiny.

Steve Hamas vs. Max Schmeling

For all their pugnacity, pro football players haven't fared very well in the boxing ring. (Exhibit A: the Bears' George Trafton staying upright for a mere fifty-four seconds against Primo Carnera in 1930.) Steve Hamas was different, though. Hamas was a boxer — a two-time collegiate champion at Penn State — who also happened to play football, not the other way around.

His NFL career was as brief as it was forgettable: a single season in 1929 as a six-foot, 195-pound fullback for the Orange Tornadoes. After that, he pulled on a pair of gloves and won his first twenty-nine professional fights — twenty-six by knockout — to become a heavyweight contender.

Hamas's big breakthrough came in 1932, when he stopped Tommy Loughran in two rounds at Madison Square Garden. Loughran was a tough customer, a former light-heavyweight champ who had beaten Jim Braddock (1929) and Max Baer (1931), both of whom would go on to win the heavyweight title. But Steve knocked him down three times in the second and "battered [him] more fiercely . . . than he ever was before in his career," the *New York Times* reported.

This earned Hamas a shot, two years later, at Max Schmeling, who was trying to regain his heavyweight crown after losing it to Jack Sharkey. Paul Gallico, advancing the bout for New York's *Daily News*, thought it would be a tough one for Schmeling. Hamas, he said, is "a rough, hard-hitting kid, a hungry fellow, who is trying to get to the top. . . . If I [were managing] a former champion, I'd try to avoid those kids on their way up. They carry something extra in their knapsacks, a little more zest, a little more zing, a little more daring, and somehow their heads clear fast when they get in trouble."

When Hamas and Schmeling met at Philadelphia's Convention Hall in February 1934, it was the most anticipated fight in the city since the first Dempsey-Tunney bout in '26, according to the *Times*. A sellout crowd of thirteen thousand turned out to see if the hard-punching American, a 12–5 underdog, could defeat the more ring-wise German.

Shockingly—to most in attendance, anyway—he did.

"Schmeling . . . was a 10-round target for Hamas's straight left in the face," Gallico wrote. "The only times the German connected solidly was [sic] when Hamas straightened up a couple of times and mixed it." Late in the fight, Hamas cut him over the left eye. "Nobody ever cut Schmeling before," Gallico said.

Here's the *Times*'s blow-by-blow of that fateful ninth round: "Hamas drove several lefts and a terrific right to the face that opened a cut over Schmeling's left eye. Schmeling was blinded by the wound and Hamas leaped after him, jabbing his left to the face and crossing his right to the eye. Hamas backed Schmeling to the ropes, jabbing him at will. Schmeling was missing most of his blows."

The decision was unanimous. Indeed, none of the judges gave Hamas fewer than eight of the twelve rounds. Alas, he never reached those heights again. At that point he should have fought Baer for the title, Gallico thought, but instead he gave Schmeling a rematch in March 1935—in Hamburg, no less, amid "the hysterical patriotism of [twenty-five thousand] Nazi excursionists," as the *Times* put it. The payday was pretty good— $25,000—but nothing else about the bout made much sense for Hamas.

In the intervening months Schmeling worked himself into top shape—he'd been rusty and strangely passive in the first fight—and Hamas seems to have gotten a little overconfident. The Associated Press noted his "lackadaisical training" and fondness for "beer and cigarettes." He'd also had knee surgery several months earlier to repair an old football injury.

Gallico, who listened to the bout over the radio in New York, correctly foresaw the outcome. "There will be blood spilled," he predicted in the days leading up to the fight. "The worst licking Schmeling ever took standing up was from Hamas. Steve couldn't knock the German out that night in Philadelphia, but he slit him as if he were boxing with razors, and humiliated him no end. Schmeling has more pride and dignity than any boxer I have ever met. . . . The German will be more dangerous than he has ever been before."

The blood spilled this time was Hamas's. By the end of the sixth round he was virtually out on his feet. In the ninth his seconds belatedly threw in the towel. Afterward he experienced temporary numbness in one of his legs—enough to cause him to stay in Germany for a couple of weeks to recuperate. He never fought again.

As for Schmeling, he fell short of his goal to become the first man to recapture the heavyweight title. But fifteen months later at Yankee Stadium, he stunned the boxing world by knocking out an up-and-comer named Joe Louis in the twelfth round. In other words, Steve Hamas, the erstwhile Orange Tornado, beat the man who beat The Man (as they say in the fight game). Let that be his pugilistic epitaph.

An Item That May Interest Only Me

After flunking out of the University of Wisconsin as a freshman, future Packers Hall of Famer Arnie Herber spent the 1929 season at Regis College in Denver. (He then signed with Green Bay at the age of twenty and helped the Pack win the '30 title.)

Another famous person who dropped out of Regis: comedian Bill Murray.

"I didn't know how to study," Murray once said of the school, "but I liked the lifestyle. You could dress any way you wanted. I was wearing pajamas and a sport coat to school and pajamas and loafers to formal events."

The Pro Game's Burden

Betting scandals in pro football's early years (read: pre-NFL) left scars that lingered through the '20s. So much so that syndicated columnist Frank Menke was moved to write,

A man who plays in the regalia of Dartmouth, Pittsburgh, Notre Dame, Southern California or any other college in the land can make a dozen fumbles in a game, fail 12 times in 12 tries at tackling and make a half-dozen other "boners" without anybody challenging his honesty.

But put the same fellow in a pro uniform the very next week before the same crowd and, if he makes so much as one error of hand or foot or brain, the very same folk who considered his bobbling of the week before as "one of the things that will happen" promptly reach the decision that his lone blunder as a pro was made with sinister intent.

Someday the scandal mongers will get tongue-tied or fate will bestow upon them a bad case of lockjaw. Then—and only then—will professional football get the "break" that it deserves and only then will the American public reach the true conclusion, which is that in pro football, practically all the players are just as honest and clean as are the collegians and that always they play to win.

Moby-Dick, Captain Ahab . . . and Football

How football can help you understand literature—courtesy of Johnny Blood, the Packers' Hall of Fame deep thinker: "Ahab had the courage of ignorance, comparable to the courage of a fullback playing his first season in professional football. He hurls himself against the line. But look at him at the age of 30. He will not be hitting the line with quite the same abandon. For the courage of ignorance, he has substituted the restraint, the caution of a little wisdom."

The All-Elmer Backfield

ELMER OLIPHANT, HB—All-league in 1921 with the Buffalo All-Americans, who finished second behind the Bears. . . . Also drop-kicked five field goals and twenty-six extra points that season—his only one, really, in the NFL. (He played one game the year before for the Rochester Jeffersons.)

ELMER ANGSMAN, HB—Ran for two 70-yard touchdowns in the Cardinals' 28–21 win over the Eagles in the 1947 title game. . . . Finished third in the NFL in rushing in both '48 and '49.

ELMER STRONG, FB—More commonly known by his middle name, Ken. . . . Three-time all-pro with Staten Island and the Giants who was inducted into the Hall of Fame in 1967. . . . Retired in 1939 but came back in '44 because of the player shortage during the war and kicked for the Giants for four more seasons, finally calling it quits at the age of forty-one.

ELMER HACKNEY, backup — Had a 78-yard run from scrimmage in 1942 (second longest in the league) and ran 30 yards for a score with a blocked punt in '43, both for the Lions. . . . Was a fairly pedestrian back, but hey, I needed another Elmer, you know? Besides, the other three were pretty good.

• • •

In the old days we lived in town and mingled with the people. Each one of us knew hundreds of fans by name and perhaps thousands by sight. They knew us and were our friends. With that mutual feeling of friendship came a deep sense of responsibility. We didn't care to face those people if we lost. And when we did lose, we wouldn't have dared face them if we hadn't put out to the limit. We had our gripes and naturally had our differences, even with the coach. But those people kept us together. — Unidentified "former Packer great" in the *Milwaukee Sentinel*

• • •

The Missus

Opponents in the '20s kept *both* eyes peeled for Bears guard Bill Fleckenstein — unless, that is, they wanted one of them blackened. Fleckenstein was legendary for "fomenting miniature riots," as Wilfrid Smith of the *Chicago Tribune* put it. He'd take a poke at anybody and everybody, even Cal Hubbard, the gargantuan Green Bay Packer. The guy was an absolute wildman.

But that's not why I bring him up. I bring him up because in February 1934, barely two years after he played his last NFL game, he married Mildred Harris. Harris's name might not ring many bells now, but she was a silent-screen star back in the day — as well as the first wife, at the tender age of sixteen, of Charlie Chaplin.

After splitting with Charlie, Mildred had a well-publicized relationship with the Prince of Wales. This is the same Prince of Wales who became King Edward VIII — before abdicating the throne to marry Wallis Simpson, the American divorcée.

And then she wed William P. Fleckenstein, the former Bears hell-raiser. Quite the trifecta.

Fleckenstein reportedly served as Mildred's agent for a time. Can you imagine sitting across a bargaining table from remorseless Bill? (It brings to mind comedian Fred Allen's famous line: "All the sincerity in Hollywood you could stuff into a flea's navel and still have room left over for eight caraway seeds and an agent's heart.")

In 1936 — thanks, perhaps, to Fleckenstein's powers of persuasion — Mildred landed a part in a Three Stooges short, *Movie Maniacs*. Maybe you've seen it. In one scene she's in the middle of a pedicure and Curly strikes a match on the bottom of her foot.

Bill, a master of mayhem himself, must have gotten a kick out of that.

Officiating, 1929

After the Portsmouth Spartans dropped a 3–0 game to their archrivals, the independent Ironton Tanks, in 1929, their fans stormed the field and attacked the officials. Umpire Ray Eichenlaub and head linesman Russell Finsterwald both got punched in the jaw.

"James Durfee of Williams [College], the referee around whom most of the spectators' displeasure seemed to center, escaped being struck," the *Portsmouth Times* reported. "Eichenlaub was a victim of mistaken identity."

The next year Portsmouth was admitted into the NFL. (Perhaps the league was impressed that the fans had let the officials live.)

A Game of Feet

Punters were high-profile players in the low-scoring '20s, field position being such a big part of the game. Somebody with a strong leg like the Packers' Verne Lewellen could be utterly dominating.

After the Pack beat Frankford 14–2 in 1929, Lewellen received this testimonial from Bob Haines, the Yellow Jackets' business manager: "Lewellen beat us. He just booted that ball to gain 30 and 40 yards on us with every exchange of punts, and at times he kicked 75 yards. He would send the oval back into our territory time and again between the 5- and 1-yard line, and when Frankford would be forced to kick on fourth down [Lewellen] would just return it on first down. We gained more ground on them through the line and also played well, but it was too much Lewellen and that's all."

Three years earlier, when Frankford won the NFL championship, the Yellow Jackets played it exceedingly safe in their season finale against Pottsville. There were thirteen punts in the first quarter alone, with "scarcely a play between them" and "nobody gaining" any advantage, according to one account.

The game ended in a 0–0 tie, which was all the Jackets needed to nose out the Bears for the title. So it sometimes went in the NFL's first decade.

Number of the Decade: 1¼

This might be the most significant number of *all time* in pro football. Any guesses what it represents?

It's the number of inches the circumference of the ball was reduced from 1912 to 1934 (from 22½ to 21¼). By the mid-'30s the pigskin no longer resembled a melon—better suited for running and especially kicking. Its shape had become much more aerodynamic—perfect for passing. The streamlining totally changed the game. (It also made Benny Friedman's twenty touchdown passes in 1929, with the fatter ball, one of the most amazing feats in NFL history.)

One and a quarter inches. That's all it took.

A player from the early days told me a story about Packers coach Curly Lambeau that relates to this. In his travels around Wisconsin, it seems, Lambeau always made a point of stopping in sporting goods stores and checking their stock of footballs. No two balls are exactly alike, of course, so whenever Curly came across one that was a little narrower than others, he'd buy it to use in games. The Pack, after all, loved to throw.

(These guys thought of everything, didn't they?)

The Adventures of Harry March

The death of Dr. Harry A. March in June 1940 was noted in newspapers east and west, large and small.

> *Syracuse Herald-Journal*: "Father of Professional Football Dies."
>
> *Ogden Standard-Examiner*: "Pro Grid Father Called by Death."
>
> *Oakland Tribune*: "The man credited with fathering professional football is dead."

And so on and so forth.

Which raises the question: Why don't we know more about this man who, clearly, had such a major impact on the game? It's almost as if there's a conspiracy at work. I mean, how many of you had even *heard* of the guy before you opened this book?

Up to now, the story of pro football's beginnings has been pretty much set in stone. The faces on the NFL's Mount Rushmore—the Founding Fathers, at least—are the Bears' George Halas, the Packers' Curly Lambeau, the Giants' Tim Mara, and the Redskins' George Preston Marshall. They're the ones who ran the league in the early years, set it on its present course (read: got the Gravy Train on the tracks), and, oh yes, won most of the titles.

Never mind that Mara didn't know a football from an Easter egg when he founded the New York franchise in 1925. Never mind that it was March who hired the coach, found the players, and, in the Giants' third season, put together a championship club that lost just once in thirteen games—and outscored its opponents 197–20. It was, after all, Mara's money, and he who has the gold rules the history books.

I'm not trying to diminish the importance of the Giants' patriarch. I'm just trying to shine a light on a figure who's been largely forgotten but who also helped make the NFL what it is today. Let's face it, those first few years in New York were crucial. If the league was going to be successful, it needed a team in the biggest market in the country. It also needed that team to do well, needed it to be a glorious advertisement for the pro game.

But there was no guarantee of that when the Giants made their debut against the Providence Steam Roller that first season. Mara's sports background was largely as a legal bookmaker, though he'd dabbled in promoting. As he told Joe Williams of the *New York World-Telegram* after Harry's death, "March got me in the game. I was managing Gene Tunney at the time, or I thought I was, and I called to see [boxing promoter] Billy Gibson about making a match. March was in Gibson's office trying to sell the New York franchise [to him]. I had never seen a football game, pro or otherwise, but my kids were always talking football, so I decided to buy the club for them. If I hadn't dropped in to see Gibson that afternoon, I probably never would have gone in for football."

Besides, who's to say Mara would have stuck with football if the Giants hadn't won that title in 1927? He'd lost quite a bit of money the season before when a rival league — the first American Football League, starring Red Grange — sprang up and attendance dropped sharply. Had that continued much longer, well, Tim knew a sucker bet when he saw one.

But the very next year the Giants beat out the Packers and Bears for their first championship, and the crowds came back. After that, Mara was all in. And he had Harry March, as much as anybody, to thank for it.

March led such a fascinating life — and such a varied one — it's hard to decide where to start this unauthorized biography. Just to give you a preview, though, among the personages appearing in the next few pages are two U.S. presidents, a Supreme Court justice, a well-known playwright, and, in a real stretch, John Wilkes Booth.

Maybe the best place to begin is aboard a boat on the Mississippi

River in August 1931. We don't know nearly enough about this boat. We don't know, for instance, whether Harry himself was behind the wheel or whether he enlisted the help of a crew. What we do know is that he used the boat to pick up players and take them back to New York for training camp.

It was no ordinary boat, either. According to one newspaper account, it was a World War I–era submarine chaser that Harry had bought from the government—presumably at a bargain price. (A sub chaser had been sold the year before, the *New York Times* reported, for $400.)

The boat was 110 feet long, almost 15 feet wide, and had a six-cylinder, 220-horsepower engine fueled by a twenty-four-hundred-gallon tank. It had been stripped, no doubt, of its depth-charge launcher—as well as its three-inch gun—but it remained a formidable vessel. Its cruising speed was twelve knots, and it could travel about two thousand nautical miles before needing refueling. It proved particularly useful in the postwar years for hauling things—bananas from South America, rum from Canada (during Prohibition), . . . and football players from the Midwest.

According to a story in the *Emporia Weekly Gazette*, March picked up five players in St. Louis—Glenn Campbell and Dale Burnett from Emporia (Kansas) State, Hap Moran from Iowa State, Marion Broadstone from Nebraska, and "Flannigan from Texas" (possibly Mack Flenniken from Centenary). They then embarked on a trip, expected to take twelve days, that took them "down the Mississippi River to the Gulf of Mexico, around Florida and up the coast to New York."

He was such an adventurer, Harry was—even in his mid-fifties (and with less than a decade, as it turned out, left to live). There he was, on the mighty Mississippi, just like his "favorite character" in literature, Huckleberry Finn. (He claimed in *Pro Football: Its Ups and Downs*, his history of the early game, that he reread part of Mark Twain's classic "every year." Indeed, *Pro Football* ends with a quote from Huck: "and so there ain't nothin' more to write and I'm rotten glad of it, 'cause if I a'knowd what a trouble it was to write a book I wouldn't have a' tackled it and I ain't a'goin to no more.")

Like Huckleberry Finn, Harry March was born under a wandering star. The last of six children in a well-to-do family from Canton, Ohio, he trooped off to the Spanish-American War and World War I — the latter as a member of the medical corps (which is where the "Dr." in Dr. March comes from) — and was on the move, one way or another, much of his adult life.

Canton was an exciting place to be at the turn of the twentieth century. The president of the United States, William McKinley, lived in Canton — lived, in fact, less than a mile from the March manse. The two families traveled in many of the same circles. Henry March, Harry's father, was the postmaster of Stark County for a while before taking a Treasury Department job in Washington — and leaving his wife to tend to the children. Harry, in other words, "had his father's restlessness," as his granddaughter, Ede Prendergast, put it.

You get the impression March knew everybody there was to know in those years. Part of it was that he had so many interests, occupied so many different orbits — medical, political, theatrical, literary.

Not only did *he* become a doctor, so did his brother Edward and sister Julia. Another brother, Harter, was a dentist. Harry also served as the county coroner for a while. Sometimes, Prendergast told me, his wife would "be very upset when she'd go downstairs in the morning and find a corpse plopped on the sofa. The body would be hauled off to the morgue later in the day. Hoddy [his nickname] was too tired to do so the night before."

When he wasn't testifying in murder trials, Harry was involving himself in Republican Party politics and going to the 1912 convention as a Teddy Roosevelt delegate. (Rugged individualist that he was, it's hardly surprising he evolved into a Bull Moose.) "It is not expediency with me," he told party members. "It is what I believe to be right, and I am not afraid to stand on that side. I was a Progressive when some of you laughed at what you thought was my folly. I'll probably be a Progressive when a lot of you have forgotten it."

Then there was Harry, man of letters. After graduating from Mount Union College, he worked for the *Canton Repository*, a paper run by the brother of his future wife. Later, while getting his medical degree at George Washington University, he wrote theatrical reviews for the *Washington Evening Times* (as well as corresponding for the *Repository*).

At the *Times* Harry assisted Channing Pollock, who would go on to fame as a playwright and lyricist. To hear Pollack tell it, he might never have made it to New York (and subsequently Broadway), broke as he was, if Harry hadn't loaned him his railway pass. "It had to be signed if and when the conductor requested," Pollock wrote in *Harvest of My Years*, "so Harry and I sat up late one night while he taught me to forge his name."

Another time the two friends decided to split the cost of a set of evening clothes. They were different sizes, though, so they had to buy an outfit that was a little too small for Harry and a little too big for Channing. After drawing up a joint-custody agreement—Harry had possession on Mondays, Wednesdays, and Fridays, Channing on Tuesdays, Thursdays, and Saturdays—Harry, lucky man, got to wear the clothes first, to a country club ball.

"Strolling about between dances," Pollack wrote, "[he] walked into an open well, ruining my half of the suit as well as his own. When they fished Harry out, our longed-for habiliments of fashion were a total loss, and I paid $27.50 for my share of a dress suit I never saw. Many years later [another writer they knew] wrote this story, and sold it for exactly 20 times our original investment."

(This is where John Wilkes Booth sneaks into our narrative— through a convenient trap door. Pollack, you see, married Anna Marble, who came from a celebrated stage family. Her aunt Emma knew John and his brother Edward well. "When John Wilkes Booth came to our house he kissed everybody in the family, including me," Emma once said. "We thought he was the nicest man.")

March returned to Canton with his MD in 1901 and wed the afore-mentioned Edith Frease, a woman who was even better connected than he was. Not only did Edith's father, a judge, help McKinley start a law practice in town, her uncle was McKinley's original partner and her brother visited McKinley at his home on North Market Street the night before he left for Buffalo—where he was assassinated in September 1901. (Edith's sister, Rachel Frease-Green, meanwhile, became a world-renowned soprano and sang at the Metropolitan Opera House in New York.)

So it was for Harry. He was never very far from the center of things. One of his lifelong friends was Luther Day, whose father, William, served as secretary of state under McKinley and was appointed to the Supreme Court by Teddy Roosevelt. In the early 1900s Harry and Luther coached the Canton McKinley High School football team. (Luther wound up marrying the niece of McKinley's wife.)

Like I said, Harry knew people, important people. Unfortunately, his was an "oil and water" marriage—essentially "arranged," according to Prendergast. At some point, the story goes, there was an episode in the nurse's dorm at the hospital, and Harry "went crashing through a window to 'escape,'" his granddaughter said. "The family said, 'Get out of town.' And he did."

It was probably around this time that March turned his attentions to theatrical producing. This was yet another side of Harry. He assembled a troupe, March's Musical Merry Makers, that performed throughout the East and Midwest. If you had a theater, Harry had a musical comedy for you, be it *The Red Widow*, *Three Twins*, *The Beauty Shop*, or some other trifle.

"Harry A. March presents . . ." it would say in the newspaper ads. One ad even had a picture of Harry—"The Man Behind the Fun."

"Since leaving Canton," Massillon's *Evening Independent* noted in 1918, "Dr. March has become prominent in theatrical circles, and his musical comedy company has played extended engagements in Louisville, Ky., Portland, Me., Erie, Pa., Trenton and Elizabeth, N.J., and in Philadelphia. The company comprises 30 people, including 18 ladies."

When March's Musical Merry Makers passed through Canton, they'd appear at the Meyers Lake Park theater. It was also at Meyers Lake, in the Minor League Baseball stadium, that Jim Thorpe and the Canton Bulldogs played their games—games that Harry, as the team doctor, never missed . . . and that taught him enough about the pro game to make him think he could run the New York Giants.

In the early '20s March moved his medical practice to Broadway and 103rd Street, just a few blocks from Central Park. He could be closer to the theater crowd—and the literati—that way. Every once in a while he'd dash off a letter to the *New York Times*, setting the paper straight on one thing or another.

But the idea of an NFL team in New York was forever rolling around in his head. He didn't have deep enough pockets to bankroll a club by himself, though. That's why he was in Billy Gibson's office that day in 1925. He needed a partner.

And Tim Mara walked in.

"Doc March was looking for an angel, and I was it," Mara said.

It was the perfect arrangement. Tim took on March as a minority partner and, being new to the game, let him call the football shots. In just a few months Harry pieced together a team good enough to go 8–4 and finish fourth in the league. The first player he signed was center Joe Alexander, the former Syracuse All-American—or rather, *Dr.* Joe Alexander, another medical man. (Alexander, a surgeon, used to wear white gloves in practice to protect his hands.)

March was able to pull this off, Mara said, because he "knew every football player in the United States. . . . That's how we got players."

Growing up in a football hotbed like Canton undoubtedly helped Harry. He'd played the game himself, of course, in high school and college. He'd also seen it played at its highest level when Thorpe and the Bulldogs were at their peak in the 1910s. Beyond that, though, he likely had a large network of "scouts"—sportswriters from all the newspapers he'd visit while on the road with March's Musical Merry Makers. You can almost picture him spending some time with the theater critic, then moseying over to the sports department and swapping stories with the editor, all the while puffing on his ever-present pipe. In those days there were few better sources of information than sportswriters.

One of his finds was guard Butch Gibson, who made the all-league team in 1931. Gibson had played at tiny Grove City College in Pennsylvania, but March knew of him because Butch had gone to Canton McKinley High.

Harry is also credited with discovering Steve Owen, a burly tackle out of another obscure school, Phillips University in Oklahoma. Owen was still with the Kansas City Cowboys when he barnstormed with the Giants after the '25 season; but once Harry saw his talent for disrupting offenses, he told Mara, "Do whatever you have to do to get this guy." Tim obliged, and Owen became an all-pro, the Giants' longtime coach (1931–53), and a Hall of Famer.

Everybody loved Harry. In *My Kind of Football* Owen recalled, "Dr. March ran the club . . . [out of] an office of an apartment. . . . All the players moved in [with] him from time to time, and the feature of the whole layout was a big checkbook on Doc's desk. It was always available to team members who needed advances on their pay. We kept Doc busy writing. But he enjoyed it, and great in all ways was his contribution to the success of professional football in New York City during those days."

People joked that Doc March did everything in the office but practice medicine. This isn't entirely true, though. Giants end Red Badgro once recounted the time he tore his chin open in practice and needed it stitched up. "I just went by his office," he said in *What a Game They Played*, "and he didn't have any of his medical equipment with him, so he got a plain needle and sewing thread out of his drawer and sewed up my chin"—eleven stitches' worth.

(Harry's granddaughter remembers visiting his office as a child.

She was very much struck by the "set of furniture in very dark wood which was carved with naked female torsos, so that when one rested an arm on the chair the hand would fall so that it rested on the ample breasts.")

Then there's this glimpse of him — courtesy of the *Providence Journal* — at a game against the Steam Roller in 1931: "Doc March typified what the well-dressed football manager shall wear, strolling out for the midfield conference with a cane hanging jauntily from one arm. But he was only another spectator to Bill Shupert, the referee. At one point in the game, Bill shooed Doc away from the sidelines as he followed the progress of the game right up to the field. Amidst the guffaws of the crowd, March ambled back to the Giant bench."

While March's medical training was a source of amusement for some, it gave him an unusual perspective on the game. "Playing hurt" might have been the rule of the day, especially with eighteen- and twenty-man rosters, but Harry thought there should be limits. He may have been influenced, too, by the death of a Canton Bulldogs player, Harry Turner, after suffering a spinal injury against Akron in 1914.

"One of the Giants went into a game with a mean boil on his arm and played [only] one quarter," March told the *Times* in 1925. "Hinkey Haines' nose was broken in a game. That happened early, and we took him out right away. It wasn't any lack of courage; it was just plain sense. . . . It might have disfigured him for life [if he'd continued playing]."

March, moreover, might have been the only executive in the league who questioned the wisdom of Red Grange's suicidal tour with the Bears late in the '25 season. (The others were too busy trying to schedule a game with Chicago after Grange dramatically turned pro as soon as his college career ended.)

"He played Wednesday in St. Louis; he plays Saturday in Philadelphia; he goes to a banquet Saturday night; he plays again Sunday in New York, Tuesday in Washington and Wednesday in Boston," Harry said. "If he doesn't slow up, he'll blow up. This isn't baseball."

Grange blew up — and missed the Bears' last two games (and parts of two others).

March also was critical of teams signing players before their college class had graduated — and pushed for a stronger league rule against the practice. As he'd told the Ohio Republicans years before, it was never about "expediency" with him. It was about "what I believe to be right, and I am not afraid to stand on that side."

After winning the title in 1927, the Giants had other outstanding teams, going 13-1-1 in '29 and 13-4 in '30, but they had to settle for second both times behind the Packers. They dropped off to 7-6-1 the next season, after which March had a falling out with Mara and sold his share of the franchise. The reason for their break is still a matter of speculation, but it isn't hard to read between the lines: Tim was simply ready to turn the club over to his sons — Jack, who was going to law school at Fordham, and Wellington, who was still in his teens but would follow his father into the Hall of Fame.

Harry moved into the league office for a few years but got forced out after running afoul of the Redskins' George Preston Marshall. He tried to launch a second football league in 1936, briefly serving as president of the second AFL, but resigned because "I did not approve of the methods [some teams were using] . . . to get some players from the National [Football] League."

Four years later, at sixty-four, he was on his deathbed in Canton. Loyal Edith, left behind decades before, took him in and nursed him to the end.

"Women adored Hoddy," his granddaughter said. "When they fell in love with him — which they did with some frequency — he'd say, 'But, my dear, I have a wife in Ohio.' . . . Many men loved [Edith], too, but she remained married as that was the thing to do."

And so we bring down the curtain on "The Man Behind the Fun," the "grand old fellow" — Badgro's description — who gave us March's Musical Merry Makers and helped turn the Giants into a team worthy of its name.

"The story of professional football is closely linked with the story of Dr. Harry A. March," *Literary Digest* said in 1933. For some reason, though, that link has been lost over the years. Doc March, it should be remembered, brought respectability to a game once overrun with "grafters, gamblers, fixers and tramp pros who played one week with one team and the next week with another," Jack Durkin wrote in the *Syracuse Herald-Journal* after Harry died.

If March doesn't belong in Canton, then he should at least be in the "Gallery of the Great." That was the name he came up with for the Hall of Fame in 1939, when it was still just a dream. Has a nice ring to it, don't you think?

What I've Learned: Dr. Harry A. March

First general manager of the New York Giants; NFL executive; author of *Pro Football: Its Ups and Downs*, the first book on the pro game

"It did not cost much to equip a football team in the 1890s. There was little protective paraphernalia. Shin guards were sometimes worn, and occasionally a man who respected the future of his nose and teeth appeared with a nose protector. . . . Instead of helmets, players wore their hair long and parted in the middle to protect their craniums from cuts and bruises."

"A player is as good as his legs. Of course, some brains are essential."

"When they legalized the forward pass, it altered the physical personnel of the players because weight was no longer the essential—the *sine non quod*—for a lineman or back."

"Proximity seems necessary for real enmity in football."

"When Jim Thorpe was right and wanted to play, Canton won [against archrival Massillon]; if he was not right or loafing—which he sometimes did—the Bulldogs lost."

"Ernie Nevers was in all-around ability second only to Thorpe and much more reliable and desirable a teammate than the Indian. His only fault was that he never gave up when he tried to gain through a line but would try again and again, regardless of consequences. He simply would not believe he could not make it yield. This error of judgment has cost him touchdowns on several occasions."

"A great blocking back is the hardest man to find for your backfield. They nearly all want to be ball carriers, passers or kickers — unfortunately the only ones that seem to attract public notice. Give a coach a reasonably heavy, fast, low-charging line and just one exceptional blocking back, and any mediocre runner can make a reputation and the headlines."

"You can't carry the mail if you dally too much with the female."

"One of the potent enemies of pro football in the beginning was W. O. McGeehan of the *New York Herald Tribune*. He early made up his mind that pro football was no good; either the pros did not try to play or if they did, they played with foul tactics. He gradually softened his animosities. One of the last columns he wrote lauded the merit and honesty of pro football to the skies."

"Some of the most brilliant and intelligent, high salaried and popular players ever in the National Football League were and are Hebrews. Without exception, Hebrew players are good men, attentive to duty, careful with their money and amenable to discipline."

"The Indians object more to playing against Negroes than do the Southern men for some reason."

"Players from small schools make up the body of every team in the league; from colleges you never heard of and never will see. Reputations do not overweigh sturdiness, good character, ability and amiability under hard coaching."

"You can't improve much on the geometric axiom that the shortest distance between two points is a straight line. Most professional attacks are built on this axiom, with just enough deviation to provide some deception in advancing the ball. The stunts, tricks and schemes of a dozen different colleges that fit into this fundamental truth make up the pro system."

"There is but one tangible menace to the pro game and that is weather. In common with any other outdoor sport, Old Jupiter Pluvius, which our lexicon tells us is the God of Rain, is the one to which we all have to bow. If weather is clear, business is good; if cloudy, it is hurt; if raining, get out your checkbook and pay the red figures."

"The reserve clause is absolutely necessary for the preservation of any league. We admit that this privilege has been abused and some injustices have been done. But on the whole, this reserve clause is rightly and fairly administered and many times it is for the players' own benefit. Men are but children of larger growth, and there are a lot of saps among professional athletes; if you don't think so, meet a dozen and see how many you would wish as a business partner."

"Men are all created free, but not all are created equal."

"'Tis better to have passed and lost, than never to have passed at all."

2.
The
1930s

1930s

NFL	1930	1939
Champion	Green Bay Packers	Green Bay Packers
Franchises	11	10
Avg. attendance	NA	19,476
Roster size	20	30
Games per season	Anywhere from 9 to 18	11
Points per game	21.2	30.8
Shutouts	34 (73 games)	12 (55 games)
0–0 ties	2	2
Yds. per game	NA	498.9
Plays per game	NA	114.8
Passes completed (%)	NA	42.5
Run/pass TD ratio	134 run, 80 pass	102 run, 99 pass
Hall of Fame players	13	17
Hall of Fame coaches	3	4

Leaders	1930	1939
Scoring (points)	Jack McBride, Dodgers, 56	Andy Farkas, Redskins, 68
Rushing TDs	McBride and Verne Lewellen, Packers, 8	Johnny Drake, Rams, 9
Passing TDs	Benny Friedman, Giants, 13	Frank Filchock, Redskins, 11
Receiving TDs	Three tied with 5	Jim Benton, Rams, 7
Field goals	Frosty Peters, Steam Roller, 2	Ward Cuff, Giants, 7

Hall of Famers who played in 1930 (13): E Red Badgro, QB Benny Friedman, HB Red Grange, QB Arnie Herber, T Cal Hubbard, G Walt Kiesling, T Link Lyman, HB Johnny (Blood) McNally, G Mike Michalske, FB Bronko Nagurski, FB Ernie Nevers, HB Ken Strong, C George Trafton.

Hall of Fame coaches in 1930 (3): Jimmy Conzelman (Providence Steam Roller), Curly Lambeau (Packers), Steve Owen (Giants).

Hall of Famers who played in 1939 (17): QB Sammy Baugh, T Turk Edwards, G Danny Fortmann, C Mel Hein, Herber, E Bill Hewitt, FB Clarke Hinkle, E Don Hutson, T Bruiser Kinard, B Tuffy Leemans, QB Sid Luckman, E Wayne Millner, T-G George Musso, QB Ace Parker, Strong, T Joe Stydahar, C Alex Wojciechowicz.

Hall of Fame coaches in 1939 (4): Ray Flaherty (Redskins), George Halas (Bears), Lambeau, Owen.

Talking Points

• Roster sizes increased from twenty to thirty in the '30s, and scoring increased from 21.2 points a game to 30.8. Anybody see a correlation? It was still the single-platoon era, but with more available bodies — that is, more substitution — you could be more adventurous on offense. (Read: Put the ball in the air.) Note that by the end of the decade teams were scoring almost as much via the pass (99 touchdowns) as via the run (102). That's a huge ground shift.

• Rule changes were largely responsible for this. After 1932 — a dull, tie-infested season — the NFL took drastic measures to open up the passing game and create more scoring. You could now throw from anywhere behind the line, and there were no longer penalties for incompletions.

Also, hash marks were added — 10 yards in from the each sideline — to give offenses more room to operate. Previously, the ball was placed wherever the runner was downed, sometimes just a yard from the sideline, which forced offenses to waste a play moving the ball back to the middle of the field.

Finally, the goalposts were returned to the goal line (after spending the previous six seasons in the back of the end zone). The result, naturally, was more field goals, a higher success rate on extra points, and fewer of those infernal ties.

• It was still a single-wing (and double-wing) world — except in Chicago, where Bears boss George Halas was tinkering with the T formation and creating the offense of the future.

• Schedules finally became uniform. In 1936, for the first time, every team played the same number of games.

• With the disappearance of the Frankford Yellow Jackets, the Providence Steam Roller, and other small-market clubs, the NFL officially became a big-city league.

• Something else that disappeared: black players. From 1934 through '45 the NFL didn't have any. The owners always claimed there was no conspiracy, but that's nonsense. They obviously decided it was easier to sell the game as an all-white enterprise.

Overlooked fact: The Bears, Packers, Redskins, Dodgers, and Lions (who started out as the Portsmouth Spartans) never had any black players, anyway, so it wasn't hard for them to continue not having them. Almost all the teams that *had* employed blacks in the early years dropped out of the league. Convenient, no?

The 1930 Census

If you want to find out where the NFL *really* stood at the start of its second decade, page through the 1930 U.S. Census sometime.

You'll learn that George Halas thought of himself, first and foremost, not as the co-owner of the Bears but as the "president" of a "real estate" firm. Tim Mara, his counterpart on the Giants, claimed his occupation as the "owner" of a "coal company." And Joe Carr, who by then had been president of the league for eight years, is identified as the "president" of "Col. Base Ball." (Translation: He ran Columbus, Ohio's, Minor League Baseball franchise, the Senators.)

Other NFL notables — and the jobs listed for them:

- Curly Lambeau, Packers coach: "agent/insurance"
- Walt Kiesling, Cardinals tackle: "athletic teacher/public schools"
- Verne Lewellen, Packers back: "District Attorney/Brown County"
- Ernie Nevers, Cardinals back: "pitcher/Base Ball"
- Ken Strong, Giants back: "professional/Foot Ball"

(Finally, an admitted football man.)

No One-Man Team

The Chicago Bears threw big money at Notre Dame fullback "Jumping" Joe Savoldi when he unexpectedly became available late in the 1930 season. (The school had kicked him out after discovering he was married.) The Bears were even willing to pay a thousand-dollar fine, which NFL President Joe Carr assessed them for signing a player before his class had graduated.

But Savoldi's career lasted just three games. When the season was over, he turned to wrestling—where he paralyzed opponents with his signature dropkick and did quite well for himself. Decades later he revealed to Frank Blair of the *Long Beach Press-Telegram* why he left football so abruptly.

Once the other Bears found out how much he was making, Savoldi said,

> they quit blocking for me. . . . Here I was getting some $4,000 a game with my cut of the gate, and my teammates in the line and backfield were being paid $50 to $125 per man. . . . If I was worth 20 times as much as they were, I could make my own touchdowns without any help. After I had been riddled a dozen times trying to hit the line or sweep off tackle, I just fell down and stayed there. I didn't have a chance.
>
> So they took me out and kept me on the bench after the second game—not because I couldn't play football, but [because] the other guys wouldn't play and block for me. I had a contract for 18 games after that first season, with a guarantee of $500 a game, but I didn't want any part of that pro football. I went into wrestling. In that business you don't need blockers.

Baseball vs. Football, 1931

A noteworthy—some might even say historic—collision took place in the sixth inning of the Red Sox's 1931 home opener. While scoring from third on a sacrifice fly, the Yankees' Babe Ruth plowed into Boston catcher Charlie Berry, who'd positioned his 185 pounds between Ruth and the plate. Both went flying, but Berry dusted himself off and finished the game. Poor Babe wound up in the hospital and was out for ten days.

Of course, what would anyone expect? The guy he ran into was a former end for the Frankford Yellow Jackets.

(And a darn good one, too. Berry led the NFL in scoring in 1925, helped Frankford win the title in '26, and made at least one all-pro team both years. But he concentrated on baseball after that, playing eleven seasons with the Red Sox, White Sox, and Athletics.)

Ruth didn't realize how badly he was hurt after his run-in with Berry and took his spot in left field in the bottom half of the inning. But when he went to chase a drive by Boston's Tom Oliver, his left leg crumpled. He initially thought it was just a bad charley horse, but the collision had actually caused nerve damage that resulted in temporary paralysis.

His first night at Peter Bent Brigham Hospital was "fitful," the *New York Times* reported. He feared "his leg was broken and that his illustrious career on the diamond had come to an end." But by the next morning he was "able to wiggle his left toes," the *Times* said. "This cheerful tiding at once was relayed from the sick chamber to the outer world, where it was received with no little acclaim."

Three days later the Bambino took the train back to New York. He was still in a wheelchair and clutched a cane in his left hand. After missing eight games, he returned to the Yankees lineup and, in a five-inning stint against the Red Sox, went 2 for 3 with a run batted in and a walk. It would be a while longer, though, before his limp went away—and he had Charlie Berry, the erstwhile Frankford Yellow Jacket, to thank for it.

"They still have the picture of that collision up in Fenway Park," Berry said in 1965. "I lowered my shoulder and drove upward. The Babe went flying into the air. According to the picture, it looks as though he was standing on his head."

Prison Football

It was just a brief item in the newspaper on November 3, 1931—two paragraphs, no more. But it would have such an impact decades later on . . . well, the movie careers of Burt Reynolds and Adam Sandler, for one thing.

The warden at Sing Sing prison, the Associated Press reported, was starting a football program and was looking for volunteer coaches. The New York Giants "immediately responded," the story said. "They announced that six players, Ray Flaherty, Glenn Campbell, Bill Owen, Butch Gibson, Dale Burnett and Ted Bucklin, would be 'incarcerated' long enough to give the Sing Sing boys a few pointers."

A few weeks earlier Giants owner Tim Mara had donated enough old uniforms and equipment to get the program started. That's right, the road to *The Longest Yard*—the 1974 Reynolds original and the 2005 Sandler remake—began in 1931 with an NFL team's generosity. (We pause now for a moment of reverential silence.)

The next year the Giants signed a Sing Sing "graduate," 220-pound fullback Jumbo Morano, and sent him to the Paterson Nighthawks of the Eastern Football League for further development. Morano never played in the NFL, though. (In fact, he kind of fell off the map after that season.) But another Sing Sing alumnus, Alabama Pitts, got into three games with the Philadelphia Eagles in 1935.

This was pretty revolutionary stuff in the 1930s. Prisons in that period were just emerging from the Dark Ages, the era of corporal punishment, No Talking Allowed, and—the ultimate symbol—striped uniforms. Sing Sing, just north of New York City along the banks of the Hudson River, was a particularly gruesome place, almost beyond description. Not only was it filled with twenty-four hundred of the hardest cases but overcrowding made it necessary to house a third of them in the Old Cellblock, a dank, dreary dungeon built by the prisoners in the 1820s . . . and condemned on more than one occasion.

The cells in the Old Cellblock were three feet three inches wide, six feet seven inches high, and seven feet long—"no bigger than a dead man's grave," in the words of one occupant. They had no windows and no plumbing (only "night buckets" that inmates would empty each morning into an open sewer).

A prison doctor described the environment thusly: "The walls are thick stone, which makes these cells look as if they have been hollowed out of solid rock. A prisoner confined to one of them for the first time invariably suffers an impression of crushing weight, closing in from all sides. Originally, the only light came from a series of small windows in the outer wall across the galleries from the cells, but some years ago this wretched condition was improved by cutting several large windows in the outer wall."

Mercifully, wardens in the 1930s were moving away from the concept of all punishment all the time and toward the idea of rehabilitation. One of the many ways Lewis Lawes, Sing Sing's enlightened leader, tried to bring this about was by forming athletic teams that would play games against outside clubs. Through healthy competition, he figured, the prisoner "learns the necessity of rules, or laws, and cooperation with his fellows. He learns to subordinate his own desires to the good of the whole team, and learns, too, that he must play the game to win. He develops a sense of proportion and values and finds that there is no royal road, or loafer's route, by which a big score can be made."

So in early November 1931, two days after a 14–0 win over the Portsmouth Spartans, half a dozen Giants went up to Sing Sing and showed the convicts how to get in a three-point stance — the first of several such clinics. In between, inmates with football experience ran the practices and coached as best they could. On November 15 Warden Lawes's warriors — the Black Sheep, they called themselves — played their first game against outside competition, taking on the local unit of the state naval militia.

Naturally, it was a home game. Where else would Sing Sing play? It also, predictably, attracted a lot of attention. Newsreel cameras were set up in the guard towers to film the historic event, and newspapers covered it like it was an Important Grid Tilt. There was so much interest, fans had to be *turned away*. (The stands could accommodate twenty-five hundred, but two thousand of the seats were reserved for prisoners.)

"I never thought I'd live to see anything like this," one older convict told a reporter.

> There's youngsters here who maybe don't understand what prison meant to the old-timers. But I have been here a long time, and I know. The days before the warden came here, every day was like the last. Nothing to think about. Exercise periods didn't mean much. The men didn't know what to do with themselves. They had to keep moving, so they'd just walk and talk. And the things they talked about wasn't good for them, or for the prison either.
>
> Football — I don't know anything about the game, but most of them do. But it's the idea — see? — playin' a fine game that the whole country talks about, and that young men like.

Clad in the Giants' red helmets and blue-and-red jerseys, the Black Sheep em-baa-rrassed the militia 33–0. This was such big news that even the *Los Angeles Times*, three thousand miles away, carried a story on the game. It only got bigger after that. The following season the aptly named John Law, who had played at Notre Dame under Knute Rockne, was brought in coach the team.

"Not only is my name John Law," he told the *New York Times*, "but the warden's name is Lawes and the football team is made up of lawbreakers. In addition to that, I'm Democratic candidate for Assemblyman from Yonkers and hope to become a lawmaker. It's really a peculiar situation."

That said, Law claimed to be "astonished" at how coachable the players were. And talk about tough! One of his men had lost three fingers in a shop accident, but the coach hoped to have him available by midseason. "Three fingers don't mean much to a good player," he said. "I knew a lad who played with Southern California who had no hand at all, only a stump, but what damage he did was plenty."

Sing Sing's games were nothing like the inmates vs. guards blood fests you see in the movies. Indeed, they were probably as cleanly contested as any in the country. The prisoners knew they had to be on their best behavior; otherwise teams wouldn't want to play them. (Visiting clubs, meanwhile, minded their manners lest they incur the wrath of two thousand convicts.)

In many respects they were just like any other football game — except for the twenty-foot walls and guards with machine guns. "Almost the only differences between this and a major intercollegiate game," the *New York Evening Journal* observed, "were a marked absence of slugging on the field and drunkenness in the stands."

(The general air of civility disappointed Westbrook Pegler, the celebrated sports columnist. After the Black Sheep lost to the Port Jervis Police Department in 1932, Pegler wrote, "There was something almost repugnant about the kind solicitude of the Sing Sing boys for the officers as they helped them to their feet and dusted them off after the [plays].")

Which isn't to say a game at Sing Sing wasn't a *little* unusual. Against the militia in '31, the second quarter was shortened to twelve minutes, the third to ten, and the fourth to seven, according to the United Press, "in order to end the game at 4:30 o'clock, when the 'lockup whistle' blew." And because the games were played in a prison, fans were frisked as they entered and had to pass through several security checkpoints before reaching the field. (Their exit was almost as painstaking, so worried was the warden that one of the convicts would escape.)

Once inside, though, fans could buy hot dogs at the inmate-run refreshment stand, laugh at the home team's zany mascot (a pony painted with black-and-white prisoner's stripes to resemble a zebra), root along with the Sing Sing cheerleaders, and be entertained by the ever-clever musical selections of the prison band.

Julius Freedman, the Marv Albert of Sing Sing, did the play-by-play of the games on the prison radio station. His listeners were largely those laid up in the hospital — or awaiting their fate on death row. A. J. Liebling, then a young reporter for the *New York World-Telegram*, offered this approximation of Freedman's style: "Here comes Jim Egan, a great fellow. He replaces Moe Bernstein. No, wait a minute, he replaces Winkie Winkle. No, friends, sorry, I've got it wrong; he replaces — well, anyway, he is a great fellow."

Sportswriters had as much fun writing about the games as the fans did watching them. The *Times* correspondent pointed out that the prisoners seemed particularly inspired in the opening quarter of one contest because "the prison gate lay in the direction of the goal they won on the [coin] toss." Another story, in a not-so-veiled reference to Sing Sing's hot seat, began, "The Big House eleven electrified its cheering section of 2,300 inmates by . . . defeating the visitors, the Poughkeepsie All-Stars, 18 to 6."

Headline writers got their jollies, too, coming up with gems like "Sing Sing Chisels Righteous Path to 20 to 0 Victory" and "Cop Team Fails to Shear Wool of Black Sheep." The "Galloping Cons of Sing Sing" were far from a joke, though. They won many more games than they lost against the likes of the Danbury Trojans, the Newark Cyclones, and the New Rochelle Bulldogs. (Of course, as the prison's athletic director noted, the team had more than just the home-field advantage. It also had "a self-sustaining nucleus"; some players never "graduated.")

Soon enough prison football had spread to Missouri State Penitentiary, to Stateville Correctional Center outside Chicago, to San Quentin in California — to just about everywhere, it seemed. But not everyone was happy about this. Some, such as Cook County (Illinois) Superior Court Judge Marcus Kavanagh, questioned the propriety of such activities.

"Jails were never meant for pity and learning but for punishment and justice," he said in an op-ed piece for the *Times*. "All things which encourage mental and moral improvement are proper, but is moral improvement attained when a burglar rolls a college boy around in the mud at a football game?"

The eye-for-an-eye crowd ultimately prevailed over the Sermon on the Mount contingent. In 1936 New York's corrections commissioner, Edward P. Mulrooney, issued an order forbidding the charging of admission to prison events. This effectively killed Sing Sing football because the team depended on the dollar it received from each paying customer to buy equipment and cover the travel expenses of visiting clubs. (During the '33 season the Black Sheep reportedly cleared a profit of $4,527.)

But the story doesn't quite end there. In 1941, six years after Alabama Pitts left Sing Sing for the Eagles, Philadelphia owner Lex Thompson announced his team would give a tryout every season to a paroled convict. The suggestion likely came from his business manager, Harry Thayer. Thayer's father, Walter, had been New York's commissioner of corrections before Mulrooney — and was a big supporter of the Black Sheep.

Walter Thayer thought football improved a prison's quality of life. "As an example," he said in 1932, "infractions of the rules at [Sing Sing] were the fewest in the institution's history for weeks prior to the games last fall. They knew that even a minor infraction would bar them from witnessing the game."

(In 1943 Thompson's club made news for trying out Don McGregor, a back who'd recently been paroled from Iowa State Penitentiary. McGregor — like Jumbo Morano, Sing Sing's Nagurski — didn't make it, but it was the thought that counted.)

Then there's the 1950 Chicago Bears. One of their preseason tune-ups, believe it or not, was a game against the Ionia State Reformatory team in Grand Rapids, Michigan. Ionia was a tad undermanned, so the Bears loaned them three players — one of whom, halfback Harper Davis, scored a touchdown for the inmates. Davis then switched back to the Bears and scored a TD for them.

Final score: Bears 53, Cons 12.

(Wish I had a few more details on the game, but unfortunately, as they say, what happens in Ionia State Reformatory stays in Ionia State Reformatory.)

Four for the Price of One

Boxers have been known to tangle with multiple opponents on the same day — George Foreman comes to mind — but the Providence

Steam Roller are the only NFL team to try anything like that. On November 22, 1931, the Steam Roller took on four semipro clubs in an exhibition game, playing one quarter against each.

In the first quarter the Roller whipped the local Watchemoket All-Stars, 27–0.

In the second they stomped the Speedways of Cranston, Rhode Island, 32–zip.

The second-half margins were a tad tighter—7–0 over the Natick, Massachusetts, Sacred Hearts and 12–0 over the East Providence town team. (The Steam Roller were probably just tired from having to run down on so many kickoffs.)

Final score: Roller 78, Four Semipro Clubs of the Apocalypse 0.

"Not one first down was made against the Providence pros, nor could a forward pass be completed," the *Providence Journal* reported. "In fact, practically every attempt of the semi-pros to advance the ball either by runs or passes was squelched completely."

It turned out to be Providence's last year in the NFL. The Steam Roller, winners of the 1928 title, were hit hard by the Depression and had to drop out of the league. The same fate befell the Frankford Yellow Jackets, the '26 champs, that season. Small-market clubs just didn't have the resources anymore to keep up with the Chicago Bears and New York Giants.

By 1934 the Staten Island Stapletons and Portsmouth Spartans were gone, too, replaced by the Philadelphia Eagles, Pittsburgh Pirates, and Detroit Lions. The only town team that survived was Green Bay's resourceful Packers.

After the four-against-one exhibition, the Steam Roller had two games left. They got pounded 38–7 by the Packers in Providence, then played a scoreless tie with the Giants in New York to finish 4-4-3, good for sixth place out of ten clubs.

Late in the Giants game, the Roller made their biggest offensive push and reached the New York 12 — with five-foot-three, 143-pound back Butch Meeker, the smallest player in the NFL, leading the way.

But the Giants' Dale Burnett picked off a pass at the 4-yard line to kill the drive.

Soon the clock ran out, and the Providence Steam Roller joined the ranks of the Watchemoket All-Stars, the Speedways of Cranston, the Natick Sacred Hearts, the East Providence town team, and all the other clubs that weren't quite major league. An era in pro football was ending.

Dining with the Dodgers

The day of the Spartans' 1931 opener, there was an ad in the *Portsmouth Times* for a one-dollar steak dinner that night at the Washington Hotel.

"Come Talk Over the Game," it said. "The Brooklyn Dodgers Will Eat with Us."

The Dodgers did indeed chow down with the locals after their 14–0 loss to Portsmouth. The dinner, staged by Spartans management for out-of-town newspapermen and "other visitors," was well attended, the *Times* reported, "and visiting scribes, who were royally entertained, voted the frolic a real one. The game was played over a dozen times around long, well-filled tables, and the air was full of football chatter."

The three officials who worked the game also attended the feast, as did coaches Potsy Clark of Portsmouth and Jack Depler of Brooklyn, who were given "a big hand" by the crowd.

The Dodgers no doubt ate well. It was the first of five straight road games for them to start the season, and they needed the sustenance.

Packers Fever

True story: A judge in Oshkosh, Wisconsin, granted a divorce to Mrs. Daisy Goldstein in 1931 because her husband, Hyman, was more devoted to the Green Bay Packers than to her.

Less than two weeks after the Packers wrapped up their third-straight NFL title, Daisy told Circuit Judge Fred Beglinger that her dearly beloved had neglected her during the season, "attending all

Packer games both at Green Bay and elsewhere [and] leaving her alone weekends," the *Oshkosh Daily Northwestern* reported. (The expense of being a superfan apparently wasn't an issue for Mr. Goldstein. He owned a chain of clothing stores.)

The Packers' unique schedule no doubt contributed to the Goldsteins' estrangement. Because of Green Bay's arctic climate, the Pack spent the first half of the season at home—when it was warmer—then played six of their last seven games on the road. One of those games was in Providence on Thanksgiving, which means Hyman spent the holiday not with Daisy but with Curly (as in Lambeau).

For her husband's "cruel and inhuman treatment," Daisy got the furniture and $200 a month support for her and their two children. As for Hyman, he was probably looking forward to the Packers' five-game eastern swing the next year that took them through Boston, New York, Brooklyn, Staten Island, and Portsmouth.

Ten Unlikely Record Holders

BILL MCKALIP, Portsmouth Spartans (1931)—McKalip tied a record by catching a touchdown pass in four consecutive games. His scores measured 42 (vs. Bears), 56 (vs. Staten Island), 63 (vs. Cleveland), and 11 (vs. Cardinals) yards. They were the only TDs of his four-year NFL career.

MARTY KOTTLER, Pittsburgh Pirates (September 27, 1933)—Kottler intercepted a Cardinals pass late in the first half and ran 99 yards for a touchdown, jump-starting a 14–13 Pittsburgh victory. His return was 3 yards longer than the previous record—held for a decade by Hall of Famer Joe Guyon—and had the added distinction of being the first TD in franchise history. It was only his second NFL game. He played in just one more.

GIL "FRENCHY" LEFEBVRE, Cincinnati Reds (December 3, 1933)—A five foot six, 155 pounder, LeFebvre scored on a 98-yard punt return in the fourth quarter to sew up a 10–0 win over Brooklyn. The crowd expected him to let Shipwreck Kelly's punt go into the end zone for a touchback, but "gasps turned to cheers," the Associated Press reported, "as the runner, who never played college football, started down the field." LeFebvre's return stood as the record for sixty-one years. It was his only touchdown in three NFL seasons.

HARRY NEWMAN, New York Giants (November 11, 1934) — Newman was a fine tailback/quarterback, but — at five eight, 179 pounds — you wouldn't expect him to set a record for rushing attempts in a game. He did, though, carrying thirty-eight times for 114 yards in a 17–3 victory over the Packers. His mark wasn't broken until 1973, when the Bills' O. J. Simpson had thirty-nine carries against the Chiefs. Years later, in *What a Game They Played*, Newman told author Richard Whittingham that his feat was "pretty stupid for a quarterback. The reason I had to carry it so often is that Ken Strong had a broken toe, Bo Molenda had a bad back, and there seemed to be something wrong with everybody else who ordinarily carried the ball."

PAT COFFEE, Chicago Cardinals (December 5, 1937) — In a season-ending loss to the Bears, Coffee threw for a record 306 yards. The total represents almost 30 percent of his career passing yardage (1,024).

RAY "BUZZ" BUIVID, Chicago Bears (December 5, 1937) — In that same 42–28 Bears win, Buivid threw five touchdown passes, which tied the record held by Hall of Famer Benny Friedman and is *still* — more than seventy years later — the most by a rookie in one game. (In fact, Buzz's name came up during the 2009 season when the Lions' Matt Stafford tossed five against the Browns.) Career TD passes for Buivid: 11.

DOUG RUSSELL, Chicago Cardinals (September 23, 1934, and November 27, 1938) — Here's an unusual double: Russell simultaneously held the records for longest kickoff return (102 yards against Cincinnati in 1934) and longest pass completion (98 yards to Gus Tinsley against the Cleveland Rams in 1938). The kickoff mark isn't too surprising; he did, after all, lead the league in rushing in 1935. But he was far from renowned as a passer. Indeed, he completed just nineteen of seventy-one for 359 yards in his career. The 98-yarder was his last completion.

DAVE DIEHL, Detroit Lions (November 26, 1944) — Diehl tied a record by catching three touchdown passes from Frankie Sinkwich in a 26–14 victory over the Cleveland Rams. (The lengths: 57, 33, and 5 yards.) He had only one other TD reception in his four NFL seasons.

FRED "DIPPY" EVANS, Chicago Bears (November 28, 1948) — Evans is the only player in league history to return two fumbles for scores in the same game. In the space of a few minutes he scooped up bobbles by the Redskins' Howard Hartley and Bob Nussbaumer and ran 10 and 16 yards for touchdowns to give the Bears a 20–0 first-quarter lead. (Chicago went on to win 48–13.) Evans's heroics came in the next-to-last game of his brief (1946–48) career. The Bears picked him up late in the season as an injury replacement, and he suited up just three times for them.

BOBBY PLY, Houston Oilers (December 16, 1962) — In a 26–17 victory over the Chargers, Ply intercepted four passes to tie a record that still hasn't been broken. He had only five other picks in his six-year career. (Three of them came the previous week against Denver, giving him seven interceptions in two games. Nobody else has had that many since they began keeping track of the stat in 1940.)

Hitting the Reset Button

The NFL was down to eight teams in the Depression year of 1932 — from a high of twenty-two just six years earlier. With rosters set at twenty, this meant that no more than 160 players were active in the league at any given time. That's barely enough for three clubs today.

The point I'm trying to make is that there were plenty of players looking for work back then — players who'd been on teams that had dropped out of the NFL, players toiling in the minor leagues, not to mention all the players pouring out of colleges. If an NFL club was unhappy with its performance and wanted to clean house — or if it brought in a new coach and he wanted to reshape the roster — it was easy enough to do, especially with everybody on a one-year contract.

The amount of turnover could be stunning. Of the thirty-four players, for instance, who suited up for the 1932 Staten Island Stapletons at one time or another, only five had been with them the previous season. That same year just six of the thirty-three players the Brooklyn Dodgers used were returnees. The two clubs still finished at the bottom of the league, though — Staten Island at 2-7-3 (after going 4-6-1 the year before), Brooklyn at 3-9 (up slightly from 2-12).

In Boston, owner George Preston Marshall was a huge fan of change for the sake of change. The Redskins had only nine holdovers in 1933 and just eight in '34 — for all the good it did. Their record stayed the same (4-4-2 in '32, 5-5-2 in '33 and 6-6 in '34).

Only one major housecleaning paid big dividends right away. After going 5-6-3 under Hal Griffen in 1930, the Portsmouth Spartans replaced him with Potsy Clark and brought back only eight players. The rebuilt Spartans placed second behind the Packers in '31 and reached the championship game the next season. Of course, their signings included one future Hall of Famer (back Dutch Clark) and four future all-pros (back Glenn Presnell, tackle George Christensen, guard Ox Emerson, and end Harry Ebding). How many teams have added five guys like that in the same year?

Obviously, not every player who disappeared from a club's roster was cut. Some would leave to take coaching jobs . . . or because they didn't like the life. But there was much more year-to-year volatility, personnel-wise, than you'd see later on — and infinitely more than there is now.

Bull Doehring

For a guy who threw just seven touchdown passes in his NFL career, John "Bull" Doehring . . . well, put it this way: It's been more than seventy years since he played for the Bears, and here I am writing about him.

Why don't we start with TD number seven? That'll give you a good sense of The Bull Doehring Experience. Then we can get into other things, like his uncanny ability to whip the ball 60 yards *behind his back* (as only a screwy southpaw can).

Doehring's last scoring pass came in November 1936 against the Eagles in Philadelphia. The final seconds of the first half were ticking away, and coach George Halas instructed him—as he often did in these situations—to throw the ball as far as he could, preferably in the vicinity of a receiver. Bull was only too happy to oblige.

From the *Philadelphia Bulletin*: "Taking the [snap from] his own 40-yard line, Doehring faded back 10 yards while [George] Corbett raced downfield, then John let the ball fly. High it soared into the heavens, higher than most punts you've seen, and far down the field. Corbett took it over his shoulder as he went into the end zone."

The pass, Stan Baumgartner of the *Philadelphia Inquirer* reckoned, traveled seventy yards in the air. "It was one of the greatest forward passes ever seen," he said, "a perfectly timed and perfectly placed heave. The spectators were so thrilled that they applauded the magnificent play for fully three minutes."

(And Baumgartner, it should be noted, had as good a view as anybody. Before sitting down to type his story, he served as the head linesman in the game.)

Bull (short for Bulldog) Doehring took your breath away. At a time when passing attacks were still fairly primitive, his throws had an almost Sputnik-like quality about them. He wasn't a great player by any stretch, but he had this one great talent—and Halas was smart enough to see the uses it could be put to. Bull could do more than just help the Bears win games; he could be a sideshow, somebody who could entertain the fans with his freakishly strong arm.

Doehring was never more of a circus act than when the Bears barnstormed around the country after the season. During a workout in Los Angeles in January 1934, he uncorked a 70-yard bomb to Bill Hewitt and "experienced the strange sensation of hearing a wave of handclapping," the *Chicago Tribune* reported. "It was such forward passing as Los Angeles grid fans—red hot as they are—had never seen. . . . The fans want to see if he can shoot such passes so far and so accurately in the heat of battle."

Much mystery surrounded Doehring—kind of the way it surrounded Shoeless Joe of Hannibal, Mo. Bull didn't make a deal with the devil, though (as far as we know). He just showed up at the Bears' practice one day in 1932 and boldly asked Halas, "Do you want the best passer in football?"

Papa Bear sized up the stranger, this sturdy kid who stood six feet tall and weighed 216 pounds, and said, "I want the best of everything."

So Doehring went out on the field and began showing off, filling the air with passes that seemed to scrape the stratosphere. It didn't take long for Halas to be convinced. He signed Bull to a contract and had him playing three days later against the Portsmouth Spartans.

Who *was* this kid? And where did he come from? The Bears would joke, when Halas wasn't around, that Doehring was his illegitimate son. In fact, he was a product of the Milwaukee sandlots who, at twenty-three, had decided to give pro ball a shot after failing his entrance exam at the University of Wisconsin. In high school he'd been a teammate of Buckets Goldenberg, who went on to win three NFL championships with the Packers. After that the free-spirited Bull had been shipped off to Illinois Military School and Kentucky Military Institute for, uh, saluting training.

"He was a character . . . a little shaky upstairs," Bears back Ray Nolting once told me. "They tell me he had a wife, and he hung her out the hotel window by her ankles."

Doehring does appear to have gotten a divorce just before he came to Chicago. A brief item in the *Sheboygan Press* in July said, "Mrs. Victoria Doehring was granted a divorce from John Doehring in circuit court in Milwaukee. Both are 22 years old." (Bull didn't turn twenty-three for four more months.) The reason for the split? "Her husband left her the next day after they were married in Wauke-gan, Ill., in May 1928."

The season was half over when Doehring joined the Bears. It didn't take him long to make an impact. In his second game, against the Brooklyn Dodgers, he had a 45-yard completion to Hewitt. The following Thursday — Thanksgiving — he burned the Cardinals with a 50-yard touchdown pass to Corbett just before halftime. (Sound familiar?) And the Sunday after that at Portsmouth, in an-other hurry-up situation at the end of the first half, he let go with a throw to Luke Johnsos — one that carried 60-plus yards — for Chi-cago's only score in a 7–7 tie.

In the space of eight days the total unknown who hadn't spent a day in college had made three huge plays. (He'd even gotten ejected from the second game for fighting with Cardinals end Milan Creigh-ton.) The TD pass to Johnsos might have been the single biggest play in the Bears' season. After all, had they lost to Portsmouth, they wouldn't have wound up tied with the Spartans in the final stand-ings . . . and there wouldn't have been any need for a playoff to de-cide the championship — which was, of course, the NFL's first title game.

During the rest of his time with the Bears — he played four more years with them and was loaned to Pittsburgh for one — Doehring was more a curiosity than a difference-maker. (You get the feeling that, after that first year, opposing defensive backs started backped-aling as soon as he came into the game.)

"He threw the ball so hard nobody could catch it," said Ookie Miller, the center on those Bears teams. "He gave Luke Johnsos a sore chest because it went right through his hands and hit him in the chest. He was the kind of guy . . . we'd have a dummy scrim-mage and just be running through things, and he'd run right into people. Hurt 'em. He was a little crazy, I think."

For a while the million-dollar question among the Chicago play-ers was: What the heck does Doehring keep in that zippered bag he's always carrying around? Finally, Nolting just had to find out.

One night he got a coconspirator to draw Bull out of his room, then snuck in and opened the bag.

"He had bottles, like rubbing compounds—about twenty of them," Nolting said.

> Another day he was in [his room], and he'd put a little [ointment] on his hands and was rubbing it into his leg, rubbing himself down. He was just an oddball. I brought four or five guys down the hall and had them look.
>
> [But] that son of a gun could throw a ball 60 yards behind his back. Accurately. George kept him as an exhibitionist. That's what he was. Maybe during the half they'd send him out. Some injured ballplayer would go out with him [and shag flies, so to speak].

If only Doehring had thrown a behind-the-back pass for a touchdown in an actual NFL game. Alas, it never happened. (And it isn't hard to confirm this because, as I said, there are only seven TDs to check out.)

In his 1947 book, *The Chicago Bears*, Howard Roberts claims Doehring zipped a behind-the-back pass to Johnsos in a 1934 rout of Cincinnati, but Luke dropped it in the end zone. The only problem is that George Strickler didn't mention it in his story for the *Chicago Tribune*—and George didn't get to be a Hall of Fame sportswriter by omitting such details.

Doehring *definitely* threw a behind-the-back TD pass on the barnstorming trail, though. (What else was there to do in those games when they started to get one-sided?) The Associated Press's account of a January 1938 exhibition in New Orleans ends with this paragraph: "John Doehring, sensational southpaw passer for the Bears, flipped one behind his back to Lester McDonald for 25 yards and the pro team's final touchdown as the Bears made a show of the game."

By then, Doehring—following teammate Bronko Nagurski's lead—had begun to do some professional wrestling. And his live arm was always attracting the attention of baseball people. The Cubs gave him a look in the early '30s, and in 1935 he could be found playing with a team run by Happy Felsch, one of the eight White Sox banned from the big leagues for throwing the 1919 World Series.

In 1938 Doehring walked unannounced into the Cincinnati Reds' training camp in Tampa and wowed manager Bill McKechnie. After he'd thrown just a few pitches to veteran catcher Spud Davis, Davis grabbed a sponge and stuck it in his glove for additional cushioning.

"I don't know when I saw a faster ball," McKechnie said. "His fastball hops like [Wild] Bill Hallahan's used to, and he has as good a curve as I want to see. He looks like a great hitter, too. Honest, I believe he's the finest prospect in all my experience."

Doehring balked at first about signing a contract because he was planning to take a deputy sheriff's job in Milwaukee. (He eventually relented.) But he didn't make it with the Reds—just as he hadn't with the Cubs. Maybe he wasn't good enough . . . or maybe pro sports were just too structured for him. There were certainly hints of that when he was in the NFL.

One night, the story goes, he missed a Bears team meeting. Halas demanded to know why.

"George, you say the same things over and over," Bull said. "I went to a movie."

John "Bull" Doehring—a true original. And just think, Braven Dyer of the *Los Angeles Times* wrote after getting a glimpse Bull's behind-the-back act, "He attained this dexterity without the aid of a college education. Had he received the benefits of higher learning, he might be able to throw a curve which would come back to him."

Pro Football's Most Famous "DNP"

One of the stranger episodes in NFL history is how Dutch Clark, the Portsmouth Spartans' Hall of Fame back, missed the 1932 championship game against the Bears because it conflicted with his off-season job—coaching basketball at Colorado College, his alma mater. That's right, folks, while the Spartans were trading bruises with

Bronko Nagurski and company, Clark was in Colorado Springs preparing the Tigers for their season opener two days later.

The scoreboard:

Bears 9, Spartans 0.

Colorado College 43, Davis and Elkins 30.

(So at least Dutch got a win out of it—even if his team did miss twenty-six of thirty-three shots in the first half, according to one report.)

Snickering aside, it's hard to fault Clark. After all, when he accepted the basketball position, no one knew there would be an NFL title game; the league had never had one before. The championship had always been awarded to the club with the best record at the end of the regular season. In '32, though, Portsmouth and Chicago wound up tied for first at 6-1 (not counting their combined *ten* ties), and a playoff was hastily arranged.

Other, less publicized factors also contributed to Clark's decision. For one thing, he was worn down by the long season and not especially anxious to play another game. Pro football, he told the *Colorado Springs Gazette*, is

> a tough racket. It's a great game, but it's certainly making an old man of me. Sixty minutes nearly every game—and 14 games is a lot of football.
>
> We carried only 17 men at Portsmouth, the smallest squad in the league, as most of them carry the National [Football] League limit of 22 players. And 14 of us out of that bunch of 17 did practically all the playing. Furthermore, our team was the lightest in the league by almost 15 pounds per man. We averaged less than 190 pounds.

Clark also revealed this bombshell: The Thursday before Portsmouth's regular season finale against Green Bay, the Spartans were putting in their offense and, being shorthanded, asked some bystanders to fill out the dummy defense—"just to stand in the positions to give us an idea of where to run our plays," he said. "This kid was at halfback. I don't know how we happened to hit, but his elbow caught me in the ear, and it looked for a while like a cauliflower. But I believe the doc has fixed it up all right."

It's possible, too, that Clark was tired of wrestling with management over money—and wasn't sure what, if anything, he'd see of the championship game take. (Let's not forget, he didn't return to Portsmouth the next season, opting to stick with college coaching.)

The Spartans were a community-owned franchise like the Packers, and paychecks sometimes bounced. The year before, Dutch had threatened to withhold his services unless the club squared accounts with him. The business manager, backed into a corner, forked over $600—in one-dollar bills.

"I had dollar bills crammed into my pants pockets, my overcoat pockets, my suit coat pockets and every other place I could find," he said in Bob Curran's oral history, *Pro Football's Rag Days.*

Put it all together, and you can understand why Clark might have preferred Davis and Elkins as an opponent rather than the no-holds-barred Bears. Still, it would have been nice if he'd played in that first title game—a game that, because of a snowstorm, wound up being held indoors at Chicago Stadium on a scaled-down field. Even in such close quarters, a slippery back like Dutch could have broken one and tipped the balance . . . and won a championship for dear old Portsmouth before it followed Frankford, Providence, and other Little Cities That Ultimately Couldn't to the NFL graveyard.

One Field Goal Is as Good as Another

Two days after missing the '32 NFL title game to coach basketball, Dutch Clark directed his Colorado College team to a 43–30 win over Davis and Elkins in the season opener at Colorado Springs. The box score:

Colorado College (43)	FG	FT	PF	PTS
Sabo, F	5	1	0	11
Glidden, F	5	0	2	10
Livingston, C	2	0	1	4
Ryerson, G	2	0	2	4
Martin, G	1	0	1	2

Boothe, F	1	0	1	2
Patterson, F	3	0	1	6
Day, C	1	0	2	2
LeMaster, G	1	0	2	2
Harter, G	0	0	0	0
Total	21	1	12	43

Davis and Elkins (30)	FG	FT	PF	PTS
Heavner, F	1	2	1	4
Vest, F	3	6	1	12
Hodges, C	3	0	0	6
Kendall, C	1	0	2	2
Martin, G	2	0	2	4
Shelton, G	1	0	1	2
Tinney, G	0	0	1	0
Total	11	8	8	30

Ad Nauseam

Even in 1932 radio listeners were revolted by the number of commercials during football broadcasts — as evidenced by this *Portsmouth Times* editorial after the Bears-Spartans championship game:

> Never was a better opportunity had to view the overemphasis of advertising on a radio program than Sunday night when a cigar company broadcast the Portsmouth-Chicago game.
>
> Every few plays the announcer told of the merits of a product, of a contest the company was conducting and how fine a Christmas present its product would be. If the broadcast did anything for this company, it harmed it, for every mention of that product in the future probably will bring back to radio listeners one of the most poorly staged broadcasts in the season of sport.

Correction

All these years we've been told the 1932 NFL championship game, staged indoors at Chicago Stadium, was played on a field only 80 yards from goal line to goal line.

Actually, it was shorter than that, Glenn Presnell once told me. Presnell, who played tailback for the Portsmouth Spartans that night, said, "The field was 67 yards long. There's been a lot written about that, but I know exactly what it was—because we kicked off from the 7-yard line."

If you doubt Presnell, check out the photo of the field, spread across two pages, in *75 Seasons*, the coffee-table book the league published in 1994. I counted thirteen stripes between the goal lines, so 67 yards is about right (allowing for a certain amount of mismeasurement, which was hardly unheard of in pro football back then).

I'm guessing the *total* playing surface, from end line to end line, was 80 yards. The end zones, after all, were shallower than normal—and sawed off on the sides by the hockey rink's dasher boards.

Sixty-seven yards. Boy, there wasn't much room to operate, was there? I mean, how could you not, at some point, run head-on into Bronko Nagurski—especially with the field not just shorter but fifteen feet narrower?

"It was just a knock-down, drag-out game," Presnell said.

Worse, "it was very treacherous footing. They'd had a circus in there the week before, and they put what they call tan bark, [wood] shavings and stuff, all over, trying to keep the dust down on the dirt floor. My best play was either running [around] end or cutting off tackle, and I can remember two or three times when I went out and made my cut and the field just skidded out from under me."

Instant Replay

After the Chicago Bears beat the Portsmouth Spartans for the 1932 championship, the teams were anxious to cash in on the attention the first NFL title game had received. So they agreed to meet again the next Sunday, Christmas Day, in a charity exhibition in Cincinnati.

Portsmouth was still without star tailback Dutch Clark, off coaching the basketball team at Colorado College, but this time it managed a 6–6 tie—thanks to a touchdown pass from Glenn Presnell to Harry Ebding. (Unless, of course, the receiver was Ace Gutowsky or John Carvosie. Every newspaper, it seems, credited a different Spartan.)

The game, according to the *Portsmouth Times*, was "replete with vicious tackling and effective blocking." Unfortunately, just two thousand fans turned out, so the players were paid only "about 25 percent of their regular salary," the *Times* reported.

The NFL had two more of these championship rematches in the next five years — after which the league outlawed them, convinced they took away from the *real* title games. A brief rundown:

1934

Title game (December 9): Giants 30, Bears 13, in New York. (The famed Sneakers Game.)

Rematch (January 27, 1935): Bears 21, Giants 0, in Los Angeles.

Giants coach Steve Owen did some spouting off before the game, probably just to build up the gate. "Those fellows from Chicago have been saying it was a fluke when we beat them 30 to 13 for the championship," he said. "Thirty to 13 is 17 points to the good. How many points does it take for a victory to be a victory and not a fluke? The Bears would have had to score three more touchdowns to nose us out. Let 'em try to score three touchdowns on us."

Owen also fussed about the officiating crew. He was particularly concerned — given the sneakiness of Bears end Bill Hewitt — about who the head linesman would be.

"I don't claim that Hewitt is offside," he said, "because he would have to be onside first. Even before a play is about to start, he will be encroaching on the neutral zone. Any one of a dozen ends in the National [Football] League could be great if they were allowed to be offside all the time."

The Bears, still riled about their loss in the title game — one that cost them a perfect season — *did* score three touchdowns on the Giants . . . before the first half was even over. Bronko Nagurski barreled over from the one-foot line in the first three minutes, and the rout was on.

Historical note: It was the final pro appearance of "The Galloping Ghost," Red Grange. In the fourth quarter he broke away for a
long gain, only to be hauled down from behind by 225-pound Giants tackle Tex Irvin.

"I realized before I reached midfield that I was through," Grange
told Richard Whittingham in *What a Game They Played.* "My legs
kept getting heavier and heavier. I knew I'd never reach the end
zone, but I knew I'd reached the end."

(You wonder if the Bears hadn't *arranged* for Grange to score a
farewell touchdown—to give the crowd of fifteen thousand one
last thrill—and someone forgot to tell Irvin. I mention this only
because when Red was tackled, "[Art] Buss, the Bears' big tackle,
threw his helmet on the ground in disgust," the *Chicago Tribune*
said, "and [end] Luke Johnsos cussed in disappointment.")

1937

Title game (December 12, 1937): Redskins 28, Bears 21, in Chicago.
Rematches: Redskins 13, Bears 0, in Dallas (January 23, 1938);
Bears 16, Redskins 10, in Miami (February 6, 1938).

Yup, once wasn't enough. They had to play twice.

The Redskins won the first rematch at the Cotton Bowl. Sammy
Baugh opened the scoring with a short touchdown flip to Wayne
Millner, and the Redskins got an insurance TD late in the game
when George Smith ran back an interception 44 yards.

The Bears, meanwhile, never got closer than the Washington
24. It might have been different if Nagurski had been able to play,
but the big fullback was in a hospital back in Chicago "suffering
from a leg injury incurred in a [professional] wrestling match," the
Dallas Morning News reported. (It was apparently caused by a rope
burn.)

The field was a muddy, puddly mess. It had rained all week, another storm hit just before kickoff, and the drops continued to fall
during the game. The attendance was only forty-two hundred.

Late that night the Redskins were celebrating a little too boisterously at a Fort Worth nightspot and police were summoned. The first two patrolmen who arrived on the scene "bounced back through the swinging doors," the Associated Press said. Two more cruisers were dispatched, then another three, and finally the "12-man line" of the "coppers . . . was too much for the battling gridsters.

"Four of the celebrators went to the police station to discuss the strategy of the post-postseason game. It was there that Ray Flaherty, coach of the Redskins, found them, talked to the blue-uniformed 'team' of coppers and got things ironed out. Damage to the café was slight."

Two weeks later at the Orange Bowl the Bears gained a measure of revenge in rematch number two. Chicago was still missing Nagurski, but Washington was without NFL rushing leader Cliff Battles, who was sidelined with "a carbuncle on his cheek," according to the *Miami Herald*. In the second half Baugh exited with a shoulder injury, and the Bears pulled away to the win.

"The game was bitterly fought throughout," the *Chicago Tribune* said, "four fist fights enlivening play" for the gathering of nearly eight thousand. "The fights, Chicago entries named first: George Wilson vs. Bob McChesney, Russ Thompson vs. Les Olsson, Milton Trost vs. Chuck Bond and Ed Manske vs. Don Irwin. All were draws."

Never again would the NFL title game be restaged in the postseason. As one columnist put it in 1935: "Suppose the St. Louis Cardinals, after winning the National League pennant and the world's [*sic*] series, extended their season until they had played a series with both the New York Giants and Detroit Tigers in California during November. Suppose, too, that in each of these series the Cardinals were severely trounced. . . . The world's series would become equivalent to . . . spring exhibition games."

• • •

Ten years ago in the National [Football] League it was survival of the fittest. Coaches encouraged roughness. There was no discipline [because] an official couldn't fine a player. — Longtime referee Bobie Cahn upon his retirement in 1943

· · ·

Highest Praise Ever Given a Punter

A one-legged man with corns could get down under his kicks in time to be waiting for the receiver to get the ball. — Don Watson, *Honolulu Star-Bulletin*, on the booming punts of the Packers' Arnie Herber

Most Ambitious Offseason Training Program

Travelers along the road from Dallas to Chicago in the summer of 1933 were greeted by a curious sight: a muscular young man in a white track outfit carrying a bale of cotton on his back.

It was pro footballer Cecil Burns getting in shape for the coming season, which he hoped to spend with the Chicago Cardinals.

Actually, there was a little more to the story than that. Allow me to explain.

Burns, a two-hundred-pound fullback, had played the previous year with the Providence Steam Roller. (The Steam Roller had dropped out of the NFL and were operating as an independent.) But the team hadn't made a profit, and he wound up being paid only a fraction of his salary.

So Burns went home to Dallas and worked a few odd jobs, none of which lasted very long in those Depression times. Then his friend Bill Hancock, an aspiring promoter, came up with an idea: Since Cecil had nothing else to do, why didn't he spend the next three months lugging a bale of cotton to the Chicago World's Fair?

The stunt could serve as a promotion for the Texas cotton industry, Hancock told him, and some cotton growers would help finance it. *I'll follow along in a car and be your manager. Just think of the condition you'll be in for football when you're done.* (Assuming, that is, the kid was still alive.)

Well, Burns replied, he *did* want to see the World's Fair. And once in Chicago, he might be able to catch on with the Cardinals, who had barely beaten the Steam Roller in an exhibition game the year before and looked like they might need players.

Nobody, of course, could lug a *real* bale of cotton a thousand miles—or even one mile. A bale weighed five hundred pounds. So Hancock concocted a frame for a hollow bale that "weighed about 135 pounds," he said decades later. "And it was cumbersome, like a piano. Red carried it on his shoulders with a harness."

Red. Oh, yeah, almost forgot. The promoter decided Cecil wasn't a suitable name for a strongman, so he changed it to "'Red Hot' Burns, the Texas Atlas."

Red Hot set out from Dallas, amid much fanfare, in June. At the Baker Hotel, with newsreel cameras whirring, he climbed up a fire ladder, bale and all, to the eighth floor.

Interesting sidelight: The famed Herbie Kaye happened to be in town with his band, and the manager of his female singer suggested she accompany Burns up the ladder (perched atop the bale, apparently). But Hancock turned him down. How was he to know the singer, Dorothy Lamour, would go on to become, well, Dorothy Lamour?

Burns almost didn't survive the first day. "Just plain misery," he recalled at the end of his journey. "I covered about 25 miles and seemed to work up a new blister on the average of every two miles. When I pulled off my shoes at night my feet were one mass of 13 blisters. I was just about ready to quit. But we had made a little money selling pictures of me"—at fifteen cents apiece—"with the cotton on my back, and I figured it might pay to push on."

This being the pre-Nike era, Burns was shod in high-topped, hobnailed shoes. (The nails, protruding slightly from the bottom, protected the sole and heel from wear.) Fortunately, after a week his feet began to callus—as did his back—and his exertions became less painful.

His route took him through Oklahoma and Missouri and on into Illinois. Burns would trudge along, inviting onlookers to grab a swab of cotton as a souvenir, while Hancock drove ahead to the next town to herald his arrival. Red Hot would make appearances at nightclubs and lift local lovelies in his bale. He'd do his ladder-climbing bit—once, in Joliet, Illinois, nearly falling off. He'd sign autographs. Crowds in the thousands would sometimes come out to greet him. *Time* magazine even mentioned his exodus. Twice.

Aside from the aches and pains, the worst problem might have been the traffic. Roads would get backed up with folks wanting to catch a glimpse of the Texas Atlas, and more than once a distracted rubbernecker ended up in a ditch. No one was seriously injured, but Hancock remembered Burns being "covered with blood one morning after helping so many people who ran off the highway and got hurt."

It was also a challenge to keep refilling Red Hot's bale after kids, being kids, would help themselves to huge handfuls of cotton. They didn't understand, he said, "that I wanted them to take just a little bit of it." Before long, "the free cotton offer was out, and we began selling little souvenir bales."

Three months and 1,170 miles later, Burns strode into Chicago—deeply tanned from all that time in the sun but little worse for the wear. Total weight loss: a mere six pounds. The venture hadn't been as profitable as he'd expected, he told the *Southtown Economist*, and he certainly wouldn't do it again, but it was still "a lot of fun."

"What got me most," he said, "was having people stare and stare at me as though I was crazy. . . . [But] right now I'm in fine shape, and if I can get lined up with the Cardinals, I'll say it was all worthwhile."

Alas, Red Hot *didn't* get lined up with the Cardinals—or any other NFL club, for that matter. (According to a 1965 story in the *Dallas Morning News*, he settled in Phoenix and became the owner of a heavy machinery firm.) Which probably explains why no pro football player since has gotten ready for the season by toting a bale of cotton from Dallas to Chicago . . . or even to Oklahoma City.

City of Brotherly Love

Walter Halas, George Halas's older brother, did some officiating in the NFL's early days. There's even evidence of him working a Chicago Bears game in 1933. Guess the league wasn't too worried about appearances back then.

The game was played in Philadelphia on November 12, 1933 — a big day, indeed. For one thing, the city council had just repealed the blue law prohibiting Sunday sporting events, and the Eagles, new to the league, were anxious to take advantage of it. For another, the great Red Grange was in town, and the Baker Bowl was bulging with a crowd of nearly eighteen thousand, including many local dignitaries.

It must have been quite a scene. There was Papa Bear, prowling the Chicago sideline and demanding, as always, that the officials give him "my fair advantage." And there was his sibling serving as the linesman on a four-man crew that also featured Paul Menton, the *Baltimore Evening Sun* sports editor.

The game couldn't have been more convenient for Walter, which might be why he drew the assignment. He was the head football coach at Drexel at the time — when he wasn't busy, that is, scouting future opponents for George. But there's no indication his officiating wasn't on the up and up. (Translation: The Eagles didn't set any records for holding penalties or anything.)

The teams wound up tying 3–3, thanks to a fourth-quarter field goal by the Eagles' Guy Turnbow. And this was a Bears club, I'll just point out, that went on to win the championship (while Philadelphia finished next to last in the East Division with a 3-5-1 mark).

Something tells me Bert Bell, the Eagles' owner, wasn't the least bit concerned that George Halas's brother might not give his team a fair shake. Years later, in fact, when Drexel deemphasized football and Walter began to take some flak for losing, Bell sprang to his defense, criticizing the college president for failing to "stand by" his coach and calling Walter "a great football man."

Familiarity Breeds (Fill in the Blank)

That same year, 1933, the Giants had seven home games. In six of them, Tom Thorp was the referee. Regardless of Mr. Thorp's abilities, this was anything but a healthy situation.

Interestingly, the only home game Thorp didn't officiate was the one against the Bears. Make of that what you will. (One possible scenario: George Halas didn't want the Giants' personal referee heading the crew in such a big game.)

Another official, Jack Reardon, did five Giants games that season, two as an umpire and three as a linesman. (One of the games was on the road, in Brooklyn.) Sorry, but it was all just a little too cozy.

In Chicago, after all, Bobie Cahn frequently did Bears games — and like Thorp, was highly respected. But when Cahn was asked to pick his all-time NFL team in 1943, the year he retired, he put six Bears on his eleven-man squad. There wasn't a single position — end (Bill Hewitt), tackle (Link Lyman and Ed Healey), guard (Danny Fortmann), center (George Trafton), or back (Bronko Nagurski) — that wasn't represented by at least one Bear. His greatest player of all time: Trafton.

Make of *that* what you will, too.

A Big, Fat Zero

The historic rule changes in 1933 — adding hash marks, moving goalposts to the goal line, loosening passing rules — were supposed to promote more scoring. But the Brooklyn Dodgers apparently never got the memo. Eight of their ten games that season were shutouts. (They won five and lost three.)

An average of 14.7 points was scored in the Dodgers' games — the fewest in the modern (post-1932) era. Indeed, you *could* say it was the most uneventful season an NFL team has ever had.

The results:

Chicago Bears	L, 10–0
Cincinnati Reds	W, 27–0
At New York Giants	L, 21–7

Chicago Cardinals	W, 7–0
Pittsburgh Pirates	T, 3–3
At Pittsburgh Pirates	W, 32–0
At Chicago Cardinals	W, 3–0
Boston Redskins	W, 14–0
New York Giants	L, 10–0
At Cincinnati Reds	L, 10–0

Integration in the '30s

There were only two black players in the NFL in 1933 — Ray Kemp, a tackle with the Pittsburgh Pirates (by way of Duquesne), and Joe Lillard, a back with the Chicago Cardinals. The next year they were gone, and the league remained determinedly all white until 1946, when Kenny Washington and Woody Strode joined the Los Angeles Rams.

I visited Kemp at his home in Ashtabula, Ohio, in 1995 and turned on my tape recorder. Some of the highlights of our conversation:

"My father's name was Ono. Mother's was Hattie. My family were Virginians. My grandmother, Helen, was a slave for the first four years of her life.

"It was a big family. My dad had three children by his first wife. She died of pneumonia. My mother had three by her first husband. He died of diphtheria, I think. He fought in the Spanish-American War, was with Roosevelt at San Juan Hill. I learned some Spanish from a book he brought back. The family migrated to Pennsylvania, bought company houses, had gardens and chickens and all that sort of thing. Went to church. My grandmother would walk to church, two-and-a-half miles. She'd put on her old shoes, carry her good shoes. We lived that kind of life."

"I saw Paul Robeson play with a Negro All-Star team that was barnstorming outside Pittsburgh — Fritz Pollard's team. [Note: Robeson, another early black player, went on to become a famous actor, singer, and activist.] They played some pickup team in Ridge View at the greyhound racing track out there. Robeson was a big, giant of a guy . . . all-everything.

"Later, he came to the University of Michigan when I was doing graduate work there, and I had a chance to shake his hand. What a voice he had. Sang Russian folk songs. Could speak six different languages. He was something else. I went to his funeral in New York. I borrowed money to go to that man's funeral.

"At the funeral, one of the fellas who went to school with him talked about what a difficult time he had at Rutgers. He said sometimes guys would go after Robeson in practice. You would have thought he was a member of the other team."

"Buff Donelli, the captain of the football team at Duquesne [and later the coach of the Steelers and Rams], taught me how to dance. I'd already learned to foxtrot, but Buff saw me out on the dance floor one time trying to waltz, not knowing whether I was coming or going, and he said, 'Go sit down, Ray. You're killing yourself.' But later he taught me how to waltz in the dormitory. I became good at it. Then I went to a black dance and started dancing, and a girl said, 'You dance like white people, Ray.'"

"I remember playing against Joe Lillard in 1933 when he was with the Cardinals. Lillard was a triple threat. Great player. Elusive as all outdoors. In the first half, he ran us crazy—kicked, passed. So we go in at halftime, and Jap Douds, our coach, says, 'Now look, we've gotta get that damn nigger the hell out of there.' I was mad, naturally. And as we're going back out, Jap pulls me aside and says, 'Ray, you know I didn't mean *you* when I said that.'"

"There were times on the road when I'd be segregated from the rest of the team. I'd stay at the YMCA. One time it happened in New York, and Walter White, the head of the NAACP, wanted to bring suit against the hotel and the Pirates. He said, 'There's no reason this should be happening, you being a college graduate and all.' But I told him I'd prefer not to go to court. I said, 'I know Art Rooney. He invited me to play for his team. He just has a couple of guys running it, no doubt, who are racist. They've never dealt with blacks. But give him a little time, and he'll straighten all this out. He probably doesn't even know this is going on' — which he didn't.

"A pioneer has to suffer the consequences. You have to start someplace. And as little as it's known, I did open the door. I was a pioneer."

Pick Six

Since the NFL started keeping track of the statistic in 1940, no player has intercepted more than four passes in a game. (Sammy Baugh was the first to do it, in 1943, DeAngelo Hall the most recent, in 2010 — both for the Redskins.)

So what are we to make of the 1935 edition of *Who's Who in Major League Football* — an official NFL publication, by the way — which contains the following passage about the Bears' Joe Zeller?

"In a battle against Philadelphia last fall he snagged no fewer than six enemy tosses."

Maybe nothing at all. The Bears, it turns out, didn't *play* Philadelphia in 1934, at least not in the regular season.

It's always possible, of course, that Zeller did it in the '33 game against the Eagles, but there's no mention of it in the newspapers.

The early years of the NFL can drive you absolutely nuts.

Football Doubleheader

The St. Louis Gunners made only a cameo appearance in the NFL — three games' worth in 1934 — but they did leave us something to remember them by: Their home games were preceded by professional soccer games. Soccer began at 1:15, and football kicked off an hour later.

Hypothetically, anyway. It sounds like the soccer games might have run a little long. After the Gunners' season finale against the

Packers, the *St. Louis Post-Dispatch* commented, "It might be wise for the Gunner officials to make some different arrangement with the soccer executives so that play might start earlier. The last two weeks, the [football] game has been finished in the darkness."

College vs. Pro, 1934

After nine years at Oregon State, Paul Schissler moved to the NFL in 1933 and coached the Chicago Cardinals for two seasons and the Brooklyn Dodgers for two more. While barnstorming with the Cards in '34, a sportswriter asked him about the differences between college and pro ball. His answer puts the lie to the notion that defenses in that era were simplistic:

> Well, it isn't the rules. Here's the big difference: In college, the coach points out the weaknesses and strengths of each opponent. Every team you meet has some players who may be classed as the weak members of that team. At a crucial point you might go for a gain over that man, but you can't do it in pro football. You might gain once, but the next play toward that fellow will go for a loss.
>
> Professional football requires a more versatile attack and a more versatile defense against forward passes. Take the Chicago Bears, for instance. Tell them the type of pass defense you are going to use and stick to it, and they'll beat you to death. The pass defense of the pro club must be so varied that it includes virtually all styles.
>
> We use about five variations. The pro clubs use very little man to man. We use a combination of man for man and zone with two variations. The zone is 6-2-2-1 or 6-3-2 or a combination, with seven-man line and box on the goal line. The diamond defense we used today was a combination of man for man and zone.

Going Really, Really Long

Is it possible the longest pass in NFL history was thrown by a lineman? Before going any further, let me clarify a couple of things:

1. By "longest pass," I mean the farthest a pass has traveled *in the air.*

I'm not necessarily referring to any of the 99-yard touchdown passes in the record book.

2. As for "NFL history," I mean that in its broadest sense. If a pass was thrown in *any* NFL game — preseason, regular season, or post-season — it counts for the purposes of this discussion.

Everybody clear on the rules? OK. Because in a 1935 exhibition between the Bears and the minor-league Washington Federals, Chicago end Fred Crawford heaved the ball from his 2-yard line to the Washington 16. Total distance: 82 yards. In all my searching, I've never come across a throw, completed or otherwise, that was longer.

Crawford, a rookie out of Duke, hadn't done much passing, according to accounts, before his Herculean arm was "discovered" in the Bears' training camp. On this night, though, with Chicago comfortably ahead in a meaningless preseason game, coach George Halas let him uncork one in the third quarter, just for the fun of it.

The play worked like this: Crawford dropped out of the line and positioned himself 20 yards deep in the backfield. The center then snapped the ball to running back Gene Ronzani, who turned and flipped it to Fred. This gave the receiver time to get downfield — *way* downfield. It also enabled Fred to get a running start before letting 'er fly. I'll let W. Wilson Wingate of the *Baltimore News and Post* take it from here:

Uphill, from the distant fringe of the sloping right-field greensward, toward home plate at Oriole Park, and against the wind, that ghostly white pigskin sailed up and out into the night. And, as it cut through the eerie half-glow of the flood lights up there where the dark began, the figure of a man in the Orange and Black of the mighty Bears sped over the turf.

On and on they flew, ball and man in a mad race for a point on the 16-yard line of the unfortunate Washington Federals.

This man, would he make it? Would he get there in time?

A hurried over the shoulder glance . . . a leap into the air . . . a deafening roar from 5,000 throats.

Ed Kawal, giant end of the Bears, had clutched the ball, even as the discomfited Federal safety clutched the receiver and all tumbled to the ground on the 16-yard line, 82 yards from the 2-yard mark at the other end of the field where the mighty passer stood.

The grand climax had been reached.

To the spectators it seemed that nothing else mattered much.

They had lived. . . .

They had seen the alpha and omega of the forward pass.

(Gives you chills, doesn't it?)

Kawal, by the way, wasn't even a receiver. He was a center who caught exactly one pass in his NFL career. No, this was the ultimate circus play, the ultimate crowd pleaser. It had been used by the Bears "in similar exhibitions," the *Sun* reported, "but never in a league contest."

Indeed, there's no indication they ever ran it in a real game that season — Crawford's one season in the NFL. Their 1935 statistics show thirteen different players throwing passes, but not Fred.

Even allowing for a certain amount of exaggeration, though — something newspapers were occasionally guilty of back then — Crawford's was an epic toss, probably the longest the NFL has ever seen. The next longest I've found — and believe me, I've looked — was "only" 70 yards.

And let's not forget, Fred was throwing "uphill" and "against the wind." There's no telling how far the ball would have gone under normal conditions.

Before Gated Communities

Getting back to that 1935 edition of *Who's Who in Major League Football* . . . the book also listed the home addresses of quite a few players. Dutch Clark, the Lions' legendary back, lived at 1131 Lake Avenue in Pueblo, Colorado. And Milan Creighton, the Cardinals' player-coach, lived at 1712 Estes Avenue in Chicago — that is, in case you had any complaints you wanted to register.

Moveable Typists

Redskins founder George Preston Marshall had one of pro football's more fertile imaginations. If he wasn't suggesting that the NFL split into two divisions — so it could stage a climactic championship game at the end of the season — he was trying to parachute Santa Claus into the stadium to cap the holiday halftime show.

But one of his best brainstorms never saw the light of day, sad to say. Marshall thought it would be cool, *Time* magazine reported in 1935, to put the "press box on a monorail to follow the plays."

Maybe in the next life.

Refusing to Belabor the Point

Contrary to popular belief, George Halas's Chicago Bears weren't entirely without pity. Take their game, for instance, against the Eagles in Philadelphia in October 1935.

The Bears, as expected, were cuffing Philly around pretty good, merrily throwing passes and laterals and building a 27–0 halftime lead. After three of the touchdowns, "Automatic" Jack Manders, their consummate kicker, booted the extra point into the stands. To the home team's dismay, the fans on the receiving end decided to keep the balls as consolation prizes.

Times being what they were — this was, after all, year seven of the Great Depression — the Eagles were left with only one usable ball. So when the Bears scored touchdowns in the second half, they were nice enough to abstain from going for the PAT. When Ed Kawal returned an interception for a TD in the third quarter, they simply lined up for the kickoff. When Gene Ronzani added another score in the fourth on a lateral from Bob Dunlap (who had received a lateral himself from George Grosvenor), they lined up for the kickoff again.

Thus was a 41–0 loss plea-bargained down to a 39–0 loss.

A suggestion that was later made — but never adopted — for solving the Football Depletion Problem: Have teams kick extra points the *other* way, from the end zone back toward the field. (The goal-posts, remember, were on the goal line in those days.)

It wasn't a bad idea, you've gotta admit. But it would have been a tight squeeze in places like Wrigley Field, where one of the end zones wasn't even ten yards deep.

• • •

There is a rule in the ranks of the Bears that forbids the use of cuss words on the bench, and Coach Halas, who wrote the regulation, en-forces it strictly, save on those occasions when he sees fit to break it in person.—From *Who's Who in Major League Football* (1935)

• • •

Double Dipping

Three weeks into the 1935 college season, Purdue had three shut-out victories and center/captain Ed Skoronski was a good bet for all-conference honors. By the end of November, though, Skoron-ski was playing pro ball for the NFL's Pittsburgh Pirates (in a game, according to one account, "punctuated by . . . the hurling of a pop bottle at umpire [Harry] Robb").

Near as I can tell, the little-remembered Skoronski is the last player to jump from the colleges to the pros in the same season. Others had done it before him, most notably Red Grange in 1925. But soon thereafter the NFL, looking to stay in the colleges' good graces, passed a rule against signing a player before his class grad-uated. Violators—and there were several—were assessed substan-tial fines.

So why was an exception made in Skoronski's case? It's not en-tirely clear. What we do know is that after the Boilermakers had got-ten off to their great start, Ed was declared ineligible when a faculty investigation discovered he had already played four college seasons. He'd appeared briefly in a game for Georgetown in 1931—before even graduating from Bowen High School in Chicago.

"He entered that university for the school year of 1930–31, then enrolled again in the fall of 1931, but soon withdrew and returned to complete his high school course," the Associated Press said. "He matriculated at Purdue in the fall of 1932."

(Obviously, the NCAA didn't pay much attention to these comings and goings back then.)

Purdue fielded one of its strongest teams in 1935. Besides Skoronski, the Boilermakers also had running back Johnny Drake and passer Cecil Isbell, both of whom would become all-pros in the NFL. But once Skoronski got booted, their season quickly unraveled. They won only one more game and finished 4-4.

Just guessing here, but maybe NFL president Joe Carr let Pittsburgh sign Skoronski because the Pirates were still new to the league—they had joined just two years earlier—and needed all the help they could get. Then, too, Skoronski's class had, technically, *already* graduated (since his college career had begun in '31), so it could be argued that no rule was being broken.

Besides, he didn't suit up for Pittsburgh until *after* Purdue's season ended—one day after, to be exact. It couldn't have been any tidier.

What simplified matters, no doubt, is that the league didn't have a college draft yet—and wouldn't until the next season. The Pirates, in other words, didn't *steal* the kid from anybody. He was a free agent . . . as all college players were in those days.

Skoronski, a solid six foot two, 213 pounds, played as a reserve in Pittsburgh's final three games that year. The next season he switched from center to end and caught eight passes, including one for his only NFL touchdown. He spent his last year in the league as a guard with the Cleveland Rams and Brooklyn Dodgers in 1937.

All in all, a rather pedestrian pro career—except, of course, for his unique place in NFL history.

• • •

Professional football is no tramp's game, and it is a good way for a young fellow to earn money in the first couple of years after college,

provided he is willing to work hard. Of course, there are some who in-
tend to play the game just as long as they are physically able to. These
players are few, however, compared with the large number who hope
to make their life's work in fields far removed from football. Why, we
even had one young fellow from Pittsburgh who went home after every game to study up on his dentistry, hoping to secure his degree next
year. — Redskins tackle Vic Carroll (who wound up playing a dozen seasons)

• • •

Secrets: Sid Luckman

In 1940, Sid Luckman's second year as the Bears' quarterback, the
Chicago Tribune ran a series of articles on the "hoodlum domina-
tion" of New York City. The June 2 installment focused on the flour-
trucking business and its infiltration by racketeers Louis (Lepke)
Buckhalter and "Gurrah" Shapiro, a.k.a. "the Gorilla Boys."

Toward the end of the piece, a harrowing tale of extortion and
murder, an interesting name popped up: Meyer Luckman, Sid's father. No connection was made, however, between the twenty-three-
year-old rising football star and this other Luckman, the mobbed-up
one who'd been convicted of killing his brother-in-law. And really,
who could have imagined such a link?

It was The Story That Never Got Written, either during or after
Sid's Hall of Fame career. Outside of New York, where Sid grew
up, few knew that his father was an "an associate" of the infamous
Lepke — as the *New York Times* described him in 1944 — and was
the central figure in what the *Brooklyn Eagle* called "one of the most
notorious scandals in the history of" the borough.

All the time Sid was making headlines for Columbia and leading
the Bears to championships, Meyer was locked away in Sing Sing
prison, where he spent the last eight years of his life. He never saw
his son throw a single pass in college or the pros.

Nowadays, of course, it would be big news if the father of a star
quarterback were being tried for murder. The quarterback would

doubtless make the rounds of the talk shows. The trial might even be carried on cable TV.

In the late '30s, however, word didn't travel quite as quickly . . . or as widely. It was possible for Meyer Luckman to bump off his wife's brother — after catching him stealing money from the family trucking business — and have it remain a largely local story.

Johnny Siegal, who grew up in Pennsylvania and played with Luckman in college and the pros, once told me he "never got the real lowdown on it. It was a hush-hush thing . . . a touchy damn subject. We knew something had gone wrong, something was amiss, but we never heard any details."

Don't ask, don't tell, circa 1935.

As was the custom then, the newspapers did everything they could to protect Sid, the local hero from Erasmus Hall High. This was the era of gee-whiz sports writing, of the Four Horsemen and the Galloping Ghost, of gods and myths. An athlete's personal life was nobody's business but his own. Too, Sid was a mere teenager, a freshman at Columbia, when the case was tried in February 1936.

The papers didn't ignore his presence in the courtroom, but they didn't dwell on it, either. Typical was the note in the *Daily News* that "Meyer Luckman's wife and his handsome son, Sidney, a promising football player at Columbia University" were seated behind the defense table. The *Herald Tribune* was even more supportive, doing everything it could to separate Sid from his murderous father (and from a cousin who was also involved in the slaying).

"The defendant Luckmans are squat, saturnine men with receding brows," it reported, "but Sidney looks like someone from another tribe, a handsome, open-faced fellow. He is so tall that he quite hid his mother, sitting beside him."

In 1938, his senior year at Columbia, Sid's dirt-smeared face filled the cover of *Life* magazine's October 24 issue. The brief article inside mentioned nothing about his father being in prison, noting only that he was "a Brooklyn truck driver." So it would always be for Sid. Feature stories about him would refer vaguely, almost in code, to this terrible chapter in his life.

> If he were to remain in college, Sid had to support himself. The family fortunes, on the upbeat for years, had collapsed virtually overnight. . . . There was no visible means of support for the family, and it is no part of an exaggeration to say that there were days when there was no food in the kitchen for Sid's mother to cook. — *Sport*, December 1949

> Luckman's public image was at its peak after a near upset of Army [in 1937], but in private he was going through deep torment. A prosperous family trucking business was on the verge of collapse." — *Sport*, December 1965

> It was during this period that the Luckman family came into hard times. His father's trucking business floundered, then collapsed. — *Pro Football Guide*, August 1970

Never was the cause of this floundering, this collapsing, discussed. Indeed, in some pieces Meyer was "killed off," as it were, said to be dead at a time when he was still very much alive — if you can call a twenty-years-to-life sentence at Sing Sing living.

"His father, a truck driver, died when he was a boy," the story would read. Or Sid would be quoted saying, "It was a difficult time for me, because I was trying to support my mother and my family, my dad being gone."

"My dad being gone" — quite the double entendre there. Naturally, most people would take it to mean Sid's father was dead, not locked away someplace.

It wasn't just the sportswriters, then; Sid also played a part in the obfuscation. His 1949 autobiography, *Luckman at Quarterback*, all but rescripts "The Meyer Luckman Story." In the introduction, for instance, Sid says his father "migrated from Germany," but according to the 1930 U.S. Census, his father was from Russia. Later, Sid talks about his family emerging from "poverty," but it's clear he experienced little, if any, of that deprivation. When he was five, the Luckmans moved out of their apartment in the lower-class Williamsburg section of Brooklyn and into a lovely place near Prospect Park, in the heart of Flatbush. Not only was the home worth $10,000, the census reveals, but the family also had a female "servant."

"She lived with us forever," Sid's sister, Blanche Fleischer, told me. "Her apple pies were so fantastic that the supermarket wanted to sell them, but she wasn't interested. She'd make pies, and then she'd give [pieces] out to all the kids on the block. The kids would sit on our stoop and wait for their apple pie."

Perhaps the most telling passage in Sid's book is his description of a family get-together at his mom's house after the Bears played in New York in 1943. "The old place was furnished anew," Sid says. "It was quieter now than usual. Ma . . . had been alone since Dad Luckman passed away early in 1943. She poured a glass of sweet wine for me in the kitchen, and as I was sipping it, she made a most surprising comment: 'You know, Sid, Pa would have loved to see this game. How proud he would have been.'"

In fact, Ethel Luckman had been alone since March 1936, when her husband was taken away in handcuffs to Sing Sing. Meyer's death, moreover, came in January 1944, three months *after* Sid and his mother sipped sweet wine in her kitchen. How great the son's shame must have been to reconfigure events the way he did.

Only once, on the dedication page, does Sid hint that anything was "amiss" — as Johnny Siegel put it. "To the late Dad Luckman," it reads, "who played the toughest game of all."

The only time the name "Meyer Luckman" shows up in the *New York Times* before 1935 is in 1901, when he would have been in his mid-twenties. "HORSE POISONING CASE FAILS," the headline says. "District Attorney Unable to Bring Crime Home to Luckman." Two horses belonging to Max Greenfelder of 55 Rutgers Street had been poisoned, the *Times* reported, and the district attorney brought charges against Meyer Luckman of 84 Chrystle Street "after receiving numerous complaints of the poisoning of horses on the east side. He was unable to prove, however, that the poison had been administered to Greenfelder's horses through the agency of Luckman."

It may or may not be ironic that Meyer went into the delivery business — the trucking of flour to bakeries (thereby accomplishing with horsepower what used to be accomplished with, well, horse power). By 1935 he and his brother Ike had a fleet of some thirty trucks. Life was good, even in the midst of the Depression. Sid often joked that he was the only one on the block who owned a football, so the other kids had to let him play quarterback.

But the Luckman Brothers firm was merely the respectable tip of the iceberg. Below the surface was what the newspapers called the "racket-ridden flour trucking business," the extortion scam that was netting Lepke and Shapiro an estimated $1.5 million a year. "By their methods," the *Times* said, the Luckmans "had obtained a virtual monopoly of the business."

Meyer used those methods on Sam Drukman when the sixty-dollar-a-week shipping clerk was found to be dipping into the company cash register to pay his gambling debts. Rather than bring the law into it, Meyer — "judge, jury and police department for the Luckmans," as the prosecution portrayed him in the trial — handled the matter himself, internally. (An interesting decision, inasmuch as Brooklyn was the cradle of Murder, Inc., the ill-famed homicide-for-hire operation. Meyer presumably could have subcontracted the job out but chose not to.)

Arrangements were made for the execution. A Ford coupe was borrowed from one of Meyer's cousins, who lived in New Jersey, and parked overnight in a garage. This was to be the vehicle, the prosecution theorized, that transported Drukman's lifeless body to the Jersey swamps, where it would be disposed of. A large canvas "body bag" was also obtained for the job.

The plan was to lure Drukman to the Luckman Brothers garage at the intersection of Moore and White Streets on the night of March 3 — a seedy and, on Sunday, deserted part of town — and do away with him. (The garage's day watchman had been fired a week before and replaced by Meyer's brother Abe, who went home early on the day in question.) You wonder if Meyer even thought of Sam as family at that point, or whether he regarded him the way Dutch Schultz regarded Legs Diamond when he was snuffed—as "just another punk caught with his hands in my pocket." The bottom line was that his brother-in-law had been found guilty of stealing, a capital offense in the underworld . . . and one that warranted the death penalty. The rules were very clear on that.

Drukman was disposed of in a manner that was equal parts bloody, painful, and protracted, a manner much like the one used by "killers of the Lepke mob," the *Eagle* reported. Meyer and two trusted employees, nephew Harry Luckman and Fred Hull, fastened a rope to his arms and legs and tied it in a noose around his neck, the result being that the noose tightened every time Sam moved. "Trussed like a chicken," was how the *Times* described him. He died, ever so slowly, of strangulation.

That might have been the end of it, except that somebody phoned the police from a store down the street while the men were still in the garage. The prosecution suspected it was Harry Kantor, Meyer's bookkeeper, who mysteriously disappeared that night—and turned up dead in Chicago eight months later. Soon enough there were cops everywhere. They broke in through a transom over the office door and found the Luckmans and Hull hiding in the shadows. The three were covered with blood. Meyer tried to make a run for it, but a warning shot stopped him in his tracks. "I don't know from nothing," he told the detective who caught him in an adjacent alley. "Six men just beat me up."

Drukman's body was discovered in the rumble seat of the Ford coupe, next to Meyer's pearl-gray fedora. Outside the garage, lying on the ground near Meyer's Nash automobile, was "the sawed-off butt of a billiard cue with bloodstains on it," the *Times* said (which presumably explained the battered condition of the deceased's skull). Meyer had $3,000 in his pocket when he was arrested; this at a time when the average annual income in the United States was about half that.

It seemed an open-and-shut case. The trio, after all, had been caught literally red-handed. But this was Brooklyn in the 1930s. Almost anything could be bought.

Two months later the grand jury considered the case and, incredibly, decided not to hand up any indictments. The three men had their bloodstained clothing and other evidence returned to them (though police kept photographs) and went on with their lives. Ordinarily, Meyer would have been able to watch Sid play football that fall, but his son was sitting out his freshman season at Columbia, practicing with the team only, so he could bring his academic work up to university standards.

Actually, the letting loose of murderers and other criminals wasn't all that unusual in those days — either in Brooklyn, which was infamous for its corruption, or elsewhere. A study by the New York State Crime Commission found that of the 19,468 arrests for felonies in New York City in 1925, only 5,622 — barely one in four — resulted in indictments and just 1,178 of the convicted wound up in Sing Sing.

(Within months of the Drukman murder, New York governor Herbert H. Lehman appointed Thomas E. Dewey as a special district attorney for New York County, his charge being to investigate organized crime. Before he moved on to the governor's mansion himself, Dewey dealt the Mob a serious blow, bringing down Lepke, Shapiro, Lucky Luciano, and many others.)

The word on the street was that Meyer had bribed his way out of trouble, that his brother Ike had disbursed about $100,000 to get the three men off. About the time Dewey set up shop, a detective wrote to Police Commissioner Lewis J. Valentine and told him the Drukman case had been fixed, but nothing came of it. (The detective claimed that Assistant District Attorney William W. Kleinman had asked him to take it easy on the Luckmans and that another man with gangland ties—who also was friendly with District Attorney William F. X. Geoghan—had offered him money. Kleinman resigned after being indicted for conspiracy the following year, though he was eventually acquitted.)

The murders might have gone unpunished had Joseph D. McGoldrick, running for DA against Geoghan in the November election, not made an issue of the bungled case during the campaign. After being returned to office, Geoghan, well aware of the public's suspicions, once again sought indictments for the trio and this time—wonder of wonders—was successful. The governor, however, thought it best to turn the prosecution over to yet another special district attorney, Hiram C. Todd. State Supreme Court justice Erskine C. Rogers was tapped to preside over the trial.

And a fascinating trial it was. You had a sequestered jury, witness intimidation, a Drukman "dummy"—all tied up in knots—used as a prop by the prosecution. And outside the courtroom you had a crowd of people trying in vain to get in, one day "nearly precipitating a riot," according to the *Eagle*.

It was front-page news for two weeks. "Drukman Case Proves Tangle of Family Ties," the headline would read, or "Mrs. Kantor Collapses" after giving testimony, or "Aged Father of Drukman Levels Finger at Luckmans."

This last scene was easily the most dramatic of the trial. While on the witness stand, Abraham Drukman—father of both Sam and Meyer's wife, Ethel—looked over at the defendants and suddenly burst out in Yiddish, "They murdered him! They murdered him! Meyer killed him!"

"The exertion weakened him," the *Times* reported, "and he collapsed against the interpreter's arm. The courtroom hushed tensely for a moment. Jurors, startled, gazed at one another. Attendants clustered around the stand. Justice Rogers leaned forward anxiously. The defendants remained taut."

The *Herald Tribune* provided additional detail:

Heavy-jowled Meyer Luckman, sixty years old, a power in the racket-ridden trucking world, . . . sat between his two stolid co-defendants, looking straight ahead. He swallowed several times.

Directly behind Meyer Luckman, staring tensely from the front spectator's bench, sat the aged witness' grandson, Meyer's boy, Sidney Luckman, Columbia University freshman football star.

Yes, nineteen-year-old Sid witnessed this horrific moment, saw his grandfather accuse his father of killing his uncle. Surely it haunted him for the rest of his days. A 1949 story in *Sport* contains an interesting passage that might well relate to this. "We were discussing the nervous, restless way [Sid] sleeps," Ed Fitzgerald writes, "and his [Bears] roommate, Fred Davis, said, 'Nobody who's got as much money as Luckman can sleep at night.'"

Forget the second part—Davis's playful jab—and focus on the first part: the "nervous, restless way" Sid slept. Fitzgerald revisits the subject later: "[Sid] sleeps fitfully and is easily awakened, especially the night before a game. 'I get very tense,' he explains. 'I'm all filled up with anticipation and anxiety.'"

Perhaps he was just the jittery type—or perhaps he never got used to his father not being there, the father who would sit on the bench beside the coach and watch his son's high school practices, the father who had the chutzpah to approach the great Benny Friedman after a Giants game and ask him to give his kid a few passing tips. (Friedman went back to the locker room for a football and then showed young Sid how to grip it.)

"Dad used to speak of football in terms of how it benefited a youngster, kept him from being spoiled, gave him self-reliance and drive," Sid says in *Luckman at Quarterback*. ". . . What affected Dad most about my rise in football was the democratic attitude he saw throughout the game, especially the unbiased ways of my coaches. Irish coaches and Italians and Bohemians, who brought a Jewish boy out of Flatbush and worked their heads off to make a high-priced football man out of him."

The Italian and Bohemian coaches, in particular—Columbia's Lou Little (the former Luigi Piccolo) and the Bears' George Halas (whose parents were Czech)—became surrogate fathers for Sid. It was Little who helped see him through the rough times after Meyer went to prison, arranging for jobs for his young tailback so he could afford to stay in school. Lou and his wife, Loretta, were childless, and Sid might have filled a void for them just as the coach did for him.

"He became very friendly with the family," Blanche said of Little. "He once gave my mother a little jewelry box with his name on it. He was always calling her and talking to her . . . and thanking her for giving him Sid Luckman."

When Sid was inducted into the Pro Football Hall of Fame in 1965, he was presented by Little, not Halas. But then it was Little who encouraged him to try pro ball when Sid was thinking of going into the trucking business with his older brother Leo. Little's influence over Sid even extended to the clothes he wore. One year with the Bears, Sid made a "Best Dressed" list; his dapper college coach, owner of fifty suits, must have gotten a kick out of that. "He dressed immaculately," Sid said a few years before he died. ". . . I emulated him in many ways."

Halas took custody of Sid from Little and tried to shield him as much as possible from the hard knocks of pro football—particularly the difficult first year, when Sid was making the transition from the traditional single wing to the newfangled T formation. When Sid signed with the Bears, he had never been out of the East except for a brief trip to Ann Arbor, Michigan, with the Columbia football team. And in training camp the veterans immediately resented him because, as the second pick in the draft, he was making much more money than they were, $5,000 as a rookie.

Early on Sid struggled with his new quarterback position—the direct snap from center, the footwork, the play calling. Halas stuck with him, though. He was convinced the kid had the right combination of talent, brains, and toughness to take the T to another level.

In later years the coach would refer to his quarterback as his "second son." Sid felt the same sense of attachment. When, near the end, Papa Bear had circulation problems in his feet, his eternally grateful protégé would drop by at night and massage them.

"We all knew he was Halas's man," teammate Al Baisi said. "You didn't dare smart-aleck him or say anything about him." Many of the Bears considered Sid a brownnoser, but that's because they didn't understand the role Halas played in his life, didn't understand that Sid sought approval from his coaches the way other players might seek it from their fathers. He would even attend Catholic services in camp, just to please the boss.

"He'd sit in the back of the room," Baisi said, " — way back, away from the rest of us."

The defense in the Drukman trial didn't call a single witness. One day during the proceedings, the *Daily News* ran a photo of the defendants looking "cheerfully" at the camera, as if they'd been arrested for nothing more consequential than a parking ticket. Was it possible the fix was still in? More than one witness had reportedly gone into hiding before testifying. A worker at the garage where the getaway car was stashed said he didn't come forward at first because "I didn't dare. I knew it was a very bad case, and I didn't want to be implicated in it. I didn't say anything because I knew I was up against bad people."

Meyer's attorney, James I. Cuff, asked the jury to entertain the possibility Drukman was killed by gangsters to whom he owed horseracing debts — the defendants' story all along. (The Luckmans were originally represented by Samuel S. Leibowitz, but the noted lawyer moved on to an even more high-profile case: that of Bruno Richard Hauptman, kidnapper of the Lindbergh baby.) Cuff also claimed that the prosecution of his client, by a special district attorney before a Supreme Court judge, was merely a "political football," an attempt to discredit District Attorney Geoghan.

The evidence, however, was too overwhelming. After seven hours of deliberations, the jury found the three men guilty of second-degree murder. (The absence of an eyewitness—e.g., Kantor—was believed to have saved them from first-degree convictions. . . and the death house.)

The next day the *Daily Mirror* published a scathing editorial, accompanied by a picture of the two Luckmans. "Look at these hideous faces," it begins,

> and be glad that they will spend 20 years in jail, even if you do think they should be on their way to the electric chair. These two, Meyer Luckman and Harry Luckman, convicted of murdering a miserable creature in their employ, are accused of torturing him before killing him, helped by a third killer, Fred Hull.
>
> If you study these faces for a moment, you will know what kind of human creatures to avoid. Skunks and rattlesnakes are gentlemen in comparison. Murderous cruelty is stamped on their vilely hideous faces. . . . Twenty years for these slimy killers is better than nothing, but you wonder what special privileges their dirty money will buy for them in prison, and whether any sloppy parole board will let them out ahead of time.

The Speaker of the New York State Assembly, Irving M. Ives, was no less disturbed. The Luckman case, he said, proved "that the long delays in the prosecution of criminal cases on the part of state law enforcement agencies are as responsible as any single factor for the flagrant flouting of the law by gangsters, racketeers and other underworld characters."

The trial dispensed with, Special DA Todd launched a probe of the bribery plot. The careers of policemen and officials would be ruined. A detective in the case, his bank records under scrutiny, committed suicide. Another of the principals went on the lam. So did Ike Luckman, dispenser of the cash. He vanished in December 1935, a few months before the Drukman trial, and didn't resurface until March 1940. He was eventually sentenced to a year in prison and fined $500, but his sentence was suspended because of failing health. The *Eagle* estimated his age at "about 69."

Sing Sing, where Meyer Luckman spent his remaining years, was one of the all-time hellholes, worse than the Lower East Side of his youth. The warden in those days, Lewis Lawes, said his earliest impression of the prison was of "dirt and filth." Inmates no longer wore striped uniforms or marched in lockstep, but there was still the rock pile—and the Old Cellblock.

The latter, a monument to a darker age, was notorious for its claustrophobic cells and lack of plumbing. Warden Lawes considered it "probably the worst cellblock in the world"—suffocatingly hot in summer, miserably cold in winter, and forever damp because of its proximity to the Hudson River. "A man can hardly breathe in those cells," he said in 1941.

This is where the father of the Columbia tailback, of the future Pro Football Hall of Famer, lived for a time—as did all new prisoners until there was a vacancy elsewhere. And how's this for pathos: One of Sid's most memorable college games, a 20–18 comeback victory over Army in 1938, was played at West Point, twenty miles up the river from the prison. It was this heroic effort that landed Sid, the "22-year-old Jewish boy . . . who once played tin-can football on the streets of Brooklyn," on the cover of *Life*. It was at Michie Stadium that he became "the most talked-of football player in the U.S."

Pathos, part two: At some point in his travels, Sid may well have taken a train that went right through Sing Sing. The New York Central Railroad's tracks bisected the prison property, separating the Old Cellblock from much of the rest of the complex. (Babe Ruth cracked a reported 620-foot homer over those tracks in a 1929 exhibition game at Sing Sing.) How strange it would have been for Sid to go speeding through his father's world—to be within a football field or so of him—and not be able to see him, talk to him, ease his pain.

His sister Blanche wasn't sure if Sid ever visited Meyer in prison. "I don't think so," she said. "I think he probably discussed it with

Lou Little, and [Little] must have told him not to go or something. [Little] didn't want Sid to get any negative publicity. He was very, very concerned about Sid."

Sid's mother also stayed away from Sing Sing. But Blanche went there regularly, one time bringing along her eight-month-old daughter, Ronnie, to meet her grandfather. Sid's younger brother David, meanwhile, stopped by the prison once a month "with a big carton of food and vegetables and all kinds of things" for Meyer and his fellow inmates.

"They would examine what he was bringing in to make sure no guns and things were in the packages," Blanche said, "but they let him bring in all this food. And the family was struggling because of what happened. The trucking business lost customers, you know, and things like that. So we were starving, and they were eating good."

According to Blanche, her father spent most of his term not in a cell but in "a little hut" with three other men, apart from the rest of the prisoners. "They cooked and they ate and they did everything in there," she said. (This is entirely possible. Older inmates were rare at Sing Sing, where the average age was twenty-three, and sometimes they received special treatment. Some years before, *New York Evening World* city editor Charles Chapin, convicted of murdering his wife, was housed in separate quarters — and gained notoriety for his horticultural skills as the "Rose Man of Sing Sing.")

Six weeks after he began serving his sentence, a story in the *Eagle* said, "(T)he rotund Harry Luckman is on a road gang, elderly Meyer Luckman is assigned to porter duty and Fred J. Hull is doing tier work." Meyer, it went on, "was in the prison hospital for some time after his arrival there. He is 60 years old and suffering from a heart ailment." Unfortunately, that's all the information we have on inmate number 91674.

One of the things that came out in the trial was that Meyer was unable to read or write English. (The 1920 U.S. Census lists him as "Myer Lukaman.") Did he belatedly learn these skills during his eight years in Sing Sing—so he could follow his son's football progress in the papers? Lawes, a progressive warden, pushed education hard. Half the prison population took classes, and school was required for anyone who tested below the fourth-grade level.

If Meyer was lucky enough to have a radio, he likely tuned it to WHN, AM-1050, on November 14, 1943. That was the afternoon they celebrated Sid Luckman Day at the Polo Grounds, and his son marked the occasion by throwing for 433 yards and seven touchdowns in a 56–7 humbling of the Giants. (The TD mark still stands, all these years later.) You wonder if Sid, with his performance, wasn't trying to communicate with his father in some way, lift his spirits, give him a reason to go on living. Meyer's heart was weak by then. He lasted only two more months.

(Sid seemed to save his best games for the New York teams. The Bears were 9-1 against the Giants and Dodgers—regular season, postseason, and preseason—while Meyer was in prison. The only loss was to the Giants in 1939, when Sid was a rookie, and he almost pulled out that one with two fourth-quarter touchdown drives. He always made sure his father could walk around Sing Sing the next day with his head held high, that he wouldn't have to take any guff from the other inmates. A dutiful son to the end, Sid was.)

Sid had just joined the U.S. Maritime Service when Meyer died on January 23, 1944. Only two days earlier Lepke, his legal appeals exhausted, had checked into Sing Sing. He soon earned the distinction of being the only Mob boss to go to the electric chair. The old gangsters were on the way out.

With his father behind bars, Sid must have felt at times like a prisoner in the Old Cellblock, must have felt like he could "hardly breathe." He dealt with it in the only way, perhaps, that made sense to him: by trying to live an exemplary life, by going to almost any lengths to ensure that no one ever spoke ill of the Luckmans again.

He never turned down an autograph request, routinely returned honoraria for speaking engagements, contributed generously to charities. He willingly shared with coaches across the country his knowledge of the T formation, the offense that would revolutionize football. (He even served on the Citizens Advisory Committee for the American Police Hall of Fame and Museum.) If his was to be the public face of the Luckmans, it would be a friendly face—not the "hideous" one of his father's, the man who, as the *Eagle* put it, "never laughs."

While accumulating titles—four of them—with the Bears, Sid also collected legions of friends. "He cannot do enough for you," one observer wrote. "He always wants to do just a little bit more."

I can speak from personal experience about that. I went to visit him once in North Miami—years, alas, before I found out about his father—and pulled out a copy of *Luckman at Quarterback*. To my surprise, he barely remembered the book. Then he began flipping through the pages, taking particular interest in some of the pictures (including one of him saluting in his Merchant Marine uniform). When he was done, he grabbed a felt-tipped pen and, without even being asked, scribbled his autograph and this inscription on the title page:

Dan—

I am glad to be your friend—you are the best of mankind.

Your admirer

Sid Luckman

Chicago Bears

#42

We had known each other for about an hour.

"He was so benevolent," his son-in-law, Dick Weiss, said. "There'd be somebody panhandling or looking for money on the street, and he'd have his driver stop the limo and he'd roll the window down. People [in vehicles behind him] would be honking their horns, and Dad would be talking to him. Nobody ever took the time to talk to these people. And you'd hear their stories, and you'd start to cry, because Dad always said, 'There but for the grace of God go I.'"

Sid's bend-over-backwards niceness masked an inner steel, an ability to just *take it*. Were he made of anything less, he probably wouldn't have survived his three years at Columbia, playing behind a line that was less than impenetrable. In the school dorms he used to supplement his income by playing craps—so much so that when the issue of *Life* came out proclaiming him college football's "Best Passer," his buddies couldn't help ribbing him. They asked if it referred to his talent for throwing footballs or for rolling dice.

In the pros Sid actually *asked* to room with Fred Davis, even though Davis had broken Sid's nose with a punch during Fred's days with the Redskins. (It was an accident; the intended target was a Bears offensive lineman.) How many players would want to live in close quarters with a guy who'd busted their beak? But the glamorous quarterback and the rugged tackle got along famously. Davis always claimed he did Sid a favor by rearranging his features. Before fist met face, he told a reporter, "Sid's nose was a utilitarian breathing instrument. The Davis alterations made it a thing of beauty."

The occasional anti-Semitism Sid encountered on the football field also thickened his hide. Baisi recalled "this one middle linebacker from Green Bay. I wanted to go over and punch him. He'd stand right over the center and say, 'Hey, Jewboy, run it up through here! Come on, Jewboy!' He was trying to get Sid riled up."

There was a lot of that in the NFL of old. During the war, particularly, the league was very ethnicity conscious. The *Official 1942 National Football League Record and Roster Manual* includes not only the players' positions, dimensions, and alma maters but also their nationalities. Lee Artoe, the Bears' take-no-prisoners tackle, was Italian; Bill Osmanski, their dentist-fullback, was Polish-Lithuanian; and Sid Luckman, their all-pro quarterback, was "Jewish." (A 1949 survey by former NFL quarterback Paul Governali found that 32 percent of the players were, like Sid, first-generation Americans.)

Sid was different from his father, sure, but it's not like they were polar opposites, not like he was "someone from another tribe" (as the *Herald Tribune* described him). Both, after all, made their mark in the physical world—and in violent worlds. A gridiron might not be as gritty as the mean streets of Brooklyn, but plenty of things happen in the heat of a game that would be criminal offenses in polite society. Indeed, you could make the argument that Sid was simply Meyer one generation removed, Meyer legitimized, Meyer's best self.

All the Luckman children did well, as it turned out, not just Mr. Football Hero. Leo captained the soccer team at Syracuse, where he was Phi Beta Kappa, and ran a successful trucking business for years. Blanche married an insurance man. David played baseball and tennis at the University of Pennsylvania, got his MBA from the Wharton School, and became a senior executive with Gimbels department store. The Luckmans were, in many ways, the American Dream incarnate. Even the Drukman scandal and their father's imprisonment didn't keep them down for long.

Over time, Meyer Luckman receded into history—to such an extent that when Sid died in 1998 at eighty-one, his father's name didn't appear in any of the obituaries. In his tribute in the *Times*, Dave Anderson talked about how the legendary quarterback not only "refined the way the position is played. He also refined the way more athletes should act: with humility and what is known as class."

In the *Daily News*, Mike Lupica reminisced with sportscaster Marty Glickman, James Madison High '35, about Glickman's schoolboy rivalry with Sid. In keeping with the occasion, the columnists concentrated on the glory and left out the gory—the night of March 3, 1935—if, indeed, they even knew about it.

Sixty-three years later, it was almost as if Meyer Luckman had never existed. Think of it as Sid's final victory.

The Games of the XI Olympiad

Bears fullback Sam Francis finished fourth in the shot put at the 1936 Olympics. His memory of the Berlin Games:

What a mass of people. We had a hundred twenty-five thousand there every day. I was so excited I ended up fouling several times. . . . One day, some of us were invited to City Hall or somewhere for a reception. That's where I shook Hitler's hand.

They served us wine in glasses that were four hundred years old. And Spec Towns — who won the high hurdles and roomed with me at these different meets — he and I decided to keep 'em. Before we left, [U.S. track coach] Lawson Robinson announced the glasses were missing and he just hoped they'd be returned. We were just like any other athletes, though — anything you can grab, grab it.

Some of the pictures I brought back were taken by Eva Braun. She was all over the Olympic Village — kind of the official photographer. I've got a good one of me and a New York runner, with Max Schmeling in the middle.

Making Way for Bronko

Tackling Bronko Nagurski, the Bears' cement-mixer-sized fullback, required a plan. If you hit him head-on, you were roadkill. And if you hit him above the shoelaces, you likely wound up in the first row.

Brooklyn Dodgers safety Joe Maniaci, who later played with the Bears after Nagurski retired, had his own technique for bringing Bronko down. "The first couple of times I hit him as hard as I could," he once told me,

> and either he bounced off or I got hurt. So the next time he came running my way, I stepped aside and tackled him from the rear.
>
> I think that might have been why [George] Halas traded for me. The players said he loved to show the film of me making that tackle. He'd say, "Look, here's a man who tackles to play another day."

The New York Advantage

How good did the New York Giants have it in the prewar years? This good:

- From 1936 to '41 the Giants played the Bears and Packers — the iron of the Western Division — eight times in the regular season. All eight games were played in New York.

- During this same period the Giants' chief rivals, the Redskins, played the Bears and Packers nine times in the regular season. Five of the games were at home, four on the road.

Granted, it was in the NFL's best interest to have big games played in New York, where they would get more media attention — and the clubs might make a few extra dollars. Still, it was an awfully nice edge for the Giants to have.

There were also two major officiating controversies during that 1936 to '41 stretch. Both took place at the Polo Grounds, and both — surprise — came out in the Giants' favor.

The first was in the 1938 championship game against Green Bay. In the fourth quarter, trailing 23–17, the Packers called one of their pet plays, and Arnie Herber threw a 17-yard completion to end Milt Gantenbein to the New York 43.

"But the officials called the play back," the United Press reported, "gave the ball to the Giants on the Packer 44 and ruled that on the shift, Gantenbein moved out of his end position and became an ineligible receiver."

The Packers flipped out. On the next play, they piled on the Giants' ball carrier and were penalized again, this time 15 yards for unnecessary roughness. (Afterward, Green Bay fullback Clarke Hinkle regretted that his team "started to get rough out there. It's silly for grown men to lose their tempers in a game," he said. "Looks bad, too.")

The call against Gantenbein, according to Joe Williams of the *New York World-Telegram*, "mystified the stands. . . . This broke up the ball game as far as the Packers were concerned. They were steaming mad at what they considered rank injustice and proceeded to show it. [Herber] looked to the sideline and motioned as if he wanted to take the team off the field."

Coach Curly Lambeau said he was almost angry enough to let him, but he thought the Packers "still had enough time left to score. . . . We had used [the play] seven times previously this year, and there never was a protest."

The Packers *weren't* able to score, though, and the Giants took the title.

The next year, in the regular-season finale in New York, the Redskins thought they'd won the division championship on a 15-yard field goal by Bo Russell in the last minute. Uh-uh. Referee Bill Halloran ruled the kick no good, giving the Giants a 9–7 win.

Halloran made a dash for the dressing room when the clock ran out, but a delegation of Washington players—along with coach Ray Flaherty—caught up with him. Punches were reportedly thrown (though the league decided none had actually landed and didn't hand out any fines or suspensions).

I'm not rendering any final judgments on the calls against the Packers and Redskins. It's difficult to reach a verdict from a distance of so many decades. I'm just saying there weren't controversies of this magnitude in Washington, Chicago, or Green Bay, that's all.

(Addendum: Something similarly suspicious happened at the Polo Grounds in the next-to-last week of the 1944 season. The Redskins' Joe Aguirre kicked a 36-yard field goal with 1:28 left to tie the Giants 16–16, but a holding penalty wiped out the score and Aguirre's subsequent try from 51 yards fell short. A tie would have been damaging for the Giants, who ended up winning the division with an 8-1-1 record to Philadelphia's 7-1-2. It would have forced a playoff with the Eagles, who'd handed them their only loss and tied them in the rematch.)

The Greatest Goal Line Stand of All Time

Or maybe I should just say: It's hard to believe there's ever been a *better* stand than the one the Bears mounted against the Rams on October 10, 1937. The Rams had eleven cracks from the Chicago 6 early in the fourth quarter—eleven!—and couldn't get in.

Unfortunately, no play-by-play exists of the game, but John Dietrich's account in the *Cleveland Plain Dealer* provides a fair amount of detail. The stand followed a 59-yard pass from Bob Snyder to Jules Alphonse that moved the Rams deep into Bears territory. And then . . .

- First and goal from the Chicago 6: Alphonse loses 8 yards trying to sweep right end.
- Second and goal from the Chicago 14: Bill Cooper throws an incomplete pass.
- Third and goal from the Chicago 14: Another pass, from Snyder to Stan Pincura, results in an interference penalty against the Bears at the Chicago 4, giving the Rams a new set of downs.

On the next three plays, Cooper and Snyder take "three smacks at the line," Dietrich says, and gain "about a yard."

- Fourth and goal from the Chicago 3: Snyder throws into the end zone, and again the Bears are called for interference.

With the ball now three feet from the goal line, the Rams try to muscle it over "in four rousing smashes at the Bear line — one by Pincura, two by Snyder and the fourth by Cooper," Dietrich reports. The Bears, being the Bears, refuse to budge.

First down, Chicago, at the 1.

(Just to review: The Rams, beginning from the 4, gained exactly 1 yard in seven running plays.)

There's no indication which Bears were in the game at the time, but it's a good bet their four Hall of Famers — linemen Joe Stydahar, Danny Fortmann, and George Musso and linebacker Bronko Nagurski — had something to do with it. At any rate, *whoever* was out there put on a goal line stand to rival any in pro football history.

For all their heroics, by the way, the Bears didn't come away completely unscathed. On the first play after the ball changed hands, Beattie Feathers tried to quick kick out of the end zone, but a bad snap forced him to run and he was tackled for a safety. That was the reason for the funny-looking final score: Bears 20, Rams 2.

When Darkness Comes

The kickoff of the 1937 title game between the Bears and Redskins at Wrigley Field was moved up from 2:00 p.m. to 1:15 — and for good reason, too. The week before, the Bears' regular-season finale against the Cardinals at Comiskey Park had ended in total darkness . . . and near-total chaos.

What kind of chaos? Well, in the fourth quarter the Bears scored a safety when a snap went whizzing past the Cardinals' punter and out of the end zone. He never saw the ball. The Cards then answered with a 97-yard shovel pass to Gus Tinsley that caught the Bears completely unawares. (It's kind of the football equivalent of Gabby Hartnett's Homer in the Gloamin' for the Cubs in '38. In fact, at the time, it was the longest touchdown pass in NFL history.)

Tinsley "ran up the sidelines," George Strickler wrote in the *Chicago Tribune*, "and was at midfield before the Bears realized anyone was loose. Even then they had their doubts, for all that was visible of the runner in the darkness was a pair of silver pants. Some Bear hero, whose identity was hidden by the night, then realized pants seldom go running around without a sponsor and gave futile chase."

As Tinsley sprinted toward the goal line, the crowd swarmed the field, forcing the officials to call the game with the Bears on top 42–28. The Cardinals didn't even kick the last PAT. It was just *awarded* to them.

At some point in the final quarter — the newspapers are hazy about when — a brawl broke out between the teams. Among the combatants were the two coaches, George Halas and Milan Creighton, who traded blows until they were sent to neutral corners.

"To add to the general confusion," the *Chicago Herald and Examiner* reported,

> the game was played under brutal conditions. The field was glazed with a sheet of ice, and the temperature was only 18 degrees above zero. The ice was sprinkled with sand, and players affected tennis shoes to improve their traction. But even at that, the footing was treacherous. . . .

Bonfires blazed in the stands through the darkness as the half-frozen spectators . . . tried to acquire some heat.

Indeed, it was all very goofy.

Anyway, to make a short story long, *that's* why the '37 title game kicked off forty-five minutes early. And not a moment too soon, if you ask me.

Called on Account of Injuries

It wasn't unheard of in the days before television for NFL games to be postponed because of the weather — or even because of light ticket sales. So why would anyone mind, Pittsburgh Pirates owner Art Rooney figured in 1938, if he put off a game because, well, a bunch of his players were banged up?

Boy, did Art figure wrong. His scheduled opponents, the Cleveland Rams, had won two in a row and were anxious to make it three against last-place Pittsburgh. The resulting disagreement led to an embarrassing few days for the league — at a time when credibility was still an issue for pro football.

Rams president Tom Lipscomb actually tried to have the Pirates' franchise revoked after Rooney insisted on postponing the October 16 game in Pittsburgh. Lipscomb sounded out other owners, and "all agreed calling off the game was an inexcusable thing to do," he said. But then NFL president Joe Carr intervened and "pointed out the far-reaching effects [of such an action], so I backed down."

Art, for his part, was much amused by Lipscomb's teeth-gnashing. "Why, that guy!" he told the *Pittsburgh Press*.

A postponement won't hurt football. It's done in the major leagues of baseball. Teams do it so they can schedule doubleheaders. Besides, I've got a lot of ballplayers hurt. The postponement won't cost him a penny, and it'll help us.

If he gets the club owners to take a vote [on whether to expel the Pirates], they might wind up throwing him out. They'll laugh at him. Why, I'm the one that went to bat for the Rams to get them in the league.

One of the reasons Rooney had "a lot of ballplayers hurt" was because his team had played an exhibition against an independent club five days before the Rams game—and just two days *after* a game against the Brooklyn Dodgers. Three Pirates had suffered season-ending injuries: center Mike Basrak (broken leg), guard George Kakasic (fractured ankle), and tackle Ted Doyle (broken arm).

But Rooney had made his own contribution to the mess. For starters, he'd invested heavily in halfback Whizzer White, the future Supreme Court justice—signing him to a reported $15,000 contract, the biggest in the NFL—and it caused dissension in the ranks. When the team started slowly, he began unloading players in hopes of changing the chemistry . . . and improving his bottom line.

After losing to Brooklyn to drop to 2-4, Rooney went into full panic mode and sold quarterback Frank Filchock to the Redskins, fullback Scrapper Farrell to the Dodgers, and blocking back Tom Burnette to the Eagles. All three were useful players, as was end Eggs Manske, who was released around the same time and rejoined the Bears.

The roster reductions left the Pirates with just twenty men, ten below the limit. That's why the injuries hit them so hard—and why Rooney felt obliged to reschedule the Rams game. He simply didn't have enough bodies.

Chester Smith, sports editor of the *Cleveland Press*, found the whole episode very alarming. "The points at issue and the discussions are entirely irrelevant, it seems to me," he wrote.

> What actually matters is that the league is run so loosely that the Pittsburgh-Cleveland game can be called off on such short notice and for the reason the Pirates' president cited. . . .
>
> The football league also has been far too free in trading and selling its talent during the course of the championship season. One of these days, if the present system persists, a center is going to snap the ball to a halfback and discover to his horror that the latter has been sold to

the opponents between the time the signals were called and the starting signal given. Then it will be up to the officials to rule which side gets the touchdown, if there is one.

According to the Rams, Rooney first tried to switch the game to Cleveland, but Lipscomb didn't think he had enough time to promote it. Then Art suggested that the teams meet December 4 in Chattanooga, Tennessee, but the Rams weren't too keen on that idea, either. The game did end up being played on that date, but it was moved to New Orleans, not Chattanooga—the first NFL game, in fact, ever played in the Big Easy.

Fortunately, the Pirates had enough healthy reinforcements to make it through four quarters. But the Rams came away with the season-ending win, 13–7, before a Sugar Bowl crowd of seventy-five hundred.

• • •

I don't care if they bet on Green Bay against the Giants, but I won't let [my players] bet on our own games. — Brooklyn Dodgers coach Potsy Clark

• • •

There's Something about Cecil

No fashion accessory in pro football history has been stranger than Cecil Isbell's chain. The Packers' all-pro passer dislocated his left shoulder in college and was worried it might pop out again, so he wore a chain—secured by a harness—that ran from his waist to his upper arm. It kept him from raising the arm above the shoulder and enabled him to play five seasons in the NFL.

"The only time I've ever noticed it was when [Alex] Wojciechowicz grabbed it instead of me in the Detroit game," he said at the end of his rookie season in 1938. "I've worn it since . . . my sophomore year at Purdue. After being gang-tackled extra hard I came up with a shoulder dislocation. Later on in the same game I dislocated it just while kicking off. I've worn the chain ever since and the wing hasn't bothered me at all."

Still, it's pretty remarkable Isbell was able to have the career he did. Single-wing quarterbacks, after all, took a pounding, and Cecil never shied from carrying the ball. In his first year with Green Bay he finished fourth in the league in rushing. But he often wondered how he would have fared in the more quarterback-friendly T formation instead of the Packers' Notre Dame Box.

"In our system," he said in Chuck Johnson's *The Green Bay Packers*, "even when I handed off, I couldn't get out of there without getting smeared. I'd usually fake and get tackled anyway."

Fortunately, Isbell threw with his *right* arm — and quite well. He and Don Hutson formed the NFL's most lethal combination — and were particularly devastating in 1942, when Hutson obliterated every receiving record of consequence by catching 74 passes for 1,211 yards and seventeen touchdowns.

At this point Isbell had thrown for a TD in twenty-three straight games — which would be a good streak *today*, never mind then. (To put it in perspective, the prolific Brett Favre, holder of the all-time mark for touchdown passes, had only one streak that long.) After the season, though, Isbell retired at twenty-seven to become an assistant coach at his alma mater. The following year he was promoted to head coach.

We'll never know what he might have done if he'd kept playing. Just as we'll never know what he might have done if his left arm hadn't been attached to a chain.

It'll Never Catch On

Sammy Baugh on a revolutionary development in pro football in 1938:

> The New York Giants have introduced something new . . . by going into a defensive huddle while the offensive team is in its huddle. I was not impressed with the defensive huddle when I saw it. It is too difficult to anticipate plays before the offensive team lines up for the center's snap. It is then that plays are usually "tipped off" by telltale actions of the offensive backs or linemen.
>
> And I actually know of a case where the defensive huddle was made

to look very stupid. Jersey City, the Giants' minor-league farm team, was in its defensive huddle in a game not long ago when the team with the ball suddenly decided to run a play before Jersey City came out of its huddle. They ran through 'em for a touchdown.

Heading for the Mountains

During the Depression, NFL teams that were struggling at the gate would play games just about anywhere they could draw a crowd (or at least be assured of a decent guarantee). In 1938 the Pittsburgh Pirates and Philadelphia Eagles met twice—in Buffalo, New York, and Charleston, West Virginia. Two years earlier, the Boston Redskins were having so much trouble selling tickets that they moved the title game against Green Bay to the Polo Grounds in New York.

It was in this spirit that the Eagles and Cleveland Rams closed out the '39 season in Colorado Springs, Colorado. The idea was to cash in on the popularity of Rams coach Dutch Clark, who had starred at Colorado College before going on to a Hall of Fame career in the pros.

Philly's Emmett Mortell, Bree Cuppoletti, and Dick Riffle drove out to the game in Riffle's four-door sedan, Mortell once told me. It took them three days to reach Colorado Springs. Emmett's memories of that week:

I remember that we got to celebrate Thanksgiving twice. FDR had moved it up a week that year [to November 23, the next-to-last Thursday in the month] to create a longer Christmas shopping season, but some states didn't recognize it. So we celebrated Thanksgiving in Philadelphia before we left, and then we celebrated it in Kansas [November 30] on the way out.

We stayed at the Broadmoor Hotel [in Colorado Springs]. You could drink the water right out of the brook. It was like carbonated water. One day we tried to drive up to Pike's Peak, but we ran into a barricade. So we parked the car and the three of us are starting to walk, and an old man came out of a ski lodge and said, "Boys, it's a long way to the top. Why don't you come in?"

So we had a couple of beers, and after the second one I said, "Boy, this is good beer!" It was Coors, of course. And the man said, "It's not the beer, son, it's the altitude. I've seen girls try to go to bed with their skis on up here."

It was the first regular-season NFL game ever played in the West. It was also, I'd be willing to bet, the first NFL game that featured an airplane flyover. "A squadron of planes from the 120th observation squadron, Colorado National Guard, will dip over the field just before the kickoff time," the *Colorado Springs Gazette* reported.

The plan was for the squadron commander to drop a football from one of the planes to the field, but it was "a failure due to the high south wind."

NFL president Carl Storck appointed four officials from the Mountain States Conference (Colorado, BYU, Wyoming, et al.) to work the game. The Eagles weren't at all happy with the job they did and "charged" umpire Bill Greim and field judge John Kraft afterward, the *Gazette* said. "Only the alertness of Officer Jim Watson of the Colorado Springs police department kept Greim from taking a haymaker punch thrown in his direction."

From the sound of things, the Eagles might have had a legitimate beef. Though the game was billed as Clark's homecoming, most of the crowd of 9,189 began cheering for Philadelphia because of "the officiating, which smacked of Class F league," according to the *Gazette*.

Five players were ejected for slugging. The Rams, scoring touchdowns in every quarter, breezed to a 35–13 win. Twenty-one years later, when this game was thoroughly—and rightly—forgotten, Colorado got a pro football team of its own.

Number of the Decade: 46.7

The United Press posed the following question to sports editors and writers in 1938: Could Jock Sutherland's number one ranked University of Pittsburgh team beat a top NFL club?

The results of the poll—135 ballots were cast—were as follows:

Yes: 38 (28.1 percent)

No: 72 (53.3 percent)

Maybe: 25 (18.5 percent)

In other words, nearly half—46.7 percent (63 of 135)—thought there was a chance the Panthers could knock off somebody like the Giants or Packers. This was the world pro football still lived in in the late '30s.

Predictably, editors and writers in college towns staunchly defended Their Game. Typical was the comment of George Alderton of the *Lansing State Journal*, who said, "Professional football is filled with silly mistakes that third-rate college teams wouldn't make. The college boys have the brains, and don't let anybody kid you that they aren't equal physically."

Eight days later, by the way, Pitt lost at home to crosstown rival Carnegie Tech, 20–10—which means they weren't even the best team in *Pittsburgh* that season. (Tech wound up going to the Sugar Bowl and finishing sixth in the final Associated Press poll, two spots ahead of the Panthers.)

For some reason, UP didn't conduct another poll asking: Could *Carnegie Tech* beat a top NFL club?

Not Hurtin' for Certain

Until the NFL passed a rule against it, it was popular in the late '30s for players to stop the clock by faking injuries. They'd do this if their team was out of timeouts or wanted to get a fresh body in the game. Packers coach Curly Lambeau once was asked how the players knew which one of them should take a dive. His classic response: "I stand on the sideline with a player next to me. If he's a right end, the right end knows it's his turn to faint. If he's a center, the center knows he must put on the act, and so on."

• • •

I'm using a new scouting system [in 1938] . . . to make sure that this young stuff we pick up is the real McCoy. I don't think that this has ever been done before. You see, I don't depend on the word of one man alone when I sign up a player. I count on three—a coach, a newspaperman and a fan. When a boy can please and win the praise of three critics such as these, I know that the kid must have something and that he can do our club some good.—Potsy Clark, Brooklyn Dodgers coach

• • •

The Pre-Combine Era

Scouting might have been more primitive in the 1930s—before television, computers, the Combine, and Mel Kiper—but NFL teams were still very good at finding players, no matter how obscure their college. If you really want to be blown away, take a look at some of the alma maters of the 1938 Giants, who won the championship:

Charles Barnard, E—Central Oklahoma

Len Barnum, B—West Virginia Wesleyan

Dale Burnett, B—Emporia State (Kansas)

Pete Cole, G-T—Trinity (Texas)

Stan Galazin, C—Villanova

Johnny Gildea, B—St. Bonaventure (New York)

Ray Hanken, E—George Washington

Larry Johnson, LB-C-E—Haskell Indian School (Kansas)

Tuffy Leemans, B—George Washington

John Mellus, T—Villanova

Kink Richards, B—Simpson College (Iowa)

Hank Soar, B—Providence (Rhode Island)

Orville Tuttle, G—Oklahoma City

And remember, this is with thirty-man rosters.

None of the aforementioned schools had big-time programs (though West Virginia Wesleyan had produced Hall of Famer Cliff

Battles). Heck, several of them—Haskell, Providence, Oklahoma City, St. Bonaventure, and George Washington—later dropped football. (Haskell brought the sport back and now competes in the NAIA.)

Barnard was just the second NFL player to come out of Central Oklahoma. Richards was the second and last to come out of Simpson. It was pretty much the same for Burnett (third player out of Emporia State), Gildea (third out of St. Bonaventure), Leemans (fourth out of GW), Soar (fourth—of a total of five—out of Providence), Cole (sixth out of Trinity), and Tuttle (sixth out of Oklahoma City).

Yet they all played for the 1938 NFL champs. Many of them had lengthy careers, too—for that era, at least. And Leemans, a do-everything back, made it to Canton.

So how did the Giants—coach Steve Owen, personnel prodigy Wellington Mara, et al.—find these guys? Answer: the old-fashioned way, by pumping former players and friends in the coaching profession for information and by catching college games whenever they could. Tips would also come from sportswriters (some of whom might even be on the payroll), from officials, from just about anybody, really.

Soar told me that Tom Thorp, a referee, helped set him up with the Giants. During a game in 1936, Thorp said to him, "Who would you like to play for in the National Football League? I've got contacts." Hank said he wanted to go to New York, and it was a done deal.

The NFL might have had teams in only eight markets in 1938, but it was very much a *national* football league, with players coming from every nook and cranny in the country—even Waxahachie, Texas (where Trinity was then located).

Secrets: Tommy Thompson

Writing about quarterback Tommy Thompson in 1942, Stan Baumgartner of the *Philadelphia Inquirer* noted, "Thompson has an engaging personality and is full of life and fun. But he wasn't always that way. Fellow players on the Eagles say that up to a year ago he was morose, surly and quiet. Liked to be by himself. Then he got married."

It's amazing what got left out of sports stories in the 1940s. Tommy, who would go on to lead the Eagles to three straight championship games and two titles, had a fairly good reason in those days for being "morose, surly and quiet," for liking "to be by himself." And he had an equally good reason for regaining his joie de vivre after getting married. It all goes back to his *first* marriage, the one no one ever talked about—assuming, that is, they were even aware of it.

Thompson, you see, made the mistake of getting married after his junior season at Tulsa. In February 1939 he wed Ruth Breene, an attractive dental assistant, in a secret ceremony—secret because, according to school rules, he would have lost his athletic eligibility had anyone found out. (College football was very anti-husband-and-wife back then.)

But somebody did find out, and Thompson's young bride was devastated that Tommy, an all–Missouri Valley back, wouldn't be able to play in the fall. So she tried to remedy the situation, tragically, by swallowing enough poison to kill herself. She literally died in his arms.

"She walked into the bathroom and came out gasping," Tommy told police. "I asked her why she did it, and she shook her head."

After burying his wife of two weeks, Tommy left Tulsa and joined the St. Louis Gunners of the American Football League. He did well enough with them in '39—eight touchdowns passing, one rushing—to attract the interest of the NFL. In his second season he moved from Pittsburgh to Philadelphia, where he became a star in coach Greasy Neale's T formation.

"I could always pass," he told Baumgartner, "but my running wasn't good enough to make me a real threat in [Pittsburgh's] single wing."

Much was made during Thompson's career of him being blind in one eye. (It was variously attributed to "a ricocheting stone when he was 10 years old" and a car accident when he was in college.) But that wasn't the biggest burden he bore, not nearly. No, the biggest burden was the memory of the wife who loved him more than life itself.

Taking a Look at Tailbacks

As you'll read elsewhere in this book, statistics keeping in the NFL's first few decades left a lot to be desired. It wasn't just the unreliability, it was the unimaginativeness. It would have been nice, for instance, if the league had done more to measure the effectiveness of single-wing tailbacks — inasmuch as it was the most important position on the field.

So I decided to do it myself. What I looked for were the greatest *all-around* seasons by tailbacks. To make the cut, you had to finish in the top five in the league in both rushing yards and passing yards. Here are the Elite Eight who did it:

Year Tailback, Team	Pass (Rank)	Rush (Rank)	Total
1933 Glenn Presnell, Portsmouth Spartans	774 (2nd)	522 (4th)	1,296
1934 Dutch Clark, Detroit Lions	383 (4th)	763 (3rd)	1,146
1934 Warren Heller, Pittsburgh Pirates	511 (2nd)	528 (T5)	1,039
1935 Bill Shepherd, Boston Redskins/Detroit Lions	417 (5th)	425 (5th)	842
1938 Cecil Isbell, Green Bay Packers	659 (5th)	445 (4th)	1,104
1939 Parker Hall, Cleveland Rams	1,227 (2nd)	458 (5th)	1,685
1943 Tony Canadeo, Green Bay Packers	875 (3rd)	489 (5th)	1,364
1944 Frankie Sinkwich, Detroit Lions	1,060 (3rd)	563 (3rd)	1,623

Another way of doing it, of course, is to look only at total yards — and to consider, in this case, tailbacks who finished in the top *ten* in the league in both categories. The results:

Year Tailback, Team	Pass (Rank)	Rush (Rank)	Total
1939 Parker Hall, Cleveland Rams	1,227 (2nd)	458 (5th)	1,685
1947 Johnny Clement, Pittsburgh Pirates	1,004 (10th)	670 (2nd)	1,674
1946 Frank Filchock, New York Giants	1,262 (5th)	371 (T9)	1,633
1944 Frankie Sinkwich, Detroit Lions	1,060 (3rd)	563 (3rd)	1,623
1939 Filchock, Washington Redskins	1,094 (4th)	413 (9th)	1,507

1940 Hall, Cleveland Rams	1,108 (3rd)	365 (9th)	1,473
1933 Harry Newman, New York Giants	973 (1st)	437 (6th)	1,410
1943 Tony Canadeo, Green Bay Packers	875 (3rd)	489 (5th)	1,364
1944 John Grigas, Chicago Cardinals	690 (8th)	610 (2nd)	1,300
1933 Glenn Presnell, Detroit Lions	774 (2nd)	522 (4th)	1,296

Finally, a handful more from the All-America Conference:

Year Tailback, Team	Pass (Rank)	Rush (Rank)	Total
1947 Spec Sanders, New York Yankees	1,442 (7th)	1,432 (1st)	2,874
1948 Sanders, New York Yankees	918 (8th)	759 (4th)	1,677
1946 Bob Hoernschemeyer, Chicago Rockets	1,266 (4th)	375 (9th)	1,641
1947 Hoernschemeyer, Chicago Rockets/			
Brooklyn Dodgers	926 (8th)	704 (6th)	1,630
1949 Hoernschemeyer, Chicago Rockets	1,063 (5th)	456 (10th)	1,519
1948 Hoernschemeyer, Brooklyn Dodgers	854 (9th)	574 (9th)	1,428

Notice anything interesting? Just two of these fourteen players —Clark and Canadeo—are in the Hall of Fame.

Which doesn't necessarily mean tailbacks have been slighted by the selection committee. Many of these backs had short careers—in some instances, no doubt, because of the wear and tear associated with the position. As for Isbell, he probably *would* have made the Hall if he hadn't retired after five seasons to go into coaching. Then there's Filchock, who killed any chance he had when he was banned from the NFL for not reporting a bribe offer before the '46 title game.

Sanders and Hoernschemeyer, meanwhile, suffer because they had their greatest seasons in Another League, though both were terrific players. Spec switched to safety in 1950 and led the NFL in interceptions, while "Hunchy" was the top rusher on the Lions' '52 and '53 championship teams.

If there's anything we can conclude from this research, it's that, even in the old days, it was a tailback's passing ability that was most valued. Sammy Baugh and Arnie Herber didn't run much, but they're in the Hall of Fame. The same goes for Benny Friedman and Ace Parker (who were a little more dangerous afoot but still did most of their damage with their arms). Then the T formation took over in the late '40s, and it became very much a throwing game.

FYI: Since 1947, when Clement did it with the single-wing Steelers, only three NFL quarterbacks have finished in the top ten in passing yards and rushing yards in the same season. And surprisingly, one of them isn't Michael Vick. The short list:

Year Quarterback, Team	Pass (Rank)	Rush (Rank)	Total
1951 Tobin Rote, Green Bay Packers	1,540 (6th)	523 (8th)	2,063
1952 Bobby Layne, Detroit Lions	1,999 (3rd)	411 (9th)	2,410
1990 Randall Cunningham, Philadelphia Eagles	3,466 (6th)	942 (9th)	4,408

Joe Carr Speaks

Inasmuch as the guy was NFL commissioner for eighteen years, longer than anybody except Pete Rozelle, you'd think Joe Carr would have at least *one* entry in *Bartlett's Familiar Quotations*. Didn't Carr, a man hailed as "professional football's balance wheel" when he died in 1939, say *anything* memorable?

He's an elusive figure in the game's history, as are plenty of others from that era. But if you're willing to crank up a search engine or ten, you can unearth, if not "The Essential Joe Carr," at least a glimmer of the mind behind the commissioner. Carr in his own words:

"Professional football last year drew crowds as large as many big league baseball games did. With the popular interest already shown and with the successful fight we are making on contract-breaking and other wildcat practices, we are confident of a big league standing before long." (1921)

"O, it's a great game, this pro football. But it's never been a great moneymaking game. Take that old team we called the Columbus

Panhandles. I organized that bunch 20 years and more ago. We made some money, but I didn't get rich. Nobody has in this pro grid game. A lot of us have gone broke thinking we would. I managed those Nesser boys and the rest of the Panhandles because I got a kick out of it. Of course I wanted to make money. But money wasn't all of it, you get what I mean?" (1926)

From a syndicated column by Billy Evans: "In the course of our conversation, Carr expressed the belief that a rule similar to the one in vogue in hockey, penalizing the player who offends by a one- or two-minute removal from the game, might make [for] less fouling and more action. . . . Carr said he intended to urge the adoption of such a rule at [that day's league] meeting." (1927)

"Our hope is to put in a team at Milwaukee. I know Milwaukee will go over in a big way in professional football. Situated as it is between Chicago and Green Bay, the traditional rivalry angle is all ready and waiting. The Green Bay Packers are a tremendous [drawing] card wherever they appear, and if a home series could be arranged between the Milwaukee and Green Bay teams, it would be a sellout." (1931)

"Spectators are opposed to drawn-out games. They want rapid action, intermingled with thrills and glamor which have made football such a great spectacle. It is our desire to open up the game and give the public as much action as possible. While we have adhered to intercollegiate rules, our players and officials handling the games have been instructed to do everything to interest the spectators." (1932)

Appearing before Portsmouth Spartans supporters, who were trying to hang on to their franchise during the Depression: "This is my second visit to your city in two months, and I'm not going to bore you with a long, tedious speech. You fans know as well as I what National League football has done for your city. It has given it your greatest advertisement. Thousands of people know all about Portsmouth and the Spartans by reason of your great team last year. It would be a pity to lose this team — and judging from your enthusiasm here tonight I don't believe you have an idea of doing this. I want to impress upon you that if Portsmouth gives up its present franchise, no other small city will be admitted into the National League. We have too many big cities knocking at our door." (1932)

"Professional football is for those who understand the game. College football was built with a background of tradition and pageantry. The professional game hasn't much tradition or pageantry yet, but it proves the hardest and most interesting competition for those who love the sport purely on its own merits." (1932)

"Usually when a team lost money in the old days, it dropped out. Also, I was always getting calls to come in and help them unsnarl their finances. Those days have passed." (1933)

"[Ted] Nesser [of the Columbus Panhandles] probably was the best defensive player the game has known. His ability to diagnose plays was amazing. He could play any position." (1934)

On dropping out of school in the sixth grade: "Nowadays a family gets the dole when they can't make a go of it. In the old days it was simpler. The boys simply went to work." (1935)

"Sports is about the only business where the hired man is really boss. The moguls own the clubs, but they know that if they are to be operated successfully they've got to be bossed by somebody else." (1935)

"We have 37 minor baseball leagues — we'll have about 40 in 1939 — which condition young and inexperienced players for the majors. There's no reason why we shouldn't have the same for football. We had more than 50 players farmed out in 1938 from the

National [Football] League clubs, and probably that number will rise next season. With new leagues spreading over the country, a place can be found for every college graduate who wants to play football. Such a system, with an agreement between the majors and minors, would help professional football and the players in many ways." (1938)

Five months after he gave that last quote, Carr died—and disappeared into a silence that is only now being broken.

Lord of the Jungle

There were pro football players who wrestled on the side, and there were wrestlers who played pro football on the side. Arthur "Tarzan" White fell into the latter group.

White, a five-foot-nine, 217-pound guard, was rolling around on the mat before he ever suited up for the New York Giants in 1937. His sister Ruby even wrestled. Newspapers billed him as the "rotund Alabama behemoth"—'Bama being both his home state and his alma mater. (For one 1938 photo he theatrically hoisted a 145-pound teammate above his head with one hand.)

After the Giants won the '38 title, they went to Los Angeles to play an exhibition game against the NFL all-stars—the forerunner of the Pro Bowl. That's when White's wrestling career really took off. He got some matches on the West Coast, unleashed his devastating flying tackle on opponents, and quickly became a marquee name.

He also attracted the attention of Edgar Rice Burroughs, author of *Tarzan of the Apes*, who was living outside of LA. Burroughs was very protective of his character—which he saw as the embodiment of virtue, athleticism, and unspoiled innocence—and was appalled to see professional wrestlers appropriating Tarzan's name.

"The other self-christened Tarzans are apes, all right," he told the United Press, "only they're muscle-bound and have broken noses. Tarzan is a copyrighted trademark, and if these plug uglies insist on using it, I'm going to insist on the right to license them and stencil the copyright number on their chests."

Burroughs sent a letter to the Giants guard asking him to kindly cease and desist. "I have not granted you permission to use . . . this name," he wrote, "and I now notify you that I do not grant such permission. Your use of this name in connection with your activities may result in confusion in the minds of the public and may result in damage to this character and its name."

The writer was merely trying to protect his interests. He'd struck gold, after all, with Tarzan. In addition to the best-selling series of books, there were Tarzan movies, a Tarzan radio show, and a Tarzan comic strip.

But Burroughs's pleadings never reached the legal stage, apparently, and White kept calling himself Tarzan for the rest of his wrestling days. Besides, it's doubtful anyone ever confused the "rotund Alabama behemoth" with Johnny Weissmuller, the sleek former gold-medal swimmer then playing Tarzan in films.

The Wreck-ord Book

Recordkeeping in the early NFL was riddled with inexactness — enough to make you wonder whether the league was using an abacus instead of an adding machine. An example:

In the last game of 1939, Jack Manders scored two touchdowns and kicked three extra points to help the Bears bury the Cardinals 48–7. In so doing, Manders "boosted his lifetime scoring total to 345 points for an all-time high," according to the Associated Press, "eight more points than piled up by Ken Strong of the Giants."

In fact, "Automatic Jack" never held the all-time scoring record. As we now know, the mark belonged — until 1942 — to Paddy Driscoll, who had racked up 402 points for the Cardinals and Bears from 1920 to '29.

(Strong, meanwhile, didn't have 337 at that stage, he had 325. But hey, who's counting?)

It was no different with the rushing record. Three games into that same season, the *Brooklyn Eagle* reported that Ace Gutowsky, the Dodgers' "powerhouse fullback," was 28 yards away from the NFL's career mark and "should complete this assignment within the next few weeks."

After the Dodgers' 23–14 win over Philadelphia on October 22, the *Eagle* ran a headline that announced, in capital letters, "PRO FOOTBALL MARK BROKEN BY GUTOWSKY." The accompanying story read, "Another mark went overboard last Sunday, according to the official figures released yesterday, when Ace Gutowsky of Brooklyn gained 7 yards to break Cliff Battles' all-time ground-gaining record by a single yard, 3,399 yards to 3,398. And he should add to that as the season moves along."

Gutowsky was, indeed, a fine runner, a member of the great Detroit Lions backfield that averaged 240.4 rushing yards a game in 1936 — still the most in NFL history. He gained 827 yards that season, which stood as the club record for twenty-four years, and would have gained more if he hadn't been hobbled several weeks.

"National [Football] League coaches insist Gutowsky is the greatest spinner back in football today," the *Eagle* said. "This, on the technical side, is his greatest asset. He's a fair blocker, hard runner and a tremendous backer-up [linebacker]. His value also lies in the fact he's a good team man. His enthusiasm is infectious, on and off the gridiron."

Two years later, in a 23–0 victory over Detroit, Green Bay's Clarke Hinkle set "a new all-time ground gaining record for the professional league, with 3,500 yards as the new mark," the United Press said. "His 33 yards gained today pushed him past Ace Gutowski, [*sic*] Detroit, whose record was 3,478."

There was only one problem: Gutowsky *didn't* break the record. And his career total wasn't 3,478, it was 3,279. Ace, it turns out, never did overtake Battles (who rushed for 3,511 yards, not 3,398 — or 3,403, as it was listed in later league publications). Which means the mark Hinkle broke early in the 1941 season was Battles's, not Gutowsky's.

Unless, of course, Battles never held the record, either. The *1941 NFL Record and Roster Manual* contains this intriguing note: "Bronko Nagurski, Chicago Bears, gained 3,947 yards in 856 attempts, an average of 4.6 yards per attempt, in eight seasons — 1930–37 — including the seasons of 1930 and 1931, two years before an official statistical bureau was established."

So maybe Nagurski was the real record holder in those years. Or perhaps it was Paddy Driscoll, whose entire career was pre–statistical bureau. There's simply no way of knowing.

As you can see, the NFL's career rushing record has had an interesting life. By 1984, when Walter Payton claimed it by passing Jim Brown, it had become one of the most prestigious marks in sports. "There's been a lot of pressure," Payton said the day he assumed the throne. "I was so nervous, so very nervous, that I was shaking."

In 1958, however, the season Joe "The Jet" Perry became the league's all-time leading rusher, "there was no countdown or anything like that," he once told me. "The newspapers weren't writing, 'Perry needs 87 yards Sunday to break the record.'" It wasn't high profile like it is today. And the record didn't have the aura it did after it had been pushed upward a ways by Jim Brown (12,312) and Payton (16,726).

"[Steve] Van Buren, the guy whose record I broke, had less than 6,000 yards rushing [5,860 to be exact]," Perry said. "He isn't even in the top twenty all-time anymore. I just didn't keep up with that stuff. I couldn't tell you, for instance, who held the record before Van Buren. There just wasn't the emphasis on records back then. And there was no whoop-de-do about it when I broke it. I think somebody came over to me and said, 'You just got the record.' And I said, 'Oh.'"

He wasn't joking. In the local papers, his only recorded comment afterward was: "What difference does it make? We lost [33–3 to the hated Rams]."

Battles, who held the record (maybe) from 1937 to '41, retired after the '37 season because Redskins owner George Preston

Marshall wouldn't give him a raise. He was twenty-seven and had just led the NFL in rushing.

Brown, who held the record (definitely) from 1963 to '84, retired after the '65 season because he was tired of football and preferred to make movies. He was twenty-nine and, like Battles, had just led the league in rushing.

And let's not forget Barry Sanders, who was closing in on Payton's record of 16,726 yards, possibly a year away, when he stunningly called it quits after the 1998 season at the age of thirty. I ask you, has any other major record—in any sport—ever been regarded so casually? (Of course, Battles didn't even know he had the mark, but still . . .)

And yet, other backs have lusted after the record—only to fall short. O. J. Simpson once reminisced about going up to Brown in an ice cream parlor across from Kezar Stadium after a game—Juice was in his early teens—and telling the great back, "Man, you ain't so tough. Look, you remember my name. I'm gonna break all your records one day."

Sure enough, Simpson broke Brown's record for rushing yards in a season, gaining 2,003 in 1973 (to Jim's 1,863 in '63). But he never bagged the Big One—Jim's career mark—missing by a little over a thousand yards.

Franco Harris was another chaser of The Record. He got closer to it than O. J. did, too—within two hundred yards at the end. Brown was miffed that Harris, a back he didn't consider in his class, might become the all-time rushing leader. How miffed? Miffed enough to talk of making a comeback at forty-seven. Miffed enough to pose for a *Sports Illustrated* cover photo in a Raiders uniform. Heck, Jim groused, I'm faster than this guy even now.

In January 1985 Harris accepted Brown's challenge and agreed to compete against him in four events over two days—racquetball, one-on-one basketball and football, and the 40-yard dash. The battle, held in Atlantic City, might have established a new low for television sports. In the much-anticipated footrace, Jim pulled up lame, and Franco chugged past him to win in a ketchup-slow 5.16 seconds.

About the only way it could have been worse, from a spectator point of view, is if Ace Gutowsky had been in lane three.

The Embodiment of Bad

The Eagles were a total train wreck in the first decade of their existence. You can say that about a lot of expansion teams, of course, but the Eagles took it to another level. Not even the Bucs, who lost their first twenty-six games, had as bad a record after ten seasons as the Eagles. In fact, it isn't really that close (Eagles 23-82-4, .229; Bucs 46-102-1, .312).

The Saints (.275) were abominable and the Broncos (.293) weren't much better, but the Eagles easily had the worst first decade of any team in the modern era. Only once did they even tickle .500 — in 1938, when they finished 5-6.

If there's one story from this period that captures the utter futility of the franchise, it might be this:

The Eagles had a player in those years named Dave Smukler, a 226-pound bruiser of a fullback. He could run. He could pass. He could kick. He could do anything you wanted. Problem was, he could also do anything *he* wanted — and he often did. One sportswriter remembered him as "a fiend for pool" during his college days. By the time Smukler got to the NFL — and started making big bucks — he was probably a fiend for many more things than that. (Think of a 1930s version of John Riggins.)

Anyway, early in the 1939 season Smukler up and quit. From the sound of things, owner-coach Bert Bell had it out with him over his dissolute ways, and Dave decided he was, in Bell's words, "tired of football."

Bell spoke about Smukler with the kind of candor you never hear in the NFL anymore. He said the fullback had habitually broken training — and had recently done it again, even though he had promised Bert he'd behave.

"In my opinion, Dave was one of the greatest players in professional football — when he wanted to be," Bell said. "But I believe for the best interests of the team and myself we can do better without him, as he was a demoralizing influence. He is a good boy but he just can't keep his promises."

At this point the Eagles were four games into the season — barely a third of the way through. When their 1-9-1 nightmare was over, Smukler, who hadn't played since October 15, was *still* their leading rusher (by 81 yards, 218–137, over Fran Murray).

That's how bad the Philadelphia Eagles were in the '30s and early '40s.

Back to School

File this one under Most Interesting Way to Spend a Holdout Year.

Champ Seibold, the starting left tackle on the division-winning 1938 Packers, couldn't come to contract terms in '39. So at the age of twenty-seven — with five NFL seasons under his belt — he enrolled at Oshkosh State Teachers College and went about finishing his degree. He even competed in basketball and track for the school.

The Pack won the '39 title without him, after which Champ decided he wasn't getting any younger and rejoined his old club. The *Stevens Point Daily Journal* reported: "The signing of Champ Seibold by the Green Bay Packers just about eliminates the big Oshkosh athlete as an Oshkosh State Teachers College football prospect for the season."

A different time, indeed.

Statistical Aside

Three of the NFL's ten teams in 1939 averaged better than 300 yards a game — the Bears (364.4), Redskins (317.1), and Packers (313.2). Only once before had a club reached that figure (the Lions in '36). This might not seem like much, so let me put it in perspective for you:

In the 2011 season, eight teams — a quarter of the NFL — averaged fewer yards than those three did *seventy-two years before*.

Translation: By the '40s, pro football was a lot more than just Push and Shove.

What I've Learned: Sammy Baugh

Redskins passing legend, 1937–52

"The home team supplied the balls back then. And sometimes when you were on the road — and you were playing somebody who didn't have a good passer — you wouldn't get the [modern] slim ball, you'd get the [old] fat ball. The Steelers would do that. I think Goldsmith used to make a ball with ten laces instead of eight, and the laces would be [raised way] up like this. It was fatter than anything. But I don't blame 'em. If I didn't have a good passer, I'd put that damn fat ball out there, too. You could throw it, but it was a different kind of ball."

"They had some of the craziest rules in pro ball in those days. For instance, if you had to be taken out of the game for any reason, you couldn't come back in until the next quarter. That's a silly damn rule when you stop and think about it, especially with 25-man rosters. If you hurt your shoulder making the tackle on the opening kickoff and had to go out, you ended up missing the whole quarter. Of course, as long as no one got hurt, everything was fine. But this is football. People get hurt."

"People don't realize how much of a difference rules make in football. They can make it a great game or they can make it a lousy one. I would've loved to play under the rules they have now. Every damn one helps the offense."

"The short passing game is the great equalizer. Even if you're the weaker team, if you've got a good short passing game, you can hit that seven- or eight-yard pass, keep the other team from putting the big rush on you, and then run twice for the first down. And while you're doing this you're using up the clock and keeping the other offense off the field. I loved to throw to my backs. They were usually quicker than my ends, and they could run with the ball after they caught it. I guarantee you, I threw more to my backs than anybody in football."

"I was lucky to play under Dutch Meyer at TCU. He was the first coach I ever heard of that had a short passing game. I remember our first [team] meeting. We were waiting for Dutch to come into the room, and up on the blackboard were three S's—one right under the other. And all us idiots, we were wondering what the S's stood for. So Dutch comes in, gives a little welcome speech, and then says, 'This is our passing attack. That first S is for short. Next one: safe. Third one: sure.' That's the first time anyone ever mentioned a short passing game to me."

"I grew up with Ki Aldrich [who played center for the Redskins in the '40s]. He lived right across the street from me in Temple, Texas. Nobody loved football more than Ki. When he was in junior high school, he'd bring his shoulder pads home on weekends and practice blocking against the corner of this old tin garage his family had. He'd be banging away, and it'd be shaking and rattling like hell. People three blocks away could hear it. They'd say, 'That's just Ki, blockin' on his damn garage again.'"

"I went to spring training with the St. Louis Cardinals in 1938. But I'd torn my sternum bone loose playing a [postseason] game against the Bears, so I couldn't do anything—couldn't throw, couldn't swing a bat. I'd always played third base, and the Cardinals tried to make a shortstop out of me. But I knew damn well I couldn't beat out Marty Marion, so it was pretty easy for me to give up baseball."

"A lot of people don't think I ever got hurt much, but I had everything that could happen to you. I had both ankles hurt, both shoulders knocked down, had the sternum broken, had both elbows hurt. For two years, I couldn't throw that damn ball 40 yards. I could throw short, but it hurt like hell to throw the ball long."

"I still don't think you make kickers. Kickers make themselves."

"Somebody should have written a book about [Redskins tackle] Wee Willie Wilkin. What a character. He drank, but he didn't try to keep anybody from knowing it, really. One day he showed up drunk—so drunk he had trouble putting his cleats on—and [coach Ray] Flaherty said, 'I'm gonna start you in this ballgame, and I'm gonna leave you in there until you die.' Early in the second quarter, a player on the other team comes over to me and says, 'Sam, could you see if you could get Willie the hell out of the game? The sonuvabitch has puked on everybody on our side of the line.'"

"[Blocking back–linebacker] Erny Pinckert always looked like a doctor to me. Always had a good suit on with a pretty tie, wore glasses, shaved good, nice talkin'. But he was one of the dirtiest players I've ever been with. You wouldn't know it to look at him, but that sonuvabitch was mean. One time against Green Bay, he and Buckets Goldenberg got into a battle, and Pinckert bit the hell out of his finger. The whole game they were fighting each other. We always hated to scrimmage when Pinckert was on the other side, because he'd do anything. He didn't know but one way to go—and that's as hard as he could go."

"I was just the opposite of Bobby Layne. I didn't chew on anybody if they made a mistake—as long as they were playing the best they could play. Dutch [Meyer] told me, 'The player already feels bad about it, so don't ever chew on him for missing a block, missing a tackle, missing a pass or whatever he's doing.' And I believe that. If a man missed a pass, I'd say I threw it too hard."

An Item That May Interest Only Me

While preparing for his role as Gus McRae in the 1989 miniseries *Lonesome Dove*, Robert Duvall visited Sammy Baugh at his Texas home. From the January 26, 1998, issue of *Time*:

> "He had a way of pointing" — Duvall cocks a finger and throws his head in the air — "and a particular way of talking. I put that in the character." Thus did an old football player become a driven cattle driver.

3.
The
1940s

1940s

NFL	1940	1949
Champion	Chicago Bears	Philadelphia Eagles
Franchises	10	10
Avg. attendance	19,328	23,196
Roster size	33	32
Games per season	11	12
Points per game	30.1	45
Yds. per game	490	623.3
Plays per game	116.2	136.3
Interceptions per game	4.05	4.12
Passes completed (%)	42.9	46.6
Field goals made (%)	39.6	45.6
Run/pass TD ratio	100 run, 100 pass	159 run, 168 pass
Hall of Fame players	17	19
Hall of Fame coaches	5	4

Leaders	1940	1949
Scoring (points)	Don Hutson, Packers, 57	Pat Harder, Cardinals, Gene Roberts, Giants, 102
Passing	Sammy Baugh, Redskins	Baugh
Rushing (yds.)	Whizzer White, Lions, 514	Steve Van Buren, Eagles, 1,146
Yards from scrimmage (RB)	Dick Todd, Redskins, 810	Roberts, 1,345
Receptions	Don Looney, Eagles, 58	Tom Fears, Rams, 77
Punt return average	White, 13.8*	"Vitamin" Smith, Rams, 15.8
KO return average	Marshall Goldberg, Cardinals, 24.2*	Don Doll, Lions, 25.5
Interceptions	Three tied with 6	Bob Nussbaumer, Cardinals, 12
Field Goals	Clarke Hinkle, Packers, 9	Bob Waterfield, Rams, Cliff Patton, Eagles, 9

*Figure is for 1941, when the NFL began keeping track of the statistic.

Hall of Famers who played in 1940 (17): QB Sammy Baugh, T Turk Edwards, G Danny Fortmann, C Mel Hein, QB Arnie Herber, FB Clarke Hinkle, E Don Hutson, T Bruiser Kinard, B Tuffy Leemans, QB Sid Luckman, HB George McAfee, E Wayne Millner, T-G George Musso, QB Ace Parker, T Joe Stydahar, C Bulldog Turner, C Alex Wojciechowicz.

Hall of Fame coaches in 1940 (5): Jimmy Conzelman (Cardinals), Ray Flaherty (Redskins), George Halas (Bears), Curly Lambeau (Packers), Steve Owen (Giants).

Hall of Famers who played in 1949 (19): Baugh, C-LB Chuck Bednarik, QB George Blanda, HB Tony Canadeo, LB George Connor, HB Bill Dudley, WR Tom Fears, WR Elroy "Crazylegs" Hirsch, QB Bobby Layne, Luckman, McAfee, WR Pete Pihos, HB Charlie Trippi, S Emlen Tunnell, Turner, QB Norm Van Brocklin, HB Steve Van Buren, QB Bob Waterfield, Wojciechowicz.

Hall of Fame coaches in 1949 (4): Halas, Lambeau, Greasy Neale (Eagles), Owen.

Talking Points

• By the end of the '40s the T formation was being used by almost everybody—and scoring and yards per game were way up. Another thing that fell out of fashion, along with the single wing, was the quick kick. Possession of the ball had become too important to simply give away, even if you were backed up in your own end. You had to take advantage of every opportunity to score.

• Note that in 1949 there were more passing touchdowns than rushing touchdowns. Pro football was continuing to evolve into a throwing game—thanks to golden arms like Sammy Baugh, Bob Luckman, Sid Waterfield, and, still relatively new to the league, Bobby Layne and Norm Van Brocklin. If you didn't have a first-rate passer, you could forget about winning a championship.

• Kickers were inching toward the 50 percent mark on field goals.

• The 1,000-yard season had started to become the standard. Steve Van Buren had 1,000 yards rushing in 1947 and '49, and four receivers also topped 1,000 during the decade—Don Hutson in '42, Jim Benton in '45, and Bob Mann and Tom Fears in '49.

• Because the war with the All-America Conference had inflated salaries, rosters were actually smaller in '49 (32) than they were in '40 (33).

Secrets: Marion Motley

Marion Motley once killed a man. It was an accident, but it easily could have derailed his Hall of Fame career before it had even begun. (And had it happened in the South, where he was born, instead of the West, which was more racially tolerant in those days, it almost certainly *would* have.)

Motley was in his first year at the University of Nevada in Reno, hadn't even broken a tackle for the Wolf Pack yet, when he drove to California with a friend in March 1940. Near Fairfield, he tried to pass a car and crashed head-on into a vehicle in the opposite lane. One of the passengers in the vehicle, a sixty-year-old Berkeley man named Tom K. Nobori, suffered a fractured skull and later died of pneumonia.

That October, three days after Motley rushed for 131 yards and two touchdowns against Eastern New Mexico, a court found him guilty of vehicular homicide. The future Cleveland Browns great spent the next week and a half in jail awaiting sentencing — and no doubt fearing the worst.

In a column in the *Nevada State Journal*, an anonymous "Old Grad" said, "All week I've been thinking of that poor kid sitting in a cell down in California after that terrible ordeal at which he heard himself adjudged guilty of negligent homicide. I'll bet the hours have seemed like weeks to him, and the thought that he may have to spend considerable more at San Quentin is more than enough to drive any man crazy, let alone a straightforward harmless boy whose most remote thought never included hurting anyone."

At this point Nevada coach Jim Aiken thought there was only "a slight chance" Motley might avoid prison. His hopes hinged on the fact that, in certain circumstances under California law, a person guilty of such a crime could be let off with probation and a $1,000 fine.

But where was Marion, who came from a poor background, going to get $1,000?

To the rescue came his friends — friends at the university, friends in the Reno community, friends from all over, really. He had played in just a handful of games at Nevada, but he had already established himself as "one of the most sensational halfbacks in [school] history," according to the *Journal*. There was no way Wolf Pack fans were going to let his life be ruined by one mistake, however regrettable.

And so a Motley Fund "thermometer" was set up on campus, and the red indicator was inched along as contributions rolled in.

Students, faculty, school organizations, downtown merchants, and Just Folks dug into their pockets to help Marion. Within a matter of days the $1,000 goal was reached.

Less than a week before Motley was to be sentenced, a contingent from Nevada appeared before Judge W. T. O'Donnell in Fairfield and handed him a check. The Reno police chief and other dignitaries then attested to Marion's good character. When they were done, the judge gave Motley three years' probation . . . and directed that $500 of the fine be given as restitution to the son and daughter-in-law of the deceased. (Five hundred dollars for a life!)

The next afternoon Marion was back on the practice field, getting ready for the Idaho Vandals. In a statement of thanks published in the *Journal*, he said to his supporters, "I cannot tell you in words how grateful I am for what you have done for me. I shall try to show it by the quality of school work I do and the service I can render in behalf of the University of Nevada and the people of this state."

Try finding *that* story on Motley's Wikipedia page.

• • •

The struggles of the earnest [college] students merely whets my appetite for some *real* football. And so the following Sunday I go to see the professionals do everything the youngsters should have done the day before. —Author Paul Gallico, an early supporter of the pro game

• • •

A Veritable Football Olympics

Say this for pro football in the '40s: It knew how to promote itself.

Before a 1940 preseason game between the Bears and Eagles in Philadelphia, the NFL staged a skills contest featuring ten of its biggest stars, past and present. To compete against Chicago's Sid Luckman and "Automatic" Jack Manders and Philly's Davey O'Brien and Franny Murray, who were already on hand, the league brought in Ace Parker and Ralph Kercheval from the Brooklyn Dodgers, Ward Cuff from the New York Giants, Parker Hall from the Cleveland

Rams, and two recently retired luminaries, Ken Strong and Tilly Manton.

It went like this: The quarterbacks had to fire the ball through hoops set up at various distances. The kickers attempted field goals of 30 to 45 yards—from both hash marks and at both ends of the field. There was also a control-punting competition where the object was to boot the ball out of bounds as close to the goal line as possible.

Parker, the winning passer, was the only one to make one of the longer throws—a 20-yarder down the middle. Cuff and Strong tied for first among the kickers by nailing 145 yards' worth of field goals. And Murray took the punting honors with an impressive exhibition, landing five of his eight tries inside the 10.

The only guy who had an off night was Kercheval, who missed six of his eight field goal attempts (converting just the two 35-yarders). But Ralph was more renowned for his punting, anyway, and he *did* finish second in that department.

There's no mention of any prize money in the *Philadelphia Inquirer*'s story, but the players must have gotten *something* for their efforts. There's also no mention of whether the kicking contest featured any dropkicks. (Manton and Kercheval both had that capability.) Nonetheless, a good time seems to have been had by all.

Passing Results from the 1940 Skills Competition

Type of pass	Parker Hall	Sid Luckman	Ace Parker	Davey O'Brien
12 yds., flat	Good	Good	Good	Good
20 yds., middle	Miss	Miss	Good	Miss
25 yds. downfield	Miss	Miss	Miss	Miss
12 yds., middle	Good	Good	Good	Good

Winner: Ace Parker, Brooklyn Dodgers. Three-way tie for second.

The Day the Ball Stood Still

Words like "best" and "worst" can be dangerous to throw around, but there's little doubt which was the worst game in NFL history. It took place September 15, 1940, in Buffalo, New York, and the participants—if you want to call them that—were the Detroit Lions and the Chicago Cardinals.

The ugly details:

- Neither team scored.
- The two clubs gained a combined 30 yards (Lions 16, Cardinals 14)—a record low . . . and 106 fewer than the next-lowest total of all time.
- Just one pass was completed (of the six that were risked).
- And here's the best part (courtesy of the Associated Press's account): "The final period saw eight successive exchanges of punts between the two [teams] without a single intervening play."

That's right, in the late going, the Lions and Cards just punted the ball back and forth without even *trying* to gain yardage. They *both* played for the tie.

In fairness, the clubs weren't *that* hopeless. The Lions had the league's leading rusher that year, Whizzer White, and finished a thoroughly respectable 5-5-1. And while the Cardinals had no star of Whizzer's magnitude, they still managed two wins and two ties. Unfortunately, a thunderstorm hit around the time of the opening kickoff and "covered the field ankle-deep with water," the *Detroit News* reported, "rendering impotent ball carriers and passers alike . . . [and leaving] the crowd of some 7,000 in drenched apathy."

(I once asked Herm Schneidman, who played in the Chicago backfield that day, how soggy it was. "You couldn't even see the center of the field," he said.)

The game should have been played at Comiskey Park, the Cardinals' home. It had to be moved, though, because the White Sox were hosting Boston that afternoon. In fact, it was Ted Lyons Day at Comiskey.

So while the baseball team was honoring its Hall of Fame pitcher—and sweeping a doubleheader before a perfectly dry gathering of thirty-nine thousand—the football team was slogging it out at Buffalo's Civic Stadium (later known as War Memorial). Such was life for the Cardinals back then.

The Lions mounted the only serious scoring threat early in the fourth quarter when Dwight Sloan—whose nickname, aptly enough, was Paddlefoot—completed a 26-yard pass to Lloyd Cardwell to the Chicago 1. But on first down Sloan lost 5 yards on an off-tackle play, and on second he was sacked, pushing him back seven more yards. Another pass play was called on third down, but the Cardinals' Gus Tinsley intercepted.

The skies were so dark, the rain so relentless, that the lights were turned on in the first quarter. Even so, it was hard to tell which players were in the game, especially when uniforms began getting muddy.

"It was impossible for any player, unaided by web feet or outboard motor, to distinguish himself," the *News* said. "Fleet Lloyd Cardwell and lumbering Bill Radovich were on a par as far as speed went. . . . The lone display of enthusiasm [by the fans] came near the end when the public address system announcer revealed, 'There are only three minutes of play left.' A spontaneous cheer" went up from the stands.

Having Their Wings Clipped

There were plenty of low points for the Philadelphia Eagles in their first decade, but the lowest might have come on October 31, 1940. That was the day—or rather, the Halloween night—they lost to the Wilmington (Delaware) Clippers, giving them the dubious distinction of being the last NFL team to be defeated by a minor-league club.

The Clippers competed in the American Association, which consisted of such juggernauts as the Jersey City Giants and the Newark Bears. In fact, they were one of strongest teams in the league, good enough to reach the championship game that year. Eleven of the players they used against the Eagles either had played in the NFL or would get there eventually. They also had the home-field advantage that night, Philly owner Bert Bell figuring he could draw a better crowd in Wilmington (where six thousand showed up) than he could at Shibe Park (where the attendance dipped as low as forty-two hundred that season).

None of this, of course, would have kept a respectable NFL club from trimming the Clippers. But the 1940 Eagles were far from respectable. They finished at the bottom of the league with a 1-10 record and, aside from Davey O'Brien's desperate throwing and Don Looney's catching, didn't have a whole lot going for them.

Wilmington spotted them a touchdown in the first quarter, then broke loose for sixteen points in the second and hung on for a 16–14 victory. One of the Clippers' TDs was set up by a blocked punt. The Eagles had three scoring chances in the late going, but each time the field goal try failed. The first, from 42 yards, was wide; the second, from 32, was blocked; and the third, from 37 in the final minute, was low.

Joe Rosentover, president of the American Association, visited the Wilmington locker room afterward and told the joyful players, "This is the first time any member of our league has defeated a National [Football] League opponent, and I offer all of you my congratulations."

The next day the headline in the *Wilmington Journal* read, "Clippers' Grid Goblins Play Halloween Prank on Eagles."

I spoke one time with Emmett Mortell, who joined the Wilmington backfield that year after spending three seasons with the Eagles. He remembered the game quite well.

"I made more with Wilmington—two hundred dollars a game —than I did with Philadelphia," he said.

And in Wilmington we only practiced two days a week.

As I recall, George Marshall, the Redskins owner, was in the stands that night. And at halftime [with the Clippers leading 16–7] he walked out, mad, and said, "This will never happen again."

And it didn't. An NFL team never lost another game to a minor-league club. Not that the Eagles didn't try. Two years later they took another trip to Wilmington . . . and were fortunate to escape with a 21–21 tie.

• • •

Risk? We're not that pessimistic — and anyway, there's more risk on the ground, especially when you're playing the Bears. But we did take the precaution of splitting up the squad. You see, we would charter two planes of about 20 seats each and then line the players up in the terminal and choose sides — one set of tackles, one set of ends, a quarterback, two guards, a left half and so on to this plane, and a similar group to the other. — Packers coach Curly Lambeau on early plane travel

• • •

Number of the Decade: 73–0

OK, so it's *two* numbers. Still, few numbers in NFL history are as recognizable as the score of the 1940 title game between the Bears and Redskins.

It still doesn't seem possible — all these years later. And it could have been worse, too. The Bears lost a fumble in the red zone, dropped a touchdown pass, missed a 32-yard field goal try, and failed to convert four extra points. In other words, they could have put up ninety-four.

Let that sink in for a minute. (Not that seventy-three isn't incomprehensible enough.)

Late in the game, the Bears were doing everything they could to score again, to land one last shot to the solar plexus. On their eighth and final interception — only a couple of plays from the end — there was actually a *lateral* during the return, Joe Maniaci tossing the ball to Harry Clark.

As for the Redskins, as hopeless as they were, they still had a first down at the Chicago 5, another at the Chicago 16, and dropped a pass at the Chicago 5 in their opening series. Without a whole lot of trouble, then, this could have been a hundred-point championship game — in *1940*, no less.

The T Formation: The Untold Story

Stratagems come and stratagems go in the NFL, but the T formation lives on. It's now in its second century, looking remarkably spry for an offense that, in its modern form, dates to the early '30s. The T is so entrenched, so seemingly eternal, we tend to forget the single wing was the formation of choice for the first twenty-five years of pro football's existence. Had the Bears not beaten the Redskins, 73–0, in the 1940 championship game — and changed the course of football history — we might still have unbalanced lines and spinner plays and tailbacks receiving the snap several yards behind the line of scrimmage.

Or maybe not. Maybe the T would have conquered pro football anyway. But it's fun to think about. And it certainly isn't hard to imagine that '40 title game turning out much differently — differently enough so that the Redskins' conventional attack (single wing, with some double wing mixed in) didn't seem quite so passé.

For instance, contrary to popular belief, the Chicago offense didn't rack up seventy-three points that day — or anything close. It was on the other side of the ball, in fact, that the Bears flirted with perfection. Their defense returned three interceptions for touchdowns, recovered a fumble at the Washington 2, and set up three other scores with a variety of big plays. Total contribution: forty-seven points (two PATs being unsuccessful).

As Sammy Baugh put it years later, "A lot of people don't realize [the Bears] were closer to scoring when we had the ball than when they had it."

But that final score, well, it got your attention. It's still the most points ever scored by a team in an NFL game. And since there was no TV then, how many fans even knew how the Bears had come by their touchdowns? In the days that followed, all they read in the papers was "T-formation" and "73–0."

"I saw the perfect football team yesterday in the Chicago Bears," Catholic University coach Dutch Bergman wrote in the *Washington*

Times-Herald. ". . . This T-formation of the Bears' is going to revolutionize modern day football. There were a horde of college coaches and pro coaches in the stands yesterday, and they received an education in offensive football. . . . The Bears' great attack is not predicated on power. The basic factor of their offense is deception, faking, the way linemen slide and the timing of the backs."

Thirteen years later, in *The Story of Pro Football*, author Howard Roberts said the effects of the 73–0 game were "so far-reaching . . . that by the start of the next season nearly every team in the land, both college and pro, had adopted the Bears' T-formation with man in motion."

But that's not the way it happened at all. Only one other NFL team, the Philadelphia Eagles, switched to the T the next season. And as late as 1944, both clubs that played in the championship game, the Green Bay Packers and the New York Giants, used the single wing or some variation.

It's a story that's hardly been touched on — this clash of offensive ideologies, T and single wing, and the making of the modern game. And it actually begins a lot further back than 1940. It begins in the late 1800s, when football more closely resembled a soccer riot . . .

George Halas — Papa Bear — is the man most closely associated with the T formation, but it's coaching legend Amos Alonzo Stagg who's credited with inventing it (at Yale in 1880s). Everybody used the T in the early days; there *was* no other offense. In the original formation, the quarterback was positioned a yard back of center, and the fullback and two halfbacks lined up in a straight line behind him, forming a *T*.

The T's limitations became clear as it evolved over the next forty years. It was an adequate, if predictable, offense for running between the tackles. It also took the thrill out of the snap, particularly in wet weather, since the ball was handed directly to the quarterback. Finally, it made the center a more effective blocker, because he could keep his head up at all times (instead of having to peek through his legs at his intended target before hiking the ball).

But the T wasn't so great for passing or running outside. The single- and double-wing formations that Pop Warner dreamed up later at Cornell and Carlisle proved more effective—and certainly more exciting. The unbalanced line (four linemen to one side of center, two to the other) gave them more power at the point of attack, and the wingback—stationed just outside the end—could be used for reverses and could get out quickly for passes.

When the NFL was formed in 1920, the Bears were the only club that used the T formation. All the others embraced the Warner system or its cousin, Knute Rockne's Notre Dame Box. But Halas had played the T all his life—at the University of Illinois, at Great Lakes Naval Training Station during World War I—and believed in it. Besides, it was what he knew.

The Bears had great success in the '20s, winning the championship in 1921 and contending most other years. But by the end of the decade the Packers—in the midst of capturing three straight titles—had emerged as the league's dominant team. So Halas decided to give the T a makeover and brought in Ralph Jones, his freshman coach at Illinois, to help him.

Jones was a prep school athletic director in suburban Chicago at the time, and "it astonished everyone" that the Bears hired him, Halas said in his autobiography. But "Ralph Jones was a sound strategist. He believed muscle, guts and spirit were not enough. He believed it also took brains to win football games. Brainwork reduced the amount of profitless and painful crashing and thrashing about. Brainwork properly applied could add excitement and make the game more attractive."

Jones did three things to bring the T formation into the twentieth century: he increased the distance between the linemen, split the ends (to provide better blocking angles on sweeps and enable them to get downfield faster), and used a man in motion. This spread the defense and created the opportunity for big gains on quick-opening plays, which required only brush blocking instead of "crash, crash, crash," in Halas's words.

The motion man was especially troublesome for the defense because it never knew whether he was going to run with the ball, catch a pass, or throw a block. Also, trying to cover him with a linebacker—the standard strategy—was risky if he was a breakaway threat like the Bears' Red Grange.

After the Bears took the title in 1932, Jones walked away, having accomplished his goal of winning a championship in three years. But the T was by no means a finished product—and wouldn't be until Clark Shaughnessy arrived on the scene. Shaughnessy was coaching at the University of Chicago when he introduced himself to Halas at a dinner one evening and started pumping him for information about the Bears' offense. By '35, Halas was paying him $2,000 a year as a consultant. It was some of the best money he ever spent.

The T formation's major shortcoming in the early '30s was that the Bears couldn't get around end consistently. But Shaughnessy helped Halas solve that problem. "Between us," Halas said later, "we worked out 21 different ways for the T to get around end. It was after that that the Bears really started to roll. We owe a lot to Jones and Shaughnessy."

Shaughnessy is one of the forgotten men in NFL history, a brilliant offensive *and* defensive mind. (In addition to his work with the T, he was one of the developers of the nickel defense.) If it were up to me, he would have been in the Pro Football Hall of Fame a long time ago.

The reason he isn't—and likely never will be—is that he was kind of a loner. Have chalkboard, will travel. Red Hickey, who played and coached under Shaughnessy, summed him up this way: "He was 10 years ahead of his time. . . . [But] he had fewer friends than anybody I have ever known."

Also, Shaughnessy was a mere assistant for most of his pro career, though he *was* the head coach of the Los Angeles Rams in

1948 and '49 and led them to a 14-7-3 record and one championship game. (One wrinkle he added to the T out there, according to Rams great Elroy Hirsch, was to turn the man in motion into a third wide receiver—the flanker. As Hirsch explained it, "When you went in motion, you had to guess who was going to cover you. With the flanker [facing the defense], you had the advantage of being able to look over the coverage before the play started.")

Shaughnessy spent most of his waking hours thinking about Xs and Os; he was very much the absent-minded professor. Tank Younger, the former Rams fullback, said, "I don't think he ever knew what my name was. I was simply Big Boy to him. I saw him six months before he died, and he still called me Big Boy."

Another sign of Shaughnessy's distraction was his habit of accumulating traffic tickets. He was too busy game planning to worry about such trivialities as stop signs and speed limits. One time he was at the courthouse to pay for a few citations, and he asked the sergeant, "Couldn't I just leave five hundred dollars here on deposit?" Or so the story goes.

The Bears provided the perfect laboratory for him. In the late '30s Halas began assembling a super team, one of the greatest of all time. He acquired the Steelers' first-round pick in '39, the second selection overall, and used it to draft quarterback Sid Luckman. He acquired the Eagles' first-rounder in '40, again the second selection, and used it to draft halfback George McAfee. And he acquired the Steelers' first-rounder in '41, the third selection, and used it to draft fullback Norm Standlee. Luckman and McAfee, of course, are ensconced in Canton, and Standlee might be, too, if World War II hadn't gotten in the way. In his brief time with the Bears, he invited comparisons to Bronko Nagurski.

Luckman was the key. As a columnist once wrote, "The T-formation without a quarterback is like tea without water." But drafting Luckman was a definite gamble. He'd been a single-wing tailback at Columbia, and nobody knew if he had what it took to run the T. The early returns weren't promising. During his first training camp he was so frustrated by his slow progress that he'd call Shaughnessy at night, sobbing.

"After about a week of training camp, three or four players went to Coach Halas," Luckman once told me. "Dan Topping owned the [NFL's] Brooklyn Dodgers at the time, and he offered Halas fifty thousand dollars to release me so I could go play with the Dodgers [a single-wing club]. The players were adamant. They probably figured Halas could use that money to give them all a raise. But Halas absolutely refused to do it."

Smart move. Luckman, as it turned out, was only a year away from the 73–0 game.

After the 1939 season the University of Chicago dropped football and Shaughnessy was hired to coach at Stanford. The Cardinal program was in the doldrums, going 3-6 and 1-7-1 the previous two years, and expectations were low. But Shaughnessy installed the T formation, and the result was magic: a 10-0 mark, including a victory over Nebraska in the Rose Bowl.

Stanford's Rose Bowl win came just three weeks after the Bears' demolition of the Redskins in the NFL title game. And since the Cardinal were the only major college team to run the T—like the Bears in the NFL—the entire football world became curious about this newfangled offense.

Curious, but not necessarily sold on it. Brooklyn coach Jock Sutherland, among others, stuck doggedly with the single wing. In 1946, after moving to the Steelers, he said, "This T comes out and people go for it, high school people especially. But I'm looking for fundamentals, not trick plays. The T is coming into popularity like all of them. Whether it will retain the permanency of the single wing and the Notre Dame Box is another thing."

The reason "nearly every team in the land" didn't immediately adopt the T formation—*couldn't* immediately have adopted it—is because only a handful of people were familiar with it. To switch the Eagles over to the T in '41, coach Greasy Neale had to get his hands on movies of the 73–0 game and Stanford's Rose Bowl victory — not so easily done back then.

"I studied [them] for four months the following winter," he reminisced in 1944. "I looked at them from 10 o'clock in the morning until 5 o'clock in the afternoon, six days a week. I checked and double-checked. I was convinced it was a better system than any I'd ever used, and I was determined to learn it — [and,] at the same time, see if I couldn't make up some deviations of my own."

Most coaches were more cautious, though. After all, the single wing and the Notre Dame Box were still very effective. The '40 Bears, it might surprise you to learn, didn't lead the league in either scoring or total offense. The Redskins (single wing) and Packers (ND Box) did. And it tends to be forgotten that two years after the 73–0 debacle, the Redskins met the Bears again in the title game and completely shut down the T. The final score was 14–6, Chicago's six points coming on a defensive touchdown. (The next time the two teams played, in November 1943, the Bears didn't score until the fourth quarter. That's right, the indomitable T came up empty against Washington for *seven straight quarters*.)

As late as 1947, Sutherland's Steelers, still plugging away with the single wing, tied for first in the Eastern Division (but lost the playoff to the Eagles). The T-vs.-single-wing debate — contrary to Howard Roberts's mythologizing — went on for most of the decade.

The early T, you see, was hardly flawless. "The big weakness at that time was that most people were playing a six-man line on defense," former Bear Aldo Forte told me, "and these ends would come storming in there on a pass play and these little backs would have to block 'em. It didn't work out very good. They were just too small to handle those big guys."

Even Luckman, in a 1945 article, wrote, "Let's not sing the swan song for single wing too hastily. . . . If an offense depends on surprise and timing [the T's forte], it also depends on power and material. . . . Even the most brilliant set of plays cannot rise above the men who are carrying out the assignments and will bog down in the hands of inferior players. Furthermore, some very good men may be far better adapted to one type of play than another. So it looks like there will always be room for 'T-totalers!'"

Luckman was wrong, of course, but the single wing did hang on until 1951, when the Steelers finally junked it. In their tenth game in the T, they scored sixty-three points against the Giants — a club record then and now.

The year before Halas had told Pittsburgh owner Art Rooney, "The single wing takes too much out of your players, Art. You do kick the hell out of the opposition physically, but the opposition is still getting the points and beating you. Remember, the other team takes that beating once; your team takes it every week."

It's an interesting tale, the spreading of the T formation gospel. Again, hardly anyone knew the offense in 1940 — except for Shaughnessy, Halas, and Bears quarterbacks past and present like Luckman, Bob Snyder, Carl Brumbaugh, and Bernie Masterson. They were the ones who began the proselytizing process.

Snyder helped the Rams and Packers put in the T. Brumbaugh lent his expertise to the Cardinals. Masterson did likewise for the New York–Brooklyn team in the rival All-America Conference. Luckman — along with Snyder — assisted Frank Leahy at Notre Dame.

In his autobiography Luckman says he and Leahy used to move chairs around at the Commodore Hotel in New York, simulating T plays. One such session included this exchange:

LEAHY: You'll find that most of your major college coaches plan their moves with hotel chairs. Name any of them — Stagg, Dobie, Bible, Waldorf — all of them are masterful chair-jugglers. The fans have no idea how many big games are won or lost beforehand in hotel rooms.

LUCKMAN: Lou Little [Sid's Columbia coach] did his best work on tablecloths in Manhattan restaurants.

LEAHY: That's another method, of course, but a mere substitute.

Later a couple of Greasy Neale's protégés — Allie Sherman (with the stubborn Giants in '49) and Charley Ewart (with the New York Bulldogs the same year) — furthered the advancement of the T formation. But nobody did more for the cause than Shaughnessy. Besides his work with the Bears and Stanford, he brought the offense to Maryland and Pittsburgh in the college ranks and served as an advisory coach for such NFL teams as the Redskins (1945) and the joint Cardinals-Steelers entry (1944).

Funny story: When the Bears played the Card-Pitts that year, they drew some delay-of-game penalties because "they were retreating 15 yards [to huddle], instead of their customary 10," the *Chicago Tribune* reported. "The reason: Clark Shaughnessy, University of Pittsburgh coach, who . . . not only gave [the Card-Pitts] the same plays [as the Bears] but didn't bother to change the numbers. Consequently, the Bears removed themselves from earshot to prevent the Card-Pitts from hearing their code."

Shaughnessy also conducted countless clinics across the country. After the 73–0 game he borrowed Luckman's car and drove out to Iowa for one such symposium. "It was my own small contribution," Sid said. "At first I thought [Halas] must be crazy to be letting his secrets out of the bag, but this is the way things are done in football circles . . . for the good of the whole game. A clinic for college coaches would spread the system out and insure stronger T-products in the future."

It would indeed. In the early '40s the Bears and the Eagles — the only two T-formation teams — drafted an unusual number of Shaughnessy's Stanford players because the Cardinal were the lone major college team using the offense. Halas drafted almost the entire Stanford backfield (Standlee, halfback Hugh Gallarneau, and QB Frankie Albert, though Albert signed with the rival All-America Conference), and Neale took four Cardinal players in 1942 alone (halfback Pete Kmetovic and center Vic Lindskog in the first two rounds and ends Fred Meyer and Arnie Meiners later on).

By the end of the decade, though, five out of seven college teams played some form of the T. Suddenly it was the single-wing Steelers who were having trouble finding players to fit their system. In their last year in the single wing, they drafted Chuck Ortman in the second round—much higher than other clubs had him rated—basically because he'd played tailback at Michigan State.

"Frankly," said Army coach Red Blaik, who became a T convert in '43,

> I got fed up trying to take out a 240-pound Notre Dame tackle with a 170-pound Army blocker. It just can't be done. Now, mind you, there's nothing more impressive to watch than a smoothly functioning single wing offense if you've got the manpower. . . . But—and it's a big but—the single wing power stuff stalls when you bump into a team that's physically superior to your own.
>
> The T formation stresses the subtle and devious approach. It depends on craft rather than force. It lacks the devastating continuity of the single wing system, but the T offense offers the weaker side a better chance to break a fast back into the open. . . . The T attack appeals to the imagination.

Things didn't end so well for Clark Shaughnessy. He was fired by the Rams after the '49 season, made the situation worse by badmouthing his successor ("When [Joe] Stydahar gets through coaching the Rams, I can take any high school team in the country and beat him"), and eventually joined forces with Halas again. By the late '50s he was coaching the Chicago defense—plotting ways to *stop* the T.

But his departure from the Bears was awkward, too. Near the end of the '62 season he abruptly resigned, announcing his decision in New York while the Bears were at home playing the Giants. Halas was caught completely off guard.

"The only communication we have had from Clark," he said, "was a telegram sent from Chicago to my secretary on Thursday. The telegram read: 'Please advise Mr. Halas that I must leave immediately for St. Paul [Minn.] to see Bill Dwyer. As you know he is a lifelong family friend and former player. Very critically ill. Cannot be at practice today.' I certainly had no idea he was in New York, and I don't know what he's doing there."

Shaughnessy left the Bears, according to news accounts, because of philosophical differences with Halas and — perhaps — a loss of authority to defensive assistant George Allen. His falling-out with Papa Bear might be the biggest reason he's never gotten the credit he deserves, Halas being so influential. Here's the saddest part, though: Had Shaughnessy coached one more year, he might be remembered a lot differently. The Bears won the title the next season, thanks largely to their defense.

His T formation, however — his and Halas's and Ralph Jones's — continues to thrive. Granted, it looks a little different than it did in 1940 — teams use three receivers, four receivers, tight ends in motion — but that's not important. As Halas once said, "T stands for total. T-formation football is total-offense football."

The seven-man line couldn't stop it. The six-man line couldn't stop it. The five-man line couldn't stop it. The three-man line couldn't stop it. Defensive coordinators have settled on the 4-3 as the best antidote to the T formation, but with the right personnel the T is a nightmare — as teams like the 1999 Rams and 2007 Patriots have shown.

Which isn't to say teams haven't tried other offenses in the past sixty years. In his first season with the Chiefs in '78, Marv Levy put in the wing-T formation — three running backs and only one wide receiver. Kansas City finished second in the league in rushing . . . but won just four games. That was the end of the wing-T experiment.

The '80s brought the wild-and-woolly run-and-shoot — four receivers and only one running back. But the NFL's flirtation with the offense lasted just nine years (1987–95), even though two of the three clubs that used it went to the playoffs (the Oilers and Falcons). It wasn't balanced enough, the league decided. It was too tilted toward the pass. Houston's inability to hold a 35–3 lead against Buffalo in the '92 playoffs didn't help the cause any.

The biggest departure from the T—the wing-T and the run-and-shoot being mere offshoots—was Red Hickey's shotgun formation, which he unveiled in San Francisco in 1960. (Yup, the same Red Hickey who coached under Shaughnessy in Los Angeles.) The shotgun operated more like the single wing; the quarterback took the snap about 5 yards behind the line and would run, pass, or hand off. Billy Kilmer, the future Redskins QB, had three straight 100-yard rushing games in the shotgun in '61. The 49ers scored an average of forty-one points in those games—and became the talk of football.

The following week, though, the shotgun misfired. The Bears blanked the Niners, 31–0—with a defense designed by Shaughnessy. Before long both the shotgun and Hickey were gone.

"Everybody said what killed the shotgun was the Bears lining up [Hall of Fame middle linebacker] Bill George on our center," Hickey told me.

> But that had nothing to do with us losing that game. What happened was, we fumbled a couple of times, then we dropped a pass and things started to get out hand. We beat ourselves, but it's hard to convince the players you beat yourself.
>
> Shaughnessy came over to me after the game and said, "Don't give up on that formation. You've got something going there." It was as sound as you could be. It looked strange, but you could do anything from it if you had the right tailbacks.

That was Shaughnessy for you—ever the adventurer, ever the idealist. So much so that sportswriter Roger Treat wondered if he'd ever "be entirely happy in the jovial thuggery of pro football, where every man has a little assassin in him."

A decade into the twenty-first century, the T formation stands totally unchallenged in pro football. But did it have to be that way? What if the Bears had only won 26–0 on that fateful day in 1940 instead of

73–0 (with their defense scoring or setting up seven touchdowns)? Would people have gone quite so gaga over the T?

What if Halas had been less patient with Luckman's rookie struggles and sold him to Brooklyn? If Dodgers owner Dan Topping was indeed offering $50,000 for him — the United Press put the figure at $15,000 — that was a lot of money to pass up during the Depression.

What if the NFL had passed a rule in 1938 — rather than waiting until '42 — barring teams from trading their first-round pick for a year (to prevent the haves from preying on the have-nots)? The Bears might never have gotten Luckman, McAfee, and Standlee — and might never have become the Monsters of the Midway.

Then again, perhaps the proliferation of the T was inevitable. Quarterbacks from the '40s will tell you it added years to their careers; single-wing tailbacks, they say, took a lot of punishment because they had to run the ball and block. And passers, after all, are the NFL's most precious commodity. You don't want them getting knocked around unnecessarily.

"I can't conceive of the single wing being used today," said Don Coryell, whose passing attacks with the Chargers in the '80s were the envy of the league. "There's so much more deception with the T, because one person can quickly hand off to several different people or pass right now. Besides, there aren't many quarterbacks who can run the ball 25 times a game, and there aren't many running backs who can throw it."

In the early days of the T formation, George Strickler of the *Chicago Tribune* wrote, "The offense itself is so elastic that few students of the game ever expect the defense to catch up with it completely." More than half a century later, those words are still true. But maybe, if a Clark Shaughnessy had come along to dicker with the single wing, that offense might have survived in some form. Heck, remnants of it can still be seen. The toss sweep, the quarterback rollout, the reverse, and the shotgun are all straight from the Pop Warner playbook. If you could just draft the right people — such as a Steve McNair–type to play tailback — you could probably still make it work.

Let's not forget, the best rushing team in NFL history (at 240 yards a game) was the 1936 Detroit Lions, a single-wing club. And the Lions — with Ace Gutowsky, Dutch Clark, and Ernie Caddel all finishing among the league's top six rushers — were no 3-yards-and-a-cloud-of-dust outfit. They averaged 4.9 yards an attempt.

One last thing: In 1950, the year after the Giants bagged the A formation — their version of the single wing — they went back to it for a game against the Chicago Cardinals. Giants coach Steve Owen had always had misgivings about the T. "We felt that in A-formation, with the [tailback] handling the ball as he does and with man-in-motion, we had captured the essentials of the T while retaining the power blocking of the single wing," he says in *My Kind of Football*. Owen also liked that his offense could shift easily from the A to the double wing and could "quick-kick at any time, which is not possible in the T, and which is a handicap of that formation."

The Cardinals were totally unprepared for the A that afternoon. The Giants scored fifty-one points and gained some 600 yards.

Not that Owen was trying to prove a point or anything.

The War Years: 1941

November 16 — Rookie Maurice Britt catches a 45-yard touchdown pass late in the fourth quarter to give the Lions a 21–17 victory over the Eagles. It's the only reception of Britt's brief NFL career. After Pearl Harbor he enters the army and becomes the first U.S. soldier to receive the Congressional Medal of Honor, the Distinguished Service Cross, and the Silver Star — the top three combat decorations — in the same war. The feat is later duplicated by Audie Murphy.

(Britt lost his right arm during the bloody battle of Anzio, Italy, in early 1944. He later told the *Chicago Tribune*, in one of a series of articles on his heroism, "There were 15 men in the room [of the house he was holed up in] when the shell struck. Five were killed, seven wounded and three escaped without injury. I still think it was a tank shell, but some of the men insist it was the 'Anzio Express,' one of those 280-millimeter railroad gun shells. It doesn't really matter now.")

Davey vs. Goliath

The NFL has had a pretty cozy relationship with beer companies over the years. So it might seem strange that one of its quarterbacks sued Pabst in 1940 for $50,000 — and took the case all the way to the U.S. Supreme Court.

Of course, the Eagles' Davey O'Brien wasn't your average quarterback. Indeed, if he played today, he'd be a perfect candidate for one of those "Got Milk?" ads. A straighter arrow, a more Boyish Scout, you'll never find. Consider: After the '40 season, his second in the league, he walked away from the game to fulfill his lifelong ambition of becoming . . . an FBI agent. To Davey, throwing touchdown passes wasn't nearly as important as throwing bad guys in jail.

O'Brien brought suit against the beer maker because it had included his picture the year before, without his consent, in a promotional calendar for Pabst Blue Ribbon. (The calendar featured photos of Grantland Rice's 1938 All-America team — of which Davey was a member — and included major college and pro schedules for the '39 season.)

Problem was, O'Brien claimed to have had only a few beers in his life, and none recently. In fact, he sat on the board of Allied Youth of America, an organization that discouraged alcohol consumption. Embarrassed by having his picture appear on the calendar, he sued Pabst for invasion of privacy.

Unfortunately for him, Texas law in 1940 didn't recognize that right. So Davey struck out in the federal district and appellate courts, and the Supreme Court chose not to review the decision. By this time, March 1942, he was out of football.

Pabst argued that O'Brien was a public figure, that the picture had been provided by his university (Texas Christian), that the company had paid for the picture, and that the quarterback had suffered no injury to his person, property, or reputation. What it may ultimately have come down to, though, was that, as appellate judge Joseph C. Hutcheson Jr. put it, the five-foot-seven O'Brien was "in physique as in prowess as a hurler, a modern David"—while the beer maker was "in bulk, if not in brass and vulnerability, a modern Goliath."

Justice Edwin R. Holmes was the one dissenting voice on the appeals panel. While acknowledging the absence of Texas law on the issue, Holmes wrote, "The right of privacy is distinct from the right to use one's name or picture for purposes of commercial advertisement. The latter is a property right which belongs to everyone; it may have much or little, or only a nominal, value; but it is a personal right, which may not be violated with impunity."

In *Sports Law*, author Patrick Thornton calls it "one of the first cases to recognize an athlete's right to his own image."

· · ·

In keeping publicity on a high, dignified plane, club publicity men are charged with the responsibility of preventing coaches and players from endorsing liquor, cigarettes or laxatives. — From the minutes of the 1941 NFL publicity clinic

· · ·

What the Well-Dressed Commissioner Wears

Speaking of endorsements, an interesting advertisement ran in the October 29, 1941, *Detroit Free Press* (and presumably other papers). The ad was for Jockey long underwear, and the product was recommended by none other than Elmer Layden, the NFL commissioner and one of the erstwhile Four Horsemen.

Unfortunately, there wasn't a picture of Layden modeling a pair of long johns. But he did have this to say about them: "One of the best aids to keeping fit I know."

And this: "Lengthen your shorts and you'll lengthen your years of activity."

(God knows where copywriters got the idea that *underwear* could enhance your physical conditioning. I mean, what are we talking about here, performance-enhancing long johns?)

Anyway, just be glad it was Layden touting skivvies and not, say, Paul Tagliabue.

The First Belichick

More than one Belichick, it might surprise you to learn, has left a mark in pro football. Long before Bill was leading the Patriots to glory, his father, Steve, was starring at fullback for the 1941 Lions. But that's not the best part of The Steve Belichick Story. The best part is that he began that season as the team's equipment manager.

It happened like this: Steve had just graduated from Western Reserve University in Cleveland, but he couldn't get a high school coaching job because he'd already been classified 1-A by the draft board. (Translation: He might be here today, but he could be gone tomorrow.) So when Lions coach Bill Edwards, his old coach at Western Reserve, offered to let him tend to the Lions' socks and jocks, Belichick jumped at the chance. At least it would enable him to stay around the game.

"You know how they paid the equipment man in those days?" Belichick once told me. "You're not going to believe this. Each player chipped in a dollar a week. And there were, what, twenty-five or thirty guys on the team?"

At the beginning of the season, maybe. But if things didn't go well for a club in those days, it often released players — that is, dumped salaries — and went with a skeleton crew. The previous year, after a particularly disappointing loss, the Lions up and fired six players. As then-coach Potsy Clark explained it, "We can lose just as easily with 25 men as with 31."

Actually, Edwards had more in mind for Belichick than just blowing up footballs. Detroit was running the same offense Western Reserve had used, an old-style single wing that revolved around the fullback — which happened to be Steve's position. So in addition to his other duties, he helped with the coaching, showing the Lions fullbacks the various steps.

One of those fullbacks, a Notre Dame grad named Milt Piepul, had trouble handling the snaps from center. His hands were decent enough, but he was "blind as a bat," Belichick said. "He was the first guy I was aware of who used contact lenses, and sometimes he had a hell of a time getting them in and keeping them in. That was a problem, because the fullback got the snap on every play except one in that offense."

(Contact lenses in 1941. What must *they* have been like? You'd think, on a football field, they could do as much harm as good. This, remember, was the pre–face mask era, and punches in the puss were a weekly occurrence. In fact, that same season the *New York Herald Tribune* reported the following: "Frank Kristufek, [Brooklyn] Dodger tackle, who wears contact lenses, got a terrible black eye [against the Giants], but the lens was removed unbroken from his eye.")

But on with our story. As the months passed, Belichick became a more active participant in practice—to the point of even running the plays. And when the Lions got off to a 1-2-1 start, Edwards said, "Heck, Steve can play fullback better than any of these other fellas"—and put him on the active roster. In his first game Detroit got demolished by the Bears 49–0. But in his second, against the Packers, he scored his team's only touchdown on a 77-yard punt return . . . and became a minor sensation.

"We were in three-deep [to receive the kick]," he said.

It wasn't a real good punt. The ball hit the ground, took a lateral bounce, and I just took it on the run. There were only a few guys up the field that I had to beat. The last one was the punter, and it wasn't too hard to fake him out.

When Bill [Belichick] went to Detroit as an assistant [in 1976], he tried to get a copy of the game film for me. I'd never seen it. But the Lions didn't have it. Later I spoke to [Green Bay general manager] Ron

Wolf, and he dug it out of the Packers' archives. He sent it to me with a note that said, "That was one hell of a run you made."

Belichick was now making $115 a game—a big improvement over his equipment manager's pay. Granted, Whizzer White, the club's franchise player, was pulling down "eight or nine hundred dollars a week," he said, but $115 was still pretty good dough. "You could buy a new Ford back then for six hundred dollars. Things were cheap. I was paying a dollar a day to stay at the Hotel Saverine [in downtown Detroit]."

Two weeks later in New York, Belichick came off the bench to score two touchdowns in a 20–13 loss to the Giants. The Associated Press's coverage of the game began thusly:

> NEW YORK, Nov. 10—After getting a load of Steve Belichick busting a line, an engaging question today around the campus of Tenth Avenue Tech—better known as the New York Football Giants—was "who called that football player an equipment man?"
>
> The Detroit Lions had little enough to roar about in the 20-to-13 mudbath the Giants handed them in the Polo Grounds yesterday, but No. 1 on the list was the work of Socker Steve, who came out from among the head-guards and hip-pads in the locker room to score both Lion touchdowns on line smashes, pick up 26 yards in four cracks, run a kick back 46 yards, intercept a pass and generally show he had a better idea of what the business was all about than any other back on the club with the single exception of Whizzer White.

From then on, Belichick was a starter. It wasn't all fun and games; Bears ruffian Dick Plasman broke his nose with a vicious forearm one afternoon. But if the war hadn't come along—after which he veered into college coaching—Steve would have been happy to keep playing. Only Whizzer scored more TDs for Detroit than he did that year (three), and no other back on the team came within a yard of his 4.2 rushing average. (And the yards came hard for the Lions. They gained fewer of them than anybody in the league.)

Belichick's now-famous son is named after Edwards, Steve's

coaching mentor—and the man who made him the most celebrated equipment manager in NFL history. Indeed, the only gripe
Steve had about his pro career was that the football encyclopedias
listed him at five foot eight or five nine, 190 pounds.

"I was 5-10¾," he said. "And I weighed 193."

Looking back from a distance of seventy years, he seems larger
still.

. . . And Don't Forget to Floss

I once asked a player who was with Jock Sutherland in Brooklyn if
there was anything about Sutherland's coaching style that told you
he was a (nonpracticing) dentist.

"We didn't drink out of the communal water bucket," Emmett
Mortell told me. "We drank out of paper cups—Dixie Cups."

Let the record show, then, that while Jock never won an NFL championship with either the Dodgers (1940–41) or the Pittsburgh Steelers (1946–47), his teams at least led the league in oral hygiene.

Footnote: Sutherland's first college head-coaching job was at Lafayette, which is located in Easton, Pennsylvania. Something else
that was located in Easton: the Dixie Cup Company.

The War Years: 1942

Drafting strategy changed in the NFL in 1942. A player's ability
wasn't nearly as important as his *availability*. The Rams' first pick
that year, Baylor back Jack Wilson, had "an eye deficiency that may
keep him out of the army," the *Cleveland Plain Dealer* reported.
Their second-rounder, Oklahoma back Jack Jacobs, was "married
and classified 3-A for army service."

November 22—Packers rookie Ted Fritsch misses the opening
kickoff against the Giants when he takes the wrong subway and
winds up in Queens instead of at the Polo Grounds. He redeems
himself by having his biggest rushing day as a pro, gaining 111
yards in nine carries and breaking a career-best 55-yard run to set

up a touchdown in the final minutes. The latter allows Green Bay to salvage a 21–21 tie.

The Lions finished 0-11 and scored a grand total of thirty-eight points. In a 42–0 loss to the Bears, they committed twelve turnovers (five fumbles, seven interceptions) and gave up a 60-yard touchdown pass on third and 34.

Brooklyn coach Mike Getto at the end of the '42 season: "I don't see how we can [play in '43]. Most of the boys will be in the service very shortly. I doubt if there will be half a dozen available next fall, and they'll be older men with families. And would it be possible to draft enough college players to build around six old men? I doubt it."

Mixing Football and Politics

The NFL needed a referee in 1942 to replace the famed Red Friesell, who had decided to retire after breaking his leg in a game the year before. The injury was so bad, in fact, that Friesell was still wearing a cast five months later.

Actually, he told Stanley Woodward of the *New York Herald Tribune*, the leg "was broken in four places. The tibia and fibula were chopped off, as if by an ax, slightly above the ankle. Three inches above, both bones were cracked through. . . . You could hear the crack all over Shibe Park."

To fill the Friesell void, the league turned to a five-foot-four, 145-pound dynamo named Sam Weiss. Weiss, a former Duquesne football captain, had been working high school and college games for nearly two decades, but that isn't what set him apart from other whistle blowers. No, what made Sam unique was that he was a U.S. congressman, the representative from Pennsylvania's thirty-first district in Pittsburgh.

(He had also, by his own count, had six teeth knocked out in his officiating travels—not that it dampened his enthusiasm any. "Football, like politics, is real excitement," he said. "And in these war times, refereeing is my one real diversion. I'm going to keep it up as long as my legs last. You'd think refereeing would tire me out. It really peps me up, makes me do a better job in Congress.")

Weiss was one of five referees on the NFL's rolls from 1942 to '47. Among the officials he worked with regularly was Fay Vincent, the father of the future baseball commissioner, who often served as his umpire. Sam wasn't assigned to any championship games, but he did get tapped for the biggest game of the 1943 regular season, the battle between the Bears, the 1940 and '41 champs, and the Redskins, the '42 champs. Despite the teams' well-known antipathy for each other, the congressman managed to keep the peace.

"The most overworked item on the field was the whistle carried by referee Sam Weiss," the Associated Press reported after Washington's 21–7 win. "He called 16 penalties excluding pass interference plays."

Weiss did more for the league, though, than just measure for first downs. He also looked after its interests in Congress. Some lawmakers, after all, would have placed greater restrictions on travel during World War II and made it more difficult for pro leagues to operate. But Sam was of the opinion that sports were "a vital factor in our all-out war effort. . . . Happy soldiers make better fighters just like contented workers make better production men. Soldier and civilian morale demands that the government permit spectator sports to continue for the duration."

Weiss even pushed to build a two-hundred-thousand-seat stadium in Washington after the war "as a giant memorial to our servicemen who have died. [It] would bring teams together from all over the world and in that manner help serve to maintain lasting peace by encouraging friendly relations in sport." It never came to pass, of course, but it was a lovely thought.

Weiss left the House in 1946, midway through his third term, when he was elected as a judge in Allegheny County. He stopped refereeing NFL games soon afterward. To his credit, he survived his years in pro football without any major gaffes — without anything like the infamous Fifth Down that Friesell gave Cornell in its 1940 game against Dartmouth.

And was Sam ever glad. "Why," he once said, "a fifth down would put me in the doghouse in Congress, and I'd be fearful about re-election."

Field of Screams

The U.S. Army War Show came to Cleveland's Municipal Stadium in September 1942. For five days, tanks, flamethrowers, motorized field artillery, and aircraft thrilled the crowds. Unfortunately, a game between the Bears and Rams had to be played there less than two weeks later.

The field was so torn up by the War Show that new sod had to be laid. But there simply wasn't enough time for it to take root. Rain the day before the game completed the catastrophe, making the turf "like so much grease," the stadium manager said.

On the Rams' first play from scrimmage, fullback Gaylon Smith swept around right end and had a "clear field ahead of him," Isi Newborn of the *Cleveland Press* wrote, "when floppo! There was Smith slipping and sprawling."

Newborn had great fun describing the players' often futile attempts to keep their feet. "The Grass Capades of 1942," he called it. "If the Pitt Panthers and the Great Lakes Naval Stadium boys are wise, they'll prepare for Saturday's clash in the Stadium by diligent practice at the art of running on conveniently scattered banana peels."

Later in his story, Newborn came up with another howler: "Running on the field yesterday was exactly like trying to comb a loose wig."

The Bears, who came away with a 21–7 win, coped with the conditions by throwing the ball and running straight-ahead plays that required little cutting by the back. On the first Chicago touchdown, a 63-yard bomb to Scooter McLean, two Rams easily could have tackled McLean around the Cleveland 30, Newborn reported, "but the first of them, Red Conkright, skidded and flopped a few feet from him, and the other, Dante Magnani, did likewise just as he was about to nail the receiver."

One Way to Combat the Wind-Chill Factor

When you think of the Green Bay Packers, you think of players toughing it out in the most extreme conditions. You think of the Ice Bowl. You think of the Frozen Tundra.

But in the 1942 season finale against the Steelers in Milwaukee —a wickedly cold December day— Packers coach Curly Lambeau decided warmth was the better part of valor. So he kept his reserves in the locker room instead of having them freeze their butts off on the sideline.

"The move occasioned a lot of surprise on the part of the fans, who couldn't figure out, at the start of the game, where the substitutes were," Don Hickok of the *Green Bay Press-Gazette* reported.

Assistant coach Eddie Kotal supervised things in the locker room. He kept in touch with Lambeau via telephone and kept abreast of the game via radio. Curly would put in a call for a player, and Eddie would send him running out the door—all nice and toasty. (The man being replaced, meanwhile, would be ordered inside, even if he wanted to stay on the bench and watch.)

It was a strange experience for the players. They were much more comfortable indoors, of course, but they didn't feel nearly as connected to the game. On the plus side, at least they had feeling in their extremities—unlike their opponents, who spent the afternoon stamping their feet and rubbing their hands together.

Near the end, Hickok left the press box and went down to the Green Bay dressing room. There, he wrote,

> Kotal sat on a table with his ear against the telephone speaker, his other ear cocked toward the radio. The players were silent except when one of them missed [the] description of the play and asked what it was.

[Packers quarterback] Cecil Isbell came in with about three minutes to play and lifted his pant-legs to display two badly skinned knees
. . . [from] when he skidded along the frozen ground. . . . So far as the
effect on the players was concerned, the field might just as well have
been paved.

The Packers held on for a 24–21 win before a chilled gathering
of 5,138. Lambeau's bold experiment doesn't seem to have been re-
peated, though, in the years that followed — certainly not by Vince
Lombardi.

The War Years: 1943

One morning in April Packers fans awoke to startling news. "Packer
Field to Be Plowed Up!" the headline in the *Green Bay Press-Gazette*
blared. "Victory Gardening to Be Only Sport at City Stadium; No
Spectators."

"After heated discussion," the newspaper said, the city council
had "decided to convert city stadium from football to food because
of the acute shortage of both fresh and canned vegetables. At first,
Johannes or Fisk Park were considered as sites, but proponents gave
way when it was pointed out that the ticket windows will make ideal
outlets for both handing out work assignments and distributing
produce. In addition, the high walls will keep out marauders."

The paper even had a picture of two horses pulling a plow inside
the stadium.

Green Bay residents, like all Americans, were used to making
sacrifices during the war, but this was too much. What kind of season could the Packers expect to have without a field to play on?

In the last paragraph the reporter let them in on the joke: It was
April Fool's Day.

To stay on the good side of the Office of Defense Transportation,
the NFL cut back on its travel in 1943 and '44 by reducing rosters
from thirty-three to twenty-eight. Also, teams primarily used day
coaches on trains instead of Pullman sleepers.

Our sport will be as good as other things that are rationed. You think meat and shoe rationing are all right, don't you? Well, our football will be the same. — Bears business manager Ralph Brizzolara

If the War Manpower Commission believes pro football players should work on war jobs, we see no reason why they can't do so and play football, too. They could start work on an early shift and be through in time to get in daily drills. If need be, they could practice at night under the lights. In the old days of pro football most of the players worked at other jobs and played football on Sunday. There's no reason why the present crop of players can't do the same thing to keep the game alive. — Packers coach Curly Lambeau

The Associated Press ran a story about Ole Haugsrud, the former Duluth Eskimos owner, placing newspaper ads to scare up talent for the Giants. "Football players wanted!" one of them reportedly said. "Play football and work in defense plants on weekdays. Earn big money."

According to the AP, Haugsrud had been scouting for Giants coach Steve Owen for several years but found it necessary to resort to ads because of gas and tire rationing. Of the "nearly 100" responses he received, he mailed contracts to "about 15."

"I can't say who they are," he said. "They're not signed yet. But you can say they're good prospects, unwanted by the military for one reason or another, none of which will interfere with their football playing."

Haugsrud's main focus was high school and college coaches whose programs had been suspended because of the war.

The Brooklyn Dodgers rushed for minus-11 yards in their first four games and were outscored 91–0.

The *Washington Post* reported that Redskins back Ray Hare "played all but 13 minutes" of the 1943 season, which included "10 league games, the Eastern Division playoff and the championship game." It figures out to "a fraction over a minute's rest in each game. Coye Dunn gave him three minutes' respite, Joe Gibson 10."

Starvation Diet

Three-hundred-pound players were rare in the 1940s, but tackle George Somers of the Steagles (the 1943 merger of the shorthanded Steelers and Eagles) showed up for camp at 310 — 45 pounds heavy. Naturally, the team made him go on a diet. After three weeks of self-denial, he decided to call it a career.

"It's not that I mind taking off the weight," he said, "but I don't like this business of eating only three times a day."

Postgraduate Work

Two weeks before their 1943 opener, the Giants beat the Lions 14–12 in a scrimmage — the *Columbia* Lions.

The New York Times described the session at Baker Field as "a one-hour contact drill" featuring — on the pros' side, at least — mostly "third-stringers." Still, one of the "third-stringers" was rookie Bill Paschal, who ended up leading the NFL in rushing that year. Paschal had a hand in both touchdowns against the collegians, throwing for the first and catching a pass for the second.

Columbia's ability to put up twelve points — it missed two PATs — tells you something about the talent level in the wartime NFL. After all, the colleges were short on manpower, too. In fact, it was probably the worst team Lou Little fielded in his twenty-seven years at the school. The Lions went 0-8 that season and were outscored 313–33 . . . while the Giants finished 6-3-1 and tied for first in the East.

The teams scrimmaged again the next day, so perhaps Steve Owen, the Giants' coach, was less than thrilled with what he saw. In the rematch he "started [his] second team against Columbia's varsity," the *New York Herald Tribune* reported. "These units battled for 20 minutes before the Giants scored." Columbia then drove to the New York 12 but lost the ball on downs.

"Seven fresh Giants were sent in at this point, three of them regulars, while Little ordered his first team to the showers," the *Herald Tribune* said. The pros pushed across another touchdown against the depleted Lions forces to make the final score 12–0.

Here's the real killer, though: Jack Kerouac might have played in these scrimmages if he hadn't dropped out of Columbia to embark on a writing career. The celebrated author of *On the Road* was a standout back on the Lions' 1940 freshman team and would have been a senior in '43.

Game of Games

Sid Luckman once threw seven touchdown passes in a game, which is still the NFL record. On that same day—November 14, 1943, against the Giants in New York—he had 433 yards passing, which broke the existing mark by 57. But his best game, the Bears Hall of Famer always said, was the one he had later that year against the Redskins in the championship game.

It's hard to argue with him. *That* game, I humbly suggest, might have been the greatest game ever played by a quarterback. The specifics:

- He completed fifteen of twenty-six passes for 286 yards and five touchdowns, with no interceptions. The TDs measured 31, 36, 66, 26, and 10 yards. Passer rating: 135.6.
- He led all rushers with 64 yards in eight carries, including a 15-yard run to the Washington 3 that set up a Bronko Nagurski score.
- He intercepted two passes, both in the third quarter. He returned the first 21 yards to the Washington 36 (and threw a touchdown pass to Dante Magnani on the next play). He ran the second back 18 yards to the Chicago 36 (and threw a 66-yard TD pass to Magnani three plays later).
- He returned two punts for 32 yards.

- *And* he punted three times. (But we won't hold his 24.7-yard average against him.)

A pretty good day's work, you've gotta admit.

The rushing yards are the biggest shock. Sid was never much of a runner. But put it all together and, well, doesn't it have to rate as the best performance ever by a quarterback? The 49ers' Steve Young and Joe Montana had fabulous passing/running Super Bowls (XXIX and XIX, respectively), and the Browns' Otto Graham put up ridiculous numbers in the 1950 championship game against the Rams (thirty-three attempts, twenty-two completions, 298 yards, four TDs, one interception, plus he led all rushers with 99 yards in twelve carries). But none of them intercepted any passes or returned any punts.

Granted, the talent level in the NFL was down during the war years, but in 1943 the Bears and Redskins were still quite capable. In fact, the Redskins had the number one scoring defense in the league and earlier in the season had held the Bears to just seven points.

On top of that, there was such wonderfully bad blood between the two teams. This was, after all, the fourth time in seven years they'd met for the title. (And Chicago, of course, had laid it on a bit thickly in its 73–0 whomping of Washington in 1940.)

It was such a bitter rivalry that in the fourth quarter that day, ahead 34–14, the Bears attempted—and recovered—an onside kick. This enabled Luckman to throw his fifth touchdown pass, a 10-yarder to running back Harry Clark . . . and wrap up the greatest game ever by an NFL quarterback.

Clutch QBs

Here's a great trivia question to wheel out at a Super Bowl party sometime: Which quarterback had the two highest passer ratings in a league championship game—NFL or AFL—prior to the 1970 merger?

I stumbled across the answer while checking to see whether Luckman's rating in the '43 title game (135.6) might be the highest for the years in question (1932–69). It isn't. Turns out the top five (minimum fifteen attempts) are as follows:

Year	QB, Team/Opponent	Att.	Comp.	Yds.	TD	Int.	Rating
1957	Tobin Rote, Lions/Browns	19	12	280	4	0	146.4
1963	Tobin Rote, Chargers/Patriots	15	10	173	2	0	145.3
1966	Bart Starr, Packers/Cowboys	28	19	304	4	0	143.5
1943	Sid Luckman, Bears/Redskins	26	15	286	5	0	135.6
1961	Bart Starr, Packers/Giants	17	10	164	3	0	130.9

Who knew Tobin Rote was such a gamer?

Don't get me wrong; I've never considered the NFL's passer-rating formula to be the truest measure of quarterbacks. (I'm still trying to figure out how the Patriots' Tony Eason could go 0 for 6 in Super Bowl XX against the Bears and still wind up with a rating of 39.6.) But the formula does give *some* indication of proficiency. So to see Rote's name at the top of this list — in the first two spots, no less — is a little mind-blowing.

After all, Rote was, at his best, a good quarterback, not a great one. He made one Pro Bowl, one AFL All-Star Game, and led the NFL in touchdown passes twice. In fact, his legs stood out more than his arm. In 1951 with the Packers he rushed for 281 yards *in the space of five days* — 150 against the Bears on Sunday and 131 more against the Lions on Thanksgiving. (His total against Chicago was the record for QBs until the Falcons' Michael Vick broke it in 2002.)

But maybe, in light of this discovery, Rote should be thought of more highly — as the Jim Plunkett, say, of premerger pro football. Sound reasonable?

Lend-Lease

With able-bodied men in such short supply during World War II, some NFL teams merged to stay alive — giving birth to the Steagles (Steelers-Eagles), the Carpets (Cardinals–Pittsburgh Steelers), and the like. The Cleveland Rams went one step further: when co-owners Dan Reeves and Fred Levy joined the Army Air Corps in 1943, the franchise simply shut down for a season.

Not every Ram went into the military, though, at least not right away. So fourteen Cleveland players were given foster homes in '43 — loaned, most of them, to other clubs. The arrangement was only for a year, however. The next season, when the Rams resumed operations, they regained the players' rights.

Cleveland had finished a respectable 5-6 in 1942, so it had some talent worth raiding. In the dispersal draft held by the league, the Bears jumped on receiver Jim Benton and halfback Dante Magnani, the Packers grabbed tackle Chet Adams, and the Redskins came away with another coveted tackle, Joe Pasqua (and later added end Joe Gibson). The Lions, with more holes to fill, had an NFL-high *four* Rams on their roster — guards Riley Matheson (an all-pro in '42) and Roy Stuart, end Ben Hightower, and halfback Bob Keene.

The other Refugee Rams were distributed thusly:

Dodgers (3): Center Red Conkright and tackles Jake Fawcett and
   Tex Mooney

Giants (1): End Steve Pritko

Eagles (1): Blocking back John Petchel

Most of them made an impact one way or another. Pritko, for instance, caught just one pass for the Giants, but he came up with a huge play in the regular-season finale against the Redskins by recovering a blocked punt in the end zone for the first New York score. The Giants went on to a 31–7 victory that forced a playoff for the Eastern Division title (which Washington won).

Then there's Mooney. He's a story unto himself. You see, his real name wasn't Tex Mooney; it was Orrin Schupbach. But after playing briefly for the Rams in 1942, he'd gone to Hollywood and embarked on a movie career. There, a studio had rechristened him "Tex Mooney" — which, understandably, was considered more suitable for a six-foot-five, 280-pound West Texan.

(If you ever get a chance to see *East of Eden*, one of James Dean's last films, be on the lookout for Tex. He has a bit part as a bartender.)

In the 1943 NFL championship game, there were no fewer than four Rams on the field—Benton and Magnani for the Bears and Pasqua and Gibson for the Redskins. But wait, it gets better: Benton and Magnani combined for three TD catches in the second half to help Chicago pull away to a 41–21 win.

That's right, the Rams scored as many touchdowns that day as the Redskins.

The temporary shuttering of the Cleveland franchise provides an interesting case study. Consider: Thirty-six players suited up for the Rams in 1942; sixteen of them—the vast majority of whom went into the service—never played in the NFL again (or in the All-America Conference, for that matter). In other words, almost half the players on the roster had their careers not just interrupted by the war but *ended* by it. When they were discharged, they found something else to do with their lives.

Two years later, with an almost entirely new team, the Rams won their first NFL title. By then only Benton, Matheson, and Pritko remained of the fourteen lend-lease players from 1943. Benton set a single-game receiving record that year with 303 yards against the Lions, and he and Matheson were voted all-pro. The next season the Cleveland Rams became the Los Angeles Rams . . . and they were all on the move again.

An Item That May Interest Only Me

Speaking of Dante Magnani—for the last time, I promise—the guy had an unusual career, maybe even unique. The Rams and Bears basically played ping-pong with him for a decade. He was the property of the Rams three different times, and he was the property of the Bears three different times. The crazy chronology:

1940—The Rams draft Magnani in the nineteenth round out of St. Mary's of California.

1943—The club closes up shop for a year because of the war, so Magnani is loaned for the season to the Bears.

1944—Magnani's rights revert back to the Rams, but he can't suit up for them because he's entered the navy.

1946—After the war Bears owner George Halas gets Magnani back, along with tackle Fred Davis, in exchange for the rights to Tom Harmon, the 1940 Heisman Trophy winner.

1947—Magnani returns to the Rams, this time in a straight-up deal for fullback Mike Holovak.

1949—The Bears purchase Magnani from the Rams for an undisclosed sum.

(Chicago released him after the 1949 season, and he spent 1950, his last year in the NFL, with the Lions.)

Dante wasn't a star, just a very useful player. He could run, he could catch, and he could defend. He was also clutch. He played in two NFL title games, both with the Bears, and caught two touchdown passes in the first (1943) and intercepted two passes—returning one for a TD—in the second ('46).

Lost in Time

"You tell somebody you played for the Cleveland Rams, their face will drop," Johnny Wilson once told me. "They don't have any idea who the Cleveland Rams were."

Wilson played end for them from 1939 to '42, when Dutch Clark was the coach. Of course, those early Rams teams didn't give us much to remember them for, as Wilson relates:

> One time we were playing the New York Giants at the Polo Grounds, and we were getting kicked pretty good. It was late in the game. We were all dog-tired. And a player comes in from the bench—one of those hotshots just off the bench—and he gets in the huddle and he says, "Come on, let's go! We'll kill 'em!" And Red Conkright, our center, hit him right in the mouth.

That same day, the coaches wanted to send another player in, a kid who had just come to us from the Cardinals, I think. It was a cold day. The field was kind of frozen. And they told him, "Now, before you go in there, warm up a little." So he ran up and down in front of the bench a few times, tripped, landed on his chin and knocked himself out.

The War Years: 1944

March 19 — Before a crowd of fifty thousand at London's White City Stadium, Eagles quarterback Tommy Thompson leads the U.S. Army to an 18–0 win over the Canadian army in the Coffee Bowl. The first half is played under Canadian rules, the second under American rules.

Sergeant Thompson throws two touchdown passes to Corporal John Bayne. "Spitfires circled over the area," according to reports, "in case the Germans tried a sneak raid."

Three days after D-Day an Austrian serving in the German army was captured in France by U.S. forces. He was sent to Colorado, where he spent the next two years working on a farm as a POW. The soldier turned out to be the father of future Colts kicker Toni Linhart, who led the NFL in scoring in 1976 and went to two Pro Bowls.

George Halas never stopped recruiting for the Bears, even when he was stationed in the jungle of New Guinea.

In August 1944, the Associated Press reported, a jeep pulled up at Lieutenant Commander Halas's navy base carrying Lieutenant Bud Ward, the U.S. Amateur golf champ, and "a big air corps corporal." George took one look at Ward's sturdy companion — at his "broad shoulders, bull neck and 210-pound frame" — and asked who he was. Ward introduced him as Chester Robertson, a former Tennessee football player.

Halas signed Robertson on the spot to play for the Bears after the war.

(Chester never made it onto their roster, but George still gets big points for his tireless personnel work.)

At the start of training camp the Redskins coaching staff noticed that Pete Marcus and Ev Sharp barely spoke to each other, even though they lined up side by side at end and tackle. Then they found out why: Both had been in the army, and Marcus, as an MP, had once arrested his future teammate.

"He got a little rowdy," Pete told the *Washington Star*. "But, you know, since we've been playing together, I like that about him. It helps me now."

Lifestyles of the Rich and Famous, Part 1

A Hollywood birthday party for actress-skater Sonja Henie was winding down in 1944 when Henie's husband punched film star Errol Flynn and sent him sprawling. What made the skirmish especially noteworthy—for our purposes—is that her husband was Dan Topping, owner of the NFL's Brooklyn Dodgers (and future owner of baseball's New York Yankees).

It wasn't clear what caused the incident. "Flynn said he supposed there was some bad ice in the drinks," the United Press reported. "Miss Henie, an expert on ice, declined comment."

Topping, on leave from the marines, insisted he and Flynn were still "the best of friends." The actor seconded that motion. "He's got to hit me harder and oftener than that to make me mad," Flynn said. "Ah—meaning no reflection on Dan's power, of course."

All in all, it was an impressive knockdown. Let's not forget, Flynn had played heavyweight champion Jim Corbett in the 1942 movie *Gentleman Jim*.

Lifestyles of the Rich and Famous, Part 2

Four years earlier Topping's marriage to another actress, Arline Judge, ended in a divorce. Judge testified in the proceedings that the Dodgers' owner drank too much and, according to the Associated

Press, once "crashed through the door of her bedroom in a Palm Springs, California, hotel, broke a bed, tossed furniture around in a fury and had to be restrained from assaulting her by her mother."

Judge received a reported $250,000 settlement. In 1947 she was married for the sixth time—to Dan's brother, Bob Topping.

• • •

I have lost 25 pounds since I reported at Bear Mountain [where the team trained]. And every pound came off as easily as skinning a live skunk.—Hall of Fame quarterback Arnie Herber on making a comeback with the Giants in 1944 after three years away from the game

• • •

Doing It All

Every now and then a quarterback will catch a pass that gets batted back to him. A laugh will go up—"Hey, he just threw the ball to himself!"—and the game will go on.

But what the Eagles' Roy Zimmerman did on October 29, 1944, was no laughing matter to the Giants. In the third quarter, from the New York 22, Zimmerman completed a 7-yard pass to end Tom Miller. As Miller was being tackled, Roy, trailing the play, got a lateral back from him and ran the rest of the way for the score.

A hook and lateral to the *quarterback*—for a touchdown. How cool is that? (And it didn't happen on a vacant lot, either. It happened at the Polo Grounds before a crowd of 42,639.)

Thus, the scoring summary read: Zimmerman 15 lateral from Miller after 7 pass from Zimmerman (Zimmerman kick).

(Yes, Roy did the booting for Philadelphia, too.)

Without those seven points the Eagles wouldn't have beaten the Giants that day 24–17. In fact, the play nearly won the division title for Philadelphia, since it gave the Eagles the head-to-head advantage (1-0-1) over New York. The Giants wound up nosing them out, though, with an 8-1-1 record to Philly's 7-1-2.

Rock Bottom

"If the war had lasted a little longer," Bears quarterback Sid Luckman once said, "the NFL might have gotten down to the level of semi-pro ball."

The league came awfully close to that in 1944, by far the worst year for scrounging up players. How bad was it? This bad: a few *teenagers* were even handed uniforms.

You can imagine the quality of play. The Brooklyn Tigers finished 0-10. So did the Cardinals-Steelers collaboration (often listed in the standings as "Card-Pitts," but referred to derisively as the Carpets).

And Ted Collins, the Boston Yanks owner—what was *he* thinking? Of all the seasons to launch a franchise . . . he chose this one.

"To put a workable squad in uniform," Tim Cohane wrote in *Look* magazine, Collins's coach, Herb Kopf, "dispatched assistant coach Tillie Manton to the four compass points with earnest instructions to waylay and wave folding money near the nostrils of any male under forty who was under the slightest suspicion of ever having been within five miles of a goalpost. Manton might just as well have been ordered to hit the jackpot on the quarter machine in a Scotch tavern two days in a row."

1944 in a nutshell:

• Only 12 of the NFL's 330 draft picks played in the league that season. (But one of them was Steve Van Buren, the Eagles' Hall of Fame back.)

• The Giants, who made it to the championship game, could field an entire backfield with no college varsity experience: Howie Livingston (Fullerton, California, Junior College), Bill Paschal (a year of freshman football at Georgia Tech), and Bill Petrilas and Joe Sulaitis (neither of whom played *any* college ball).

• Giants physician Doc Sweeny: "One day at Bear Mountain we'd have 30 guys practicing, and the next day there'd be 50. [Coach] Steve [Owen] never knew where half of 'em came from—or went. Lots of guys—most of 'em out of shape—came to . . . try out for the team. What a sight that was. After one of Steve's wind sprints, they'd be heavin' all over the field."

• In their season opener the Redskins missed four extra points in a 31–31 tie with the Eagles. A bad snap sabotaged the first; the next three were blocked.

• Frank "Tiger" Walton rejoined the Redskins as a guard and assistant line coach after being out of the league for *nine years*. It's still the longest gap in an NFL career. Walton had left the Redskins after the 1934 season—they were based in Boston then—to coach high school ball in Beaver Falls, Pennsylvania.

• Brooklyn was assessed twenty-two penalties, an NFL record, in a September 17 game against the Packers. The Bears tied the mark eight weeks later against the Eagles. Only one other time in NFL history has a club been penalized that much. (The 49ers had twenty-two against Buffalo in 1998.)

• After an 0-5 start Brooklyn fired coach Pete Cawthon. "I hated do it," general manager Tom Gallery said, "but you've got to give the fans something. This kind of football we've played at home I wouldn't give 30 cents to watch. I couldn't go on asking our patrons to pay $2.40 to see it."

• Cawthon responded by marching down to the bank with his severance check—which amounted to two years' salary—and cashing it (fearful Gallery might stop payment). He then shoved the money into a briefcase and flew to Detroit, where he finished out the season as Gus Dorais's assistant.

• Brooklyn end Bill LaFitte was eighteen years old. He caught one pass for 15 yards before being called into the service. (It set up a touchdown.) Boston quarterback Frankie Santora was also eighteen. He had a 27-yard kickoff return in the Yanks' opener—and was never seen in pro football again (though he later played Minor League Baseball).

• The Cleveland Rams had two players who were blind in one eye —halfback Mike Kabealo and end Al Gutknecht. The fans never would have guessed in Kabealo's case, the *Cleveland Press* reported, "unless they were tipped off by the one concession to Mike's handicap—his switch to left halfback on defense in order that his good eye can be toward play."

Yup, 1944 was a real keeper.

Let's Go to the Tape!

There was a bit of a problem before the Rams-Lions game on October 15, 1944. Both teams showed up in blue jerseys—though the Lions' Honolulu blue was a touch lighter.

Detroit, the home club, wanted to send out for its white road jerseys and have the Rams put *those* on. But the jerseys were across town, and it would have caused a lengthy delay. So Rams general manager Chile Walsh agreed to "a compromise in which strips of [athletic] tape were pasted on the shoulders of [his team's] jerseys to distinguish them," the *Cleveland Plain Dealer* reported.

Three touchdown passes were thrown that afternoon, so the quarterbacks must have had *some* success identifying their receivers. The Rams won 20–17.

The 1944 AP Service All-America Team

The NFL might have been experiencing a talent shortage in 1944, but the U.S. military certainly wasn't. Take a good look at the Associated Press Service All-America team from that year. Four players, including almost the entire backfield, went on to the Pro Football Hall of Fame (Joe Stydahar, Otto Graham, Charlie Trippi, Bill Dudley), and all but one member of the squad played at least four seasons of pro ball. Note, too, that Stydahar and Russ Letlow were already in their thirties. If this team had played the '44 NFL champs, the Packers, it probably would have won by four touchdowns. Unless, of course, it won by five.

Position, player, team	Age	Pro career
E, Sgt. Jack Russell, Randolph Field	25	1946–50 New York Yankees (AAC/NFL)
T, Lt. JG Joe Stydahar, Fleet City NTS	32	1936–42, 1945–46 Chicago Bears

G, Spec. A1C Buster Ramsey, Bainbridge	24	1946–51 Chicago Cardinals
C, Cadet George Strohmeyer, Iowa Pre-flight	20	1948 Brooklyn Dodgers, 1949 Chicago Hornets (AAC)
G, CPO Russ Letlow, Camp Peary	31	1936–42, 1946 Packers
T, Ens. John Woudenberg, St. Mary's Pre-flight	26	1940–42 Steelers, 1946–49 49ers (AAC)
E, 2nd Lt. Nick Susoeff, Second Air Force	23	1946–49 49ers (AAC)
B, Cadet Otto Graham, North Carolina Pre-flight	22	1946–55 Browns (AAC/NFL)
B, Sgt. Charlie Trippi, Third Air Force	22	1947–55 Chicago Cardinals
B, Lt. Bill Dudley, Randolph Field	24	1942, 1945–51, 1953 Steelers/Lions/Redskins
B, Lt. Len Eshmont, Norman NAB	27	1941 Giants, 1946–49 49ers (AAC)

A Soldier's Story

Packers halfback Hal Van Every went into the Army Air Corps after Pearl Harbor and got his wings in July 1942. He was on a bombing run over Germany in 1944, piloting a B-17 Flying Fortress, when his plane was hit by artillery fire. He spent the next year in a prison camp. The tale he told me:

I got shot down May 12, 1944, on the way to Leipzig. It was the 10th mission I'd flown. There were ten in the crew, and they all survived the bailout—other than a sprained ankle by, I think, my tail gunner. The four officers—the pilot, copilot, navigator and bombardier—were taken to one camp and the other six, the enlisted men—the radio man, ball turret [gunner], top turret [gunner], waist gunners and tail gunner—were taken to another camp. Every one of us made it home.

I didn't have my regular navigator with me that day. He'd let another guy take his place so the guy could complete his thirtieth mission. After thirty, see, you got to go home. But we got shot down, so he didn't get to go. About two or three weeks later, we heard my regular navigator got shot down and killed. We thought *he* was lucky [for missing the bombing run to Leipzig], but it turned out we were the lucky ones.

[The Germans] put us immediately on a train for Frankfurt. Frankfurt was the main interrogation center for almost all airmen. I was there for about ten days, and then they took us to our permanent camp. Of course, we couldn't tell 'em much that they didn't already know. They held me a little longer because I was a captain, and they figured they might get more out of me — secret equipment we might have, or more advanced stuff as far as the war effort. They'd withhold food to try to get you to talk, but I just kept repeating the same story.

I didn't even tell them I was the pilot, but they knew because my crew had told them. [The Germans] knew everything about you. They'd say, "We know you graduated from Bakersfield or Sacramento in 1942, and you were in this class." They'd gotten books on all this. I did get away with one lie, though. I told them I'd taken the *Queen Mary* over to England, when in fact I'd flown the Atlantic — flew over Greenland, landed in Iceland and went over [to England]. I didn't want to give 'em the route, in case they tried to sabotage it. They didn't question my story about the *Queen Mary*.

We were flying out of a little base in England called Rattlesden, between Ipswich and Norwich. Of course, almost every mile in England, in that whole south-southwest corner, there was a bomb base. What happened that day was . . . our group commander and our wing got attached to the wrong formation. It's easy to do when you're trying to get a thousand bombers organized. So we had to take a three-hundred-sixty-degree turn with about a hundred or so airplanes, and by the time we got turned around we were ten minutes behind. And you can't catch up.

Because of that, we didn't have any fighter [planes escorting] us, and when we came over the continent they just shot the crap out of us, shot down six out of seven of us in the upper squadron. The whole right wing of our plane was on fire. That's where the gasoline tanks are, so we bailed out.

We wound up in a POW camp in Sagan, Poland, a hundred twenty miles southeast of Berlin. It was called Stalag Luft III. You know that movie, "The Great Escape"? That was the camp I was in. In fact, the escape had happened just before I got there. Eighty guys got out, as you remember, and they caught fifty of 'em and shot 'em, put 'em all in one little cement-slab grave. When I walked in, there was a big picture of the grave in the outer entry of the barracks. Over the picture, in big letters, it said, "Gentlemen, escape is no longer a sport."

Living conditions were not the best. It was one of the coldest winters they've ever had. It got down to twenty below. And we'd only have nine lumps of coal every day that we'd have to make last. You had twelve in a room there. Very low on food. I lost about fifty pounds, and bigger guys lost more than that. [That spring there was a story in U.S. newspapers about Van Every, while being held prisoner, writing a letter to Packers coach Curly Lambeau. "Just heard Green Bay won the [1944] Western Division title," the letter read. "I'm a scatback now." Hal's usual playing weight was 195; subtract 50, and it means he got down to 145.]

If it wasn't for the parcels we got from the Red Cross, we wouldn't have existed, I don't think. We'd use the food we got in the parcels, which was in cans, to supplement the food they gave us in the camp. But once they started making us go on these marches, they could hardly provide any food. And we were forced to march out of there, because the Russians almost liberated us.

So they moved the whole camp — ten thousand men. It was awful cold. You'd lay down in the road and be almost dead. If your buddy didn't kick you, you wouldn't get up. We'd come into a town and try to get a little something to eat, some warm soup maybe, and look for a place to stay — usually a barn. The guards would have a police dog with 'em, but they'd march right with us. Most of 'em were just like us, really. They were kinda marching for their lives, too.

We marched for two days and two nights. Then we took box cars to Nurnberg [Nuremberg] and stayed in a prison camp there for two months. After that, they knew the Americans were coming, so they marched us to Moosburg in southern Germany. We had [over a hundred thousand] prisoners there. Along the way, we could see the [American] planes bombing the cities at night.

Ol' General Patton [and the Third Army] arrived on April 29, 1945. He told the Germans they had to give up the camp by 10 in the morning or he was coming in, and by golly, at 10 o'clock he came rolling in.

Opened the gate . . . what a sight. He was our hero. I went up to his tank and whatnot. Most of the prisoners did.

A bunch of the Germans in charge of our camp went down and held up in a church in downtown Moosburg. They thought they'd be safe there. It's my understanding that Patton told 'em to get out of there or he was coming in, and I guess he just pulled out the artillery and leveled that church. He wasn't going to let 'em get away with that.

I had to wait another two weeks before I got out of there. I finally got a sixty-day leave, and then I was reassigned to Colorado Springs [Colorado]. Second Air Force. I helped coach the football team that season. The team was called the Superbombers. See, that's the heavy bomber headquarters.

I could have played pro ball when I came back. I got offered a contract. But I hurt my back bailing out over Germany, and on the marches it just got worse. It causes me nothing but pain now through the legs and ankles. I've been to the Mayo Clinic four or five times, trying to get some answers. They did a spinal fusion in '55, and it worked on one side and not the other. Yeah, I could have played for another year or so, but being in a prison camp for a year. . . . That's not the best training place for football.

• • •

Unless the Bears' pugilistic penchant is curbed next autumn, some club is going to retaliate, and the carnage will be something to behold. I'm certain the National [Football] League doesn't want anything like that to happen. It would be bad for professional football, but the players on other clubs are growing mighty tired of having to combine football maneuvers and judo gyrations while keeping their hands up in self-defense. —Cleveland Rams coach Buff Donelli

• • •

Bellying up to the Barbell

You barely heard a whisper about weightlifting in the NFL until the mid-'50s, and it didn't became a certified craze until well after that. So what are we to make of the Redskins' Bob Seymour pumping iron in 1944?

It's impossible to say whether Seymour, a six-foot-two, 205-pound fullback out of Oklahoma, was the first pro football player to lift weights, but he's the earliest I've come across. Lewis Atchison of the *Washington Star* described his regimen: "Seymour has been working out at the 'Y' and also at home, balancing the weight on his shoulders and slowly coming up from a squatting position. About 45 minutes of this daily is guaranteed to get the legs in shape or else leave you in a state bordering on collapse. It has had a salutary effect on Seymour, as the records show."

Sure enough, Bob had his best season that year, leading the team in rushing, finishing fourth in receiving, scoring six touchdowns, and even helping out with the punting. It would be years, though, before anyone drew a correlation between weight training and performance. After all, weight lifting made you "muscle-bound" (or so the thinking went back then).

• • •

The league will buy one of the Army's big C-47 transports. It will hire a pilot, copilot, steward and two maintenance men on a full-time basis and haul the clubs on all the trips. One of those big ships can fly the longest jump in the league in four hours, and the way our schedule is arranged it will be no trick at all to transport five teams on roundtrips every weekend. — Lions owner Fred Mandel's fascinatingly off-base prediction about travel in the postwar NFL

• • •

The War Years: 1945

From the March 30 issue of *Touchback*, a newsletter the NFL published for its players in the service: "Lt. Bill Osmanski [of the Bears] saved a fellow officer from death in a quicksand pit in New Guinea after their canoe had capsized in a crocodile-infested stream. . . .

They were on a banana hunting expedition. . . . The other officer was in up to his armpits before Bill got him loose."

While the Lions' Whizzer White was on furlough in Detroit, owner Fred Mandel kidded him about his Bronze Star and cluster. "What's that for, getting to meals on time?" Mandel said.

"Oh, no," White replied. "Something much easier than that."

Whizzer had been aboard the uss *Bunker Hill* two months earlier when it was hit by two kamikazes.

During his twenty-seven months in the medical corps in Australia, the Packers' Bob Adkins collaborated with a Melbourne sports editor to invent a game that merged American football with Australian rugby. Austus, it was called.

There were eighteen men on a side, just like the Australian game, "and the Americans were restricted to passing for scoring," Adkins told the *Chicago Tribune*. "There were two high goal posts at the ends of the field and also a short post near the two large ones. If a ball was kicked through the tall posts or an American caught a pass in that sector it was good for six points. If the score was made between the large and small ones it was one point. So our scoring was about the same."

Excerpt from a letter written by the Giants' Marion Pugh, postmarked Pilsen, Czechoslovakia: "Pilsener beer is really good. Only there is a drastic shortage, and it is all the fault of those Britishers. They received the mission to bomb the Skoda Arm Works. And what do they do? They bomb the brewery, the louses! But you can get a glass if you know the right fellow."

Redskins rookie John "Tree" Adams, rejected multiple times by the military because he was six foot seven, asked one day to change his jersey number to 4-F.

"Why?" owner George Preston Marshall wanted to know.

"Then when I run on the field," Adams said, "maybe the draft board will leave me alone."

The Steelers bought halfback Art Van Tone from the Lions two games into the 1945 season, but he decided to quit after learning of their murderous practice schedule. The team was subjecting its players to "twice-daily workouts on Wednesday and Thursday and scrimmages twice each week," the *Pittsburgh Press* reported. "The arrangement is usually discarded after preseason drills for daily practice sessions, but because of the frequent arrival of discharged veterans has been continued this fall."

Colts Hall of Famer Art Donovan reminiscing about his war experience: "[Giants quarterback] Charlie Conerly and I were in the same division in the Marine Corps. I got a medal. You know how I got a medal? I was running, and I got shot in the ass."

• • •

The . . . war did something for the football writer. It made him temper his regard for the nobility and intrepidity of individuals who were operating only as athletes. — Stanley Woodward, *New York Herald Tribune*

• • •

Pro Football's Pete Grays

Baseball fans in 1945 thrilled to the exploits of Pete Gray, the one-armed outfielder for the St. Louis Browns. Not that we're having a contest or anything, but the NFL had *two* one-armed players that year, Ellis Jones and Jack Sanders.

Jones was the more famous of the pair. A six-foot, 190-pound guard-linebacker for the Boston Yanks, he'd captained the team at Tulsa and played in the College All-Star Game that summer against the defending NFL champion Packers. The Yanks drafted him sixty-ninth overall, so clearly he had some talent.

A childhood fall from a tree had cost Jones his right arm. Blood poisoning set in, and doctors had to amputate eight inches below the shoulder. But none of this made him any less determined to go out for football at Abilene (Texas) High School. And it just so happened that one of the assistant coaches there, Jack Christian, had lost a hand in an accident at an ice plant.

"He will always be my favorite player," Christian once said of Jones. "Because we both had the same handicap, perhaps we were drawn together. I realized that Ellis' chances of making the grade were slim, so I tried to make a placekicking specialist out of him."

But Jones was capable of doing a lot more than just booting extra points. He was fast enough to run the 100 and 220 in track—and even played on the golf team. (He was also smart enough to make the honor roll.) By his junior year he was starting on varsity. That led to two seasons at San Angelo Junior College, after which he became a star at Tulsa.

Or as he put it, "I get along all right. It seems to bother the other fellow more than it does me."

Bill Stern spotlighted Jones on his national radio show. Grantland Rice mentioned him in his syndicated sports column. Ripley's featured him in one of its *Believe It or Not!* cartoons. There weren't many linemen in 1945 more publicized than Ellis.

Jones compensated for his missing arm in any number of ways. On offense, he relied heavily on the cross-body block; on defense, he often tackled with his legs. ("Just like a mowing machine!" Yanks coach Herb Kopf said.) His quickness, meanwhile, helped him contend with bigger opponents—and there were plenty of those.

Ellis's NFL career lasted only a season. He went into the oil business after that. Years later he told the *Tulsa World*, "It never occurred to me that I could not keep playing football. I guess I was too dumb to think I couldn't do it."

Jack Sanders's story is a little different. Sanders, a guard like Jones but thirty pounds heavier, had lost his left hand and wrist in an explosion while serving with the marines on Iwo Jima. He'd also suffered shrapnel wounds and partial hearing loss, and one of his legs was broken in three places.

When Sanders returned home, he was still the property of the Pittsburgh Steelers, with whom he'd spent his first three NFL seasons (1940–42) after graduating from SMU. But the Steelers loaned him to the Eagles so he could receive treatments at Philadelphia Naval Hospital (where he also got a specially made brace and pad for his arm).

Sanders made his first appearance with Philly in a preseason charity game. A crowd of ninety thousand was on hand—including tens of thousands of servicemen, many of them wounded. The *Philadelphia Inquirer*'s description of the scene:

> The thunderous crescendo rolled from one side of Municipal Stadium and back again as Lieutenant Jack Sanders of the Marine Corps ran onto the field to take his place in the Eagles' starting lineup. . . . Every eye was focused on the courageous athlete, who lost part of his left arm at Iwo Jima. The sincere wishes of every man, woman and child in the huge stadium went with him as he stepped forward to make his comeback—a personal ambition for him as well as a shining example for other fighting men who have returned from the battlefronts wounded.

Sanders got into three games that season before retiring at twenty-eight and going into coaching. The Eagles hosted Jones's Yanks in the final week, but Jack didn't play that day, so he missed the chance to line up against Ellis. Darn.

In an interview with the *Corpus Christi Times* in 1951, Sanders said his steel-and-cowhide arm guard, which weighed five or six pounds, actually made a pretty good club. Besides, he added, opponents were terribly nice to him, since he was a wounded veteran and all.

"If I fell down on the ground," he said, "those guys would dust me off and help me up."

Wounded Warriors

Jack Sanders wasn't the only war veteran to play in the NFL after being seriously wounded. The Redskins had *three* players who fell into that category.

Guard Fred Boensch lost part of his jaw when he was hit by a Japanese sniper's bullet, but he returned—with the help of a special helmet—to play for two seasons.

Center Clyde Ehrhardt suited up in 1946, sat out the next year because of complications from a gunshot wound, and came back for two more seasons.

Then there's tackle Tom Dean. Just after the Redskins traded for him in 1948—after he'd spent two years with the Boston Yanks—he was forced to retire because of a head injury suffered in the service. (He kept getting severe headaches in training camp.)

And that's just one team. What was happening in Washington was happening all over the league.

In Chicago, for instance, Cardinals back Mario "Motts" Tonelli survived the Bataan Death March—and forty-six months in Japanese prisons—but saw his weight drop from 190 to 113. His mother was convinced all he needed was some home cooking. "I've got the spaghetti kettle ready, and the points to get him plenty of meatballs," she said. "My cooking is going to help him get ready to crack the line again."

But Tonelli never played in another game—though the Cards and the All-America Conference's Chicago Rockets were dearly hoping he could. Unfortunately, he was thirty by the time he went to training camp with the Rockets in 1946 and still had "the spell of his years in a Nipponese prison . . . hanging heavily over his head," Wilfrid Smith wrote in the *Chicago Tribune*. The newspaper later reported that he was "still subject to bouts of tropical fever" and had to be put on the inactive list.

The story of Bears guard Pat Preston has a happier ending. Preston was on Okinawa with the marines when a Japanese machine-gun bullet shattered his right ankle. While he was lying in a field hospital, Bears fullback Bill Osmanski came by. Osmanski was in charge of evacuations from the island, and he quickly got his future teammate on a plane to Honolulu. (Pat had been drafted by the Bears just before going into the military and had yet to play for them.)

Preston's recovery was slow. For months, he couldn't even stand on the ankle. Doctors looked at the x-rays, shook their heads, and told him his career was over. But he got back on the field in 1946 and helped the Bears win the championship.

Late that season, when Osmanski was returning to the lineup after being slowed by leg injuries, Preston told a reporter, "Sometime Sunday, I'd like to open a hole that'll get Bill through the line as fast as he got me out of Okinawa." (Bill didn't do anything spectacular in the next game, but he did run for touchdowns of 12 and 10 yards the week after that. Wonder if Pat had anything to do with it.)

Preston played with the Bears through '49, after which he took a job at Wake Forest coaching the line. All things considered, he was one of the lucky ones.

$\cdots$

The end of a football game is always marked by the blowing of a whistle or the shooting of a gun. Chicagoans prefer the shooting of a gun. — Corinne Griffith (wife of Washington owner George Preston Marshall) in *My Life with the Redskins*

$\cdots$

Ten Great Players Who Never Played in the NFL

PAT O'DEA, FB — The Australian-born "Kangaroo Kicker" starred for Wisconsin at the end of the nineteenth century, long before pro football became organized. But what a weapon he would have been in the '20s. He drop-kicked a record 62-yard field goal against Northwestern and punted the length of the field, then 110 yards, against Minnesota. Imagine O'Dea and Cardinals Hall of Famer Paddy

Driscoll booming kicks back and forth. It would have been worth the price of admission.

GEORGE GIPP, TB — How could we leave out the Gipper? I'm guessing he would have joined Curly Lambeau, his old Notre Dame buddy, in Green Bay when he was done in South Bend — that is, if a throat infection hadn't killed him in 1920. And had that happened, the Packers might have started winning championships sooner than 1929. Gipp was your classic triple threat, a true natural. It's a little scary, though, to think that George, a frequenter of bars and pool rooms, could have been teammates with the inimitable Johnny Blood, a frequenter of . . . everything.

BRUD HOLLAND, E — Holland was an All-American at Cornell, a terror of a two-way end, but the NFL wasn't hiring blacks in 1939. So he stayed in school, got his master's and PhD degrees, and later was president of Delaware State and Hampton Institute. In his autobiography, *Luckman at Quarterback*, Sid Luckman speaks admiringly of Holland. "He was voted by sports writers the best end in the country in 1938," says Luckman, who quarterbacked Columbia that year, "and when I faced him one Saturday he carried my vote, too."

NILE KINNICK, QB-HB — Here's all you need to know about Kinnick, the 1939 Heisman Trophy winner from Iowa: in the College All-Star Game the next year against the NFL champion Packers, he *drop-kicked* three extra points (in addition to firing a 56-yard touchdown pass). Nobody in pro football was drop-kicking anymore, but Kinnick was a throwback — and would have made a fine pro, even though he was a bit undersized at five foot eight, 167 pounds. Alas, he lost his life in a plane crash during World War II.

DOC BLANCHARD, FB — There weren't many fullbacks in the mid-'40s who could run 100 yards in ten seconds flat. In other words, Blanchard might have been dubbed "Mr. Inside" at Army, but he had outside speed. The 49ers tried to sign both him and teammate Glenn Davis — the first Heisman Trophy–winning backfield in college football history — but Blanchard decided to stay in the military. (Davis wound up with the Rams.)

GLENN DOBBS, TB-QB — Dobbs, who came out of Tulsa, was the only AAC superstar who didn't cross over to the NFL. Instead he went to Canada, where the money was better. There was hardly anything he couldn't do on a football field. With the Brooklyn Dodgers in 1946, the year he was voted MVP, he led the league in passing yards (1,886) and punting average (47.8), returned a punt 78 yards for a touchdown, intercepted two passes, and rushed for 208 yards. His '48 season with the Los Angeles Dons was even better in many ways: 2,403 passing yards, twenty-one TD passes (eight more than in '46), 539 rushing yards, and a 49.1-yard punting average. Dobbs was as big as today's quarterbacks — six foot four, 210 pounds — and he needed to be, since he rarely came out of the game.

"[Rival quarterbacks] Otto Graham and Frankie Albert never got their suits dirty," he once told me. "I was always down in the mud and everything else. I'd lose 15, 20 pounds during the season. But I wouldn't have had it any other way. I really enjoyed playing both ways."

JACKIE JENSEN, RB — In 1948 Jenson finished fourth in the Heisman voting, was third in the nation in rushing — averaging 7.4 yards an attempt — and carried California to the Rose Bowl. Problem was, he was just as good a baseball player. As an outfielder with the Red Sox in the '50s, he won a Most Valuable Player Award and led the American League in RBI three times. Still, he had serious NFL prospects.

DICK KAZMAIER, TB — Maybe I'm being overly romantic. After all, Kazmaier was a five-foot-eleven, 171-pound *Ivy Leaguer.* But he *did* win the 1951 Heisman and led Princeton to number six national rankings his last two seasons. Check out the game he had against number twelve Cornell as a senior: fifteen of seventeen passing for 236 yards and three touchdowns, eighteen rushes for 124 yards, and two scores. Unfortunately, the Tigers operated out of the single wing — an offense that was perfect for his all-around talents but nowhere to be found in the NFL. No matter. Kazmaier wasn't interested in pro ball, anyway, and opted for Harvard Business School.

Had he come along five years earlier, though, when the single wing still had a few breaths of life, it would have been interesting to see what he could have done against the big boys.

JOHNNY BRIGHT, RB — Bright, from Drake, graduated the same year Kazmaier did. The Eagles took him with the fifth pick of the '52 draft but, like Dobbs, he found the pay better in Canada — and the attitude toward blacks more tolerant. In thirteen seasons with Calgary and Edmonton, he won three Grey Cups, a Most Outstanding Player Award, and rushed for 10,909 yards, a CFL record at the time. He could even throw if needed. In the NFL, I'm convinced, he could have been a back along the lines of Joe Perry . . . especially if he'd gotten to play with Norm Van Brocklin in Philadelphia.

ERNIE DAVIS, RB — Never mind Bright teaming with Van Brocklin, how about Davis joining forces with Jim Brown? That's the backfield the Browns were envisioning when they traded with the Redskins for the top pick in the 1961 draft — and used it on Davis, the Heisman winner from Syracuse. Then leukemia struck, and Ernie died without ever playing pro ball. I once asked Bucko Kilroy, as astute a scout as there was in those days, what recent running back Davis most reminded him of. His reply: "Marcus Allen." Translation: Ernie was a little on the tall side for a back — six two — but he was fast, elusive, tireless, and could catch the ball. What a loss.

1940s AAC

All-America Conference	1946	1949
Champion	Cleveland Browns	Cleveland Browns
Franchises	8	7
Avg. attendance	24,589	26,734
Games per season	14	12
Points per game	39.5	42.6
Yds. per game	508.4	637.9
Plays per game	110.7	119.2
Interceptions per game	3.3	3.4
Passes completed (%)	48.4	47.4
Field goals made (%)	48.5	40.8
Run/pass TD ratio	128 run, 133 pass	118 run, 104 pass
Hall of Fame players	6	10
Hall of Fame coaches	2	2

Leaders	1946	1949
Scoring (points)	Lou Groza, Browns, 84	Alyn Beals, 49ers, 73
Passing	Otto Graham, Browns, Glenn Dobbs, Dodgers	Graham
Rushing (yds.)	Spec Sanders, Yankees, 709	Joe Perry, 49ers, 783
Yards from scrimmage (RB)	Sanders, 968	Chet Mutryn, Bills, 1,029
Receptions	Dante Lavelli, Browns, Beals, 40	Mac Speedie, Browns, 62
Punt return avg.	Chuck Fenenbock, Dons, 18.7	Sam Cathcart, 49ers, 17.0
Kickoff return avg.	Fenenbock, 28.2	Ray Ramsey, Hornets, 29.1
Interceptions	Tom Colella, Browns, 10	Jim Cason, 49ers, 9
Field Goals	Lou Groza, Browns, 13	Harvey Johnson, Yankees, 7

Hall of Famers who played in 1946 (6): C Frank Gatski, QB Otto Graham, T-K Lou Groza, WR Dante Lavelli, FB Marion Motley, MG Bill Willis.

Hall of Fame coaches in 1946 (2): Paul Brown (Browns), Ray Flaherty (New York Yankees).

Hall of Famers who played in 1949 (10): DE Len Ford, Gatski, Graham, Groza, Lavelli, Motley, FB Joe Perry, QB Y. A. Tittle, DT Arnie Weinmeister, Willis.

Hall of Fame coaches in 1949 (2): Brown, Flaherty (Chicago Hornets).

Talking Points

• With so many players pouring out of the military after World War II, the time was right for a second league. But the Browns took a lot of the fun out of it by being so much better than everybody else (52-4-3, counting the playoffs). After four seasons, most of the AAC was shuttered—while Cleveland, the San Francisco 49ers, and the Baltimore Colts were absorbed into the NFL.

• Though top-heavy, the league gave us some memorable individual performances. Spec Sanders, the tailback in the New York Yankees' single wing, had 1,442 yards passing *and* 1,432 yards rushing in 1947. The next year Chet Mutryn of the Buffalo Bills not only rushed for 823 yards, he also caught thirty-nine passes for 794 yards—a 20.4 average. (That's 1,617 yards from scrimmage, folks, a total that wouldn't be surpassed in pro football until Jim Brown gained 1,665 a decade later.)

• Historical footnote: In 1946 the Browns' Lou Groza became the first pro player to lead the league in scoring without scoring a touchdown. "The Toe" did it all with his, well, toe, booting thirteen field goals and forty-five extra points for eighty-four points. (Unlike today's kickers, though, Lou also played a position, sharing the center spot with Mike Scarry. Specialization in the kicking game was still a ways off.)

Pride of the AAC

The All-America Conference's vice president during its first year of existence was none other than Eleanor Gehrig, widow of the late, great New York Yankees first baseman.

"I was a football fan before I ever saw baseball," she said.

Eleanor was one sharp cookie (as they said back then). She originally heard about the league from sports promoter Christy Walsh, Lou's former business manager, who had bought the Los Angeles franchise with actor Don Ameche.

"Oh, that sounds good," she told him. "Can I get in there, too?"

For a time, when the AAC was still being organized, Eleanor was part-owner of the New York Name To Be Determineds. (According to one report, she "loved" the sound of Wolves.) She was the first female owner in pro football history—and later, of course, the first female league executive.

"I suppose there must be some who will shake their head and regard me as a misguided female who is investing all of [her] husband's savings in a sports gamble," she said. "I want to clarify that here and now. I don't regard the league as a gamble. I believe postwar sports interest will see a boom comparable to that of the '20s. . . . But more important, the money is my own. Every cent is what I have earned myself over the past four years . . . [as] a saleswoman for the Consolidated Cork Company, the second-largest manufacturers of bottle tops in America."

But before the AAC kicked off its first season in 1946, Eleanor sold her interest in the franchise and was given a position with the league. Her name was prominently displayed on the office door at the Empire State Building, just below Commissioner Jim Crowley's.

One day, before a big charity dinner at the Hotel Commodore, she asked Crowley for the afternoon off to buy a new hat.

"Why do you need a hat?" he asked.

"They tell me Babe Ruth is going to be at the dinner," she said, "and I *have* to look prettier than he does."

Telling the Players without a Scorecard

The American Football League always gets credit for being the first to put players' names on jerseys. But the Hollywood Bears of the Pacific Coast Football League were doing it long before 1960—in 1946, in fact. What's more, the Bears didn't just have their names on the backs of their jerseys, they had 'em across the front, too. That's *really* going Hollywood.

Most Interesting 2,000-Yard Season

The 2,000-yard season was just a dream for running backs in 1946. Nobody could possibly gain that much ground in an eleven-game schedule. The record for rushing yards in a season was 1,004 (the Bears' Beattie Feathers, 1934), and the record for yards from scrimmage by a back was 1,178 (ditto). That's barely halfway there.

But if you add up all the yards Bill Dudley *accumulated* for the Steelers in 1946 — he did just about everything — you get, by my count, 2,115. Here's the breakdown:

Category	No.	Yds.	TD
Rushing	146	604*	2
Passing	90	452	2
Lateral passing	5	13	0
Receiving	4	109	1
Punt returns	27	385*	0
Kickoff returns	14	280	0
Interceptions	10*	242*	1*
Fumble yardage	7	30	0
Total	303	2,115	6

*Led league

Notes

If you're wondering what "lateral passing" means, it's yardage gained on laterals. The league considered it a separate category . . . Dudley recovered five fumbles on offense and two on defense and advanced them 30 yards.

He also punted sixty times for a 40.2-yard average — I didn't count those yards — and kicked two field goals and twelve extra points. No wonder he was voted Most Valuable Player (and is now in the Hall of Fame).

Sammy Baugh told me a funny story about Dudley once. He said Bill was the only player in the league who seemed to know when Baugh was going to quick kick—and was often able to catch the ball on the fly (and keep it from bouncing far downfield).

Near the end of his career, Dudley was dealt to the Redskins. Great, Baugh thought. Now I'll find out his secret.

So one day Sammy sidles up to him in the locker room . . .

BAUGH: Tell me something, will ya, Bill? You're always able to anticipate when I'm about to quick kick. Am I doing something to tip it off?

DUDLEY: I can't tell you.

BAUGH: Why not?

DUDLEY: Because I might get traded again. This might not be the last team I play for.

Sammy was still wondering, all those years later, how Bill did it.

Once a Polar Bear . . .

Of all the coaches who've won NFL championships, Adam Walsh might be the most improbable. Walsh won his title—in 1945 with the Cleveland Rams—while "on leave of absence" from Bowdoin College, a Division III school in the wilds of Maine.

Walsh, a Knute Rockne product, came to Bowdoin in 1935 and coached the Polar Bears quite contentedly—not to mention successfully—for eight seasons. But in '43 the college shut down the program until the war was over, and Adam asked for a leave so he could return to Notre Dame and, in the interim, coach the line.

Two years later, when Rams coach Buff Donelli went into the navy, Walsh agreed to replace him. (It would have been hard for Adam to say no; the Cleveland general manager was his brother, Chile Walsh.) Adam got immediate results. With a roster that featured, at one time or another, nineteen rookies, the '45 Rams shocked the pro football world by winning it all, beating Sammy Baugh and the Redskins in the championship game, 15–14.

The next season the franchise moved to Los Angeles, and the

Rams finished second behind the Bears in the Western Division. Adam had a contract that ran through 1949, but it included an escape clause after the second year if he decided the NFL wasn't for him. He decided to exercise it—sensing, perhaps, that owner Dan Reeves intended to become more involved on the personnel side. (Indeed, early in '47 Reeves bought out Chile's contract and assumed the GM duties.)

Adam reportedly received offers from the NFL, the All-America Conference, and other colleges but opted to return to Bowdoin. "It's like going home to be among friends again," he said. "I spent [eight] very happy years at Bowdoin . . . and have been on leave of absence."

The feeling in Maine was mutual. "Bowdoin men everywhere got a lift with their coffee this morning when they read Adam Walsh had decided to return as football coach of the Polar Bears," *Portland Press Herald* columnist Blaine Davis wrote. "A lot of wives who hadn't heard a word at the breakfast table for months probably were pleasantly astonished. Anyway, astonished. . . . The State Series didn't seem the same last fall without the big, blond, bespectacled Walsh roaming the sidelines."

On September 27, 1947, nine months after he'd coached the Los Angeles Rams to a 38–17 win over the Green Bay Packers—and twenty-one months after he'd taken them to the NFL title—Adam Walsh led the Bowdoin Polar Bears into battle against the Tufts Jumbos. The opposition spoiled the occasion, though, by turning three Bowdoin fumbles into touchdowns and holding on for a 21–12 victory.

There would be other Saturdays, though, for Walsh, who stayed at the school for twelve more seasons. The main thing was, he was back where he belonged.

Breaks of the Game

The Redskins' 1947 media guide claimed that Wilbur Moore, their just-retired back, "played so vigorously he suffered more broken bones than any other player in the league's history: arm (twice), shoulder (twice), collarbone, ribs (four times), leg, hand (twice) and nose (three times)."

That's fifteen broken bones in eight seasons — if you're willing, of course, to overlook the fact that the nose is made of cartilage.

The Game-Ready Coach

Pro football coaches have strolled the sideline in suits, hooded sweat-shirts, and everything in between, but only one has ever donned an actual uniform (player-coaches aside, that is). That would be Cliff Battles, who coached the Brooklyn Dodgers of the All-America Conference in 1947.

Battles, a decade removed from his Hall of Fame days with the Redskins, didn't go overboard and wear a helmet or pads. Nor was there any mention in the newspaper stories of a mouthpiece. But he did wear a Dodgers jersey, football pants, and cleats during a pre-season game against the Los Angeles Dons in Portland, Oregon.

Prescott Sullivan, the *San Francisco Examiner* columnist, was slightly aghast. "Battles," he wrote, "was the first football coach to wear a football suit we ever heard of — much less ever saw. . . . Why was he so attired? Did the cleaner fail to get his double-breaster back in time, leaving Battles with the choice between a football uniform and a barrel?"

Cliff took the ribbing good-naturedly. Actually, he told Sullivan, he wore the uniform "because I wanted to wear one. What's more, I'm going to continue wearing one all season. In my opinion, it's the practical outfit for the football coach to wear. He doesn't have to worry about mud-splashed players brushing up against him, and it gives him the appearance of being much closer to his work than is possible in blue serge."

(Raise your hand if you think ol' Prescott might have massaged that quote just a little.)

"Football is an earthy business," Battles went on. "And it is my conviction that the coach should not be above sharing its sweat and grime with the players. That's why I'm going in for working clothes."

The sight of Battles in uniform didn't bother Sullivan *too* much because Cliff was still fairly close to his playing weight. "Nevertheless," Prescott said, "we dread the widespread acceptance of this idea."

He needn't have worried.

Most Politically Incorrect Newspaper Lead*

From the September 29, 1947, *Green Bay Press-Gazette*:

> The Green Bay Packers tomahawked the Chicago Bears and then scalped them in a 29–20 massacre at City Stadium Sunday afternoon.
>
> Indian Jack Jacobs, whose ancestors taught him the rudiments of skinning bears and lifting attached toupees, presided at the killing before 25,461 partisan fans.

> *Or rather, it *would* be the most politically incorrect newspaper lead if there had been such a thing as political incorrectness in 1947.

Best Unconfirmed Story

As a player-coach with the Cardinals in 1947, Dick Plasman once kicked off while wearing a camel hair coat.

The episode is mentioned in the Steelers' 1958 media guide. (Dick was an assistant with them that year.) According to his bio, it was bitter cold that November day in New York, so he was standing on the sideline wearing "a dressy camel hair coat" over his uniform. After the Cards scored a touchdown in the seesaw game, "there was so much excitement that before anyone on the bench realized it, Plasman was out on the field, kicking off in his expensive coat. Fortunately, he didn't have to make the tackle."

The story has a certain ring of truth because, well, Plasman was the last NFL player to play without a helmet (in 1941). It just *sounds* like something he'd do. Also, '47 was his last season, so it was a perfect time to pull the stunt.

Alas, none of the newspapers mentioned anything about it. In fact, Plasman's name isn't even in the box score—which doesn't mean he didn't play in the game. It could just mean that, with his coat covering up his number, no one realized he was out there.

Good Thing He Didn't Listen

Joe Maniaci, the erstwhile Bears fullback, was coaching at St. Louis University in the late '40s when he got a call from Vince Lombardi, his old Fordham teammate. Lombardi had been coaching the freshmen at his alma mater and was looking to move up.

"He wanted to be my line coach," Maniaci once told me.

And I said, "Vince, football coaching is not for me, and it's not for you. Football coaching is a dead end. There's going to come a time when you haven't got the material, you've got a losing record—and you're out. You were a good student. [Coach Jim] Crowley used to have you work with the boys who needed help to stay in school. You wanted to be a CPA, you wanted to be a chemist—you're an intellect. Stick with that. Don't get into coaching."

And of course, you know what happened. He went to Green Bay and made an ass of me.

Rookie Hazing, Giants Style

In his autobiography, *Footsteps of a Giant,* Hall of Famer Emlen Tunnell described the horrors of The Gantlet, the cruel and unusual punishment all of the Giants' rookie backs were subjected to in the '40s. It basically involved running the length of the field with the ball under your arm and being tackled by everybody else on the team, one at a time.

"The rookie could not juke, or fake, the tackler," Tunnell said. "This was enough to guarantee that he would be tackled violently at least 75 times a day. . . . For the first time in my life, I thought seriously of quitting a team."

Now Drop and Give Me Twenty

Could there have been a more brutal practice, in all of pro football history, than the one the New York Yankees were subjected to on September 10, 1948?

A little background: The Yankees had arrived in San Francisco late the night before after a typical—for those days—twelve-hour flight. All the time they were in the air, the stewardesses kept feeding them "sandwiches and junk," tackle Derrell Palmer, the team's captain, once told me. "There wasn't anything to do except eat, read magazines and shoot the breeze."

The next day at practice—this was the Friday before the game against the 49ers—one of the players vomited during calisthenics. "I don't think he felt good, anyway," Palmer said. "But he'd just eaten too much."

Coach Ray Flaherty, a Hall of Famer who'd led the Washington Redskins to two titles before the war, went ballistic. For openers, he had the players do thirty minutes of vigorous exercises. Then he started running them—and didn't let up for over three hours.

To make matters worse, it was a wickedly hot afternoon to be in full pads (as was the custom then)—ninety-one degrees. Another Yankees player, end Jack Russell, recalled "somebody bringing water out so the players could have something to drink, and Flaherty ran over and kicked the bucket over."

Bruce Lee of the *San Francisco Chronicle* witnessed the whole spectacle . . . and wrote about it in great detail in the next day's paper. He called the workout—which, by his watch, ran three hours, twenty minutes—the worst he'd ever seen, "almost cruel."

"One man, halfback Wilson 'Bud' Schwenk, collapsed from heat exhaustion and was semi-conscious for 10 minutes," Lee reported. "Seven men were sick and lost their lunch. Eighteen men were down on their hands and knees, gasping for breath. . . . The coaches drove the Yanks unmercifully. . . . Every man was straining every minute. And all the time the driving, the pounding, the verbal flogging by the coaches. 'Force yourself, force yourself. When you're tired, reach down for some guts and force yourself on,' line coach Jim Barber would roar."

In the first part of practice the players chased after long passes, one after another. Then they sprinted down under punts—and sprinted back with the returner—until their legs were rubbery and their lungs ready to burst. Finally, they began working on their offensive and defensive game plans. At 5:20 the pitiless ordeal ended . . . "with five minutes of wind sprints," according to Lee.

There might have been more to Flaherty's madness than just a player puking. The Yankees, All-America Conference finalists the previous two seasons, had been unimpressive in splitting their first two games, and he no doubt was getting some heat from owner Dan Topping.

At one point, Palmer said, he went up to the coach and said, "Ray, you're killing this dadgum football team. We couldn't win a ballgame if you keep this up. We won't be able to play."

To which Flaherty replied, "Don't give me any of that crap. You're gonna pay. You guys are not in shape."

Afterward, Palmer said, "we had a big open shower with about ten or fifteen shower heads, and some guys went in and just lied on the floor of the shower and let the water wash over them. Some were standing up *drinking* the shower water—because they couldn't have any during the workout. There wasn't anybody who went anywhere after practice. As soon as they could get to a bed and lie down, that was it."

The game two days later, before a record crowd of 60,927 at Kezar Stadium, went as badly as Palmer envisioned. The Yankees' Bob Kennedy fumbled the opening kickoff, the ball was recovered in the end zone for a touchdown, and the 49ers ran away to a 41–0 win. After another uninspired loss dropped the Yanks to 1-3, Flaherty was forced to resign.

"The game had passed him by, I think," Russell said. "The game was changing—and we were still running the single wing."

Nowadays, of course, we probably wouldn't have known about any of this. The practice would have been closed to the media.

Another reason to love the old days.

Third and Forever

In an All-America Conference game against the Baltimore Colts in 1948, the Los Angeles Dons found themselves in a third and long late in the first half.

Actually, it was a little longer than long. It was third and 72.

Alas, the newspapers didn't explain with much specificity how the Dons found themselves in this predicament. The *Los Angeles Times* merely said, "[Quarterback Glenn] Dobbs being smeared on an attempted pass and penalties set up the unusual statistical situation."

Just as bad, none of the papers mentioned what play was run in such dire circumstances — or whether Dobbs, a fabulous punter, merely quick kicked.

Sigh.

Or Is It Dr. Poole?

Barney Poole played eight years of college football before turning pro in 1949 with the New York Yankees of the All-America Conference.

No, that's not a misprint.

During the war years, when the eligibility rules were basically thrown out the window, something like that could actually happen. Here, in four easy steps, is how Poole pulled it off:

1. He spent his first two seasons, 1941 and '42, at Mississippi.
2. He played the next year at North Carolina because he'd enlisted in the marines' v-12 officer training program and that's where they sent him.
3. In 1944 he received an appointment to West Point and put in three seasons there.
4. When he was done, he returned to Mississippi for his final two years.

And it was all perfectly legal. The three seasons at Army and the one on North Carolina's preflight team didn't count in the eyes of the NCAA (which viewed them, loosely, as military service).

Poole never lost a game at Army (27-0-1). And in his second stint at Ole Miss, he set a college record in '47 by catching fifty-two passes, most of them thrown by future Giants quarterback Charlie Conerly. (That was season number seven.)

Funny story about Conerly. When he got to the NFL, people somehow had forgotten he spent three years in the marines. As a rookie in '48, his age was listed as twenty-four (rather than twenty-seven). It wasn't until a decade later that it was corrected. He suddenly went from being thirty-three in the Giants' '57 media guide to being thirty-seven in their '58 guide.

In other words, when Conerly was throwing passes to Poole at Ole Miss in '47, they were a combined fifty years old (Charlie twenty-six, Barney twenty-four).

And Barney, let's not forget, was still a "junior."

Poole's six seasons in pro ball were relatively nondescript. In 1950 he signed with the NFL's itinerant New York Yanks . . . and moved with them to Dallas in '52 and Baltimore the year after. In 1954, the last season of his career, he was reunited with Conerly on the Giants. He was the third Poole brother — all ends — to play for the club, following Jim (1937–41, 1945–46) and Ray (1947–52).

• • •

Farm kids have the best chance to succeed in pro football today. They lead a more rugged life than the city youngsters. That's why you have so many Texans in pro ball, fellows like Sammy Baugh, who have roughed it on ranches and are rugged. Take the Texans out, and pro football would have a tough time surviving. — Rams line coach Joe Stydahar

(Or as Bears tackle Russ Thompson, a farm kid from Nebraska, once said of the pro game: "It beat the hell out of sittin' out in the country and milking a cow.")

• • •

It's All a Matter of Timing

The New York Bulldogs and Green Bay Packers were locked in a scoreless battle in 1949 when the Bulldogs' Nick Scollard tried a field goal in the third quarter—a very long field goal. Earlier he'd missed a chip shot, a 15-yarder, but this one cleared the crossbar from 55 yards away. And 55 yards, come to think of it, was a yard longer than the NFL record, a mark that had stood for fifteen years.

So why haven't you heard of this Nick Scollard fellow? Because the kick of his life came in a *preseason* game, that's why.

When I said "kick of his life," by the way, I wasn't kidding. Scollard, who also played some end, spent four seasons in the league and made a modest six field goals in eighteen attempts. His longest field goal in an actual game measured 38 yards—17 shorter than the one he boomed between the uprights on September 11, 1949, in Rock Island, Illinois.

Sometimes, life ain't fair.

Three Hundred Pounds of Trouble

If the trial hadn't been held in the hinterlands of East Texas, *State of Texas v. Forrest P. Grigg Jr.* would have caused much more than just a local media stir. And if it had taken place in 1987 instead of 1977, the cable television carnival surely would have come to town.

The defendant, Forrest "Chubby" Grigg, was one of pro football's first supersized players, a six-foot-two, three-hundred-plus-pound defensive tackle who had played on three championship teams with the Browns in the '40s and '50s. From the stands Grigg might have looked a bit blubbery, but as one rival discovered, his roll of fat "was like an inch of rubber around a concrete piling."

"I loved to eat, but not like Chubby," his Cleveland roommate, Derrell Palmer, told me. "He'd take a hot dog, put mustard on it and just stick it in his mouth. Whole. He just shoved it in there and started chewing. One day we were on a bus headed to Yankee Stadium, and the bus got stuck in traffic. So Chubby rolled down the window and bought a couple of hot dogs from a street vendor. And he sat there eating them on the way to the ballgame. *Loved* to drink beer and eat hot dogs."

Grigg may well have been the first player to have a weight clause in his contract. If he strayed above 280, it cost him $1,000. One year, Palmer said, Chubby was well over the limit when he reported to camp, "but he took all these laxatives and sweated it off in the whirlpool and starved himself. He was so weak, we had to help him get up on the scale. He got the thousand dollars, though."

Being from the same part of Texas as Grigg, Palmer enjoyed his company and tolerated his excesses. Derrell could still laugh about the time he asked Chubby, as he often did, for "just a little swig" of his soda . . . and wound up sipping furniture polish.

As funny as Grigg could be sometimes, though, he also had a mean streak. Palmer saw him spit tobacco juice in an opponent's face once to goad him into a penalty. Then there was the time Chubby, doing his very best Lou Groza imitation, kicked a Chicago Bear in the ribs.

In 1976 Grigg was a retired restaurateur living in Ore City, not far from his hometown of Longview, when his temper flared again, tragically. His only son, Mike, had developed a drug problem, and Chubby was frustrated by his unwillingness to enter a rehab program. He was also embarrassed by his son's increasingly derelict behavior. (Mike got caught burglarizing the high school, was expelled his senior year for "violating the hair code," according to the *Dallas Times Herald*, and quit one job after another.)

Finally, Chubby could take no more. On Halloween night Mike drove his car into a ditch—not the first wreck he'd had, Palmer said. Chubby went and picked him up, got him into bed, and, after a few moments of tortured deliberation, put a bullet in his sleeping son's head with a .22 pistol.

"I went to see him afterward," Palmer said. "He talked about it very matter-of-fact, just like I'm telling you. He said, 'I decided the only way I could stop it was just to kill him. . . . I should never have done it.'"

The case was tried in Upshur County District Court in Gilmer. Grigg pleaded temporary insanity. When the jury couldn't reach a verdict, District Attorney Harry Heard accepted a lesser plea of involuntary manslaughter, and Judge Virgil Mulanax gave Chubby a suspended five-year sentence.

"I thought it was murder," Heard said. "[But] I don't believe a jury anywhere would have sent him to the pen."

Mulanax couldn't bring himself to do it, either. Putting Grigg in prison, he said, made no sense to him "as far as any deterrent for him committing the act again. As far as any rehabilitation of him, I don't know what it would take to rehabilitate him from what he's been through."

Six years later Chubby died, beset by diabetes. He was fifty-seven. Not long before, he'd called Palmer and told him doctors wanted to amputate one of his legs, but he wasn't going to let them.

His survivors, the obituaries said, included two daughters and a granddaughter. There was no mention of his son.

The Great Extra Point Derby

If there was ever a time to get excited about the extra point — and I'm not saying there was — it was in 1949. In the NFL the Eagles' Cliff Patton and the Cardinals' Pat Harder both cruised past the record of seventy-two consecutive PATs that had stood for a dozen years. And over in the All-America Conference Harvey Johnson of the New York Yankees and Joe Vetrano of the 49ers had point-after streaks going that were even longer than Patton's and Harder's.

The extra point was becoming automatic. Indeed, Patton said on a radio show the night before the November 13 game against the Redskins that he thought he could keep his streak going "forever."

No streak is forever, though, and Patton's — almost predictably — ended at eighty-four the next day when he pushed one wide in the second quarter. That opened the door for Harder to claim the record, but he missed later that same afternoon against the New York Bulldogs, ending his run at eighty-one.

Johnson and Vetrano were playing for even higher stakes—to be the first to boot one hundred PATs in a row. Harvey beat Joe to it, but at the end of the season the scoreboard read Vetrano 104, Johnson 102 (thanks to the Niners' higher-scoring offense).

At that point the two leagues (partially) merged, and Vetrano went off to Canada to kick. But Johnson played one more season—1951 with the New York Yanks—and increased his streak to 133. He never made it into the record book, though, because the AAC's statistics weren't recognized by the NFL.

Actually, Vetrano's streak may have been the most impressive of the bunch. Right in the middle of it, in a game against the Browns in 1948, he had to improvise mightily when a bad snap eluded the holder. He alertly picked up the ball and *drop-kicked* it through the goalposts. In fact, it was pro football's last successful dropkick . . . until the Patriots' Doug Flutie got cute in 2005.

What I've Learned: Jimmy Conzelman

Player-coach of 1928 champion Providence Steam Roller; coach of '47 champion Chicago Cardinals; after-dinner speaker extraordinaire

"Ever since I was a kid playing high school football, football has meant to me the burning of the autumn leaves. And every year, when I smelled those first leaves burning, I knew it was time for football."

"[In one game] I saw an opening and started down the sideline. . . . I'd gone about three yards when [Jim] Thorpe came along. He didn't try to tackle me. He just hit me with his hip, and I flew over a short fence about six feet away. I thought someone had fired a big shell. The funny part is that Thorpe used his hip in a tackle as often as his arms and shoulders. Jim had a hip that seemed to jump out of joint. Especially when you tried to tackle him. He had both offensive and defensive hips."

"Those were the times when the cure-all for any football injury was a dab of iodine and four fingers of bourbon."

"When I quarterbacked for the old Providence Steamrollers, just about everybody in the human race had a higher standing than a pro football player. The colleges frowned on us. They threatened to [take away] the letters we had won in school. On top of that, we were playing before 'poverty' crowds. Then Red Grange came into the act."

"In the good old days, all that a football coach needed to get a job was a journeyman knowledge of the off-tackle play and a yen to kick anyone who happened to be in a crouching position. If he had the vocabulary of a longshoreman and spun his own clothes, so much the better."

"I once had a team so weak that it never won a coin toss all season."

"I went completely nuts [in 1925] and bought the Detroit franchise for fifty dollars. I was the owner, triple-threat halfback, coach, press agent, ticket manager and groundskeeper. I finally sold it for two hundred fifty dollars. When that same franchise was purchased a few years ago the price was more than 3.5 million dollars. That alone should show you how I conduct my business affairs."

"Money can't buy friendship, affection or the finer things in life. Of course, I mean Confederate money."

"Watch a group of 9- and 10-year-old boys playing tag. Notice that kid who is always the last one touched. He is a potential ball carrier and will become one if he likes to play football. . . . That speed, that wiggle, that change of pace are tricks that some forgotten ancestor might have used to fool a nasty man armed with a bow and arrow. The boy inherited it."

"When I arrived in Chicago [to coach the Cardinals in 1940] all dewy-eyed from campus, I found that the best I could muster on short notice was a squad of eight castoffs, 22 rookies and three Eagle scouts. . . . I inherited a team that was used to losing, and when players are used to losing you can't do much about it, so I got rid of them."

"I drafted [halfback] Elmer Angsman [sixteenth overall in 1946]. And there was a peculiar reason. He'd had eight teeth knocked out in a Notre Dame game on Saturday, and on Monday he reported for practice. Well, now I don't care who you think you are, the chances are you might stay home and hurt a little."

"I like to say [my teams are] not very deep. That way I can show what a terrific coaching job I've done."

"These old emotional talks don't work with the pros. They have heard them all. Occasionally there may be some high-pitched exhortations in the dressing room. But, by and large, the time is devoted to discussions about second-half changes in defensive and offensive strategy."

"[Pros play] football for a living, not for a mess of glory. Football is their profession, not some schoolboy hobby, and when they walk on a field and the whistle blows, their reputations are at stake. They can't afford to look bad. If they could afford to, they probably wouldn't be out there playing pro football, and taking a chance of winding up injured."

"There are no super men in football and no super systems. Power will prevail most of the time."

"The great thing [Bears coach George Halas] has done is convince them the game is fun. He has built plays that please their vanity, that make them proud of out-thinking and out-witting the other guy."

"Halas is the nicest rich man I know. . . . We always exchange Christmas gifts, and this year George gave me a pair of moccasins — water moccasins."

"Anybody who threw the old and bigger football had to have a hand like a ham even to grip the ball. Then it was cut down to its present size, and almost anybody could throw it—and this was a tremendous boost for the game."

"I was talking to [Redskins owner] George Marshall last week in Washington. No, you'd better change that to George was talking to me. Marshall gave me a lot of advice. He said that the thing that built pro football in Washington was that he gave the folks a show—good vaudeville between halves, colorful uniform for the band and so on. I told him, 'Listen, if I had Sammy Baugh on my team I could draw a crowd playing a banjo between halves.'"

"[A] coach has to speak a lot. There are high school dinners, luncheon groups and all that. That talking business was alien to me. My talks were gruesome, ghastly. My nervousness was horrible. . . . So I decided to talk at every opportunity. I had to lick that fear. In 1933 I gave exactly 157 talks, before every kind of organization available. Sometimes three a day. And I licked that nervousness. I got some confidence and poise. I developed a pattern for a speech, and the listeners began to laugh. I began to collect my expenses for speeches. Then I could charge 50 dollars, then 100 dollars, and they paid gladly. In fact, they think more of you if they have to pay."

"Talk about what you know—that ought to narrow it down considerably for you."

"When I enlisted in the Navy at Great Lakes [during World War I], my official title was hospital corps apprentice, second class—the amoeba form of Navy life. It doesn't sound very impressive, I'll admit—and it wasn't. But the Navy offers great opportunity for the man who works, who has a burning ambition and who really wants to make something of himself. . . . When I was mustered out in 1919, my manly bearing and fierce devotion to duty had rewarded me with the rank and the grandiloquent title of hospital corps apprentice, first class."

"Pro football has a definite place, duty and responsibility [during World War II]. The airplane has wiped out battle lines. This war is not the First World War. That was a soldiers' war; this is everybody's war. If the air raiders come, we all are in the trenches, and we're all under strain. Sports have a big job in preventing that strain from reaching the cracking point."

"The war has been a big boost for the football coaching profession. Football coaches always have been apologists, going around defending their game from attacks by those who think it has no place in our college program. Now the military men have acknowledged the benefits of tough, rugged sports. The men in the Naval Air Cadet schools are being taught to be tough and mean on the theory that to beat a brutal, low-punching enemy you've got to know all the tricks. Football teaches a man to take it and dish it out."

"The strange part is that violence, which terrifies the average fellow, isn't one-tenth as bad as you think it is once you're exposed to it. People go to football games and gasp when a 160-pound back is hit by a 220-pound lineman. They think the little guy will be broken in two; they're surprised when he gets up and goes on playing. You ask the little guy if he was afraid of being hit by the big ox with all the muscles and he'll laugh at you. That's what training can do."

"Who can tell what things will be like when this [war] is over and everybody begins to cut loose after the tension of war has been removed. I figure one thing as almost certain: People are going to demand rugged sports. They won't be interested in the soft stuff. They will be tougher mentally after this widespread involvement in war."

"I'm a man who is unfamiliar with anything mechanical. The workings of an automobile engine or of a front-door bell are utter mysteries to me. Hence, I have an acutely developed fear of the unknown. On top of that, I have a set of nerves which haven't been helped any by 22 years of coaching football. All that accounts, perhaps, for my distaste for . . . air [travel]."

"When I go to New York, I check my bags at Toots Shor's [restaurant] and stay there until I'm ready to go home."

"I've shared with [a certain New York writer] the four progressive stages of drink: the Rosy-Glow stage, the Discussion of World Affairs stage, the Brotherhood of Man stage and finally the Misplaced Articles stage."

"He is not drunk who from the floor . . . can rise again and drink some more. But he is drunk who prostate lies . . . and cannot drink and cannot rise."

"[When he was young and lived in Greenwich Village] I was always afraid I might come home a little worse for the wear. So I sculpted a little statue and placed it under the bushes. If I found the statue, I knew I was home."

"It's a rough business, this winning. Before we played the Bears, I thought of a spread formation, so I called a secret practice. I locked all the doors, and we sprang that spread [in the game]. Bulldog Turner of the Bears looked across our line, grinned, and said, 'Oh, here comes that spread, boys.'"

"I had to quit because I was just getting too clever for my own good. In the old days I had lousy teams. So I could relax and tell funny stories. That gave us a lot of publicity. But once the Chicago Cardinals started to win championships, I was always too worried to tell funny stories."

"I guess football coaches are a lot like the actor Frank McGlynn, who himself attempted always to be a perfectionist. The actor spent his life doing Lincoln, both on the legitimate stage and in the movies. In his living room he assumed Lincoln postures, he walked like Lincoln, dressed like Lincoln. On this particular day he was coming out of his apartment in the habiliment of Lincoln — top hat, frock coat, striped trousers — and when he reached the sidewalk he surveyed one end of the block, and then the other, very deliberately, and then with long strides, very similar to Lincoln's, he walked up the street. A fellow standing across the street watching him said, 'Look, that guy will never be satisfied until he's assassinated.'"

4.
The
1950s

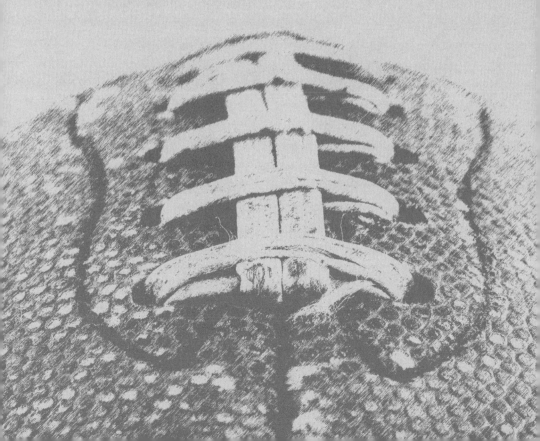

1950s

NFL	1950	1959
Champion	Cleveland Browns	Baltimore Colts
Franchises	13	12
Avg. attendance	25,356	43,617
Roster size	32	36
Games per season	12	12
Points per game	45.9	42.7
Yds. per game	640.1	627
Plays per game	134.6	123.9
Turnovers per game	7.5	5.6
Passes completed (%)	46.6	50.0
Field goals made (%)	44.2	46.8
Run/pass TD ratio	208 run, 220 pass	159 run, 197 pass
Hall of Fame players	34	48
Hall of Fame coaches	5	5

Leaders	1950	1959
Scoring (points)	Doak Walker, Lions, 128	Paul Hornung, Packers, 94
Passing	Norm Van Brocklin, Rams	Charlie Conerly, Giants
Rushing (yds.)	Marion Motley, Browns, 810	Jim Brown, Browns, 1,329
Yds. from scrimmage (RB)	Glenn Davis, Rams, 1,008	Brown, 1,519
Receptions	Tom Fears, Rams, 84	Raymond Berry, Colts, 66
Punt return avg.	Herb Rich, Colts, 23.0	Johnny Morris, Bears, 12.2
Kickoff return avg.	"Vitamin" Smith, Rams, 33.7	Abe Woodson, 49ers, 29.4
Interceptions	Spec Sanders, Yanks, 13	Three tied with 7
Field goals	Lou Groza, Browns, 13	Pat Summerall, Giants, 20

Hall of Famers who played in 1950 (34): QB Sammy Baugh, C-LB Chuck Bednarik, QB George Blanda, HB Tony Canadeo, LB George Connor, T-G Lou Creekmur, DT Art Donovan, HB Bill Dudley, WR Tom Fears, DE Len Ford, C Frank Gatski, QB Otto Graham, T-K Lou Groza, Elroy "Crazylegs" Hirsch, WR Dante Lavelli, QB Bobby Layne, QB Sid Luckman, HB George McAfee, FB Marion Motley, DT Leo Nomellini, FB Joe Perry, WR Pete Pihos, DT Ernie Stautner, QB Y. A. Tittle, HB Charlie Trippi, S Emlen Tunnell, C Bulldog Turner, QB Norm Van Brocklin, HB Steve Van Buren, HB Doak Walker, QB Bob Waterfield, DT Arnie Weinmeister, MG Bill Willis, C Alex Wojciechowicz.

Hall of Fame coaches in 1950 (5): Paul Brown (Browns), George Halas (Bears), Curly Lambeau (Cardinals), Greasy Neale (Eagles), Steve Owen (Giants).

Hall of Famers who played in 1959 (48): DE Doug Atkins, Bednarik, WR Raymond Berry, FB Jim Brown, T Rosey Brown, DB Jack Butler, Creekmur, DE Willie Davis, QB Len Dawson, Donovan, LB Bill George, HB Frank Gifford, T Forrest Gregg, Groza, G Gene Hickerson, HB Paul Hornung, LB Sam Huff, FB John Henry Johnson, G-T Stan Jones, DT Henry Jordan, QB Sonny Jurgensen, CB "Night Train" Lane, S Yale Lary, Layne, CB Dick LeBeau, DE Gino Marchetti, HB Ollie Matson, T Mike McCormack, WR Tommy McDonald, HB Hugh McElhenny, HB-WR Bobby Mitchell, HB Lenny Moore, LB Ray Nitschke, Nomellini, G-T Jim Parker, Perry, LB Les Richter, C Jim Ringo, DE Andy Robustelli, LB Joe Schmidt, QB Bart Starr, Stautner, T Bob St. Clair, FB Jim Taylor, Tittle, Tunnell, QB Johnny Unitas, Van Brocklin.

Hall of Fame coaches in 1959 (5): Brown, Weeb Ewbank (Colts), Sid Gillman (Rams), Halas, Vince Lombardi (Packers).

Talking Points

• The decade of calm between two storms (i.e., the wars with the All-America Conference in the late '40s and the American Football League in the '60s). Canadian teams picked off some players during the '50s, but not enough to make a difference. The NFL was probably never more competitive than it was in these years, inasmuch as there were only a dozen clubs (down from as many as eighteen in the two leagues in the previous decade).

The talent was so concentrated that the 49ers—a team that never won anything—had a backfield composed entirely of Hall of Famers (Y. A. Tittle, Joe Perry, Hugh McElhenny, and John Henry Johnson). At the same time (1954–56), they had not one but two Hall of Fame tackles, Bob St. Clair on offense and Leo Nomellini on defense. And yet they never even made it to the championship game. That's how good even the also-rans were.

Meanwhile, the Rams, who did win something (the '51 title), were blessed with two Hall of Fame quarterbacks—Bob Waterfield and Norm Van Brocklin—and alternated them for several seasons.

Here's another way to look at it: At the end of the '40s there were nineteen Hall of Famers playing in the NFL. At the end of the '50s there were forty-eight . . . an average of four a club.

• The previous two decades had seen big spikes in scoring—45.3 percent from 1930 (21.2 points a game) to '39 (30.8) and 49.5 percent from 1940 (30.1) to '49 (45). It flattened out in 1950 (45.9), though, and only once since has it risen above that figure (in 1965, when it hit 46.1 before dropping back to 43.4 the next season).

Kinda startling, isn't it, given all the hoo-hah about offense these days? Oh, offenses are gaining a few more *yards* now, but they aren't scoring any more points than they were from 1948 (an all-time high of 46.5 points per game) to '50. In fact, they're scoring less. Consider: In '48 — and again in '49 — four pro teams (three in the NFL, one in the AAC) averaged 30 or more points a game. It's never happened again, though the NFL came close in 2011 with the Packers (35 per game), Saints (34.2), Patriots (32.1), and Lions (29.6).

• The reason scoring stopped going up, up, up — indeed, dipped a little — is that the T formation wasn't so new anymore, and coaches came up with better ways to combat it. The 4-3 defense (which supplanted the 5-2 and was more successful against the short passing game) was the main breakthrough. Also, bump-and-run pass coverage, which kept receivers from roaming quite so freely, was introduced.

Beyond that, though, clubs began paying more *attention* to defense, spending more time on it. And fewer and fewer players were playing both ways as the decade wore on, so you had more defensive specialists.

• After holding steady at ten franchises in the '40s (save for 1943), the NFL finally grew again in the '50s, adding three teams from the AAC (one of which folded). Nonetheless, it ended the decade with barely more clubs than it had in 1930 (eleven) — though its reach had expanded to include the West Coast (Los Angeles, San Francisco). There were still plenty of markets that wanted to join the pro football party . . . and if the NFL wouldn't let them in, the AFL would.

A Total Lock

The 1950 issue of *Pro Football Illustrated* included an item about a woman — Mrs. Anna Kadlitz of Hersfield, Germany — who'd won $3,600 the year before in a pro football pool.

"Her system is interesting and bears watching," the magazine said. "She made selections 'exactly the opposite of my husband,' she says."

Mr. Inside

Houston was the birthplace of pro football's first Dome Team — in 1968, when the Oilers moved into the Astrodome. But the birth might have taken place nearly two decades earlier if the NFL had been willing to grant the city a franchise.

At the January 1950 league meetings, Glenn McCarthy, a wealthy oilman, "appeared before the owners and really captured the imagination of many," New York's *Daily News* reported. "He brought all sorts of graphs, charts and pictures" — not to mention architectural plans. It was his intention, if the NFL gave Houston a team, to build a huge indoor stadium just southwest of town, only a few blocks from his luxurious Shamrock Hotel. The facility, he figured, also could be used for conventions, exhibitions, livestock shows, you name it.

According to the *New York Herald Tribune*, the "seating capacity . . . could be juggled anywhere from 110,000 to 130,000." Among the features were a retractable roof that could open in five minutes and escalators that transported fans to the upper levels. Construction costs — estimated at $6.5 million — were to be paid by public and private financing.

"An architect's sketch gives the stadium the appearance of a giant circus tent," the *Herald Tribune* said.

McCarthy told the owners the stadium would take a year to build. In the meantime, he said, the team could play at the high school field, which seated twenty-seven thousand but could be expanded to forty-five thousand. (It was the same stadium — Jeppesen Stadium — that the Oilers first used.) All he asked for in return was "assurances that we'd get a fair shake. We would want a real football team and a chance to give football a real try."

The month before, McCarthy had shown his organizational chops by bringing the All-America Conference All-Star Game to Houston. Well connected with the Hollywood community, he got Jack Benny, Dinah Shore, and Phil Harris to perform before the kickoff and, despite wet weather, drew a crowd of twelve and a half thousand.

But the NFL, intrigued though it may have been by his futuristic ideas, simply wasn't ready to take a chance on Houston, not after fighting a financially draining four-year war with the AAC. And let's not forget: In those days, before big TV contracts, it was still possible for a franchise to fail—as the (original) Baltimore Colts, New York Yanks, and Dallas Texans all did in the next three seasons.

More than a decade later Roy Hofheinz would be celebrated as a visionary for getting the Astrodome built for his baseball team, the Astros. But Glenn McCarthy, owner of the NFL Franchise That Wasn't, was the first to dream of such wonders.

• • •

Officials, by and large, do a good job. I've never had an official score a touchdown against me yet. I've seen 'em get to the 1-yard line—but never score a touchdown.—Giants coach Steve Owen

• • •

The Price Is Wrong

Things weren't going well for the Baltimore Colts in their first year in the NFL. They began the 1950 preseason with three straight losses, and interest in the team was waning. The weather—typically steamy in August—wasn't helping attendance much, either.

Abe Watner, the Colts' neophyte owner, got so desperate he tried to buy his way out of the next home exhibition game. He called 49ers owner Tony Morabito and asked if he'd be willing to cancel the game for $3,000. Morabito refused. Watner upped his offer to $3,500, $5,000, and finally $7,500, according to the *San Francisco Examiner.*

But Tony was no dummy. The Niners were guaranteed three times that for playing in Baltimore and, even with travel expenses, figured to net quite a bit more than $7,500. "We would like to help," he told Watner, "But we can't see our way clear to do it just now. To put it bluntly: We've gotta be hard."

So the 49ers came east and handed the Colts another defeat, 27–14. Only six thousand showed up, and Watner was one step closer to being an ex-owner.

Being Black

In 1950 Bob Mann was coming off one of the best seasons an NFL receiver had ever had. His sixty-six catches were the third-highest total in history. His 1,014 yards were also number three all time. The only reason he didn't go to the Pro Bowl was because there *was* no Pro Bowl in 1949.

Lions management considered Mann's many contributions and offered him a big fat . . . pay cut. Welcome to the world of the black player in the postwar NFL.

Pro football had begun to reintegrate in the late '40s, but economic equality was still decades away. In a 1951 doctoral thesis by former NFL quarterback Paul Governali, an unnamed player talks about a black star in that era getting paid "chicken feed" because his bosses "feel that he can't get a job anyplace else on account of his color."

There was clearly some of that at work in Mann's case. The problem the Lions ran into was that Bob wasn't just any old player. He was an extremely bright guy who, after his playing days were over, became a lawyer. Naturally, he balked at the idea of his salary being reduced (by $1,500, according to reports).

So the Lions traded him to the New York Yanks, who apparently had no use for him. The Yanks cut him at the end of training camp—the day after he'd caught a 56-yard touchdown pass against the Redskins for his team's only score in a 24–7 loss.

"The Yanks never gave me a chance to make their ballclub," he said later that season. "I don't think they ever intended to." His only game action was in the Washington exhibition, and they put him in for just "two minutes."

It wasn't until the end of November that Mann was picked up by another team—the desperate 2-7 Packers, whose passing attack was the worst in the NFL. A few weeks earlier he'd wondered whether he hadn't been "railroaded" out of the league because of his unwillingness to accept Detroit's insulting contract offer.

"I must have been blackballed," he said. "It just doesn't make any sense that I'm suddenly not good enough to make a single team in the league."

His charges smoked out Edwin Anderson, one of the Lions' owners. "The most ridiculous thing I ever heard of," Anderson said. If Mann couldn't find a job, it had to be because clubs were looking for "something more from an end than pass-catching ability." Besides, he added, the kid had asked to be traded.

Mann started in the Packers' remaining three games. The following year he was again one of the NFL's top receivers, finishing among the leaders with fifty catches (fourth), 696 yards (fourth), and eight touchdowns (tied for third). Indeed, only three players in the league scored more TDs than he did.

(Imagine the season he would have had if he'd possessed more than just "pass-catching ability.")

It was one of the more shameful episodes in NFL history, especially when you consider the Lions' racial track record. From 1950 to 1956 they didn't have a single black on the roster. The only other team you could say that about was the Redskins, who were the last in the league to integrate, in 1962.

The Lions' coach for most of those years — very successful years in which they won two championships — was Buddy Parker. I once asked Buster Ramsey, Parker's longtime assistant and close friend, why Buddy didn't have any blacks on his team until 1957, his last year in Detroit.

"I ain't gonna tell you," Ramsey said. "You can figure it out."

I suppose we can.

When Mann died in 2006 at eighty-two, the Lions put out a news release calling him "a trailblazer in professional football." Hall of Famer Lem Barney sang his praises. "Bob was a great example to everyone," Barney said. "He not only was a great football player but a man who gave of himself to the city and the entire community. I have tried to pattern myself after great men like Bob."

Too bad Mann had to do most of his trailblazing in football somewhere other than Detroit.

One Last Thing . . .

Bob Mann's sixty-six catches for the Lions in 1949 figure out to 5.5 per scheduled game. It wasn't until 1995 — forty-six years later — that a Detroit receiver averaged more. Herman Moore (123 receptions) averaged 7.7 a game that season and Brett Perriman (108) averaged 6.8.

Who Needs a Quarterback?

Only five times in modern NFL history has a team gone an entire game without passing — the last in 1950, when the Browns did it against the Eagles. Amazingly, four of the clubs that stuck entirely to the ground came away with a victory, and the other tied. Take a look for yourself:

Date	Team	Vacationing passer	Result
October 8, 1933	Packers	Arnie Herber*	Beat Portsmouth, 17–0
September 10, 1937	Lions	Bill Shepherd	Beat Rams, 28–0
November 16, 1941	Steelers	Boyd Brumbaugh	Beat Brooklyn, 14–7
November 13, 1949	Steelers	Joe Geri	Tied Rams, 7–7
December 3, 1950	Browns	Otto Graham*	Beat Eagles, 13–7

*Hall of Famer

The record of the non-passing teams would be a perfect 5-0 if the Rams hadn't scored with twenty-four seconds left in 1949 to salvage a tie. "At first it appeared that Elroy (Crazy Legs) Hirsch had scored the Rams' touchdown," the United Press reported, "but later when the teams went to their dressing rooms it was confirmed that [Fred] Gehrke carried over. The uniforms of both teams were so muddy that it was nearly impossible to identify the players in the gathering dusk."

(That's the other thing about these games: four of them were played in the rain. Only the Steelers and Dodgers in '41 had dry conditions.)

An Item That May Interest Only Me

The 1950 Baltimore Colts were a truly awful team. They finished 1-11, allowed the most points per game in NFL history (38.5), and dropped out of the league when the season was over. (The Indianapolis Colts are descendants of the *second* Colts franchise, which was launched in '53.)

But here's the thing: only five quarterbacks have ever thrown seven touchdown passes in an NFL or AFL game, and *three* of them played for that hopelessly horrid Colts club—Y. A. Tittle (seven TD passes for the Giants vs. the Redskins in 1962), Adrian Burk (seven for the Eagles vs. the ever-helpful Redskins in 1954), and George Blanda (seven for the Houston Oilers vs. the New York Titans in 1961).

So the '50 Colts have *that* going for them, which is nice.

At Least There Weren't Any Doubleheaders

What follows is, in my estimation, the worst schedule in modern pro football history. At a time when the NFL was supposed to be becoming more equitable, the 1950 New York Yanks . . . boy, did *they* ever get the shaft. Take a look, and then we'll discuss it:

September 17 (Sunday)—at San Francisco 49ers

September 22 (Friday)—at Los Angeles Rams

September 29 (Friday)—vs. Detroit Lions

October 8 (Sunday)—at Green Bay Packers

October 12 (Thursday)—vs. San Francisco 49ers

October 19 (Thursday)—vs. Green Bay Packers

October 29 (Sunday)—vs. Chicago Bears

November 12 (Sunday)—at Chicago Bears

November 19 (Sunday) — vs. Los Angeles Rams

November 23 (Thursday) — at Detroit Lions

December 3 (Sunday) — at New York Giants

December 10 (Sunday) — vs. Baltimore Colts

The highlights:

- Back-to-back road games at San Francisco and Los Angeles to begin the season — with just four days' rest in between (September 17, 22). The 49ers had finished second the year before in the All-America Conference; the Rams had been runners-up in the NFL.
- Two games in five days against the Packers and 49ers (October 8, 12).
- Another two-games-in-five-days stretch against the Rams and Lions (November 19, 23).
- Consecutive games against the ultra-physical Bears. Granted, they were separated by a bye week, but still . . .
- The Yanks' only nonconference opponent: the crosstown Giants, who tied for first that season with a 10-2 record. Naturally, it was on the road.

All this with a thirty-two-man roster. Brutal. Just brutal.

Part of the problem was that, being utterly insignificant, the Yanks were moved from the American (read: Eastern) Conference to the National (read: Western) Conference that year to make room for the Browns, who had just been absorbed from the AAC. This stuck them with road games at Los Angeles *and* San Francisco, as well as at Green Bay, Chicago, and Detroit. (And plane travel in those days, I'll just remind you, was no joyride, particularly when you went cross-country.)

But what made the schedule almost inhumane was the *three* short workweeks the Yanks had — Sunday–Friday, Sunday–Thursday, Sunday–Thursday. Which makes you wonder: Was it something owner Ted Collins said?

Well, yeah, maybe it was. In a priceless first-person piece in *Look* magazine in 1945, Collins, then boss of the Boston Yanks, said, "National Football League schedule making is second cousin, once removed, from a Nazi plebiscite. The New York Giants, Green Bay Packers, Washington Redskins and Chicago Bears hold a private caucus and whack up the choice dates. Teams like the Detroit Lions, who have had a taste of gridiron riches, squawk until they are purple, to no avail. The country cousins like us keep quiet."

No organization, after all, likes to have its inner workings compared to the Third Reich's. (Especially if the comparison is valid.)

I'm kidding about the Yanks' schedule being an act of retribution. It was just the way things worked back then in the wild, wacky NFL. (The Giants, for instance, didn't have *any* short workweeks.)

To their credit, Collins's warriors wound up 7-5, good for third in the conference behind the Rams and Bears. But there's no telling what they might have done with a less suicidal schedule. Their offense was the second best in the league, averaging 30.5 points a game, and their quarterback, George Ratterman, threw more touchdown passes than anybody, twenty-two. Coach Red Strader got them off to a 6-1 start before, almost predictably, they hit a wall and lost four straight to drop out of contention.

Anyway, whenever you hear a team complain about its schedule, think of the 1950 New York Yanks. It'll help put things in perspective.

Record-Shattering

With offenses opening up in the postwar years, some records weren't just broken, they were obliterated. Five examples:

1. JIM BENTON, RAMS, 303 YARDS RECEIVING VS. LIONS, NOVEMBER 27, 1945

Old record: 237 by the Packers' Don Hutson vs. Dodgers, 1943.

Raised record by: 27.8 percent.

Record stood until: 1985 (forty years). The Chiefs' Stephone Paige broke it with 309 yards vs. Chargers.

Current record: 336 by the Rams' Flipper Anderson vs. Saints, 1989.

How many yards you'd need today to break the record by as much as Benton did: 430.

2. DON CURRIVAN, BOSTON YANKS, 32.6-YARD RECEIVING AVERAGE, 1947

Old record: 24.9 by Hutson, 1939.

Raised record by: 30.9 percent.

Record stood until: Currivan's mark still stands.

What you'd have to average today to break the record by as much as Currivan did: 42.7.

3. TOM FEARS, RAMS, 18 RECEPTIONS VS. COLTS, DECEMBER 3, 1950

Old record: 14, shared by four players.

Raised record by: 28.6 percent.

Record stood until: 2000 (fifty years). The 49ers' Terrell Owens broke it with 20 vs. Bears.

Current record: 21 by the Broncos' Brandon Marshall vs. Colts, 2009.

How many catches you'd need today to break the record by as much as Fears did: 27.

4. NORM VAN BROCKLIN, RAMS, 554 PASSING YARDS VS. NEW YORK YANKS, SEPTEMBER 28, 1951

Old record: 468 by the Bears' Johnny Lujack vs. Cardinals, 1949.

Raised record by: 18.4 percent.

Current record: Van Brocklin's mark still stands.

How many yards you'd need today to break the record by as much as Van Brocklin did: 656.

5. JIM BROWN, BROWNS, 1,527 RUSHING YARDS, 1958

Old record: 1,146 by the Eagles' Steve Van Buren, 1949.

Raised record by: 33.2 percent.

Record stood until: 1963 (five years). Brown broke his own mark with 1,863 yards.

Current record: 2,105 by the Rams' Eric Dickerson, 1984.

How many yards you'd need today to break the record by as much as Brown did: 2,805.

Temp Work

Bobby Thomason did a nice job at quarterback for the Packers in 1951. He had the highest completion percentage in the NFL (56.6), the lowest interception percentage (4.1), and the fourth-highest passer rating (73.5) — all while splitting time with Tobin Rote.

Here's what really stood out about his performance, though: He didn't even belong to Green Bay. He was the property of the Los Angeles Rams, who'd drafted him in the first round in 1949 and then *loaned* him to the Packers for a year.

The deal worked like this: if, at the end of the season, the Pack wanted to keep him, they had to give the Rams their number one and two picks in '52. Otherwise, he returned to L.A.

It was a win-win situation for both sides — weird, but win-win. Green Bay desperately needed a second quarterback, and here they were being given one, free of charge, for a season.

The Rams, meanwhile, could spare Thomason because they were set at the position with Bob Waterfield and Norm Van Brocklin. By letting the Packers borrow him — test-drive him, really — they were getting his salary off the books while still retaining his rights. They were also giving him a chance to develop — and giving the rest of the league a chance to see what he could do (in the event Green Bay sent him back and the Rams wanted to trade or loan him to another team).

The NFL allowed this sort of arrangement in those days because — in theory, at least — it helped prop up the weaker clubs. But occasionally a team would bend the rules a bit too far. In 1934 Pittsburgh owner Art Rooney caused an uproar when tried to loan his best player, tailback Warren Heller, late in the season to the Giants, who were making a playoff run and needed a replacement for injured Harry Newman. Heller had actually started practicing with the Giants when league president Joe Carr ordered him back to Pittsburgh.

The NFL bylaws were very clear on the subject:

> A player under contract with one member of the League may be loaned
> to play temporarily with another member, provided the President shall
> have given permission in writing for such temporary transfer and the

members of the League immediately are notified by the Secretary. The spirit of this section is to permit a member whose team is seriously weakened through injury or other unavoidable cause to borrow one or more players temporarily to reinforce his team to normal strength. It is not the spirit of this section, however, to permit a member to add additional strength to his team by borrowing one or more of the best players of another member in an effort to win a certain game or games.

(Rooney was just trying to do his old buddy/bookie Tim Mara a favor by slipping him Heller, who tied for fifth in the league in rushing that year. Art, being Art, didn't see any harm in it. Pittsburgh's season, after all, was already over. The Giants still had three games left, though, because of the NFL's screwy scheduling.)

But getting back to Thomason . . . The strangest part of his year in Green Bay might have been the two games he played against his real team, the Rams. It would have been a great story if he'd torn them up, but he didn't do much damage, completing twenty-six of fifty-two passes for 251 yards and no touchdowns as the Packers lost both.

In the end, Green Bay coach Gene Ronzani decided the price was too high for Thomason and shipped him back to Los Angeles. With the first of the two picks he saved, he drafted Babe Parilli, who found success late in his career with the AFL's Patriots but was little more than a journeyman in the NFL. With the second pick Ronzani took Billy Howton, who went on to break Don Hutson's career records for receptions and receiving yardage.

But the Packers didn't necessarily come out ahead in the deal. The Rams turned around and traded Thomason to Philadelphia, where he played in three Pro Bowls and threw a league-best twenty-one touchdown passes in '53. Rote-Thomason would have been a much more potent combination for Green Bay than Rote-Parilli. So maybe the Pack *should* have exercised their option to buy.

Players were still being loaned in the '60s. One of them, quarterback Jacky Lee, took it personally when the Houston Oilers rented him out to the Broncos in 1964. "I have no desire to come back," he said. "I'm going to get a lawyer and fight this thing if Houston tries to get me back."

The Oilers got him back anyway. He played for them in '66 and part of '67 before being dealt—this time with no strings attached—to the Chiefs.

Soon after, loaning players was outlawed. It had ceased being a way to aid struggling clubs and had become merely "another form of hiding people," as Chargers coach Sid Gillman put it. Besides, he argued, quite rightly, "How can a player ever know who he belongs to if he's loaned out to another team?"

• • •

No team figures to take two straight on the coast. Too much to beat—travel, the climate and another thing I wouldn't mention.—Lions coach Buddy Parker in the midst of a two-game West Coast swing in 1952

• • •

Groza, Part 1

Brain Twister: Lou "The Toe" Groza kicked on five consecutive plays in the Browns' 1952 season opener against the Rams. Can you figure out how he did it? (No, there weren't any penalties involved that would have caused him to re-kick. They were five straight *legal* plays.)

Answer:

1. In the last minute of the first half, Groza boots a 49-yard field goal to give Cleveland a 20–0 lead.
2. Groza kicks off, the Rams' Woodley Lewis fumbles, and the Browns gain possession.
3. On the next play Groza boots a 14-yard field goal to make it 23–0. Eight seconds remain in the half.
4. Groza kicks off again. The half ends during the return.
5. Groza kicks off to start the second half.

(How close did you come?)

What's a Guy Gotta Do?

Decades before the NFL kept track of sacks, the Eagles' Norm "Wild Man" Willey had a huge day against the Giants on October 26, 1952. Exactly how huge, though, is a matter of debate.

Willey has claimed he sacked Charlie Conerly and Fred Benners seventeen times—ten more than the modern record, set by Chiefs Hall of Famer Derrick Thomas in 1990. But future *Sports Illustrated* writer Paul Zimmerman, who was at the game, said he marked Willey down for eight sacks and Philadelphia's other defensive end, Pete Pihos, for six. (And anyway, the stats credit Philly with "only" fourteen sacks, so Wild Man couldn't have had more than that.)

I'm not here to quibble, though. No matter how many sacks Willey racked up that afternoon, it was one of the greatest defensive performances of all time. I just want to point out that in the *New York Times* the next day—in a game story measuring well over a thousand words—Wild Man's name *isn't even mentioned.*

Which raises the question: What game was reporter Louis Effrat watching?

(Effrat *was* nice enough to note that "aerial attempts by Chuck Conerly and Fred Benners were smothered for huge losses"—without specifying who was doing the smothering. "All the News That's Fit to Print," indeed.)

"The Big D" Gets an F

The NFL's first foray into Dallas—with the Texans in 1952—was an utter disaster. The ownership group, unprepared for the financial losses, forfeited the franchise after an 0-7 start, and the league operated the team out of Hershey, Pennsylvania, for the last five games (all on the road). The Texans are the last NFL club to fail . . . and it's hard to imagine that ever changing.

One of their few bright spots was safety (and occasional receiver) Tom Keane, who finished second in the league with ten interceptions. "I was supposed to go to the Pro Bowl that year," he once told me, "but it never came down. I guess maybe being on the road they couldn't find us."

Some of his other recollections from that wreck of a 1-11 season:

"I was one of the eleven players the Rams traded to the Texans for [linebacker] Les Richter. A year later, I was the only one still in the league."

"There was always talk about whether the team was going to move. One day, our coach, Jimmy Phelan, handed us our paychecks and said, 'Gentlemen, I'm not saying these checks aren't any good, but we're going to call practice off. You'd better get to the bank.'"

"Phelan would put in at least one trick play a game, some flea-flicker or something like that. One of them I remember very well. It started with a lateral pass to the left, followed by another lateral pass to the right, followed by *another* lateral pass back to the quarterback in the middle of the field, . . . followed by a pass to me. It worked."

"On our last road trip before we went to Hershey — we were going up to play Detroit — I noticed our trainer, Chief West, wasn't on the plane. The next day I saw him in the locker room. I said, 'Where the hell you been?' He said, 'They wouldn't pay my way, so I thumbed up.'"

"In Hershey, we were pretty much on our own, except for the games. Our workouts consisted of . . . we'd go out and play volleyball over the goalpost with a football. We probably ended up with the best volleyball team in the league."

"Our only win was over the Bears in Akron [27–23 in Week 10]. On one play they threw me the ball at about the [Chicago] 2-yard line, and Don Kindt, who was covering me, intercepted the pass. As he came down, though, I took the ball away from him and fell at about the 1." [Two plays later, with just thirty-four seconds left, Texans quarterback Frank Tripucka sneaked over for the deciding score.]

"[Bears coach George] Halas went crazy. When Don went off the field, Halas walked up to him and—boom!—kicked him right in the shins."

• • •

The point after touchdown has no place in professional football. It's so easy that it is almost automatic. Besides, it isn't in keeping with the spirit of a team game. Only the center, the fellow who holds the ball and the fellow who kicks it take any real part in the play.

But the real reason I want to see the point after touchdown eliminated is to beat the gamblers. They've made a pretty good thing out of it. Gives them a chance to offer half-point spreads and they keep the ties. The suckers go for it and get hurt.—NFL Commissioner Bert Bell

• • •

Number of the Decade: 433

The 49ers' Joe Perry led the NFL in rushing in 1953 with 1,018 yards—a modest figure by today's standards. His year becomes a lot more impressive, though, when you consider he ran for another 433 yards in the *preseason*, including 101 against the Eagles and 117 against the Giants.

Not that anyone was counting.

When comparing players across generations, it tends to be forgotten that guys in Perry's era gained thousands of yards—off-the-books yards—in exhibitions. In the case of Joe the Jet, who played sixteen years, we're probably talking about 3,000 or 4,000 yards, maybe more.

Nowadays, of course, franchise backs get a handful of reps in the preseason and save themselves for the real games. But in the less prosperous '50s teams took exhibitions much more seriously—in hopes of exciting the fan base and spurring ticket sales. As a result, starters stayed on the field longer.

The Niners played seven preseason games in 1953—six against NFL clubs and one against a service team, the Fort Ord Warriors. Even in the tune-up against the soldiers, Perry was a busy man, scoring three touchdowns. It might have been "only an exhibition," but it was still a work day, even for the best running back in the league.

The Rockne Diaspora

Among the NFL's dozen head coaches at the end of 1953 were Curly Lambeau of the Redskins, Buck Shaw of the 49ers, Joe Bach of the Steelers, and Hugh Devore of the Packers. Why, you ask, have I singled out these four? Answer: Because they all played under Knute Rockne at Notre Dame.

Rockne's impact on the pro game was almost as great as it was on the college game. So much so that in '53, twenty-two years after his plane crashed in a Kansas wheat field, *a third* of the head coaches in the NFL were former players of his. Indeed, it's possible no one—outside of maybe George Halas—had more influence on the first half century of pro football than Rock.

Consider:

• Every year from 1920, when the NFL was formed, to 1964, there was at least one Rockne pupil—and usually more than one—working in pro ball as either a head coach (eighteen in all), general manager (four), or commissioner (two). (Note: The term "pro ball" also includes the All-America Conference, which gave the NFL stiff competition in the late '40s.)

• Five of Rockne's players coached teams to NFL championships —Norm Barry (1925 Chicago Cardinals), Lambeau (1929–31, '36, '39, and '44 Packers), Hunk Anderson (co-coach of the 1943 Bears), Adam Walsh (1945 Cleveland Rams), and Shaw (1960 Eagles). Total titles: ten.

• As for the GMs, Chile Walsh, Adam's brother, put together the Rams' '45 championship club, and Vince McNally won a pair of titles with the Eagles in '49 and '60. (That's right, both the coach *and* GM of the '60 Eagles were graduates of the Rockne school.)

• The two commissioners, in case you were wondering, were Elmer Layden (NFL, 1941–45) and Jim Crowley (AAC, 1946).

Of course, unlike a lot of fuddy-duddy college coaches in his era (e.g., Amos Alonzo Stagg), Rockne was a supporter of the pro game. He even played some pro ball himself in the pre-NFL days and coached pro teams on the side when he was an ND assistant. One of his biographers, Ray Robinson, writes in *Rockne of Notre Dame*, "He couldn't overlook how much he had learned by playing and coaching in the professional ranks; he remained grateful for the extra money he earned as a pro and felt that he shared a common bond with many of those men who were involved in the sport."

Harry Stuhldreher, one of the famed Four Horsemen, explained the coaching success of Rock's players thusly: "Remember, there were no large coaching staffs in those days. Rockne relied upon his senior lettermen to help impart his know-how. I was fortunate enough to be tutored by varsity quarterback Frank Thomas. It was a valuable experience for me. I was not surprised years later when he developed into a top flight coach at Alabama" —where he turned out Don Hutson, pro football's first great receiver.

Though the T formation took hold of the game after World War II, some Rockne disciples still used his Notre Dame Box offense —a variation of the single wing that featured a balanced line. Jim Leonard, for instance, switched the Steelers from the T to the ND Box in 1945. And Joe Kuharich, who played at Notre Dame a few years after Rockne's death, worked some ND Box–type plays into the Redskins' offense as late as 1954. (As the *Oakland Tribune* described them: "The quarterback crouched under center, then started drifting back to his right. As he stepped back, the ball was snapped to the left half back.")

And let's not forget, the last game Rockne ever coached was a charity affair in December 1930 between his Notre Dame All-Stars and the New York Giants at the Polo Grounds. Unfortunately, it wasn't much of a contest. Some members of the ND team were retired as players and in less than peak condition. The Giants, on the other hand, had finished second in the league that year and had the wondrous Benny Friedman throwing passes for them.

It was a great advertisement for the NFL, though: Pros 22, Rockne's boys 0. Call it Rock's parting gift to pro football.

"Rockne . . . would be in the National [Football] League today himself if he had missed that West-bound plane," *Chicago Tribune* sportswriter George Strickler once said. ". . . It was Rock who kept Lambeau in the game with constant encouragement during the dark days. Lambeau spent a great deal of time with Rockne. Short, unannounced visits, like the one the night before Notre Dame opened the 1930 season against Southern Methodist. Sitting in a car in front of the Oliver Hotel . . ."

One more thing: After the nostalgic Shaw-McNally collaboration in 1960, the NFL was essentially taken over by Vince Lombardi's Packers for the rest of the decade. Lombardi didn't play under Rockne, but he did play under Crowley — another of the Four Horsemen — at Fordham.

Groza, Part 2

Lou Groza's kicking statistics for the 1953 Browns were so ridiculous, they almost didn't seem real. In a season when the rest of the league made 41.3 percent of its field goal tries, Lou "The Toe" was good on twenty-three of twenty-six — 88.5 percent.

When you break it down kick by kick, though, it becomes a little less awe-inspiring. For one thing, Groza booted only four field goals longer than 30 yards. He just happened to be very good at not missing the gimmes — of which there were many. But that alone gave Cleveland a huge edge, especially with the Giants successful on just three of twelve attempts, and the Eagles (four of fifteen) and Steelers (four of twelve) not doing much better.

Lou's 1953 field goal log:

Yds.	No. made (distance)
0–9	1 (9)
10–19	7 (15, 16, 15, 14, 11, 18, 19)
20–29	9 (29, 20, 27, 29, 23, 20, 26, 28, 24)
30–39	3 (37, 30, 30)
40–49	2 (42, 41)
50+	1 (50)

Average distance: 24.9 yards

• • •

One day I was talking with [49ers owner] Tony Morabito about signing for the next year, and I asked for more money. He said no. I asked him three times. No, no, no. This went on for about half an hour. Finally, I said, "OK, I'll take what you're offering." There was maybe a fifteen-hundred or two-thousand-dollar difference between my figure and his.

So he called his secretary and said, "Bring in the contract." And when he handed it to me, I saw it was made out for the salary *I* wanted. I said, "What in the world . . . ?"

Tony said, "I just wanted to see if you'd take less." —Lowell Wagner, Niners defensive back, 1949–55

• • •

Bert Rechichar's 1953

We all have our soft spots for certain players and certain seasons. Me, I never cease to be amazed by the year Bert Rechichar had for the Colts in 1953.

Rechichar, a six-foot-one, 209-pound cornerback, didn't punt the ball to the moon like the Lions' Yale Lary or return kicks like the Giants' Emlen Tunnell, but he did just about everything else you could ask of a DB. A summary of Bert's contributions in '53 (a twelve-game season):

- Seven interceptions (tied for eighth in the league), one of which he returned 36 yards for a touchdown.

- Three fumble recoveries. (The man was always around the ball.)
- Five field goals (tied for eighth in the league). The first—which came on his *first attempt as a pro*—was a 56-yarder that broke the NFL record, a mark that had stood for nineteen years. Another of his field goals, from 52 yards, was the third longest in league history. (Rechichar wasn't Mr. Automatic by any means, but he did have a strong leg. In the Pro Bowl after the '56 season he single-footedly beat the East by booming field goals of 41, 44, 44, and 52 yards in a 19–10 West win. Naturally, he was voted MVP of the game.)
- Three receptions for 151 yards. Two went for TDs of 66 and 55 yards, and the other was good for 30 yards.

See what I mean? The guy might not have been a Hall of Famer, but he was all football player. And his 1953 was, for a defensive back, about as good as it gets.

Otto Graham and Dr. Sam

In 1954 America's most famous quarterback found himself linked to one of America's most infamous murders. It just so happened that Otto Graham, the Browns' consummate QB, was a good friend of Dr. Sam Sheppard, the suburban Cleveland osteopath who was found guilty of bludgeoning his pregnant wife to death.

The case became a national sensation, and Graham, out of loyalty to Sheppard, didn't shy from the publicity. The Browns would have preferred that he kept a low profile, but Otto told syndicated columnist Bob Considine, "Friendship comes first. I'd do the same thing over again. I don't know if he did it or not. . . . But if they start putting people like that in jail we're going to have a real boom in jail-enlarging. . . . If the trial ended today and a lot of things still weren't cleared up, I'd put my life in his hands."

The Grahams and Sheppards lived just half a mile apart in the exclusive community of Bay Village. They often went waterskiing together on Lake Erie. Three days before Marilyn Sheppard was killed, the two families—Otto had three children, Sam one—took in the stock car races. Marilyn mentioned the outing "in the last letter she ever wrote," Considine reported.

Police let Graham view the murder scene. "There was blood all over the walls, like someone had painted it there," he said years later. He was also one of the select few allowed to visit Sam in the hospital, where the doctor was recovering from injuries he claimed to have suffered while fighting the "bushy-haired" intruder who had murdered his wife. The Grahams even gave statements to investigators, though they didn't think they added much to what was already known.

At one point a New York paper published a story that Otto's wife, Beverly, was having an affair with Sam. The real story, Otto said, was quite different. At a party, Beverly wanted to go for a ride in Sam's new two-seater sports car, so "he drove her from the party in it, and I followed in another car. That's all there was to it."

Over time Graham changed his mind about his friend. To him, Sheppard's refusal to take a lie-detector test or to help much with the investigation suggested Sam had something to hide. Otto remained convinced of the doctor's guilt even after his verdict was overturned in a second trial in 1966.

Following his release, Sheppard married a German divorcee who had written to him in prison. The woman's half sister—you can't make this stuff up—was the wife of Joseph Goebbels. So not only was there a connection between Otto Graham and Dr. Sam Sheppard, there were just three degrees of separation between Otto and Adolph Hitler's propaganda chief.

Catching 'Em Napping

One of the more notable football deaths in 1954 was the passing of the Sleeper Play. The end was quick and relatively painless. On the season's first play from scrimmage, the Rams' Skeet Quinlan hid out near the sideline, undetected by the Colts secondary, and caught an 80-yard touchdown pass with no one around him. The next day, without even summoning a quorum, NFL Commissioner

Bert Bell condemned the play as "unsportsmanlike" and declared it illegal. (Though it's still used in touch football games across the country, especially on Thanksgiving morning.)

"This thing should never have happened in the first place," Bell said. "No matter how many good rules we have, somebody also comes up with something that we have to correct."

The Sleeper Play (a.k.a. the Hideout Play) was a neat bit of trickery, as old as football itself. It was particularly effective in the days before stadium lights. Clubs would wait until dusk, when the fringes of the field were less visible, then spring it on unsuspecting defenses.

It usually worked like this: A receiver would jog toward his bench—as if he were going out of the game—but would stop just inside the sideline. There, his uniform would blend in with those of other players standing in the area, and he'd practically disappear. At the snap of the ball, he'd bolt downfield . . . and be totally uncovered.

The Bears' Luke Johnsos once pulled the stunt in *broad daylight* by using the linesman, three-hundred-pound Wilfrid Smith, as a screen. Nobody on the Giants defense noticed Johnsos until the 29-yard TD throw was on its way. It turned out to be the only score in a 6–0 Chicago win, one that enabled the Bears to tie Portsmouth for first place in 1932 and force a playoff for the title, the league's first championship game.

But there was always something a little cheesy about the play, a little unmanly. Far from being clever, it seemed one step removed from slipping the ball under your jersey. That's where Bell was coming from when he made his ruling. "We're too good for this," is what he basically was saying.

And he was right, of course. It wasn't the 1920s anymore. Clubs didn't need to resort to such dubious tactics to put points on the board. Heck, the Rams scored *forty-eight* that day in their shutout of the Colts.

A few things about the Last Sleeper Play: It wasn't just the first scrimmage play of the season, it was the first scrimmage play of

Weeb Ewbank's Hall of Fame coaching career. How's that for a housewarming gift? (He'd just left Paul Brown's staff in Cleveland and taken over the Colts.)

Also, the cornerback who was burned on the play was none other than Don Shula (who was also the Colts' defensive signal caller). Years later, when he was well on his way to Canton himself, Shula told *Sports Illustrated*'s Paul Zimmerman, "I remember thinking: Where in hell is [Rams quarterback Norm Van Brocklin] throwing the ball?"

Maybe the best part, though, is that the teams met again in the next-to-last game of the season, and the Colts avenged their 48–0 humiliation by upsetting the Rams 22–21 in Los Angeles. Victories don't get much sweeter than that.

Most Brutal Way to Break Up the Wedge

No play better illustrates the sheer nastiness of the '50s than a kickoff that took place at Kezar Stadium on October 24, 1954.

Early in the second quarter, the Lions' Gil Mains ran downfield to bust up the wedge and—in a moment of temporary insanity—flew *feet-first* into it. One of his cleats plunged into the thigh of the Niners' Hardy Brown, who needed fifteen stitches to repair the damage.

"His cleats raked Hardy along the chest and arm," the *Oakland Tribune* reported, "and then one ripped through his pants to inflict the deep cut. However, with the wound closed by stitches, Brown came back to play the entire second half on defense."

Ouch.

Mains was no ordinary projectile, either. He was a six-foot-two defensive end who weighed 243 pounds, a healthy fifty more than his victim. In other words, the injury could have been a lot worse—as Brown was well aware.

"When I first looked down [at all the blood]," he supposedly said later, "I thought I was Christine Jorgensen." (Historical note: Jorgensen had one of the first sex-change operations, in 1952.)

Two weeks later, according to the *Tribune*, Brown still had "a hole the size of a golf ball" where Mains had landed on him. Not that there were many tears shed for Hardy. He was a ruthless player in his own right who left much wreckage behind in his career — broken noses, broken jaws, broken cheeks, broken everything.

Still, what Mains did was pretty extreme, even by the (low) standards of the times. Turns out he'd gotten the idea from Lions roommate Bob Dove, who had regaled him with stories about the Giants' Nello Falaschi, back in the '40s, planting his cleats in the chest of the Redskins' Willie Wilkin on a kickoff.

"It looked like three white stripes on Willie's chest," Dove told me, " — the scar tissue from the cleats."

Anyway, there was Mains, flying down the field on the kickoff, "and here comes Hardy Brown," Gil once said.

> And I'm thinking: *Oh, Christ*. I'd been told all these [scary] stories about him. He wasn't that large, but he was built like a fireplug.
>
> And I don't know what made me do it, but just as he got to me, instead of getting hit, I jumped up feet-first and went straight at him. . . . He went off the field, got stitched up, came back out in the second half and damned if, on the second or third play, he didn't hit [Lions fullback] Bill Bowman and break his nose.

That wasn't the only time Mains led with his cleats, apparently. He also tore into the Rams' Les Richter, he claimed. ("The official came over and said, 'That's the dirtiest thing I ever saw.' And I said, 'Well, run the film of the last time we played, and watch when he comes up and hits me on the back of the head when I'm not looking.'")

Finally, after Mains had cut open a few players, Commissioner Bert Bell phoned him and said, "Son, you can't do that." So Gil stopped doing "that."

"It's not all glory," he said. "I remember one time I went in cleats-first, and when I jumped up they all scattered. It had rained, and I hit on my bottom and looked like a speed boat going through the water."

Slowing Down "Hurryin' Hugh"

Few hits in NFL history have reverberated quite like the one the 49ers' Hugh McElhenny took on October 31, 1954. Sure, Chuck Bednarik's splattering of Frank Gifford several years later got tons of attention—it happened, after all, in New York—but it didn't change the way the game was played. McElhenny's separated left shoulder did.

At the time, you see, it was still legal for the ball carrier to get up after he was knocked down and scramble for more yardage—as long, that is, as his forward progress hadn't been stopped. Naturally, this led to plenty of late hitting and piling on, which in turn led to plenty of injuries. As far back as 1932, Commissioner Joe Carr questioned the wisdom of the pros' dead-ball rule, which was meant to create more excitement but posed greater dangers than the college rule.

"When a player, who has momentarily stopped and is partially on the ground, is struck, opportunities for injury are great," Carr said. On top of that, rarely had "any player who once had been thrown [to the ground] ever made any appreciable gains."

Still, ball carriers would take the risk. That's what McElhenny was doing late in the fourth quarter against the Bears when rookie safety Stan Wallace, according to the *Oakland Tribune*, "apparently leaped into the pileup, driving McElhenny's shoulder into the ground." As Hugh was being attended to on the Chicago sideline, the *Tribune* reported, Bears coach George Halas and "a number of his players" could be heard sniping at him, "What's the matter? Can't you take it?"

McElhenny had been off to the greatest start of his Hall of Fame career. He was leading the league in rushing with 515 yards and averaging a ridiculous 8 yards a carry. (He still cracked the top ten in rushing that year, even though he missed the last six games. And his running mates in San Francisco's "Million Dollar Backfield," Joe Perry and John Henry Johnson, finished 1-2.)

The Niners wound up losing to the Bears, 31–27, the beginning of a three-game skid that dropped them from 4-0-1 to 4-3-1 . . . and out of contention once again. But some good did come of their—and McElhenny's—misfortune. After the season the NFL wised up and rewrote Article 1, Rule 7, Section 7, Item 1, Part 3 so there would be an "immediate whistle to kill [the] ball when [the] runner touches the ground with any part of his body, except hands and feet, while in the grasp of an opponent(s), irrespective of [the] grasp being broken."

Even the crusty Halas could agree with that. In the modern game, he said, "the extra yard is so unnecessary, compared to what it used to be, that it is foolish to try to make it. . . . In the case of McElhenny, think how many yards the 49ers were deprived of through the injury. If he hadn't been hurt needlessly, he is such a runner that he might have made 50–60 yards on the next play. Instead, he was lost for many games."

• • •

There isn't enough money in the world to get anyone to play football. Money is just the excuse you give your wife for playing. If I'm back next year, it's only because I like it. — Rams running back Skeet Quinlan

• • •

The Military Pipeline

Service teams turned out some darn good players in the postwar years. Joe Perry went straight from Alameda (California) Naval Training Station to stardom with the 49ers, and Night Train Lane, another Hall of Famer, did likewise with the Rams after serving in the army.

Then there's Big Daddy Lipcomb, the Colts' Pro Bowl defensive tackle, who learned his football in the marines, and Packers fullback Howie Ferguson, the number two rusher in the league in 1955, who was a product of Navy ball.

And let's not forget "Touchdown Tommy" Wilson. As a rookie with the Rams in '56—a year after playing for the Shaw Air Force Base team—he set an NFL record by rushing for 223 yards in a game.

All of these guys—and others like them—spent little or no time in college. But the training they got in service ball enabled them to carve out successful pro careers.

Meanwhile, in the CFL . . .

Highlights from October 20, 1956:

When the third quarter of the Winnipeg-Calgary game ended, timekeeper Jimmy Dunn took out his gun, pointed it skyward, and pulled the trigger, just like he always did.

This time, though, he got a very different result: a dead duck plopped at his feet.

You might say Dunn was startled. As Gab Grundy of the *Winnipeg Free Press* wrote, "Dunn always thought his timer's gun was a most un-lethal weapon."

Turns out a fun-loving fan had sneaked the deceased fowl into the stadium and hurled it at Dunn as he fired the gun.

"Not many people saw it, which was a pity," Grundy said. "It was one of the few bright spots in the Bomber defeat."

That same night the Montreal Alouettes beat the Hamilton Tiger-Cats 82–14—still the most points ever scored by a Canadian team . . . by twelve. (It's also nine more than the NFL record set by the Bears against the Redskins in the 1940 title game.)

Even more amazing, Montreal did of all its scoring in *the first three quarters*—on twelve touchdowns, nine extra points, and one rouge (a punt into or through the end zone that isn't returned). The Alouettes gained 799 yards, also a mark that still stands, forced nine turnovers, and, somehow, still managed to punt three times.

But wait, it gets better.

A week later the two teams met in Hamilton—and the Ti-Cats, bent on revenge, blew out the Alouettes 50–14.

A 104-point swing in the space of seven days. Now *there's* a record that will never be broken.

Because I don't bleed if I don't know I'm cut. — Rams coach Sid Gillman on why he didn't read newspapers

· · ·

Attack of the Soccer-Style Kickers

Imagine this happening today — in anything but a Disney movie:

A recreational soccer player from London flies to the United States to visit his older brother. He's never seen an American football game. Just for fun, they start going to a nearby field with a football; the older brother holds while the younger one kicks.

Little Brother picks it up so quickly that Big Brother sends letters to several pro teams, asking for a tryout. The Falcons grant one but don't offer a job. Then the kid brother auditions for the Lions, and they sign him to a contract. In his fifth game, just five months after arriving in this country, he boots six field goals to break an NFL record that had stood for fifteen years.

That, amazingly, is how Garo Yepremian broke into the league in 1966 (before going on to greater fame with the Dolphins in the '70s). He — and his kooky, side-footed technique — rocked pro football like a Dick Butkus hit. Granted, the transition from straight-on kickers to soccer-stylers took more than twenty years to complete. (The Browns' Mark Moseley was still toeing 'em through as late as the '86 season.) But the revolution was underway, a revolution that, for better or worse, would bring football closer to its roots, make it more about the foot again.

It's one of more significant developments in the game's history, and yet few fans know much of the backstory. For instance, not only was Yepremian *not* the first sidewinder — as they were called in those days — neither was Pete Gogolak, who broke in, amid great ballyhoo, with the Bills two years earlier. They were merely the first soccer-style kickers *in the pros*.

No, the tale goes back quite a bit further than that. In fact, it begins in a Nazi labor camp outside Salzburg, Austria, in 1942. It begins with Fred Bednarski.

Bednarski was the University of Texas junior who — against Arkansas in 1957 — booted college football's first soccer-style field goal. There's been a lot of confusion about that. A 2001 story in the *Cincinnati Enquirer* claimed Hank Hartong, a soccer player from the Netherlands who played for the University of Cincinnati, was the first sidewinder in 1961, kicking an extra point two weeks before Gogolak did for Cornell.

"Hey, I invented something," Hartong is quoted as saying.

Uh, no, you didn't, Hank. Fred Bednarski did. (Unless, of course, somebody in some remote outpost came up with the idea before he did. In the pre-ESPN era, you can never be 100 percent sure.)

As for Hartong, he wasn't even the second soccer-styler . . . or the third. Ever hear of Evan Paoletti, a kicker for the Huron College (South Dakota) Scalpers in 1958? (Talk about off the beaten path.) How about Walt Doleschal, who did the booting for Lafayette College (Pennsylvania) from 1959 to '61? They, along with Bednarski, are The Forgotten, the first wave of side-foot kickers.

Bednarski, a strong-legged fullback, had been serving as the Longhorns' kickoff man when he was sent in to try a 38-yard field goal that day in '57. It was early in the game, and coach Darrell Royal was hoping to come away with *something* after Texas had driven deep into Razorbacks territory.

The week before Royal had had him try a 55-yarder against Oklahoma, not expecting much. "If you miss," he told Bednarski, "it'll be better than a punt, anyway, so go on in there." That boot, at the limit of Fred's range, had landed short; but the kick in Fayetteville — with Arkansas governor Orval Faubus in the crowd, rooting on his tenth-ranked Hogs — was nothing out of the ordinary. He'd made field goals that long many times in practice.

And sure enough, Bednarski knocked it through — with plenty of room to spare — to give the Longhorns a 3–0 lead. Still, it got barely a mention in the Sunday newspapers, just a sentence in the stories about Texas's 17–0 upset: "Fred Bednarski, a soccer-type kicker who uses a sideways foot motion, kicked the field goal after the Longhorns had been halted . . . in the first quarter" (Associated Press); "The kick, executed in Bednarski's distinctive soccer style, came early in the opening period" (United Press).

Far bigger news was the presence of Queen Elizabeth II at the Maryland–North Carolina game. That got lots of play in papers all over the land. Besides, who could have envisioned soccer-stylers taking over the game the way they have, literally *changing* the game? Back then, Bednarski was just a curiosity, like an ambidextrous quarterback or a three-hundred-pound lineman. He was a sideshow, somebody to entertain the fans with his booming kickoffs and quirky technique.

Heck, soccer hardly existed in the United States in 1957, and in Texas it was just a rumor. That's why Bednarski, who had grown up with the game in Europe, turned to football when his family sought refuge here after the war.

It's somewhat miraculous, really, that Bednarski even made it to this country. He was just five when the Nazis uprooted his family from their home in Poland and herded them into the aforementioned labor camp. The conditions there were almost unlivable.

"In the wintertime, we had to melt snow to have enough water just to wash up," Bednarski, who later settled in Austin, Texas, once told me. "There was only one toilet at the end of the barracks. In our room we had two families — ours and an older couple. We used a blanket to separate us. There were triple-decker beds, no mattresses. We slept on straw with a sheet over it."

There wasn't much food, either, just servings of watery carrot soup and meager portions of black bread. His parents would try to get by on less so the children could eat a few morsels more. "It really was kind of a slow starvation," he said. "We were just lucky to be liberated by the Americans when we were. My mother weighed about 75, 80 pounds at the end of the war."

Long hours were spent in bomb shelters, waiting for Allied planes to dump their loads on the nearby radio and cannon factories where the men worked. When the skies cleared, the kids would come out —Jews, Poles, Ukrainians, Russians, Czechs—and play soccer with a ball fashioned from rolled up socks. Or maybe someone would have a tennis ball. This was where young Fred learned to kick soccer style, under the gun of the Germans.

After arriving at Ellis Island in 1950, the Bednarskis were supposed to go to North Dakota, where a job was said to be waiting. But there was a problem with the paperwork, and the family wound up on a dairy farm in Smithfield, Texas. Fred's first exposure to football—watching the local high schoolers play under the Friday night lights—didn't exactly make him run out and join a team.

"I couldn't believe what these people were doing—fighting each other!" he said. "But I went out anyway and tried to play with the guys [on the playground], even though I didn't know how to tackle or anything. I guess I just stuck my foot out to see if I could make a tackle that way."

One day in junior high a game was going on during recess, and Fred was called over to give the ball a kick. He was barefooted—times being what they were—but didn't think twice about it. Approaching from an angle, as soccer players do, he proceeded to blast the ball about 40 yards, much farther than his schoolmates had.

Witnessing all this, disbelievingly, was the football coach, Floyd Martine.

"Who *is* that kid?" he said.

"The Polish boy," came the reply.

"Try it one more time," he told Fred. "Let me see you do it again." The Polish boy obliged—and launched another long one.

"He invited me to come out the next day for football and gave me some shoes," Bednarski said. "And that's really when I started learning to play ball."

Almost all the early soccer-stylers have stories like that, stories of smirking onlookers, soaring kicks, and dropped jaws. Jim Long, Paoletti's coach at Huron College, remembered Evan picking up a ball on the practice field, giving it a twirl so it spun upright on the ground, and side-footing it right between the goalposts.

"So he became our kicker that year," Long said. "Kicked extra points [sixteen in all]. I was always open to anything that would help me win a ballgame. I assume he might have tried a field goal or two, too, but we very seldom went for field goals. We were one of the top small college teams in the country and had a very dominant running game."

Paoletti was the exception—the pioneer sidewinder who was actually born in the United States. He'd grown up in St. Louis and been a member of the St. Cecilia Parish soccer team, one of the best in the state. But he'd played football in high school and—here's the funny part—kicked in the conventional fashion, straight on, with a square-toed shoe the school had issued him.

"Well, the school took it away after my senior year—I suppose so they could give it to the next guy," said Paoletti, who gravitated to the Phoenix area after college and scouted teams for the Fiesta Bowl. "So after two years of junior college, I went up to Huron—to play baseball on a scholarship-type thing—and decided to try out for football. I was wearing a pair of soccer shoes I'd brought with me, and at first I was kicking the ball with my toe like I always had. But it didn't work as well with a pair of soccer shoes, so I kinda started messing around with a tee, kicking them sideways. I got more length and accuracy and everything else right off the bat."

His holder, quarterback Dave Bowe, was a little unnerved by the experience at the outset. "I thought he was going to kick me right in the teeth the first time," he told the Associated Press. But it was obvious Paoletti—and Bednarski before him—were on to something. To Evan the logic was inescapable: by using his instep, he was getting "about six inches of my foot against the ball," giving him much more of a margin for error than a straight-on kicker.

It seems hard to believe now, given how fast news travels, that Bednarski and Paoletti had no awareness of each other's exploits. For most of his adult life Paoletti was convinced *he* was the first soccer-styler. Not that he yearned for the recognition, mind you, "but my boys are kinda fond of telling their buddies about it," he said. "Then I found out there was another guy, but I'd never heard of him."

Back at Lafayette College, Walt Doleschal was equally in the dark about Bednarski and Paoletti. Like Bednarski, Doleschal had been a displaced person after the war, a Czechoslovakian forced to live under Nazi rule when Hitler swiped the Sudetenland. One day in 1950 he and his mother, Emilie—his father had died years before—boarded a Scandinavian Airways flight in Hamburg and came over to live with an aunt in New Jersey. An all-state football career at Memorial High in West New York got him recruited by Lafayette, where he starred as a halfback and all-purpose kicker.

The soccer skills he'd developed in his homeland came in handy on the gridiron. He learned to kick in the conventional style—"a pendulum kick," he called it—but on the shorter ones he'd use the side of his foot. He even punted soccer style. On one pet play of Lafayette's, he'd fake an end sweep to draw up the safetymen and quick kick the ball, end over end, over their heads. The ball would roll forever.

"He throws the ball high up in the air, just like a soccer player," his coach, Jim McConlogue, told United Press International. "Then, somehow, he gets off a 50- or 60-yard kick. He gets the job done, but it sure is hard on my nerves."

That was the thing about sidewinders: their method was so, well, foreign, that it made coaches uncomfortable (and their strange accents didn't help any). Some coaches also feared that soccer-stylers booted the ball too low and were more susceptible to blocked kicks. And in the pros there was the issue of roster sizes. In 1957 NFL teams were allowed to carry thirty-five players, eighteen fewer than today. Only three kickers in the league that year could be described as specialists. The others either started at other positions or provided depth.

Which brings us to George Squires. He was another early side-footer, an English immigrant who settled in Laramie, Wyoming, and kicked for the Wyoming Cowboys. Squires told me he was booting soccer-style for Laramie High in 1957, and in just his fourth varsity game at Wyoming in 1962 he sent three field goals through the uprights, setting a school mark. (The next day he scored three goals for the Cowboys' soccer team in a 4–2 victory over Colorado.)

Squires had the stuff to make it in pro ball. He could have been the second soccer-styler after Gogolak. He even went to training camp with the Denver Broncos in 1965 — and was doing well.

"I was hitting 50-yarders," he said. "Then one day the head coach, Mac Speedie, puts me in at running back [the position he'd played in college before concussions sidelined him]. So I run a curl route over the middle, two linebackers hit me and blow my knee out and that's the end of my career. I came back the next year and kicked well again, but they said they just couldn't take a chance on me because the injury was to my plant leg."

Over time, though, the soccer-stylers proved their worth. They were just too good to keep off the roster, even if they had only one function. You can debate whether they boot the ball farther than straight-on kickers, but there's no question they're more reliable. In 1957 NFL kickers made 52.2 percent of their field goal tries; in recent seasons they've made better than 80 percent. There's no comparison.

Beyond that, though, it was just time. Kicking was the most undeveloped area of the game, something teams might spend a few minutes a day practicing. The field goal in pro football's early days just wasn't that big a weapon. Consider: Only once before 1962 was a pro title game decided by a late three-pointer — in 1950, when the Browns' Lou Groza kicked a 16-yarder in the last seconds to beat the Rams. It was a game of touchdowns, not field goals.

But that changed in a hurry. By 1977, two decades after Bednarski's kick, twenty of the NFL's twenty-eight teams had soccer-stylers, most of them from other countries. There were kickers from Austria, from Poland, from Mexico, from Norway. Once it was clear sidewinders were here to stay, clubs went to great lengths to find one of their own.

In the 1960s the Cowboys staged cross-country Kicking Karavans—and looked at anybody with even one good leg. The first year (1967) they drew fourteen hundred candidates in twenty-nine cities, thirty of whom were invited to a four-day "kick-off" at the Cotton Bowl. Three of the finalists, two kickers and a punter, wound up playing in the NFL.

The Chiefs, meanwhile, held tryouts at London's White City Stadium—where they discovered Bobby Howfield, who would go on to kick for the Broncos and Jets. And sometimes a soccer-styler just fell in a team's lap. (See Yepremian.)

Nowadays, of course, kickers are among the biggest impact players in the game and routinely spell the difference between winning and losing. In the past decade or so we've had the Patriots' Adam Vinatieri settle the Super Bowl with a 48-yarder in the final seconds—then do it again two Roman numerals later with a boot from 41 yards.

The kicker has become football's thief in the night, stealing victories from Foxborough to San Diego. And it all started with Fred Bednarski, the Polish Gogolak, in that Texas-Arkansas game half a century ago.

1957 VS. 2010

Little-known fact: Scoring in the NFL has risen from 39.7 points a game in 1957—the year Texas's Fred Bednarski sparked the soccer-style revolution—to 44 in 2010. This increase can be almost entirely attributed to kickers becoming more accurate.

But, hey, don't take *my* word for it. Let's do the math:

In 1957 kickers made 52.2 percent of their field goal tries (128 for 245) and 95.8 percent of their extra-point tries (338 for 353).

By 2010 their success rate had climbed to 82.3 percent for field goals (789 for 959) and 98.9 percent for extra points (1,207 for 1,221).

But if kickers had the same success rate in 2010 as they did in 1957, they would have made 288 fewer field goals, 38 fewer PATs, and scored 902 fewer points. This would have dropped the per-game scoring average from 44 to 40.5 — just *eight-tenths of a point* more than in '57.

Improved kicking has helped disguise the fact that fewer offensive touchdowns are scored today than in the late '50s. The numbers:

1957–59: 1,072 rushing and passing TDs, 5.0 per game

2008–10: 3,411 rushing and passing TDs, 4.4 per game

You'd never know it, though, given all the hullaballoo about the West Coast offense, about four- and five-receiver packages, about Tom Brady throwing for fifty touchdowns in a season and LaDainian Tomlinson scoring thirty-two. (In fact, if anything, the downward trend makes Brady's and Tomlinson's feats even more remarkable.)

Kickers are kind of like three-point shooters in basketball. They've changed the way the game is played — and won.

Outsourcing

By 1977 — twenty years after Polish-born Fred Bednarski kicked college football's first soccer-style field goal — half of the twenty-eight teams in the NFL had imported sidewinders . . . and several others had American ones. Where they came from:

Austria (three): Toni Fritsch (Houston Oilers), Toni Linhart (Baltimore Colts), Ray Wersching (49ers)

Mexico (two): Efren Herrera (Cowboys), Rafael Septien (Rams)

Poland (two): Chester Marcol (Packers), Richie Szaro (Saints)

Canada (one): Roy Gerela (Steelers)

Cyprus (one): Garo Yepremian (Dolphins)

England (one): John Smith (Patriots)

Hungary (one): Steve Mike-Mayer (Lions)

Italy (one): Nick Mike-Mayer (Eagles)

Norway (one): Jan Stenerud (Chiefs)

West Germany (one): Fred Steinfort (Falcons)

U.S. soccer-stylers (six): Chris Bahr (Bengals/born in State College, Pennsylvania), Rolf Benirschke (Chargers/Boston), Joe Danelo (Giants/ Spokane, Washington), Pat Leahy (Jets/St. Louis), Allan Leavitt (Bucs/ St. Petersburg, Florida), Bob Thomas (Bears/Rochester, New York)

Straight-on kickers (eight): Jim Bakken (St. Louis Cardinals), Don Cockroft (Browns), Fred Cox (Vikings), John Leypoldt (Seahawks), Carson Long (Bills), Errol Mann (Raiders), Mark Moseley (Redskins), Jim Turner (Broncos)

The Eagles used *three* foreign-born sidewinders that season. Besides Mike-Mayer, they also had Horst Muhlmann, a West German native, and Ove Johansson, who was from Sweden.

• • •

With speed we have the kind of football which fills the field like a circus, with split lines and spread formations, extremely long pitchouts and passing attacks which go sideline to sideline. Never before has so great an area of the field been opened to the scrimmage play; it has come to the point where every blade of grass must be defended. The field, in fact, is not big enough for today's wide open game. — Giants scout Jack Lavelle on pro football becoming a faster game in the '50s

• • •

Bear in Winter

By 1955 the year-round grind of NFL coaching had begun to take its toll on George Halas. Before the season was even over he announced he was through, was "no longer willing to give up the time coaching consumes during April, May, June and July.

"Those are four long months of tedious preparation when the coach is required to stay in there and slug it out over his films, diagrams and scouting reports," he said. "Those are the months when you may win or lose the championship. I'm 60 years old now, and I've had my fill of the ordeal."

Three years later, though, Papa Bear was recharged and ready to deal with The Ordeal again. He was still, despite his advancing age, the same old Halas — stomping up and down the sideline, fighting for every yard and call. Sometimes, depending on how the game was going, his theatrics were the best part of the show.

Dick Hyland of the *Los Angeles Times* once described George's gyrations this way: "He was up, he was down, he was kneeling, he was walking, he turned his back, he clenched his fists and rammed them into his pockets. He unbuttoned his coat, buttoned it, snapped his hat brim up, snapped it down. He yelled at his players and yelled at the officials."

But getting back to our story . . .

Early in the fourth game of 1958, Halas took exception to the way the Rams' Les Richter and Don Burroughs rode Bears receiver Harlon Hill out of bounds. Racing to the scene of the crime, he screamed for a penalty, demanded — as only one of a league's founding fathers can — that these hoodlums be brought to justice.

Did he, in his righteous anger, breathe a little too heavily on Burroughs, possibly even bump him? Hmmm . . . could be. What we do know is that the Rams defensive back eyed the Grumpy Old Man before him and, according to the *Long Beach Independent*, "shoved [him] nearly off his feet."

Abe Gibron, Chicago's double-wide offensive guard, was quick to defend his boss and pushed Burroughs back. But Halas defused the situation before it got out of control. The Bears played in a barely disguised rage the rest of the afternoon, forcing six turnovers and routing the Rams 31–10. George Strickler of the *Chicago Tribune* called it "one of the roughest and most bitter contests seen in Wrigley Field since the days of the old Packer-Bear donnybrooks. . . . Officials were repeatedly breaking up budding brawls."

The following Sunday in San Francisco, Halas found himself in the eye of another storm. Late in the second quarter, with George politicking from the sideline, referee Ron Gibbs reversed a fumble ruling and gave the ball to Chicago. The Kezar Stadium crowd went crazy—and held up the game for a good five minutes with its booing.

At halftime, as Halas was walking to the locker room, a 49ers fan—one William Dunn of Palo Alto—came out of the stands and grabbed him by the shoulder. In a flash, a swarm of George's assistants began pummeling the assailant. (There was even a photo the next day in the *San Francisco Chronicle*—one of the greatest photos in pro football history, for my money—of Halas's son, George Jr., kicking Dunn squarely in the . . . behind.)

"Bear assistant coach Phil Handler went ahead on points with a couple of jolts to the whiskers," the *Chronicle*'s Bob Stevens reported, "and George Allen, who helped Luke Johnsos work the press box phones, scored. An unidentified member of the Bear sideline family, late arriving on the scene, jarred Dunn with a crisp right hand as Dunn was struggling to break free from the encircling arms of the law."

Dunn was no bottle-waving lowlife; he was a thirty-three-year-old chemical engineer—dressed in a *suit coat*, no less. He was just tired of seeing Halas get his way. And clearly, the flip-flop on the fumble had contributed to the Bears' 27–14 win.

"First they gave the ball to the 49ers, then after Papa Bear straightened them out they gave it to the Bears," Dunn said. "I was just going to give him a piece of my mind. I . . . was going to tell him we have plenty of officials out there and don't need his help. I never took a swing at him. [He] just got me riled. I apologize to all concerned."

The incident raised once more the issue of Halas's sideline antics, particularly his habit of wandering far outside the coaching box. Rams coach Sid Gillman had one of the stronger opinions on the subject. "No coach," he said, "should be allowed to roam all over the place. If I was an official, a coach walking up and down the sidelines yelling at the decisions certainly would affect me."

NFL Commissioner Bert Bell, as was his wont, refused to make a big deal of it. But he did send the league's supervisor of officials to the Bears' next game, in Los Angeles, to monitor the situation.

A mere 102,368 showed up at the Coliseum that Sunday, a league record that stood for decades.

So ended eight days in the life of George Halas in 1958, eight days in his — and the NFL's — thirty-ninth season. His eighth and last championship was still five years away.

Fearsome Foursomes

Pro football's original Fearsome Foursome, near as I can tell, was an offensive backfield — which makes sense when you stop and think about it. After all, in 1949, when Frank O'Gara of the *Philadelphia Inquirer* dubbed the Eagles' backs "Football's Fearsome Foursome," there were no four-man defensive fronts in the NFL. The five-man line, with a middle guard, was the norm.

(Besides, quarterback Tommy Thompson, halfbacks Steve Van Buren and Bosh Pritchard, and fullback Joe Muha *were* pretty scary back then. The Eagles won their second straight title that year, dropping only one game.)

In the '50s and '60s, though, the nickname was attached to several front fours, at least five by my count. The Giants had the first Fearsome Foursome, but soon they were getting competition from the Colts' Fearsome Foursome — to be followed by the Chargers', Lions', and Rams' Fearsome Foursomes. Talk about identity confusion. Fortunately, people got Fearsome Foursomed out and started coming up with other nicknames for D-lines, like the Purple People Eaters and the Steel Curtain.

Brief thumbnails on the various Fearsome Foursomes:

GIANTS (1958–63)

From left to right: Jim Katcavage, Dick Modzelewski, Rosey Grier, Andy Robustelli.

Hall of Fame: Robustelli.

Pro Bowls: Robustelli 7, Katcavage 3, Grier 2, Modzelewski 1.

Average height, weight: 6-2¼, 250.3.

League leaderships: Scoring defense (three times), total defense (once), rushing defense (once), sacks (once), interceptions (once), turnovers (once). The Giants also had the best pass defense—if you go by their opponents' quarterback rating—one year, and that's at least partially the result of pressure from up front.

Notes: By far the smallest of the Fearsome Foursomes. . . . Went 0-4 in championship games—and lost another in '63 when John LoVotere replaced Grier at right tackle. . . . Did win a championship in '56 with Walt Yowarsky starting at left end and Katcavage, then a rookie, filling in at multiple spots.

Fear factor (on a scale of 1 to 5 screams): 4 screams.

COLTS (1957–60)

From left to right: Gino Marchetti, Art Donovan, Big Daddy Lipscomb, Don Joyce.

Hall of Fame: Marchetti and Donovan.

Pro Bowls: Marchetti 11, Donovan 5, Lipscomb 3, Joyce 1.

Average height, weight: 6-3¾, 261.

League leaderships: Rushing defense (twice), pass defense (thrice), interceptions (twice), turnovers (twice).

Notes: Beat the Giants for the '58 (23–17) and '59 (30–16) titles. . . . Forced New York to punt in overtime of the '58 game, setting the stage for Johnny Unitas to drive the Colts to the winning touchdown. . . . Finished next to last in sacks in '59 but still picked off eighteen more passes than anybody else (forty total)—which shows you how misleading sacks can be. . . . Marchetti, Lipscomb, and Joyce all made the Pro Bowl in '58. . . . When Big Daddy, a six-foot-six, 284-pound behemoth, was suitably inspired, this unit was a total nightmare.

Fear factor: 5 screams.

CHARGERS (1961–62)

From left to right: Earl Faison, Bill Hudson, Ernie Ladd, Ron Nery.

Hall of Fame: None.

AFL All-Star Games: Faison 5, Ladd 4, Hudson 1.

Average height, weight: 6-6, 269.3.

League leaderships: Scoring defense (once), total defense (once), pass defense (once), interceptions (once), turnovers (once).

Notes: The tallest and heaviest of the Fearsome Foursomes. . . . Ladd's length in the middle of the line—he was six nine—was particularly troublesome for quarterbacks. . . . Didn't stay together long, but had a fabulous year in '61, when they led the AFL in every major department except rushing defense and sacks. (They were second in both categories.) . . . The "D" had forty-nine interceptions and forced sixty-six turnovers that season, mind-boggling numbers that are still AFL-NFL records. . . Broncos QB Frank Tripucka compared playing against Ladd and Company to "throwing in a forest. Those big so-and-sos make you throw the ball up in the air to get it over them. You're laying it up there to get picked off." . . . Lost the '61 championship game to Houston, 10–3, despite intercepting six more passes.

Fear factor: 3 screams (2½ of them generated by the humongous Ladd, who was a pro wrestler on the side).

LIONS (1962, 1964–65)
From left to right: Darris McCord, Alex Karras, Roger Brown, Sam Williams.
Hall of Fame: None.

Pro Bowls: Brown 6, Karras 4, McCord 1.

Average height, weight: 6-4, 258.3.

League leaderships: Total defense (twice), rushing defense (once), sacks (twice).

Notes: Much of their reputation stemmed from their Thanksgiving Day mauling of the mighty Packers in '62. Before a national television audience, they sacked Bart Starr *eleven* times, once for a safety, returned a fumble for a touchdown, and held Green Bay to 122 yards in a 26–14 win. (It was 26–0 after three quarters.) . . . And that might very well have been Vince Lombardi's greatest team. The Pack didn't lose another game all year. . . . Say this for the Lions' foursome: they put the quarterback on the ground, averaging fifty-two sacks in '62, '64, and '65 . . . '63 doesn't count because the incorrigible Karras was suspended that season for betting on games. . . . Never made it to the title game because the Packers kept getting in the way.

Fear factor: 3½ screams.

RAMS (1964–68)

From left to right: Deacon Jones, Merlin Olsen, Rosey Grier, Lamar Lundy.

Hall of Fame: Jones and Olsen.

Pro Bowls: Olsen 14, Jones 8, Grier 2, Lundy 1.

Average height, weight: 6-5½, 267.8.

League leaderships: Scoring defense (once), total defense (once), rushing defense (twice), sacks (once — tied), pass defense (once), interceptions (once — tied).

Notes: Never finished out of the top five in any significant defensive department after George Allen took over as coach in '66. . . . Jones and Olsen played side by side for a solid decade (1962–71). It doesn't get any better than that. . . . Lundy, a fine basketball player at Purdue, stood six foot seven. He started his NFL career as a tight end and probably would have developed into one of the best if he hadn't switched to defense. . . . Grier, of course, came from the Giants' Fearsome Foursome. When Rosey retired after the '66 season, the Rams got Roger Brown, one of the Lions' Fearsome Foursome, to take his place. . . . Grier was on the downside, though, when he joined the Rams — as was Brown. . . . Amazingly, this line didn't win a single playoff game. But that didn't keep Jones, Olsen, and Allen from reaching the Hall.

Fear factor: 4½ screams. (Awarded half-scream bonus for appearing as a group on *Shindig*, a rock 'n' roll show on ABC in the '60s, and singing "Since You're Gone." The Rolling Stones were on the same night and performed "Heart of Stone.")

A Kinder, Gentler Paul Brown?

For a book we collaborated on two decades ago, *The Pro Football Chronicle*, Bob O'Donnell dug up a version of the speech — or rather,

The Speech—Paul Brown gave at the start of the Browns' training camp every year. It's an absolute classic. Years later I came across an earlier version of The Speech that ran in the *Canton Repository* in 1956. I couldn't help noticing a few differences, such as:

1956 speech: "If you're a drinker, you may as well leave now. The smoking should be stopped for your own good, but if you must have one don't do it around here or in public. Again, you will be looked up to by youngsters, and nothing is worse for a youngster than to see his football hero smoking."

1959 speech: Makes no mention of drinking or smoking.

1956: "We will have a bed check, and if you sneak out after the check and we find out about it, don't bother to come back for your belongings—we'll send them to you."

1959: "For the player who sneaks out after bed check there's an automatic fine of $500."

1956: "From time to time you will be interviewed by members of the press here at Hiram [College]. Treat them as you would me and answer their questions. We've always had good relations with the press, and the writers at the camp won't ask you any embarrassing questions. They have been here for several years, all of them, and if you start talking out of turn I'm sure they will clean it up. They aren't interested in making a fool of any of you players."

1959: Doesn't mention the newspaper guys. (Then again, maybe he did and the reporter scribbling down The Speech, Gordon Cobbledick of the *Cleveland Plain Dealer*, omitted it—for any number of reasons . . . such as self-preservation.)

At any rate, in the '56 speech Brown comes across as a real hardass; whereas in '59 he seems to have mellowed a bit. Of course, in '56 he was coming off ten straight championship games. He was invincible. By '59 he'd had a taste or two of humility—and the world was changing.

Hoopla

Most NFL clubs in the '50s had off-season basketball teams that toured around playing games against high school faculties. It was good way to mingle with the fan base and, oh yes, pick up some extra change.

But the 49ers took it to a whole new level in February 1958. They played a four-game series against the Harlem Globetrotters in San Jose, San Francisco, Oakland, and Sacramento. The total attendance was 26,293, with a high of 14,430 at the Cow Palace that, according to the *San Mateo Times*, was "just short of the Pacific Coast record."

Make no mistake, the Niners could play some hoops. R. C. Owens had been a star at the College of Idaho, and Gordy Soltau (Minnesota), Billy Wilson (San Jose State), Clyde Conner (Pacific), Joe Arenas (Nebraska-Omaha), and Bob St. Clair (San Francisco) had all lettered in the sport. St. Clair stood six foot nine, and the six-three Owens could really jump. Against Bay Area competition they were nigh unbeatable.

The 49ers put in some trick plays for the 'Trotters. One involved Hugh McElhenny dribbling up court behind a flying wedge of blockers. Another had Y. A. Tittle throwing a baseline-to-baseline pass to Owens — just like his "Alley-Oops" to R. C. on the football field. Also, Soltau, the Niners' kicker, wasn't bad at placekicking the ball into the basket.

Meadowlark Lemon and his mates won all four games, of course, but they were nice enough to keep the scores respectably close. From the sound of things, the first halves were played relatively straight, and in the second halves the teams clowned around.

"The big crowds both nights [in San Francisco and Oakland] were more a tribute to the popularity of the 49er football players briefly essaying a basketball role than the Harlemites' worldwide reputation," the *Oakland Tribune*'s Alan Ward wrote. "Abe Saperstein's 'Trotters for years have played in the Bay Area, but not in recent seasons to such crowds as those of the current weekend."

Four days that didn't quite shake the basketball world — but were still a blast:

Date	Site (attendance)	Score	49ers' high scorer(s)
February 6	San Jose (3,300)	'Trotters, 58–43	Billy Wilson, 10
February 7	San Francisco (14,430)	'Trotters, 56–45	Wilson/Joe Arenas, 10
February 8	Oakland (5,876)	'Trotters, 77–66	Gordy Soltau, 16
February 9	Sacramento (2,687)	'Trotters, 58–52	Arenas, 15

Life Is a Bowl of . . . Cereal

Shipwreck Kelly and Chris Cagle are fondly remembered as the last player-owners in the NFL. They bought the Brooklyn Dodgers in 1933, and Kelly still had a piece of the club as late as '41 (by which time he was retired).

In 1958, though, Rams halfback Ron Waller tried his darnedest to buy the Chicago Cardinals — and might have succeeded if he hadn't been dealing with a buffoon like Walter Wolfner, who ran the Cards for his wife, owner Violet Bidwill.

Waller was just twenty-five and beginning his fourth year in the pros. As a rookie, he'd finished fourth in the league in rushing and played in the Pro Bowl. This hardly made him a rich man, though. He was just lucky enough to be married to Marjorie Durant, heiress to the Post cereal fortune. Marjorie's famed grandmother, Marjorie Merriweather Post, was "anxious for me to get out of the contact part of football, into management," Waller said. "It was her suggestion that we buy a team."

Since the Cardinals were one of the league's weak sisters, perennially fighting a losing financial battle with the Bears, Waller offered $1.5 million for them. This, for the record, was *sixty times* what Kelly and Cagle had paid for the Dodgers a quarter century before. Waller had big plans for the franchise. He wanted to move it to Miami, and he wanted to get his old Rams teammate, Hall of Famer Norm Van Brocklin, to be his quarterback. (Van Brocklin had "retired" in hopes of forcing a trade — and wound up going to the Eagles.)

But Wolfner rejected the bid, as he had others he'd recently received for the Cardinals. "I seem to make one mistake," he said. "When the phone rings I pick it up and say hello. When I show people the courtesy of answering the phone and listening to them, everybody gets the idea the Cards are for sale. I'm going out to Lake Forest tomorrow and sign a contract for our training there next summer. Maybe that fact will help to convince people we're staying in Chicago."

Two years later Wolfner moved the Cardinals to St. Louis.

Waller was still optimistic he'd get a team — in a couple of years, perhaps, when he expected the NFL to add two franchises. And the league did add two franchises, the Cowboys and the Vikings. But by then his marriage to the cereal heiress was on the rocks. In 1961, the year after he finished his career with the Chargers, he was divorced.

Judge Charlie

Nobody remembers today, but the head linesman in the 1958 NFL title game — the celebrated Sudden Death Game between the Colts and Giants — was Charlie Berry. The reason this matters is that less than three months earlier Berry umpired in the World Series (won by the Yankees over the Braves in seven games). In fact, he called the balls and strikes in games two and six.

It was the third and last time he accomplished this double. No one else has done it even once. The other times were in 1946 (Red Sox legend Ted Williams's only Series) and 1950 (when he was the plate umpire for the final game of the Yanks' sweep of the Phillies).

In the '46 Series, by the way, the umpiring crew included not only Berry but also Pro Football Hall of Famer Cal Hubbard. Cal umped the plate in two of the games, Charlie in another. (Unfortunately, none of them was the game in which Williams, frustrated by the Cardinals' shift, got headlines for laying down a bunt.)

Berry was the sports equivalent of a Supreme Court justice. He'd played professionally in both baseball (Athletics, Red Sox, White Sox) and football (Frankford Yellow Jackets) and, for more than twenty years, easily moved from one to the other every October.

The Quarterback-Golfer

Early in his career, when he wasn't throwing passes to R. C. Owens, the 49ers' John Brodie spent a few off-seasons trying to make it on the PGA Tour. He was a good enough golfer to win the 1958 Northern California Amateur, and in '59 he qualified for the U.S. Open. He missed the cut at Winged Foot, though, shooting 76-77—153. (On the plus side, he did finish a stroke ahead of an amateur named Jack Nicklaus.)

"I like both golf and football," he said, "but have no intentions of giving up football. The two sports simply fit well into my schedule. I can play golf up to July 10, take three weeks to get in shape for football and then report to the 49ers around August 1."

Three weeks of preparation for the season. Welcome to the NFL in 1959.

Brodie was perfectly capable of shooting a low score on the Tour. He just had trouble putting four decent rounds together. At the 1961 Lucky International, for instance, he fired a 66 on the first day—a stroke off the lead—but wound up missing the cut. In the end, he just shot too many "Red Granges." (That's what golfers in that era called a 77, which was Red's jersey number.)

Here's all you really need to know about Brodie's pro golf experience: In the second round of the 1959 Bing Crosby Pro-Am at Pebble Beach, he knocked his tee ball on the 110-yard seventh hole right into the cup.

Unfortunately, he'd hit his first tee ball into the ocean—and had to write a "3" on his scorecard.

A Different NFL

It's hard to believe how young the NFL was in 1941, the last year before the war. Only eleven players in the league were thirty or older — eleven! — and Frank Bausch, the Eagles' center, was the oldest at thirty-three. Four teams didn't have *any* players as old as thirty. One, the Rams, didn't have any older than twenty-seven.

Almost half the coaches — the Steelers' Buff Donelli (thirty-four), the Rams' Dutch Clark (thirty-five), the Lions' Bill Edwards (thirty-six), and the Redskins' Ray Flaherty (thirty-eight) — were in their thirties. Even the owners were kids. The Dodgers' Dan Topping and the Rams' Dan Reeves were twenty-nine, and the Eagles' Lex Thompson (thirty) and the Lions' Fred Mandel (thirty-three) were in their early thirties. It was, in every respect, a young man's game.

The NFL wasn't nearly as spry in 1959 — the last year before a different war began, the decade-long battle against the American Football League. No fewer than sixty-six players were in their thirties that season, and four clubs had eight thirtysomethings — almost as many as there were in the entire NFL in '41. There wasn't a single coach under forty-two; the youngest owner, Reeves, was forty-seven.

What caused this change? Several things, it would seem. First, the league had become more stable, more profitable, and with this came more continuity. Eight of the dozen franchises in '59 had the same owners (or families owning them) as they did eighteen years earlier.

Also, the game was radically different. Single-platoon football was out, and free substitution was in; the single wing had been replaced by the less-punishing T formation; and salaries, of course, kept going up. All this led to longer careers. Pro football had ceased being merely a means to an end; it was becoming an end in itself.

The same goes for the coaches. They were just another part of the NFL's increasing professionalism — a more experienced ruling class to go along with the more experienced worker class. In the early years you had player-coaches and players who, upon retirement, stepped right into head coaching jobs. No longer. (Indeed, only one more player would move directly into the coach's office after calling it a career—Norm Van Brocklin, who quarterbacked the Eagles to the title in 1960 and took over the expansion Vikings the following season.)

Granted, the NFL was bigger in 1959, too—432 roster spots vs. 330 in '41. But that hardly explains a sixfold increase in thirty-and-over players. No, pro football wasn't just getting better, it was getting older.

"The Turk" Run Amok

With more thirtysomethings on NFL rosters in the late '50s, it was harder for rookies to make teams, even high draft picks. In 1958 the Colts actually cut their second-rounder, running back Bob Stransky—*the twenty-fourth overall selection.* The next year the Giants cut their first- and second-rounders, quarterback Lee Grosscup (tenth) and receiver Buddy Dial (twenty-second).

The Colts and Giants were the two best teams in the league, though, so it was hard for anyone to second-guess them. Also, dumping a high pick wasn't nearly as costly back then because rookies didn't usually get big signing bonuses—and wouldn't until the AFL began competing with the NFL for talent in the '60s.

Besides, Stransky and Grosscup (who has the dubious distinction of being the last number one pick to get cut) were drafting mistakes, pure and simple. Neither had much of a pro career. Indeed, Lee is more remembered for his work as a TV analyst than for anything he ever did on a football field.

Dial was another matter, though. The Steelers were happy to claim him off waivers, and he quickly became Bobby Layne's favorite target. In his second season he was second in the NFL with 972 receiving yards—222 more than the Giants' top wideout, Kyle Rote—and had the highest per-catch average (24.3). In fact, from 1960 to '63 he made two Pro Bowls and put up these numbers: 203 receptions, 4,295 yards, 21.2-yard average, 36 touchdowns.

(More Buddy trivia: From November 1959 to October '61 he had at least one TD grab in eighteen of twenty-one games — including a streak of eleven straight, which tied a league record that wasn't broken for another twenty-seven years. Jerry Rice's best streak: seventeen of twenty-one. Don Hutson's: sixteen of twenty-one.)

So, yeah, the Giants might have been a bit hasty with Mr. Dial. The guy they chose over him — Joe Biscaha, their twenty-seventh-round pick — caught exactly one pass in the NFL. But again, it wasn't like the Giants were hurting for receivers the next few seasons. They reached the championship game in '59, '61, '62, and '63.

Still, you can understand why the timing might have been right for the AFL, why the NFL might have been vulnerable to a second league at this stage. That '59 draft, after all, was a disaster for the NFL. Look at what happened to some of their top picks:

1 QB Randy Duncan, Packers — Signed with CFL.

4 QB Don Allard, Redskins — Signed with CFL.

7 RB Don Clark, Bears — Signed with CFL.

10 QB Lee Grosscup, Giants — Cut.

13 RB Alex Hawkins, Packers — Cut, withdrawn from waivers, and sold to Colts (who had claimed him).

18 G Charley Horton, Lions — Signed with CFL.

20 B Don Brown, Rams — Placed on "sick and unavailable list"; never played in the NFL.

22 WR Buddy Dial, Giants — Cut.

26 RB Wray Carlton, Eagles — Signed with CFL.

27 B Jimmy Butler, Cardinals — Went to camp with them but never played in the NFL.

30 C Ron Koes, Lions — Cut. Went to CFL.

The NFL was ripe for the picking, all right. It had gotten used to being a monopoly, generally conducted itself like one, and that isn't the best way to respond to an outside threat — as the next decade would show.

Driving with Bobby Layne

By the end of his career Bobby Layne's drinking escapades had stopped being funny—if indeed they ever were. Twice in less than two years in the late '50s the Hall of Fame quarterback was arrested for drunk driving. In addition, there was an episode recalled by Steelers owner Art Rooney in Ray Didinger's *Pittsburgh Steelers.*

On that night, according to Rooney, Layne "got pinched for driving into the side of a street car," though he claimed he hadn't had a drop. The cops just assumed he was smashed because, well, he was Bobby Layne.

"And he was telling the truth," Rooney said. "It just happened that his tires stuck in the trolley track, and he lost control of the car. He said to me the next day, 'Shoot, if I was drunk I would have never hit that car. I'm only a bad driver when I'm sober. I don't have that much practice at it.'"

Layne was full of pithy comments about his boozing. Another one was, "When I want a drink, I go to the best saloon in town and I use the front entrance. My obligation is to be fit and ready to play, and in 12 years in this business I've always been exactly that."

Except maybe for the Steelers' season finale against the Cardinals in 1958, when Rooney said Layne was hung over from a night of partying with Bob Drum, the *Pittsburgh Press* sportswriter. But Bobby had his greatest game as a Steeler that snowy day, throwing for 409 yards and two touchdowns in a 38–21 win, so nobody minded that he wasn't exactly "fit."

Neither of Layne's DWI arrests led to a conviction, by the way. The first came in September 1957, when he was still with the Lions. Detroit police stopped him around 2:00 a.m. after they saw his car straddling the center line—with the lights off—for more than a block.

On the witness stand Layne estimated he'd had "about six scotches with water" but insisted he was "not under the influence to the point where it hurt me." After two officers testified that Bobby's speech was slurred and his face flushed, his attorney argued that they'd simply misinterpreted his Texas drawl.

A jury of eleven women and one man acquitted him. (The Lions, after all, had a big game coming up that Sunday against the Browns.) One of the female jurors explained the decision thusly: "Layne stuttered on the stand and had a flushed face. That seems to be his natural appearance."

In August 1959, after a preseason game with the Steelers in Austin, Texas, Layne was booked again. This time he'd driven into a parked car, then left the scene in a taxi with three players who were with him.

The case never even got to trial. The players — teammate Len Dawson and Cardinals Bill Koman and Jack Patera — all lived outside of Texas, and the district attorney's subpoena power didn't extend across state lines. All he could do was ask them to testify voluntarily. Naturally, they refused. Without their testimony, which the prosecutor considered "indispensable," he felt obliged to drop the matter.

Bobby Layne 2, John Law 0.

(Or perhaps the score should read Johnnie Walker 2, John Law 0.)

The following September, amid much fanfare on a Saturday night, the expansion Cowboys made their NFL debut by hosting the Steelers in Dallas. That same weekend the AFL's Texans made *their* home debut, but the game wasn't until Sunday.

"Maybe we could arrange for Bobby to be picked up by the cops at the airport for being drunk and disorderly," an AFL official said. "That'd take the edge off Saturday night's game."

Make Way for the Tight End

A new term was added to the pro football lexicon in the late '50s: tight end. You couldn't really call it a new position, because ends had been lining up tight — that is, right next to the tackle — forever. But teams were now distinguishing their split ends from their tight ends.

On October 6, 1958 — the earliest reference I've found — the *San*

Mateo Times reported that the 49ers had "operated a tight end and back formation, splitting only [R. C.] Owens out," in a 33–3 loss to the Rams. That means Clyde Conner, who caught four passes for 46 yards that day, worked out of the tight end spot.

The next year Rams coach Sid Gillman benched tight end Leon Clarke and replaced him with Lamar Lundy. His explanation to the *Los Angeles Times*: "We have to get more blocking. Lundy played right, or the tight end, the last two years. He knows the job. We can only hope that he'll give us what we need at this position."

What the Rams needed at the position is what teams have always needed: a pass-catching people-mover, a guy who can score touchdowns but also help out with the heavy lifting.

Lundy is better remembered as the right *defensive* end in the Rams' Fearsome Foursome in the '60s. But when he was just starting out, he was also used—all six feet seven, 245 pounds of him—as a tight end. In 1959, his second season, he caught twenty-five passes for a 15.8-yard average and three touchdowns.

By the early '60s tight ends were playing prominent roles on many clubs. The Bears' Mike Ditka, the Colts' John Mackey, the Packers' Ron Kramer, the Eagles' Pete Retzlaff, the Lions' Jim Gibbons, the Chargers' Dave Kocourek—all were stars. (And the Cardinals' Jackie Smith would soon become one.)

In the 1961 title game Kramer caught two touchdown passes in Green Bay's 37–0 rout of the Giants. (Though if you look at the film you'll see Vince Lombardi sometimes moved him away from the tackle a bit so he could get a quicker release.) But at that point, certainly, you could state unequivocally that the tight end had arrived.

In fact, some of the greatest seasons ever by a tight end came in that first decade, which suggests defenses took a while to adjust to the threat posed by Ditka and the rest:

Year, tight end, team	Rec.	Yds.	Avg.	TDs
1960, Willard Dewveall, Bears	43	804	18.7	5
1961, Mike Ditka, Bears	56	1,076	19.2	12

1961, Dave Kocourek, Chargers	55	1,055	19.2	4
1963, Pete Retzlaff, Eagles	66	1,190	18.0	10
1967, Jackie Smith, Cardinals	56	1,205	21.5	9

Note: Keep in mind Dewveall had 804 receiving yards in just a twelve-game season. That projects to 1,072 for sixteen games.

Then again, that was a phenomenal group of tight ends — probably the best until the current generation. Ditka, Mackey, and Smith are all in the Hall of Fame, and you could make an argument for one or two others.

Thanks for the Memories

The Steelers held a day in the late '50s for Jack Butler, their Hall of Fame defensive back. "They had a halftime show and presented him with a car and all these gifts," his teammate, Dale Dodrill, once told me.

The next week, I asked Jack, "Where's your new car?"

He said, "Oh, it's down at the dealer. There's a couple of thousand dollars that's owed on it yet, and before they give it to me I've got to pay the two thousand dollars." The car hadn't been completely paid off, and the dealer wouldn't let him have it until it was. Jack said, "I got a car pretty cheap, but it wasn't free."

The Greatest Hoax Ever Perpetrated

"The Greatest Game Ever Played." What a load of crap. — Art Donovan, Colts defensive tackle, on the 1958 NFL championship game

Even the participants are convinced that the '58 title game — the hallowed Sudden Death Game — is overrated. "When you think about it," the Giants' Frank Gifford told the *New York Times* in 2008, "it was a lousy game."

Was it unique? Sure. It was the first and — as of this writing — only NFL championship game to go to overtime.

Did it have drama? Plenty. The Giants rallied from a 14–3 half-time deficit to take the lead before the Colts' Johnny Unitas began working his magic.

Were the teams well stocked with future Hall of Famers? Absolutely. Both had six, and there were three more on the coaching staffs.

But until the fourth quarter it was a fumble-filled affair that could hardly have been considered a "classic," never mind a "game for the ages." Every sport has its myths, though, and that seems to be the function of the '58 championship game. It tends to be looked at as a defining moment, a turning point—one that catapulted pro football out of the past and into the future.

If you study the attendance figures, though, you'll see this simply isn't true. In terms of ticket sales—the lifeblood of any club in those days—the Sudden Death Game did nothing to alter the NFL's trajectory. In fact, the league had bigger attendance increases after the '56 and '57 title games than it did after the '58 game. (Which raises the question: How come nobody ever calls one of *them* the Greatest Game Ever Played?) Check out the numbers:

Year	Avg. attendance	Change
1950	25,356	+9.3%
1951	26,570	+4.8%
1952	28,502	+7.3%
1953	30,064	+5.5%
1954	30,425	+1.2%
1955	35,026	+15.1%
1956	35,434	+1.2%
1957	39,393	+11.2%
1958	41,752	+6.0%
1959	43,617	+4.5%
1960	40,106	-8.0%

Pretty clear, isn't it? There were only two seasons in the '50s when the NFL had a smaller attendance spike than it did after the '58 championship game. Then the AFL came along in 1960, and attendance actually went *down* for a few years. It wasn't until 1964 (46,562) that the NFL topped its '59 figure (43,617) and started heading toward the stratosphere.

If you break down the numbers even further—that is, team by team—you discover something else. Take a look at this chart:

Team	'58 attendance	'59 attendance	Change
New York	294,237	390,603	+96,366
Philadelphia	174,532	216,484	+41,952
Chicago Cardinals	121,126	160,438	+39,312
Green Bay	167,636	190,018	+22,382
Baltimore	321,849	343,373	+21,524
Pittsburgh	140,592	159,870	+19,278
Washington	160,135	169,717	+9,582
Chicago Bears	261,748	266,194	+4,446
San Francisco	339,600	330,906	-8,694
Detroit	321,727	308,090	-13,637
Cleveland	370,581	338,380	-32,201
Los Angeles	502,084	444,476	-57,608

Source: Carroll, *Total Football*

For starters, outside of the Colts and Giants, who could be expected to have attendance bumps after making the title game, there were nearly as many losers (four) as gainers (six). But here's what's really interesting: the combined increase in New York and Baltimore (117,890) accounts for *82.6 percent* of the league increase (142,702). Or to put it another way, the other ten teams sold a mere 24,812 more tickets than they did in 1958—a 0.97 percent jump.

The Greatest Game Ever Played?

As Donovan said, pure manure.

Biggest Missed Opportunity

In the 1959 preseason the Packers played back-to-back games in Portland, Oregon, and Bangor, Maine. What, they couldn't find a suitable stadium in *Portland*, Maine?

Ten Defunct Nicknames

Nicknames had become a lost art by the end of the '50s. It had been years since the NFL had had an "Ox," a "Mule" or a "Tuffy"—let alone a "Pug" or a "Jug." Some other nicknames, even more popular than those, that had fallen by the wayside (or were about to):

Nickname	The last one
Bull	Bull Karcis, B, Giants, 1943
Chief	Chief Johnson, LB, Redskins, 1944
Doc	Doc Morrison, C, Brooklyn Dodgers, 1934
Dutch	Dutch Elston, C, 49ers, 1948
Heinie	Heinie Weisenbaugh, B, Redskins, 1936
Monk	Monk Williams, WR, Bengals, 1968
Rip	Rip Collins, B, Packers, 1951
Swede	Swede Johnston, B, Steelers, 1940
Tex	Tex Coulter, T, Giants, 1952
Tiny	Tiny Croft, T, Packers, 1947

Of course, one reason "Doc" fell out of fashion was that there were no longer any players going to medical school in their off hours. The game had become too time consuming—or something.

Hawaii

We tend to remember the Hula Bowl as a *college* all-star game, the tropical version of the Senior Bowl or East-West Shrine Game. It wasn't always thus, though. In the '50s scores of NFL players suited up in the Hula against the collegians—until the league started squawking about it, that is.

The game was set up a little differently back then. It pitted a team of All-Americans (a.k.a. the "Mainland" team) against a Hawaiian squad composed of local legends, players from U.S. military bases and—to level the playing field a bit—pro ringers.

Hula Bowl officials, well aware that offense sells tickets, almost always brought in a top NFL quarterback to throw the ball around, be it Sammy Baugh, Otto Graham, or Y. A. Tittle. Plenty of other Hall of Famers also played for the Hawaiian club, including backs Joe Perry, Hugh McElhenny, and Doak Walker and receivers Crazy-legs Hirsch, Tom Fears, and Dante Lavelli.

As the decade progressed, the games got wilder and more wide open. In 1956 the Hawaiians won 51–20 as Tittle passed for six touchdowns. The next year they romped 52–21 with Norm Van Brocklin throwing for five scores (and, better still, *drop-kicking* four extra points). It might have looked more like touch football at times, but it sure was entertaining.

Not coincidentally, it was also in also in '57 that the NFL began discouraging players from going to Honolulu. Commissioner Bert Bell was worried the Hula Bowl might start to upstage the Pro Bowl, which was held a week later in Los Angeles. Injuries were another concern. When Duane Putnam, the Rams' star guard, played in the Hula that year—and didn't get to LA in time for the first Pro Bowl practice—Bell booted him off the West team.

Naturally, Putnam was upset. It was hard for him, he said, to pass up the $700 he earned in Hawaii. "I'm just a lineman. I don't make much money." He also wondered why *he* was being singled out when, in the past, several players had been allowed to play in both games (e.g., Graham, Walker, Hirsch, and Lou Groza).

A year later the Giants' Frank Gifford got bounced from the Pro Bowl for the same reason. But the issue really came to a head in 1959, when Steelers QB Bobby Layne and Rams running back Ollie Matson announced they were blowing off the Pro Bowl to play in the Hula.

The way Layne looked at it, "I accepted the invitation to play in Honolulu long before the Pro Bowl people contacted me."

Matson, meanwhile, was under the impression "the [standard NFL] contract was for only the regular season. I was not informed that any action would be taken against me if I did not play in the Pro Bowl," he said.

Actually, NFL players had long been barred from postseason games that weren't sanctioned by the league. Bell was good enough to look the other way for a while, but then the Hula Bowl started attracting more attention and the number of pro players in the game grew to eleven or twelve. At that point he felt compelled to put his foot down.

And understandably so. The Pro Bowl, after all, was just a decade old, and the NFL was trying to develop it as a major postseason attraction. It didn't need competition from this Other Game, this Pro Bowl Lite.

Thus the 1959 Hula Bowl was the last to feature NFL players. To celebrate the occasion, Layne threw for five TDs, Hirsch came out of retirement to catch a pass for an extra point, and the Hawaiian club won big again, 47–27. The following year the Hula became an all-college affair . . . and in 1980 — you've gotta love this — the Pro Bowl was moved from Los Angeles to Honolulu, where it made its home for three decades.

What I've Learned: Joe Perry

Onetime NFL career rushing leader; helped reintegrate football with the 49ers after World War II

"I got along with everybody. But I don't take no shit off of nobody."

"I forged my mother's name on the permission slip so I could play football. She wanted me to stick with the books. And the first day out for practice I broke a bone in my ankle. The first day! At first I wouldn't tell her, though. For three days I walked on that ankle. And finally it hurt me so bad, it was so big and so black and blue, that I had to confess.

"'OK,' she said. 'If you want to kill your damn fool self, go ahead.' And from that day on she was my greatest fan."

"Look, Jackie Robinson was a great man, a pioneer. We all know that. But in terms of the physical danger he faced—come on. We were out on that field, and they weren't just tackling us, they were kicking us, punching us, calling us everything but a child of God. He didn't have eleven guys pummeling the crap out of him when they got him down, saying, 'Nigger, I'm gonna kill you if you come over here again.'"

"Sex with twenty thousand women? I don't see how Wilt [Chamberlain] could have done it. Physically impossible. I know; I tried. I used to bring my bowling ball with me on road trips to try to keep myself out of trouble."

"Alcohol was the drug of my generation. The heavy drinkers, you could smell 'em a mile away. It's a distinct smell, kind of a garlic-and-alcohol mix. Norm Standlee was a great beer drinker, and he used to get polluted and come to practice, and you couldn't get within twenty yards of him. You just didn't want to be in the huddle with him. And [coach] Buck Shaw would know it. Buck never swore. He'd just say, 'Dammit it to hell, I'm gonna run ya today.' And I can remember Norm just retching. Buck would run him until he puked."

"The Million Dollar Backfield [featuring running backs Perry, Hugh McElhenny, and John Henry Johnson and quarterback Y. A. Tittle—all Hall of Famers] got along fabulously. People might have a hard time believing that today, but it's true. We rooted for each other, blocked for each other. None of us ever got the ball enough, of course. We'd get ten, eleven, twelve carries a game. In the huddle you'd hear:
    "'Give me the ball.'
    "'No, give me the ball.'

"'No, give *me* the ball.'

"But maybe that extended my career. Who knows?"

"Running is mostly instinct, and you can't teach instinct. You can't teach somebody to run like McElhenny or Perry or [Jim] Brown or John Henry. That's their own, and it's God-given. It's like a fingerprint."

"If we had won a championship, would I be better known today? Don't know. I was the first to rush for a thousand yards in back-to-back seasons, but I didn't get much exposure. What if I'd been in New York and did that? Hell, you'd never forget my name. Look at the exposure O.J. Simpson got, and how bad the [Buffalo] teams he played on were."

"I don't think modern players owe us anything, but without us they wouldn't be where they are today. Football players, I think, are too selfish. Story: In 1949 we played the Browns for the championship of the All-America Conference. There were thirty-three of us on the team, and our [losing] share was $172.61 a man. Some of us wanted to cut the trainer and the equipment man in, which would have cost each player ten bucks. Do you know the team voted not to? Is that selfish? Ten freakin' dollars, and they voted not to. So what do you think today's football player is going to do?"

5.
The
1960s

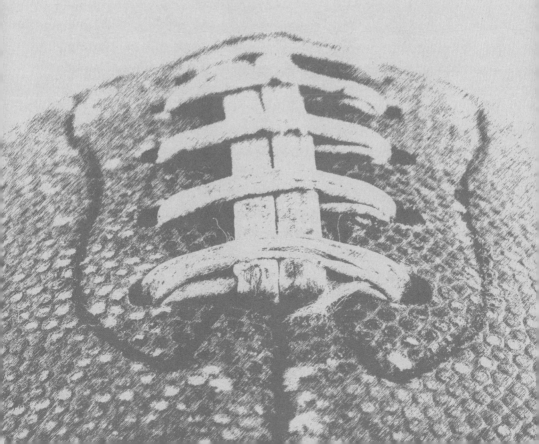

1960s NFL

NFL	1960	1969
Champion	Philadelphia Eagles	Minnesota Vikings
Franchises	13	16
Avg. attendance	40,106	54,430
Roster size	38	40
Games per season	12	14
Points per game	43.1	41.8
Yds. per game	607.5	598.9
Plays per game	123	122.7
Turnovers per game	5.7	4.7
Passes completed (%)	50.2	52.6
Field goals made (%)	56.2	52.7
Run/pass TD ratio	161 run, 221 pass	197 run, 323 pass
Hall of Fame players	48	45
Hall of Fame coaches	5	6

Leaders	1960	1969
Scoring (points)	Paul Hornung, Packers, 176	Fred Cox, Vikings, 121
Passing	Milt Plum, Browns	Sonny Jurgensen, Redskins
Rushing (yds.)	Jim Brown, Browns, 1,257	Gale Sayers, Bears, 1,032
Yds. from scrimmage (RB)	John David Crow, Cardinals, 1,533	Tom Matte, Colts, 1,422
Receptions	Raymond Berry, Colts, 74	Dan Abramowicz, Saints, 73
Punt return avg.	Abe Woodson, 49ers, 13.4	Alvin Haymond, Rams, 13.2
Kickoff return avg.	Tom Moore, Packers, 33.1	Bobby Williams, Lions, 33.1
Interceptions	Two tied with 10	Mel Renfro, Cowboys, 10
Field goals	Tommy Davis, 49ers, 19	Fred Cox, Vikings, 26

Hall of Famers who played in 1960 (48): DE Doug Atkins, C-LB Chuck Bednarik, WR Raymond Berry, FB Jim Brown, T Rosey Brown, DE Willie Davis, QB Len Dawson, DT Art Donovan, LB Bill George, HB Frank Gifford, T Forrest Gregg, T-K Lou Groza, G Gene Hickerson, HB Paul Hornung, LB Sam Huff, FB John Henry Johnson, G-T Stan Jones, DT Henry Jordan, QB Sonny Jurgensen, CB "Night Train" Lane, CB Yale Lary, QB Bobby Layne, CB Dick LeBeau, DE Gino Marchetti, HB Ollie Matson, T Mike McCormack, WR Tommy McDonald, HB Hugh McElhenny, HB-WR Bobby Mitchell, HB Lenny Moore, LB Ray Nitschke, DT Leo Nomellini, G-T Jim Parker, FB Joe Perry, LB Les Richter, C Jim Ringo, DE Andy Robustelli, LB Joe Schmidt, QB Bart Starr, DT Ernie Stautner, T Bob St. Clair, FB Jim Taylor, QB Y. A. Tittle, S Emlen Tunnell, QB Johnny Unitas, QB Norm Van Brocklin, S Larry Wilson, S Willie Wood.

Hall of Fame coaches in 1960 (5): Paul Brown (Browns), Weeb Ewbank (Colts), George Halas (Bears), Tom Landry (Cowboys), Vince Lombardi (Packers).

Hall of Famers who played in 1969 (45): CB Herb Adderley, Atkins, CB Lem Barney, T Bob Brown, LB Dick Butkus, Davis, TE Mike Ditka, DE Carl Eller, DT Joe Greene, Gregg, LB Chris Hanburger, WR Bob Hayes, LB Ted Hendricks, Hickerson, Huff, CB Jimmy Johnson, DE Deacon Jones, Jordan, Jurgensen, HB Leroy Kelly, S Paul Krause, LeBeau, DT Bob Lilly, HB Floyd Little, G Tom Mack, TE John Mackey, Nitschke, DT Merlin Olsen, DT Alan Page, CB Mel Renfro, TE Charlie Sanders, HB Gale Sayers, TE Jackie Smith, Starr, QB Roger Staubach, QB Fran Tarkenton, HB-WR Charley Taylor, Unitas, WR Paul Warfield, CB Roger Wehrli, LB Dave Wilcox, Wilson, Wood, T Rayfield Wright, T Ron Yary.

Hall of Fame coaches in 1969 (6): George Allen (Rams), Bud Grant (Vikings), Landry, Lombardi (Redskins), Chuck Noll (Steelers), Don Shula (Colts).

Talking Points

• It's easy to accuse the NFL's old guard — George Halas, the Maras, et al. — of conservatism, greed, and a general lack of clairvoyance in their failure to head off the AFL threat. Had they just placated Lamar Hunt, Bud Adams, and maybe Ralph Wilson with franchises, the thinking goes, they wouldn't have had to exchange forearm shivers with a rival league for the next decade.

But those times, we tend to forget, were so different from these. In 1960 the prosperity — indeed, the primacy — pro football now enjoys was hardly inevitable. For one thing, the NFL hadn't tapped into the TV mother lode yet. Not collectively, at least. The first league-wide contract was still a few years away.

The '50s, moreover, hadn't been entirely smooth sailing. One team had failed; others had struggled and relocated. Halas and his lodge brothers, having lived through the Depression and two world wars, weren't the type to take anything for granted. Were they a little too reluctant to alter the status quo — to share the spoils, to take on new partners? Perhaps. But they had built the game from nothing, and you couldn't blame them for being a little possessive . . . or even a lot possessive. Besides, they hadn't gotten to where they were without being smart, *careful* businessmen.

• And anyway, who would have wanted to miss the NFL-AFL slugfest? It was ten of the best years in pro football history — the AFL maturing from a seven-on-seven passing drill into a worthy adversary, the NFL being carried kicking and screaming into the future, preemptively expanding to Dallas, Minnesota, Atlanta, and New Orleans, and emerging from the merger stronger than ever.

• It was hard not to notice that many of the quarterbacks who helped make the AFL a success—George Blanda, Len Dawson, Tobin Rote, and Jack Kemp—had either washed out of the NFL or been cycled out. Eight of the AFL's ten championships were won by those QBS, which suggests that the NFL was either choking on talent or having trouble identifying it.

• The Cowboys got to the championship game in their seventh season (1966). The Vikings got to the Super Bowl in their ninth (1969). And in the late '50s the Colts won the title in their sixth (1958). Never had pro football been more equitable.

• From 1950 to '69 the number of turnovers per game dropped from 7.5 to 4.7. Ergo, it was becoming less and less a game of mistakes (and more one of execution).

• By the '60s kickers had become more reliable than quarterbacks. Translation: The success rate on field goal attempts was higher than the success rate on pass attempts (something that had been true, off and on, in the previous decade). The gap would only get wider.

1960s AFL

AFL	1960	1969
Champion	Houston Oilers	Kansas City Chiefs
Franchises	8	10
Avg. attendance	16,538	40,620
Roster size	35	40
Games per season	14	14
Points per game	48.3	42.3
Yds. per game	646.8	603.9
Plays per game	131.4	123.3
Turnovers per game	6.5	5.4
Passes completed (%)	48.5	49.8
Field goals made (%)	44.2	57.8
Run/pass TD ratio	135 run, 186 pass	119 run, 194 pass
Hall of Fame players	4	26
Hall of Fame quarterbacks	1	4
Hall of Fame coaches	2	5

Leaders	1960	1969
Scoring (points)	Gene Mingo, Broncos, 123	Jim Turner, Jets, 129
Passing	Jack Kemp, Chargers	Greg Cook, Bengals
Rushing (yds.)	Abner Haynes, Texans, 875	Dickie Post, Chargers, 873
Yds. from scrimmage (RB)	Haynes, Texans, 1,451	Mike Garrett, Chiefs, 1,164
Receptions	Lionel Taylor, Broncos, 92	Lance Alworth, Chargers, 64
Punt return avg.	Haynes, Texans, 15.4	Bill Thompson, Broncos, 11.5
Kickoff return avg.	Ken Hall, Oilers, 31.3	Thompson, Broncos, 28.5
Interceptions	Goose Gonsoulin, Broncos, 11	Emmitt Thomas, Chiefs, 9
Field goals	Mingo, Broncos, 18	Turner, Jets, 32

Hall of Famers who played in 1960 (4): QB George Blanda, WR Don Maynard, T Ron Mix, C Jim Otto.

Hall of Fame coaches in 1960 (2): Sid Gillman (Chargers), Hank Stram (Texans).

Hall of Famers who played in 1969 (26): WR Lance Alworth, LB Bobby Bell, DE Elvin Bethea, WR Fred Biletnikoff, Blanda, CB Willie Brown, DT Buck Buchanan, LB Nick Buoniconti, FB Larry Csonka, QB Len Dawson, QB Bob Griese, S Ken Houston, WR Charlie Joiner, LB Willie Lanier, HB Floyd Little, G Larry Little, Maynard, Mix, QB Joe Namath, Otto, G Billy Shaw, T Art Shell, HB O. J. Simpson, K Jan Stenerud, CB Emmitt Thomas, G Gene Upshaw.

Hall of Fame coaches in 1969 (5): Paul Brown (Bengals), Weeb Ewbank (Jets), Gillman, John Madden (Raiders), Stram.

Talking Points

• The AFL wasn't just another football league, it was an alternate universe — in the first half of its existence, at least. If there was a quint-essential early AFL game, it was Oakland's 52–49 win over Houston in 1963, a fireworks show that featured six touchdown passes by the Raiders' Tom Flores, five by the Oilers' George Blanda, over 1,000 yards of offense, and best of all, practically no punting. The NFL just didn't have games like that.

In the AFL's first five years the points-per-game averages were 48.3, 48.9, 46.2, 46.3, and 46.5. They're the five highest in NFL-AFL history. But here's the thing: By the end of the decade the two leagues were in pretty much the same place. In the average NFL game in 1969, 41.8 points were scored and 598.9 yards were gained. In the average AFL game that year, the figures were 42.3 and 603.9. (And they would only go lower in the '70s, until the NFL legislated against bump-and-run pass coverage and loosened the blocking rules for offensive linemen.)

What happened? Defense happened. In the AFL's last few years, the Raiders and Chiefs were outstanding on that side of the ball, and the Jets and Oilers weren't far behind. The league had simply become better balanced — as all good leagues must. The NFL might have leaned more toward zone coverage in the secondary and the AFL more toward man-to-man, but in the end the two leagues were more alike than different. So why not merge?

• Seven of the original eight AFL franchises played in the title game at some point. (The Broncos were the only exception.) Six of the eight won the title. (The Patriots made it to the championship game in 1963 but got blown out by the Chargers.) And this, I'll remind you, was in just a ten-year period. It's one of the many reasons why the AFL was such a hit. The All-America Conference, the last league to challenge the NFL, was hurt by the Browns' invincibility. In the AFL just about everybody had a turn at the top.

• In the last year of the AFL five of the ten coaches and four quarterbacks were Hall of Fame bound. That's remarkable — and further explains why the league was able to stand up to the NFL. (The NFL, which by then had grown to sixteen teams, had six coaches and five quarterbacks in 1969 who were headed to Canton.)

Narrow Escape

As loaded as Vince Lombardi's Packers were on defense, they probably would have won a few championships even without Hall of Fame linebacker Ray Nitschke. But he sure was nice to have around, and he almost wasn't after a bizarre incident in practice before the 1960 season.

Nitschke, then an unknown third-year linebacker, was standing in the wrong place when the wind kicked up and knocked over a twenty-five-foot photographer's tower. Not only did the five-thousand-pound structure land right on top of him, a bolt from the tower pierced his helmet and "stopped just short of his skull," according to newspaper reports.

This was miraculous in two respects, the second being that Nitschke was even *wearing* a helmet. Most of the players, after all, had already taken off their equipment — it was only a light workout — but Ray had put his helmet back on when it started to rain.

"I didn't want to get this wet," he said, pointing to his thinning dome.

To refresh your memory, 1960 was only Lombardi's second season in Green Bay. He hadn't even *taken* the Packers to a title game yet, much less won one. And he came *this close* to losing his running-back-munching middle linebacker.

Nitschke's teammates eased him out from under the tower, and he continued practicing. Except for a twisted ankle—one he was already nursing after spraining it three weeks earlier—he was unharmed.

In the locker room afterward, fellow linebacker Dan Currie said, "I guess we had better offer a prayer that Ray's still with us."

Amen to that.

The Element of Surprise

One of the many things that have gone out of pro football is the halfback option pass. Oh, teams will try one every now and then, but not like they did in the old days, when it was a staple of offenses.

Consider the 1960 season. Looking back, that was probably the option pass's last roar. Guys like the Steelers' Tom Tracy, the Cardinals' John David Crow, the Packers' Paul Hornung, and the Raiders' Tony Teresa were throwing them all over the lot. Check out their passing stats that year:

	Att.	Comp.	Pct.	Yds.	TDs	Int.	Rating
Tracy	22	9	40.9	322	4	1	108.9
Crow	18	9	50.0	247	2	1	109.7
Teresa	18	9	50.0	111	1	3	48.4
Hornung	16	6	37.5	118	2	0	103.6

Crow attempted at least one pass in the Cardinals' *last eleven games*. The others threw pretty much every week, too. It was what clubs did back then if they had a back with a decent arm and wanted to keep defenses honest. Besides, why not take advantage of the fact that Hornung (Notre Dame) and Teresa (San Jose State) were former college quarterbacks?

In the opener against Dallas, Tracy had the kind of game you don't see any more. He rushed fourteen times for 64 yards, caught four passes for 82—including a game-winning 65-yard touchdown catch in the last three minutes—and attempted three passes, completing one for a 70-yard score to Buddy Dial.

That's twenty-one touches for 216 yards—a terrific day then, now, or anytime. (Alas, nobody paid much attention. The eyes of Texas were all on Bobby Layne, the former Longhorn, who threw for four TDs in the Steelers' 35–28 win at the Cotton Bowl.)

As the '60s wore on, the halfback pass fell out of fashion. The Colts' Tom Matte and the Cowboys' Dan Reeves did their best to keep it alive — along with Tracy's successor in Pittsburgh, Dick Hoak — but it was no longer the weapon it used to be. It just got to be too risky . . . or something. Pity.

Colossal Comebacks

Bears Stadium in Denver was a veritable ghost town by the end of the Broncos' game against the Bills on November 27, 1960. It had snowed in the first half, turned freezing in the second, and a twenty-mile-per-hour wind never stopped blowing. Besides, late in the third quarter the home team was getting killed 38–7.

Only about twenty-five hundred fans were still around when the Broncos staged one of the most remarkable rallies of all time. It began with an 80-yard touchdown pass from Frank Tripucka to Lionel Taylor. It ended with a 19-yard field goal by Gene Mingo with nine seconds left. In the final twenty minutes Denver scored thirty-one points to snatch a 38–38 tie from the jaws of defeat. It's still the biggest regular-season comeback in pro football history . . . even if it didn't actually result in a win.

How did the Broncos do it? Well, one move that helped was putting in two fullbacks, Red Brodnax and Don Allen, to block for Tripucka. The Denver QB had been getting pounded to the frozen turf all afternoon by the Bills' rush — that is, when he wasn't throwing one of his career-high five interceptions. But with Brodnax and Allen buying him a little extra time, he tossed three TD passes to Taylor to close the gap to 38–28.

"We weren't able to complete our pass patterns until the fullbacks gave Tripucka that protection," coach Frank Filchock said.

That's the thing about comebacks — most of the greatest ones haven't ended in victory. In fact, only once in the regular season has an NFL team rebounded from a twenty-eight-point deficit to win—once in nearly a century. (That was in 1980, when the 49ers trailed the Saints 35–7 before Joe Montana rallied them to a 38–35 overtime victory. But don't forget, had the game been played in 1960, when the Bills-Broncos barnburner was, it likely would have ended in a tie because there was no OT back then.)

Anyway, I've come across six cases of a pro club wiping out a twenty-eight-point lead . . . and *not* winning. I've already regaled you with the story of Denver's miraculous deadlock with Buffalo. Here are the particulars on the other five:

1. SEPTEMBER 24, 1944: CHICAGO BEARS AT GREEN BAY PACKERS

Biggest lead: Packers, 28–0 (second quarter).

The comeback: Late in the first half Chicago finally got on the scoreboard with a 60-yard trick play, a hook-and-lateral from Sid Luckman to George Wilson to Scooter McLean. Luckman threw two more touchdown passes in the second half, both to Wilson, and Bob Margarita tied the game with a 5-yard run in the fourth quarter.

What happened next: The Packers, with gale-force momentum against them, pulled out the victory in the last few minutes on a 42-yard run by Lou Brock and a 50-yard interception return by Ted Fritsch.

Final score: Packers 42, Bears 28.

Notes: Luckman obtained a leave from the U.S. Merchant Marine to play in the game, and Green Bay fans were pretty irate about it—so irate that Sid was genuinely "worried about slipping into a football suit," he wrote in his autobiography, *Luckman at Quarterback*. The Packers crowd booed him (and worse) all day. "The most disturbing thing I ever faced in my career," he said. "I still worried about it aboard a ship a week later when our Merchant Marine crew was suddenly called on another trip to France."

2. NOVEMBER 23, 1947: CLEVELAND BROWNS AT NEW YORK YANKEES

Biggest lead: Yankees, 28–0 (second quarter).

The comeback: Early in the second half, still up 28–7, the Yankees drove to the Cleveland 1, but the Browns made "a miraculous [goal line] stand," the *New York Times* reported. Cleveland then went 99 yards for a touchdown, most of the yards coming on an 82-yard pass from Otto Graham to Mac Speedie. TD runs by Marion Motley (10 yards) and Jim Dewar (5) pulled the Browns even.

What happened next: In the last minute the Yankees moved to the Cleveland 31 but got pushed back to the 38 by a Spec Sanders fumble (which teammate Buddy Young recovered). They ran one more play—a *running* play, for some strange reason—but the clock expired before kicker Harvey Johnson could attempt a field goal.

Final score: Yankees 28, Browns 28.

Notes: The game at Yankee Stadium, pitting the two best teams in the All-America Conference, drew the biggest pro football crowd in New York history up to then—70,060. . . . Yankees offensive tackle Derrell Palmer: "The Browns always had small guards. Good tackles, but small guards. And so I told [Yankees coach] Ray [Flaherty], 'If you just let us run straight at 'em up the middle, we can run 'em out of the ballpark.' Which we did in the first half. But we just flat ran out of gas."

3. OCTOBER 3, 1948: PHILADELPHIA EAGLES AT LOS ANGELES RAMS

Biggest lead: Eagles 28, Rams 0 (third quarter).

The comeback: After recovering an Eagles fumble at the Philadelphia 44 late in the third quarter, the Rams exploded for four touchdowns in the last eighteen minutes. Three came on Bob Waterfield passes, the last a 20-yarder to Jack Zilly with thirty seconds to go.

What happened next: The Eagles got a 50-yard field goal try in the air on the final play, but "the hurriedly kicked ball barely cleared the heads of the linemen and bounced on the 20-yard line," according to the *Long Beach Independent*.

Final score: Eagles 28, Rams 28.

Notes: The Eagles were so mad, they beat their next two opponents 45–0 (Giants) and 45–0 (Redskins). . . . They went on to win their first NFL title—the first of back-to-back titles, as a matter of fact.

4. OCTOBER 7, 1951: PITTSBURGH STEELERS AT GREEN BAY PACKERS

Biggest lead: Packers 28, Steelers 0 (second quarter).

The comeback: After Green Bay won the first eighteen minutes 28–0, Pittsburgh won the next eighteen minutes 33–0. A safety late in the second quarter—defensive end Charley Mehelich tackled Packers fullback Jack Cloud in the end zone—made it 28–23, and Jim Finks gave the Steelers the lead on the first play of the second half by picking off a Tobin Rote pass and running 25 yards for a touchdown. Joe Geri increased the cushion to five points with a 26-yard field goal.

What happened next: Craziness. In the fourth quarter the Packers drove to within an inch of the Pittsburgh goal line—only to get stopped. The Steelers were forced to punt, though, and Rote marched the Pack back downfield and threw a touchdown pass to Bob Mann—only to have it nullified by a penalty. So Rote threw *another* TD pass to Mann, a 16-yarder with under five minutes to play, and this one counted.

Final score: Packers 35, Steelers 33.

Notes: The Steelers were still using the single wing—the last NFL team to do so (on a regular basis, at least). . . . Finks, who threw twenty touchdown passes the next season when they switched to the T, played mostly cornerback. (It's the same Jim Finks, by the way, who later became a Hall of Fame general manager with the Vikings, Bears, and Saints.)

5. SEPTEMBER 25, 1994: MIAMI DOLPHINS AT MINNESOTA VIKINGS

Biggest lead: Vikings 28, Dolphins 0 (second quarter).

The comeback: With Minnesota's Warren Moon throwing the ball all over the lot, Dan Marino decided he'd better respond—and he did. He hit O. J. McDuffie, Greg Baty, and Keith Jackson for touchdowns, and Bernie Parmalee's 10-yard scoring run with 10:34 remaining made it a tie game.

What happened next: Moon responded to Marino's response and put ten more points on the board—on a 3-yard run by Scottie Graham and a 38-yard field goal by Fuad Reveiz. That was enough to offset one last Dolphins TD.

Final score: Vikings 38, Dolphins 35.

Notes: Had Miami won, Moon might never have been able to live it down. After all, he'd also taken part in the Houston Oilers' historic playoff collapse against Buffalo in January 1993, when the Bills dug themselves out of a 35–3 hole. . . . Miami coach Don Shula: "It could have been one of the greatest comebacks, and we would have loved to be associated with that. This has got to be one of our most disappointing losses."

Tag-Team Kickers

As late as the '60s teams that didn't have a stud kicker like Lou Groza or George Blanda would sometimes compensate by using *two* kickers—one for short ones, one for long ones. Heck, in 1965 Raiders coach Al Davis was *still* splitting the job between Gene Mingo (field goals) and Mike Mercer (extra points). After Mingo missed eleven of his first nineteen tries, though, Davis turned everything over to Mercer.

You can't blame clubs for improvising. Kicking, after all, wasn't that specialized a skill until the latter part of the decade. Often, it was just another thing a guy did . . . along with, say, playing quarterback (Bobby Layne), offensive guard (Jerry Kramer), or defensive end (Lou Michaels). Punter-kicker hybrids (e.g., Mercer) were common, too. Given the smaller rosters back then—in '63 the NFL limit was only thirty-seven—versatility was a necessity.

Some of the more notable kicking tandems were the Lions' Doak Walker (short) and Pat Harder (long), the Colts' Gary Kerkorian (short) and Bert Rechichar (long), the Cardinals' Bobby Joe Conrad (extra points) and Gerry Perry (field goals), and the Steelers' Layne (short), Rechichar (long), and Tom Tracy (long). Also, George Halas's last championship team, the '63 Bears, divided the duties between Bob Jencks (thirty-five extra points) and Roger LeClerc (thirteen field goals).

Just to give you a visual, here's the season Layne (short) and Jim Martin (long) collaborated on for the Lions in 1956:

Opponent	Layne	Martin
Packers (A)	12	48
Colts (A)	—	36
Rams (H)	—	33
49ers (H)	27, 17	—
Rams (A)	11, 15	43
49ers (A)	30	—
Redskins (A)	22	—
Colts (H)	11, 10	—
Packers (H)	22, 15	—
Bears (H)	—	—
Steelers (H)	13	—
Bears (A)	—	—

Total: Layne twelve field goals, 17.1-yard average; Martin four field goals, 40-yard average

Note: Figures are lengths, in yards, of field goals.

Going back and forth between kickers—especially in the same game—might seem strange, but at times it worked well. Take a 1954 matchup between the Colts and Rams. In that one Rechichar booted three field goals (44, 39, and 32 yards) and Kerkorian two (25, 13), the second with thirty-one seconds left, to provide the Colts with most of their points in a 22–21 win.

The last time two kickers from the same team booted two or more field goals in a game was November 27, 1960. Tracy and Layne did it for the Steelers against the Redskins. The box score:

Pittsburgh Steelers	6	7	3	6–22
Washington Redskins	0	0	7	3–10

Steelers—FG Tracy 37
Steelers—FG Tracy 31
Steelers—Tracy 28 run (Layne kick)
Redskins—James 49 pass from Guglielmi (Khayat kick)
Steelers—FG Layne 21
Redskins—FG Khayat 9

Steelers—FG Tracy 36

Steelers—FG Layne 11

God 1, Mother Nature 0

The 1960 Redskins couldn't do much of anything right. The only team they beat was the expansion Cowboys, who didn't beat *anybody*. They ran poorly (3.2 yards per rush), threw worse (4.4 yards per attempt), and allowed the most points in the Eastern Conference (309, an average of 25.8 per game).

So why should anyone have been surprised when they couldn't get the tarp off the field one Sunday—and a game against the Giants had to be played on top of it?

In the Redskins' defense, the Washington weather *was* pretty wacko that December 11 morning. It rained at first, which brought out the tarp. But then it started snowing—about a foot's worth.

The grounds crew tried mightily, but it just didn't have the equipment to remove that much snow that quickly. It was able to roll up only one 25-yard strip of tarp at one end of the field.

Referee Bill Downes surveyed the wintry scene at Griffith Stadium and asked Redskins general manager Dick McCann what he wanted to do. "Why, play, of course," McCann said.

"I want this understood," Downes said. "I'll make all the decisions on whether or not a play is in bounds, and I'll do all the measuring. My word goes. I'm going to be God out there."

McCann: "Aren't you always?"

The game finally started forty-one minutes late—mostly because "the workmen couldn't budge the heavy corrugated spool they were winding the tarp on," the *Washington Post* reported. "Trucks were pressed into service and kept butting it a few yards at a time to get it off the field. The good-natured crowd, that numbered 14,077 by turnstile count, cheered each lunge as if it were a fullback hitting the line."

Neither team could do much under the conditions. The Giants had minus-1 yard rushing, the Redskins minus-6 passing (which was sack yardage, since they failed to complete any of their seven throws and had two intercepted). Shovels were brought out to clear the footing for kickers—and New York's Pat Summerall and Washington's Ed Khayat both managed to boot field goals. The Giants wound up winning 17–3 on a touchdown pass from Charlie Conerly to Joe Morrison and an interception return for a score by Tom Scott.

The stat of the day, though, was this: despite the rain, the snow, and the Redskins' wretchedness, thirty-four tickets were sold at the box office.

Quick Turnarounds

In 1958 the Packers (1-10-1) and Eagles (2-9-1) finished with the worst records in the NFL.

In 1960 they met in the championship game—with the Eagles winning, 17–13.

Two teams, two years, worst to first. It's the only time it's happened in league history.

That's how egalitarian pro football became after World War II. If you were down and stayed down, it wasn't because the Giants, Bears, Packers, and Redskins ran the show—as might have been the case before. It was because you didn't know what you were doing. *Everybody* had a legitimate shot at the title.

A Peach of a Performance

Milt Plum wasn't a great quarterback, but he did have one off-the-charts season for the Browns in 1960. He didn't throw his first interception that year until the tenth game, and going into the finale against the Giants his numbers looked like this:

Attempts: 210

Completions: 132

Completion percentage: .629

Yards: 2,001

Touchdowns: 17

Interceptions: 1

Plum's passer rating at that point was 119.2—in 1960, I'll remind you again. That's a better rating than the Patriots' Tom Brady (117.2) had when he threw fifty TD passes in 2007. In fact, the only higher ones in NFL history are Aaron Rodgers's 122.5 for the 2011 Packers and Peyton Manning's 121.1 for the '04 Colts.

Too bad Plum couldn't quite finish it off. He had four scoring tosses against New York to help Cleveland win 48–34, but he also had four picks. Thus he wound up with a rating of "just" 110.4—which, incidentally, is still the ninth best of all time.

Nobody back then, though, had any awareness of this. The passer rating hadn't been invented yet, and quarterbacks that year were ranked according to a kooky formula that included total TD passes, total completions, and total yards as well as completion percentage, interception percentage, and average gain per attempt.

Plum easily won the passing title over future Hall of Famers Norm Van Brocklin (second), Johnny Unitas (third), Bobby Layne (fifth), and Bart Starr (sixth)—and earned the first of his two Pro Bowl berths—but there was little sense of how large his margin was.

Put it this way: His passer rating was nearly twice that of the rest of the quarterbacks in the NFL (a combined 57.8). Imagine a QB doing that today. Actually, don't bother; it's impossible. Even if your rating were perfect (158.3) it wouldn't be enough, because the average league rating these days is in the low eighties.

For Plum, it was, by any measure, a season for the ages. Just wanted to give it its proper due.

. . . And One That Got Away

Speaking of Fearsome Foursomes (as we were in the previous decade), how do you think this one would do?

LE — Willie Davis

LT — Art Donovan

RT — Henry Jordan

RE — Doug Atkins

Four Hall of Famers as a first line of defense. Would you even need a second line of defense?

Well, guess what? Paul Brown, the Cleveland coaching legend, drafted the whole lot of them in the '50s . . . and then traded them away — for virtually nothing.

Could the Browns have kept winning championships after 1955 — Otto Graham's last season — if their coach had seen the greatness in these linemen, the greatness that became so evident later on? You could certainly make that argument. You could also argue that Brown wouldn't have been fired in '63 — a year in which Atkins, Davis, and Jordan all were picked for the Pro Bowl (Donovan had hung 'em up) — if they'd still been wearing Cleveland uniforms.

Brown got away with dealing them — at first, anyway — because for much of the '50s he had studs like Bill Willis, Len Ford, Don Colo, and Bob Gain in the defensive line. But in the '60s the Cleveland defense began to decline, and by '65 it had slipped to eighth in the league in points allowed and thirteenth in yards allowed. Sure, the Browns reached the title game that year, but they lost to a Green Bay team that was stronger defensively because, among other things, it had Davis and Jordan up front.

It's truly startling how little Brown got in return for his four future Hall of Fame linemen. Only one of the players he acquired so much as *played* for Cleveland — receiver A. D. Williams, who caught exactly one pass in his brief time with the club. (Brown swapped Davis for him in 1960 because he was reportedly worried that starting wideout Billy Howton might retire.) Most of the others never even made it in the NFL.

It's almost as if the Grid God was angry at Brown for letting all this talent get away. Consider: A decade later, when Paul was running the Bengals, he had a Pro Bowl defensive tackle named Mike Reid. Have you heard this story? While still in his prime, Reid suddenly retired, decided he'd rather bang out country music songs than bang helmets with Larry Little. The next season Brown retired himself, never having won a playoff game in Cincinnati.

Not to pile on or anything, but Brown also drafted *another* notable defensive lineman in this period—and got rid of him, too. I'm talking about end Jim Marshall, who was sent to Minnesota in 1961 and proceeded to play in 282 straight games, a record that stood until 2005. Which raises the question, how can a coach be smart enough to draft all these guys . . . and dumb enough not to keep any of them?

The details of Brown's regrettable deals:

1951—Drafts Donovan in the fourth round (fiftieth overall). Art had already been in the NFL for a year but was thrown back in the pool because his previous team, the Baltimore Colts, had folded. During training camp Brown trades him and rookie offensive guard Sisto Averno to the New York Yanks for third- and eighth-round picks in '52. The Browns select quarterback Don Klosterman with the number three and end Stan Williams with the number eight. Neither ever plays a down for Cleveland.

(Note: Williams and another rookie were shipped to the Dallas Texans for George Ratterman, who spent five seasons with Cleveland as a backup quarterback. Klosterman also wound up going to the Texans in a separate transaction for a third-round choice in '53, which turned out to be offensive tackle Jim Hietikko. Hietikko broke his arm in camp, prompting him to give up the game and take a high school coaching job.)

1953—Drafts Atkins in the first round (eleventh overall). When Doug is slow in developing, Brown deals him to the Bears, along with safety Ken Gorgal, for Chicago's number three and number six in '56. The third-rounder yields end Larry Ross; the sixth-rounder brings offensive tackle Sherman Plunkett. Both fail to stick. Ross winds up signing with a Canadian team; the mammoth Plunkett later latches on with the Colts and Jets and plays in two AFL All-Star Games (as well as the third Super Bowl).

1956 — Drafts Davis in the fifteenth round (181st overall). Willie spends two seasons in Cleveland as an end and tackle before he's traded to Green Bay for A. D. Williams, an unproven receiver. Williams lasts only a year with the Browns and catches just fifteen passes in the NFL.

1957 — Drafts Jordan in the fifth round (fifty-second overall). After two seasons Henry is packed off to the Packers for a number five in 1960. In his first year under Vince Lombardi, he's voted to the Pro Bowl. With the fifth-rounder the Browns take fullback Bob Jarus, but he can't crack the roster — or the one in Green Bay, which gives up a number eight in '61 for him. Jarus eventually opts for the CFL.

(Note: Cleveland spent the Packers' eighth-rounder on kicker Fred Cox, who had a very successful career . . . with the Vikings. Not quite ready to replace Lou "The Toe" Groza, Brown included Cox in a four-player package in '62 for Minnesota's '63 sixth-rounder. Fred led the league in scoring twice for the Vikes and totaled 1,345 points in fifteen seasons. The Browns used the number six on offensive tackle Ernie Borghetti, but he spurned them and signed with the AFL's Kansas City Chiefs.)

1960 — Drafts Marshall in the fourth round (forty-fourth overall). The next year Brown sends him and five other players to the expansion Vikings for their numbers two and eleven picks in '62. Neither selection bears fruit. The second-rounder, defensive tackle Chuck Hinton, fractures an ankle in camp and is later cut. Hinton also washes out the following year in Baltimore, but he catches on with Pittsburgh in '64 and plays seven seasons there — and nine in the NFL in all.

As for the eleventh-rounder, end Ronnie Myers, he's the answer to a great trivia question — or part of it, at least. Myers was one of the players let go by the Browns on the same day they released basketball Hall of Famer John Havlicek (who was trying out as a receiver before going on to greater glory with the Boston Celtics).

Final totals:

- Donovan: four all-pro teams, five Pro Bowls, two titles with the Colts (1958 and '59)
- Atkins: one all-pro team, eight Pro Bowls, one title with the Bears (1963)
- Davis: five all-pro teams, five Pro Bowls, five titles with the Packers (1961, '62, '65, '66, and '67)
- Jordan: five all-pro teams, four Pro Bowls, five titles with the Packers (see Davis)
- Marshall: two Pro Bowls, four Super Bowl appearances with the Vikings (after the '69, '73, '74, and '76 seasons), immortality as a member of the famed "Purple People Eaters" defensive front

Add it all up, and you get fifteen all-pro teams, twenty-four Pro Bowls, and thirteen rings.

I'm still not sure what Paul Brown got.

Firefight

Bears tight end Willard Dewveall was the first NFL player to play out his option and jump to the rival AFL. When the signing was announced in January 1961, Houston Oilers owner Bud Adams couldn't resist rubbing it in a little, saying, "Dewveall said he was tired of playing with a losing team, and that he wanted to play for a championship team." (The Oilers had won the first AFL title the previous year.)

Chicago owner George Halas wasn't going to put up with that. "Adams' statement is typical bush league and characteristic of him," he shot back. "The biggest mouth west of the Mississippi has spoken again. You can quote me."

(As it turned out, Halas didn't suffer too much from the loss. He replaced Dewveall with first-round draft pick Mike Ditka, who proceeded to have a Rookie of the Year season — fifty-six catches, 1,076 yards, twelve touchdowns — en route to the Hall of Fame. Willard, used as both a tight end and a split receiver in Houston, was never much more than a second or third wheel in the Oilers' passing attack, behind Charley Hennigan and Bill Groman.)

Still, Dewveall satisfied his desire to play for a championship team. The Oilers won another title in 1961 and made it to the championship game the next season. The season after that, though, the Bears took the NFL crown, so Halas gained a bit of revenge.

Erroneous Headline of the Decade

As the owner of baseball's St. Louis Browns, Bill Veeck once sent a midget up to bat. As the owner of the Chicago White Sox, he gave us the exploding scoreboard. We can only imagine what stunts he might have pulled if this headline had been true:

VEECK BUYS OAKLAND FOOTBALL CLUB!

It was stripped across the top of the *Chicago Tribune* sports section on January 14, 1961 (barely a dozen years, for those of you scoring at home, after the *Tribune* had informed its readers that "Dewey Defeats Truman"). Veeck "and a group of associates, mostly Chicagoans, have concluded negotiations for the Oakland club of the new American Football League" for $175,000, the non-bylined story read. The plan was to move the team to Chicago, where it would share Comiskey Park with Veeck's White Sox — and bring in revenue during the baseball off-season. (The Chicago Cardinals, who had called Comiskey home for more than three decades, had relocated to St. Louis the year before.)

The story was very believable. The Raiders had been a last-minute entry in the American Football League and had lost an estimated $270,000 in their first season. They had stadium issues (which forced them to move their games to Candlestick Park in *San Fran-*

cisco), attendance issues (average: 12,397), ownership issues (Ed Mc-Gah and Wayne Valley didn't get along), all kinds of issues.

At the AFL's recent league meeting, the *Tribune* reported, one of Veeck's partners had tried to get a franchise for Chicago, but the league had decided to hold off on expansion. Buying an existing team like the Raiders was the only alternative.

The next day everybody was denying everything. Veeck said he'd "like to have a tenant for Comiskey Park in the offseason, but I wouldn't go as far as buying Oakland to get one." Valley called the report "completely untrue."

Too bad. Veeck would have fit right in with the Foolish Club, the adventurous souls who brought the AFL into being. Maybe he would have staged the first Throwback Game . . . and had his players wear leather helmets along with their vintage uniforms. Or maybe he would have gotten Ernie Nevers, the old Cardinals great, to come out of retirement and drop-kick an extra point. (Ernie was only fifty-seven then. He might have had one more in him.) Or maybe he would have let the fans vote on which play to run (as he did one day with the St. Louis Browns).

Of this you can be sure: every time the team scored, there'd have been fireworks.

Wildest Off-season Rumor

For a few days in February 1961 there was a story floating around that the Browns had tried to trade Jim Brown for the Cardinals' John David Crow and that—here's the best part—the Cards had *turned them down*. Sounds crazy today, of course. Crow was a nice all-around back, sure, but Brown was arguably the greatest runner in pro football history.

Several things gave the rumor legs. First, the strong-willed Brown had been critical of coach Paul Brown's offense, which he considered too conservative. He'd also reportedly upset the front office by not showing up for a couple of public appearances—and was even said to be considering playing out his option and becoming a free agent.

Crow, meanwhile, was coming off one of the greatest years a running back had ever had. Check out these numbers, accomplished in a twelve-game season:

Rushing: 183 attempts, 1,071 yards, 5.9-yard average, 6 touchdowns.

Receiving: 25 catches, 462 yards, 18.5-yard average, 3 TDS.

Passing: 18 attempts, 9 completions, 247 yards, 2 TDS. (Yes, he could throw, too.)

Crow finished third in rushing that year behind Brown (1,257) and the Packers' Jim Taylor (1,101), and his 1,533 yards from scrimmage led the league. In fact, he was only the third NFL back to gain 1,500 yards from scrimmage in a season. (Brown and Lenny Moore—two Hall of Famers—were the others.) And 1,533 yards in twelve games, I'll just point out, is the equivalent of 2,044 in sixteen games.

Suddenly, a Brown-for-Crow swap doesn't seem so farfetched, does it? Besides, they were about the same age; John David was twenty-five, and Jim was almost twenty-five.

Paul Brown finally put the rampant rumormongering to rest. "Pardon me while I laugh," he said when told of the report while on vacation. The story, he figured, must have come out of a "jesting conversation" he'd had with Cardinals boss Walter Wolfner at the league meetings.

"We were talking about Crow not starting in the Pro Bowl game," Brown said. "Walter seemed put out about it, and I asked him if he wanted to trade Crow. So he kept the kidding going by bringing up the name of Jim Brown. No, Jim is not up for trade."

And that was that.

Crow, by the way, never had another season that compared to 1960. And four years later the Cardinals did, indeed, trade him—to the 49ers for Abe Woodson, an all-pro return man who also played cornerback.

Mr. Warmth

In a 1961 issue of the *Saturday Evening Post* Redskins owner George Preston Marshall declared football the national pastime — and trashed just about every other sport in the process. Some of the highlights:

Baseball: "A bloodless, unemotional spectacle . . . [beset by] chronic bellyaching." Women "buy new hats or suits" to go to football games because they're social events. "For baseball a woman will wear any old rag."

Golf: "I have studied golf for years and found only this — you hit the ball and then walk after it."

Boxing: "A freak show for characters in pool rooms, bars, bookie joints and barbershops."

Horseracing: "With no betting, how many people would watch horses run?"

Bowling: "A stupid game. . . . The participants wear the shabbiest clothing in sports."

Fishing: "The only thing I can say on behalf of fishing is that it is least susceptible to corruption of any sport. There has yet to be a case of anyone caught trying to bribe a fish."

Group Brainlock

Good thing the Packers beat the Giants 37–0 in the 1961 championship game. Otherwise folks might still be yelping about the fifth down the officials gave Green Bay in the third quarter.

The nightmare for referee George Rennix and his crew began just after the second-half kickoff. The sequence of plays went like this:

First and 10 from the Green Bay 36 — Paul Hornung gains a yard up the middle.

Second and 9 from the GB 37 — Bart Starr scrambles 21 yards to the New York 42 but fumbles when hit by cornerback Erich Barnes. Giants safety Jimmy Patton picks up the ball at the 37 and runs it back to the 42.

At this point, all hell breaks loose.

The officials rule Starr was down when he fumbled, enabling the Packers to retain possession. The play is wiped out, though, by an illegal motion penalty. So Rennix walks back to the Green Bay 40 and steps off the 5 yards. Unfortunately, the original line of scrimmage was the 37, which makes it only a 2-yard penalty. (The chain gang had apparently moved the sticks during all the confusion and "did not return them to the same place," the Associated Press reported.)

When the Packers line up for the next play, the down marker reads "1." (After Starr's fumble, you see, everybody thought it was going to be the Giants' ball, first down.) Nobody catches the mistake. So Green Bay ends up getting a second down, a third down, a fourth down, and a fifth down.

First and 15 from the GB 35 (down number two), Hornung sweeps right for 10 yards.

Second and 5 from the GB 45 (down number three), Jim Taylor picks up a yard over center.

Third and 4 from the GB 46 (down number four), Starr trips and falls after taking the snap, gets up, and bounces a pass to Boyd Dowler in the left flat.

Fourth and 4 from the GB 46 (down number five), Dowler punts. What a disaster.

Worst Grasp of Public Relations

Former NFL quarterback Don Heinrich after signing with the Raiders in 1962: "I've never even seen an AFL game on television."

• • •

The only change in Chicago in the last 30 years is that Al Capone is dead. — Vikings coach Norm Van Brocklin, upset with the officiating after a last-second loss at Wrigley Field in 1962

(George Strickler of the *Chicago Tribune* seconded the motion, writing, "Referee John Pace and his associates, especially back judge George Smith, contrived to remain as popular as Hitler with the contestants and the 46,984 spectators through a series of decisions that most likely will not be accepted as illustrations of proper officiating technique in the next league manual.")

• • •

Re-jected!

R. C. Owens's basketball background—he starred at center for the College of Idaho—served him well in the NFL. He was a rookie sensation with the 49ers in 1957, leaping high to catch lobs from Y. A. Tittle for touchdowns. The Alley Oop, the play was called (and still is).

Several years later Owens found another use for his unusual jumping ability and height (six feet three): blocking a field goal. R. C. did it a little differently, though. Rather than block the kick at the line, he stood back at the goalposts and batted the ball away just before it went over the crossbar.

As far as anyone knows, Owens is the only NFL player who's ever done that. And he did it just once in a real game—against the Redskins on December 8, 1962, the year he joined the Baltimore Colts.

It happened in the first quarter. Washington's Bob Khayat had a longish 40-yard attempt and tended to boot the ball low, so Owens went in and stood at the goal line, hoping to get lucky. As the kick tumbled toward him, R. C. timed his jump perfectly and knocked it to the ground— "just like blocking a shot in basketball, except that it is harder," he said later. "The ball is smaller, and it comes faster."

The crowd at Memorial Stadium went crazy. The next day the photo of Owens's history-making play—his cleats well off the ground—appeared in newspapers all over the country. "The kangaroo Colt," the Associated Press dubbed him.

"I just got my hand in back of the ball in time to keep it from going over," he said. ". . . Man, I've been just waiting for the chance to do that. What a thrill. The first time it's happened in the history of football, and I do it on national TV."

Owens had blocked a kick in practice before, he said, but the few times he'd tried it in a game things hadn't quite worked out. One time the kick was wide. Another time, earlier that season, it was short—and R. C. ran it out to the Baltimore 43.

"Now that I've done it," he said, "you don't think they're going to outlaw it, do you?"

No, goaltending continued to be allowed until 1985, when the owners decided there was no longer any place for it in the No Fun League. Unless they change their minds, Owens will remain the first, last, and only player to reject a field goal attempt just like Wilt Chamberlain.

The Ubiquitous R. C.

For a player who caught a modest twenty-two touchdown passes in his career—one less than Randy Moss did in a single season (2007)—R. C. Owens sure left his mark on pro football. Besides the Alley Oop and the World's Most Unique Way to Block a Field Goal Try, he also got headlines for becoming a free agent in 1962 and jumping from the 49ers to the Colts.

It tends to be forgotten today, but for a brief period in the '50s and '60s players enjoyed a certain amount of freedom. They didn't have as much as they do now, but it was better than nothing.

Here's how it worked: The standard contract back then—in every sport—included an option year. When a player reached that year, he had two choices: re-sign with his team (which he usually did) or play out his option for 90 percent of his previous year's salary and, at the end of the season, shop himself around. (Sometimes, of course, a player would play out his option just to gain negotiating leverage with his club and force it to pay him a little more.)

Owens played out his option with the Niners in 1961 and had the best season of his career—fifty-five catches (seventh in the league) for 1,032 yards (sixth) and five touchdowns. Naturally, he got some offers from other teams. Across the bay the Oakland Raiders reportedly put together a lucrative package, as did another AFL club, the New York Titans. But Colts owner Carroll Rosenbloom wanted to give Johnny Unitas somebody else to throw to, so he signed R. C. to a one-year deal worth an estimated $17,000.

"You can only perform so long under certain conditions," Owens said. "I've got peace of mind now, and that's worth everything."

This didn't sit well with other NFL owners. They were used to seeing players jump to rival *leagues* like the AFL (e.g., Browns quarterback Len Dawson, Bears tight end Willard Dewveall, Steelers cornerback Fred Williamson) or CFL (e.g., Lions QB Tobin Rote and scores of others), but never before in the modern era had a player jumped to a rival *club*. If more followed Owens and Rosenbloom's lead, they decided, it might undermine the NFL's competitive balance—and, oh yes, significantly increase payrolls.

Teams were already concerned that players playing out their options might be holding back—to keep from getting hurt, maybe. The year before Lions coach George Wilson had said of Rote, "I'm not saying that a guy didn't give 100 percent, because there's no way you can prove it. But I do say that there were times when I questioned whether a guy was giving his best."

So after the 1962 season NFL owners passed a rule that basically said: Players are free to move within the league after their contracts expire, but their new team has to compensate their old team. And if the teams can't agree on compensation, Commissioner Pete Rozelle will decide what's fair. This became known as the Rozelle Rule, and it pretty much kept a lid on free agency—within the NFL, at least—until 1977, when the league replaced it with a compensation formula. Only a handful of times did Rozelle have to step in.

Really Deep Threat

As a rookie with the Baltimore Colts in 1962, Bake Turner finished with these odd-looking statistics: one reception, 111 yards, 111.0 average, one touchdown.

Even in Canada, where the fields are 110 yards long, you can't average 111 yards a catch. So how did he pull it off? This way (if you must know):

In Week 5 against the Bears, Turner took a lateral from R. C. Owens after a completion and ran 37 yards. This gave him 37 receiving yards but no reception (which was credited to Owens).

In the fourth quarter of the season finale against the Vikings, Turner caught his only pass of '62 — and went 74 yards for a touchdown.

Thus his 1-111-111.0-1 line.

The next year the Colts cut Turner, and he signed with the AFL's New York Jets. In his first appearance, a preseason game against the Patriots, he returned the opening kickoff 95 yards for a TD.

So at that point he was averaging 111 yards a catch in the NFL and 95 yards a kickoff return in the AFL.

Some guys don't know when to quit.

Invisible Man

One of the NFL's longest-standing records is Night Train Lane's fourteen interceptions for the Rams in 1952. What makes it doubly impressive is that it was set in just twelve games . . . yet it hasn't been broken even in a sixteen-game schedule. It's entirely possible, given the low interception rates these days, the mark will last another fifty-odd years.

Except . . .

Lane's record really *has* been broken — sort of. Ever hear of a safety in the early years of the AFL named Tommy Morrow? In an eleven-game stretch for the Raiders in 1962 and '63, Morrow had fifteen interceptions.

That's right, he picked off one more pass than Night Train — in one less game.

Too bad nobody noticed.

The particulars:

1962

Week	Opponent	Int.	Quarterback(s)
8	New York Titans	2	Johnny Green
9	Houston	1	George Blanda
10	Buffalo	0	Jack Kemp, Warren Rabb
11	Dallas Texans	1	Len Dawson
12	San Diego	1	·John Hadl
13	Houston	1	Blanda
14	Boston	1	Tom Yewcic

1963

Week	Opponent	Int.	Quarterback(s)
1	Houston	3	Blanda 2, Jacky Lee 1
2	Buffalo	1	Daryle Lamonica
3	Boston	2	Babe Parilli
4	New York Jets	2	Dick Wood

Total: 11 games, 15 interceptions

Morrow also had interceptions in eight straight games during that stretch. *That's* what he's in the record book for. It's the longest such streak in AFL-NFL history. But his more significant accomplishment—fifteen picks in eleven games—has fallen through the cracks.

It's a little like the Tiger Slam, Tiger Woods's four consecutive major championships (2000 U.S. Open, British Open, and PGA and 2001 Masters). Because Tiger did it over two years, less importance is attached to it. "It wasn't a true Grand Slam," purists say.

Still, Morrow's feat is pretty remarkable. Granted, the early years of the AFL were pass-crazy—and interception-crazy—but his picks, I'll just point out, came at the expense of two Hall of Famers (George Blanda, Len Dawson) and several other recognizable names (John Hadl, Daryle Lamonica, Babe Parilli).

Morrow's amazing run might have received more attention if the Raiders hadn't gone 1-13 in 1962. At that point they weren't even on *Oakland's* radar screen, never mind pro football's. He also suffered from a severe case of second-place-itis. Even though he had more interceptions in those two years (nineteen) than anybody else in the league, he finished second in interceptions to the Titans' Lee Riley in '62 (11 to 10) and second to the Oilers' Freddy Glick in '63 (12 to 9).

Another reason Morrow isn't remembered, of course, is that he didn't wind up in Canton like Night Train did. In fact, he played only one more season in the pros, picking off four passes. He was cut at the end of camp in 1965.

From the sound of things, Tommy was the center fielder–type of safety, and Raiders coach Al Davis preferred defensive backs who punished the opposition (e.g., Fred "The Hammer" Williamson and, later, Jack Tatum and George Atkinson). Then, too, the AFL was improving rapidly, and more than a few of the early stars had trouble keeping up.

For two seasons, though, Morrow was a takeaway machine. Don't hold your breath waiting for somebody else to intercept fifteen passes in eleven games. Nowadays, lots of *teams* would have trouble doing it.

• • •

We should've won, but [Johnny] Unitas is a guy who knows what it was to eat potato soup seven days a week as a kid. That's what beat us.—
Vikings coach Norm Van Brocklin (yes, him again) after Johnny U. led the Colts to a last-minute victory in the '60s

• • •

The Fighting Forty-Niner

Listen, my friends, this is no jive,
Charley Powell must bow out in five.
—Muhammad Ali (then known as Cassius Clay)

In January 1963, barely a year before he took the heavyweight title from Sonny Liston, Muhammad Ali fought Charley Powell at the Pittsburgh Civic Arena. It was the same Charley Powell who'd played defensive end for the 49ers (1952–57) and Raiders (1960–61) — when he wasn't, that is, pursuing a boxing career that saw him climb to number nine in the *Ring Magazine* rankings.

Powell cracked the top ten in 1959 after flooring the number two heavyweight, Nino Valdes, three times en route to a stunning eighth-round TKO. He was far from a great fighter (record: 25-11-3), but at six foot three, 226 pounds, he punched with plenty of power, enough to knock out seventeen opponents. Had he not suffered a succession of broken hands, he might have gone even further than he did.

By the time he climbed in the ring with Ali, though, he was thirty years old and near the end. Muhammad, meanwhile, was twenty-one and invincible — and had just polished off Archie Moore in four rounds. Still, Powell talked a good game in the days leading up to the fight.

"In football," he said, "you have to play against 11 men. In boxing, it's only one. And I don't think [Ali] is as tough as the Green Bay Packers. . . . As soon as I land a good punch, it could be over."

He also claimed to be undisturbed by The Greatest's constant yapping. "I'm a married man," he said, "and I get that all the time."

Ali, being Ali, happily returned fire. "I hear you're a football player," he told Powell at the weigh-in. "Well, tonight you're going to make the first touchdown."

He also revised his original prediction — and promised the bout would end even earlier. "I don't like the way he's popping off," he said, "so now I'm going to knock him out in three rounds [instead of five]."

And Ali did knock him out in three rounds — with a wicked left hook at the end of one of his signature barrages. The crowd of 11,238, an arena record, "lustily booed" the perfect timing of Powell's exit, the *Pittsburgh Press* reported, but Muhammad offered no apologies.

"They can't say it was a fix," he said. "Just take a look at Powell.

He's got a lump on his head, his eyes are swollen, his nose is split and one eye is hanging out."

He was exaggerating, of course. Charley wasn't in nearly that bad shape. In the second round, moreover, he'd landed a right that Ali admitted had "shook" him. "This was my roughest fight—for three rounds," Muhammad said.

Powell had one more bout of consequence. In December 1964 he took on Floyd Patterson, then on the comeback trail after losing his heavyweight crown to Liston. The fight, held in San Juan, Puerto Rico, went six rounds, Floyd finishing him off with a left hook followed by a right cross.

"Referee Joe Walcott counted him out," Gay Talese wrote in the *New York Times*. "Patterson helped him up, shook his hand and later offered him a job as a sparring partner. Powell will think about it."

To sum it all up, Charley might not have won the heavyweight championship, but he fought Muhammad Ali and Floyd Patterson, was counted out by Jersey Joe Walcott, and was written about by Gay Talese. Not bad for a guy who used to chase quarterbacks for the 49ers.

The Buddy System

Sandy Koufax and Don Drysdale, the Los Angeles Dodgers' 1-2 pitching punch, threw some serious chin music at baseball owners in 1966 when they staged a joint holdout. For more than a month, it was a huge national story.

Koufax and Drysdale might have gotten the idea from Philadelphia Eagles quarterbacks Sonny Jurgensen and King Hill, who'd walked out of training camp together three years earlier to speed up contract talks. Jurgy and Hill didn't need nearly as long to get their situations resolved, though. They were back at practice the next day, with Sonny proclaiming, "We both got what we wanted."

It was a pretty gutsy move nonetheless. Players, after all, had little power in 1963. They had only recently formed a union, and agents were almost unheard of.

But Jurgensen and Hill had some leverage: they were the only two quarterbacks in the Eagles' camp. On top of that, Sonny was one of the NFL's best passers, making the Pro Bowl in '61 and tying the league record by throwing for thirty-two touchdowns. Hill wasn't nearly in his class, but he did have the usefulness of being able to punt.

Both had entered the option year of their contracts. This gave the club the right, if they didn't re-sign, to cut their pay by 10 percent. Jurgensen's salary reportedly would have dropped from $25,000 to $22,500, Hill's from $20,000 to $18,000. That, as much as anything, is what they were trying to avoid.

After General Manager Vince McNally capitulated, the Eagles proceeded to have a thoroughly miserable 2-10-2 season. Jurgensen missed five games and substantial parts of three others with a jammed thumb and fractured throwing shoulder. Then Joe Kuharich came in as coach, and Sonny was traded to Washington — at least partially out of spite, you figure, because of his walkout the previous summer.

And that, my friends, is how the Redskins got a Hall of Fame quarterback — and franchise icon — in exchange for Norm Snead.

Brush with History, 1963

Sift through the archives of the Kennedy assassination and you might come across a picture of the president visiting downtown Fort Worth on that fateful November 22, 1963. The husky guy in the hat — standing to John F. Kennedy's immediate left — is Lon Evans, longtime sheriff of Tarrant County . . . and two-time all-pro tackle with the Packers in the '30s.

Afterward the presidential motorcade went to Carswell Air Force Base for the short flight to Dallas's Love Field. In his autobiography, *The Purple Lawman*, Evans said a Secret Service man told him, "I have an eerie feeling about going to Dallas. . . . I wish we could take off right now and head directly for Austin."

Happily, there are other things to remember Evans for. Consider the year he had in 1936: In March he was a member of the *Mutiny on the Bounty* cast that won the Academy Award for Best Picture, and in December he was a member of the Green Bay team that won the NFL title. Has any other player ever pulled off a double like that? (He was also voted all-league that season.)

Alas, by the time the film editor got through with *Mutiny*, Evans said, his role had been reduced to a cameo—"a mutineer for a few minutes." As a two-way lineman for the Packers, though, Lon always loomed large.

How large? Well, the story goes that the *Saturday Evening Post* once commissioned Redskins owner George Preston Marshall to write a piece about the best lineman in pro football. The magazine assumed Marshall would pick Turk Edwards, his future Hall of Fame tackle. But instead he opted for Evans, whom he'd tried unsuccessfully to sign coming out of Texas Christian University.

Lon said Marshall always used to kid him about choosing the Packers over the Redskins. George would tell him that "if I had accepted his offer, I wouldn't be 'freezing my tail off playing football in a hick town in Wisconsin.'"

Heads or Tails?

You might call the 1963 AFL season the Year of the Coin Flip.

It all began when quarterback Tobin Rote became available after his contract ran out with his Canadian team, the Toronto Argonauts. The Buffalo Bills had Rote's rights but figured they were set at QB with veteran Jack Kemp. That left the Denver Broncos and San Diego Chargers to fight over him.

Rote, who had just turned thirty-five, was a potentially huge catch. He'd led the Detroit Lions to the 1957 NFL title and, after leaving the club in a salary dispute, had been the CFL's top passer in two of his three seasons with Toronto.

The Broncos and Chargers agreed to settle the matter by having Commissioner Joe Foss flip a coin. San Diego won—and gave Buffalo a player and two draft picks as compensation. The following December the Bolts annihilated the Boston Patriots in the title game, 51–10, with Rote throwing two touchdown passes.

"That coin flip determined the 1963 championship," coach Sid Gillman said.

Two weeks later Gillman coached the West team in the All-Star Game. Since the Raiders had finished second behind the Chargers, he wanted to add one of their quarterbacks — Tom Flores or Cotton Davidson — to his roster. So he tossed a coin. It came up Cotton.

In the fourth quarter, with the West trailing 24–17, Davidson was sent in to replace Rote. He promptly directed two drives to pull out a 27–24 victory, the winning score coming on a 25-yard pass to Oakland teammate Art Powell with just forty-three seconds left.

The league championship and the All-Star Game . . . both decided by the turn of a coin.

Some other memorable coin flips in pro football history:

1940 — Early in the season Turk Edwards, the Redskins' Hall of Fame tackle, went out for the pregame coin toss. As he turned to go back to the sideline, he "wrenched his knee," according to reports, and never played again.

1951 — The third pick in the draft was up for grabs among the 49ers, Packers, and Redskins, all of whom had finished 3-9 the previous year. Niners general manager Lou Spadia won the coin flip, enabling him to select Hall of Fame quarterback Y. A. Tittle, who had already played three seasons with the Colts but had been thrown back in the pool after the Baltimore franchise folded.

1958 — The day before the NFL championship game NBC television announcers Chris Schenkel and Chuck Thompson tossed a coin to see who would do the play-by-play of the first half and who would do the second. Schenkel won and, of course, chose the second. But when the Colts and Giants went into overtime, it was Thompson's turn again. That's how Lucky Chuck, who lost the toss, got to do the climactic minutes of pro football's first Sudden Death game.

1961 — In his autobiography, *A Proud American*, Foss recalled resolving another issue with a coin, this one among the Raiders' original owners. Two of the owners, Wayne Valley and Charlie Harney, were so incompatible, he wrote, that at one point in the meeting, "Charlie hauled back and swung his cane at Valley. It whistled past the left side of [Wayne's] face, just missing his nose. It could have killed him if it had hit him on the temple." The Valley faction wound up winning the flip—and with it the right to buy out the Harney faction and take total control of the club.

Voting with Their Feet

The Cleveland Browns drew 570,648 fans to their eight home dates at Municipal Stadium in 1963—one preseason (83,218), seven regular season (487,430).

Why is this number significant? Because it's 8,141 more than the Cleveland Indians drew for their eighty-one home baseball games that year (562,507).

Near as I can determine, it's the first time a pro football team outdrew a Major League Baseball team that shared the same facility. A pretty big watershed, you have to admit.

And lest anyone think it was a fluke, the Browns did it again the next season (712,614 to 653,293).

Of course, the Browns won the NFL title in '64 and were nearly as good in '63. The Indians, on the other hand, finished 79-83—and in the middle of the American League pack—both years.

Clevelanders obviously were more interested in watching Frank Ryan throw to Paul Warfield than in watching Jack Kralick throw to Joe Azcue. Can't blame them.

Who Wants To Be a Millionaire?

If you're ever trapped at a party with a football know-it-all and want to stump him with a trivia question, try this one: Who are Frith-jof Prydz, Erik Jansen, and Rolf Prydz, and what role did they play in NFL history?

Give up? They're the three guys who finished ahead of Montana State's Jan Stenerud in the 1964 NCAA ski jumping championship.

Who knows? Had Stenerud won, he might have stuck with his

original sport instead taking up kicking . . . and going on to a Hall of Fame career with the Chiefs, Packers, and Vikings. After all, he came to the United States from Norway on a skiing scholarship and didn't boot a football for the first time until later in '64. The following season he made a 59-yarder for the Bobcats and was on his way to immortality.

The top five in the ski jumping competition at Hanover, New Hampshire:

Skier, school	1st jump	2nd jump	Points
Frithjof Prydz, Utah	139	135	214.5
Erik Jansen, Denver	133	134	214.5
Rolf Prydz, Idaho	123	139	204.2
Jan Stenerud, Montana State	127	127	201.5
Aarne Valkama, Denver	133	121	201.4

Note: Distances are in feet. Prydz was declared the winner because he jumped farther, though Jansen scored more style points.

An Item That May Interest Only Me

Here's a backup trivia question for the football know-it-all (in case he happens to be a ski jumping buff): What does Y. A. Tittle, the Hall of Fame quarterback, have in common with Bartolo Colon, the Cy Young Award–winning pitcher?

Answer: Their last names are also punctuation marks.

Everybody, I suspect, is familiar with the colon (:). Well, the tittle—little-known fact—is the dot over the *i*—as in, uh, Tittle. (It can also be an accent or a vowel mark, according to the grammar books.)

One of the many reasons to appreciate Jack Kent Cooke, who became a part-owner of the Redskins in the '60s, is that he would actually use the word *tittle* in conversation. "I don't care a tittle or a jot" about such and such, he would say. In this case, though, *tittle* means "one iota"—or some reasonable approximation.

Class dismissed.

By Mrs. Frank Ryan

In 1964, the year of the Browns' last NFL title, the wife of quarterback Frank Ryan began writing a column for the *Cleveland Plain Dealer*. It ran twice a week, on Wednesdays and Sundays. Back-Seat Brown, it was called.

Joan Ryan wasn't the first pro football spouse to dabble in newspapering. Several years earlier Perian Conerly — wife of Charlie, the Giants' QB — had written a similar column, one that gave a woman's-eye view of the game. Perian even got hers syndicated; the *New York Times* was among the papers that picked it up.

But while Mrs. Conerly displayed a certain literary flair, Mrs. Ryan was more provocative, more opinionated — and frankly, gave readers better behind-the-scenes dirt. One day she recalled meeting her husband at the airport after a loss — this was when Paul Brown was still coaching the team — and being surprised "to see the players jovially patting Frank on the back and laughing as they came into the terminal."

This was followed by the sight of Brown limping noticeably as he went by. "What on earth is going on?" she wondered.

Frank smiled and told her "he had accidentally cleated [his coach] in the pregame warm-up. The players were hopeful that Brown might miss the next game because of the injury."

You'd never catch Perian saying something like that about Jim Lee Howell or Allie Sherman. She was too much the Southern lady.

Another time Joan wrote of watching the telecast of a Cowboys-Cardinals game and blurting out, "I think St. Louis will stomp Dallas because Don Meredith is a loser." This caused a bit of an uproar in the Big D, even if Dandy Don did play poorly that day in a 10–10 tie (fifteen of thirty-four, 203 yards, no touchdowns, three interceptions).

The next week the Cowboys came to Cleveland amid much hoohah about the remark made by the Quarterback's Wife. Sure enough, "loser" Meredith threw four picks and the Browns won 30–21. In the Monday sports section the *Plain Dealer* happily reminded its readers that "Joanie was so right yesterday."

You had to love her. She badmouthed the offensive line of Frank's previous team, the Rams. ("The first time I saw him throw four consecutive passes STANDING UP was the first time I saw him play for the Browns.) She ripped the Redskins' uniforms. ("The minute the Redskins prance onto the field they are all but beaten. The psychological letdown of having to go into a locker room on a bleak day and don mustard-gold pants with a maroon-and-gold jersey would make me want to forfeit. They look like frumpy old grandmothers.") And as if that weren't enough, she dumped on the Redskins' helmets, too. ("I always have to stop and think whether the wide decorative strip running down the center of the helmet is supposed to represent a feather or a missing scalp.")

When Frank joined the Redskins in 1969, Joan continued her column, writing for the *Washington Star* and later the *Post*. By then, apparently, folks had forgotten — or forgiven — her cracks about the Redskins' uniforms and helmets.

One-Two Punch

The 1964 Buffalo Bills did something no pro football team has done since: win a championship while rotating quarterbacks. Veteran Jack Kemp started thirteen of the fourteen games, but second-year man Daryle Lamonica routinely came off the bench and, several times, sparked the Bills to victory.

They complemented each other well. Kemp — the future U.S. senator and vice presidential candidate — was the team's leader and a classic pocket passer. "He probes the defense," coach Lou Saban said. "And Lamonica has, just by nature, learned to take advantage of Jack's experience and knowledge."

Lamonica, meanwhile, was a terrific deep thrower and dangerous runner. In fact, he led AFL quarterbacks in rushing that year with 289 yards — and had as many rushing touchdowns as anybody in the league (six) — even though he took fewer than half the Bills' snaps.

Toward the end Saban wavered a bit. He played Lamonica the whole way in the next-to-last game, a 30–19 win over the Broncos. The kid, after all, had really been coming on—while Kemp had struggled with interceptions (and would end up throwing twenty-six, a career high).

But Saban turned back to Kemp in the season finale against the second-place Patriots. With the division title on the line, Jack went the distance in a 24–14 victory. "He needed a chance to redeem himself," Saban said. "And we were going to go with him come heck or high water."

In the championship game win over the Chargers, Saban again stuck with Kemp for the full sixty minutes. But the Bills never would have gotten that far without their co-quarterback, Lamonica.

Week by week with the two QBs:

Opponent	Score	Kemp	Lamonica
Chiefs	W, 34–17	34-15-218-3-3	0-0-0-0-0, rushing: 3-5
Broncos	W, 30–13	18-8-136-0-4	5-2-58-0-0, rushing: 6-47, 1 TD
Chargers	W, 30–3	19-8-95-0-1	2-2-68-1-0, rushing: 3-21
Raiders	W, 23–20	26-10-173-0-2	10-7-164-1-0; rushing: 2-2, 1 TD
At Oilers	W, 48–17	26-14-378-3-3	3-2-27-0-0; rushing: 2-6
At Chiefs	W, 35–22	23-14-256-3-3	2-1-20-0-1; rushing: 7-48
Jets	W, 34–24	16-8-220-1-1	11-4-127-1-1; rushing: 4-14, 1 TD
Oilers	W, 24–10	7-2-43-0-1	11-5-69-0-2; rushing: 8-61
At Jets	W, 20–7	7-2-26-0-1	24-11-267-1-1; rushing: 2-(-2)
Patriots	L, 36–28	41-16-295-2-2	12-4-77-0-1; rushing: 0-0
At Chargers	W, 27–24	20-8-136-0-1	7-4-40-0-0; rushing: 6-6, 1 TD
At Raiders	L, 16–13	6-2-23-0-1	18-7-131-1-1; rushing: 6-48
At Broncos	W, 30–19	0-0-0-0-0	21-6-89-1-1; rushing: 6-33, 2 TD
At Patriots	W, 24–14	24-12-286-1-3	0-0-0-0-0
Chargers	W, 20–7	20-10-188-0-0	rushing: 1-2

TOTALS

Kemp: 289-129-2,473-13-26

Lamonica: 128-55-1,137-6-8; rushing: 55-289, 6 TD

Note: Passing figures are attempts-completions-yards-touchdowns-interceptions. Rushing figures are attempts-yards.

FYI: Two other modern-era clubs won titles while alternating quarterbacks—the '51 Rams, with Bob Waterfield and Norm Van Brocklin, and the '56 Giants, with Charlie Conerly and Don Heinrich. It wasn't a widespread practice by any means, but coaches were still open to the idea. The game, let's not forget, wasn't that far removed from the single-platoon era, and in those days the passing was often shared by two or more players—tag teams like the Packers' Arnie Herber and Cecil Isbell and the Redskins' Sammy Baugh and Frank Filchock.

The problem was finding a second guy who was almost as good as the first. The Rams hit the lottery with Waterfield and Van Brocklin, two Hall of Famers, but how easy is *that* to duplicate?

Still, teams tried—the Lions with Bobby Layne and Tobin Rote and the 49ers with Y. A. Tittle and John Brodie, to name two. The '50s might have been the last time pro football was flush with quarterbacks—not because there were more of them, but because, after the NFL merged with the All-America Conference, there were only twelve clubs left. On every roster, then, you had a backup quarterback who'd be a starter in today's thirty-two-team league. Heck, most of the *number three* quarterbacks would be starters now. (That changed in the '60s, though, when expansion to Dallas, Minnesota, Atlanta, and New Orleans—coupled with the arrival of the AFL—ended the stockpiling of QBs.)

Sid Gillman, the Hall of Fame coach with the Rams and Chargers, was among those comfortable with a two-quarterback system. Indeed, his '64 San Diego team, which met the Kemp-Lamonica Bills in the championship game, rotated John Hadl and Rote.

"It's just like baseball," he said. "When your starting quarterback is off with his control, you bring in another man from the bullpen right away."

But it wasn't that simple. Most quarterbacks don't thrive when they're constantly being taken out and put back in. They can lose their feel for a game, even their confidence. Also, when you divide the quarterback duties, you risk dividing the team — and the fans, too. The Rams might have won with Waterfield and Van Brocklin, but the situation wasn't always harmonious. Billy Wade, who later shared the QB job with the Stormin' Norman, once said of him, "The only help Van Brocklin ever gave anyone [of his competitors] was a shove off the field."

Years after the '64 Bills took the title, Tom Landry was still alternating quarterbacks in Dallas. With Landry, it was almost a crusade. He rotated veteran Eddie LeBaron and young Don Meredith in the early '60s, Meredith and young Craig Morton later on, and in 1971 was still going back and forth between Morton and Roger Staubach. Of course, he'd been on the Giants' coaching staff in '56, when Conerly and Heinrich had meshed so brilliantly, so he'd seen firsthand how it could work.

Finally, midway through the '71 season, Landry threw in the fedora and switched permanently to Staubach. The Cowboys proceeded to win their final ten games and their first Super Bowl. And that's the last time any coach has been very enamored with using two quarterbacks.

Even so, Tom couldn't quite admit defeat. "There's nothing wrong with the two-quarterback system," he said after the last game of the Morton-Staubach experiment. "It would have worked today if we hadn't made so many mistakes."

Speaking of Lamonica ...

Daryle Lamonica's nickname was "The Mad Bomber." It's easy to understand why. Here are the distances, in yards, of his first dozen touchdown passes in pro football ('63 playoff game against the Patriots included): 74, 35, 23, 93, 40, 44, 44, 80, 38, 46, 30, 74.

Average: 51.8 yards a TD throw.

Has any quarterback ever broken into pro football with more of a bang?

Lamonica might not be a Hall of Famer, but he put up some interesting numbers. In his first seven seasons — four with Buffalo, three with Oakland — his regular-season record as a starter was 40-4-1, a winning percentage of .900. That's better than Otto Graham's first four years with the Browns in the All-America Conference (47-4-3, .898).

What separates them is that Graham went 5-0 in the postseason over that stretch, while Lamonica went 3-3.

Next Time, Try a Wooden Stake

How hard were the Packers to beat during the Vince Lombardi era? This hard:

On October 24, 1965, the Cowboys sacked Bart Starr five times and held the Packers to minus-10 passing yards, the worst passing performance by any Lombardi-coached team. Final score: Green Bay 13, Dallas 3.

On September 24, 1967, the Bears forced eight Packers turnovers (three fumbles, five interceptions), the most by any of Lombardi's clubs (and committed just one themselves). Final score: Green Bay 13, Chicago 10.

9 + 1 Rookies Who Signed Contracts with Both the AFL and NFL

The AFL-NFL war rarely burned hotter than when leagues fought over a rookie who, in a moment of temporary insanity, signed with both sides. The roll:

Year, rookie	Signed with	And later with	Who won
1960 RB Billy Cannon	LA Rams	Houston Oilers	Oilers
1960 RB Johnny Robinson	Detroit Lions	Dallas Texans	Texans
1960 FB Charlie Flowers	New York Giants	LA Chargers	Chargers
1960 DE Don Floyd	Houston Oilers	Baltimore Colts	Oilers
1960 FB Bob White	Houston Oilers	Cleveland Browns	Oilers
1960 QB Bob Ptacek	Saskatchewan Roughriders (CFL)	LA Chargers	Saskatchewan
1963 RB Tom Woodeshick	Buffalo Bills	Philadelphia Eagles	Eagles

1963 DE Jim Moss	Buffalo Bills	St. Louis Cardinals	Bills
1964 FB Tony Lorick	Oakland Raiders	Baltimore Colts	Colts
1965 OT Ralph Neely	Houston Oilers	Dallas Cowboys	Both teams

Final Score: AFL 6, NFL 2, CFL 1, 1 tie

• The fates of Cannon, Robinson, and Flowers were decided in U.S. District Court.

• Neely's case went a step further, to the U.S. Court of Appeals. His suit dragged on until November 1966, the middle of his second season with the Cowboys, when an appellate court reversed the previous finding and said he belonged to the Oilers. To hang on to their future all-pro offensive tackle, Dallas compensated Houston with four draft picks—a number one, a number two, and two number fives—and agreed to play three preseason games against the Oilers. The only one of the picks who became a Pro Bowl player was cornerback Zeke Moore.

• When Lorick changed his mind, Raiders boss Al Davis didn't press the issue because, as he put it, "The courts will always side with the boy."

• Cannon and Robinson, who went first and third in the NFL draft, had the best careers of the bunch. Cannon won two AFL titles with Houston, another as a tight end with Oakland and played in six championship games and two All-Star Games. . . . Robinson switched to safety, won three titles with the Texans/Chiefs, and was a six-time all-pro. There's still a chance he'll make the Hall of Fame, especially considering his fifty-seven interceptions. . . . Woodeshick was another good one. In 1968, his one Pro Bowl season, he was third in the NFL in rushing (947) and second in yards from scrimmage (1,275).

• White played just one season with the Oilers, appearing in six games in 1960 (and accumulating no offensive stats). . . . Moss tore up his left leg during his first training camp with the Bills and never suited up for them.

• Ptacek was actually a *second*-year quarterback—one who hadn't yet thrown an NFL pass. But he's included in the list because his indecision affected *three* leagues, not just two. Cleveland didn't pick up his option in 1960 because it wanted to trade his rights to the Saskatchewan Roughriders for defensive end Jim Marshall, who had left Ohio State a year early and gone to play in Canada. (The Browns drafted Marshall in the fourth round in '60.) After signing with Saskatchewan, though, Ptacek turned around and signed with the Chargers, too. But AFL commissioner Joe Foss didn't approve the contract, and Ptacek wound up playing for the Roughriders. See how confusing things could get in those days?

• Floyd, a fixture at right end for Houston for much of the '60s, issued the most heartfelt mea culpa. Unlike many of the others, he didn't try to wriggle out of his first contract because another club offered more money. It was just that the AFL's New York Titans had drafted him, he explained, and he had no desire to play in the big city. Then Oilers owner Bud Adams told him he could acquire his rights if he wanted to play in his home state—Floyd was from Midlothian, Texas, by way of TCU—and the kid's head started spinning.

"I signed the Houston contract," Floyd said.

> That was about 6 o'clock. At 10 o'clock I talked to Mr. [Don] Kellett [of the Colts]. I was worried about whether Mr. Adams could get my release from New York, so I signed with Baltimore also.
>
> I made a mistake.

They all did, one way or another. And in their naïveté—if not their duplicity—they only added more fuel to the AFL-NFL fire.

• • •

There are no longer any dirty players in the NFL. Now they have guys who are trained to injure you scientifically. —Henry Jordan, Packers defensive tackle

• • •

A Wizard, a True Starr

Here's something you don't see every day. In fact, it might be the only time it's happened in pro football history:

In the 1967 season opener against the Lions, the Packers' Bart Starr completed two passes longer than 50 yards *on the same drive*.

The sheer mathematics of it are enough to give anyone a migraine. The field, after all, is only 100 yards long.

Even more mind-boggling, the drive measured a mere 76 yards . . . and *neither* completion went for a score.

How Starr did it (according to accounts in the *Milwaukee Sentinel* and *Wisconsin State Journal*):

1. From his own 23 late in the third quarter, he hit receiver Carroll Dale for a 51-yard gain to the Detroit 26.

2. A sack and a holding penalty (which in those days was 15 yards *from the spot of the foul*) pushed Green Bay back to its 45. On third and 39 Bart tossed a screen to Jim Grabowski, and the fullback chugged 53 yards behind a wall of blockers to the Detroit 2.

Elijah Pitts ran it in on the next play, narrowing the Lions' lead to 17–14. The game ended in a 17–17 tie (but it didn't keep the Packers from winning their third straight NFL title).

"He got lucky," Lions defensive tackle Alex Karras said of Starr's second 50-yarder. "Third-and-[39] and he calls a screen pass. Even if you don't expect it, you should get 25 yards and that's all."

Bart agreed, saying the Packers went with the play only because "I didn't know of anything else we had run all day we could get 40 yards with."

Which is why, I guess, he's in the Hall of Fame and we aren't.

A Fight to Remember

One football brawl isn't much different from the next—except, maybe, when an *owner* gets involved. That's what happened in 1967 when the expansion New Orleans Saints paid their first visit to New York.

It all started when the Saints' Tom Hall caught a pass late in the game and ran out of bounds near the Giants' bench. The way New Orleans coach Tom Fears saw it, "The play was over, and then this guy came off the bench and dropped him."

The "guy" in question, center Greg Larsen, had a slightly different view. "He was coming right at me," he said. "I couldn't get out of the way." (The Giants' game film showed it to be a shove rather than a forearm or elbow, as the Saints had suspected.)

When the game ended, New Orleans linebacker Steve Stonebreaker raced across the field and nailed Larsen with a punch. "It was a cheap shot and Larson knew it," he said. "I popped him, and I'd do it again."

Soon enough, others were joining in, including John Mecom, the Saints' young owner, who'd been watching the game from the sideline.

"Somebody took a punch at me," he told the *New York Times*. "I think it was number 81. I got emotional and lost my cool. I threw a punch at number 81. I missed and hurt my arm."

Number 81 was Freeman White, the Giants' six-foot-five, 225-pound linebacker.

A few spectators even got caught up in it before order was restored. Norm Van Brocklin, the analyst on the Saints' telecasts, called it "the best fight in Yankee Stadium in years." (Probably since 1959, when Ingemar Johansson TKO'd Floyd Patterson to win the heavyweight title.)

When Stonebreaker was fined by Commissioner Pete Rozelle, contributions from Saints fans poured in. He received so much money — some of it nickels and dimes from kids — he reportedly could have paid the fine several times over.

Double-Edged Hammer

If you whack a man so his teeth chatter and his eyeballs bleed a little, he's looking for you instead of the ball. — Fred "The Hammer" Williamson, Chiefs cornerback

Fred Williamson claimed to have put cracks in thirty helmets with "The Hammer," his merciless karate chop of a tackle. By the end, though, it was as big a threat to him as to opponents. Twice in his last two seasons he suffered serious injuries—a separated shoulder in 1966 when he tried to knock out the Bills' Glen Bass (for the *fourth* time) and a broken arm in '67 when he got a bit overzealous with the Jets' Don Maynard.

(In between, just to remind everybody he was still around, he dropped "The Hammer" on the Dolphins' Howard Twilley and fractured Twilley's cheekbone.)

After the Maynard mishap, Williamson insisted there was "no way" he'd remove his signature tackle from his arsenal. "I've got about three more years left in the game," he said. "When I'm gone, football can be played by the nice guys again."

As it turned out, he only had about three *months* left. He returned to the lineup in October, managed to keep from hurting himself in the final eleven games, and was waived in the off-season at the age of thirty—after which he headed to Hollywood to make movies (including one, naturally, titled *Hammer*).

Historical note: In the next-to-last game of his career, Williamson picked off a pass by the Jets' Joe Namath and ran it back 77 yards for a touchdown. These things can be hard to verify, but I wouldn't be surprised if it was the first time in the annals of pro football that a pass thrown by a quarterback wearing white shoes was intercepted by a defender wearing white shoes and returned for a score.

But don't forget, Fred would always tell people, "I wore them before Namath. Originally, I wore powder blues. But they got dirty too quickly and I couldn't obtain the powder to clean them."

• • •

"The Hammer" is a stiff-armed tackle aimed in the area of the Adam's apple, much like Night Train Lane's old clothesline tackle. Only difference is I've refined the trick.

You can throw "The Hammer" two ways. You can throw it in a perpendicular plane to the earth's latitude or you can launch it from a horizontal plane. Night Train used to clothesline them when they got the ball. I wait until after they catch the ball before chopping them down. I personally favor the perpendicular stroke because it lands on top of the head and tends to stun the opposition. — Fred Williamson expounding on his most lethal weapon

• • •

Glue-Fingered

You'll find references to Stickum — that gooey adhesive players used to coat their fingers with — as far back as the 1940s. By the '60s it was so prevalent guys would talk openly about it.

Colts quarterback Johnny Unitas on an interception by safety Andy Nelson in 1962: "He just reached up in the air with one hand, like a baseball fielder, and the ball stuck. Andy has so much stickum on his hand it had to stick."

Vikings receiver Paul Flatley after a 202-yard day against the 49ers in 1965: "For me to go without stickum would be like going without a helmet. The body heat only increased its effectiveness."

The substance came in particularly handy in hot weather, when sweat made the ball slippery. But it had its drawbacks, too, as the Jets' Joe Namath once discovered.

In 1968 Namath returned to Legion Field in Birmingham, Alabama, where he'd played in college, for a game against the Patriots. On a third down early in the second half, he dropped back near his goal line to throw a screen pass to Bill Mathis, but the ball stuck to his hand as he let it go. It fluttered right into the arms of defensive end Mel Witt, who could have walked into the end zone.

Stickum giveth, and Stickum taketh away.

But mostly, Stickum gaveth — too much — which is why the NFL outlawed it in 1981 (and replaced it with tacky gloves, which accomplish essentially the same thing, only much more neatly).

Word of Namath's mishap must have gotten around. A decade

later in the Super Bowl the Cowboys called a halfback pass that Robert Newhouse wasn't quite expecting. "I had stickum all over my hands," he said. "I started wiping it off on my pants and started licking my fingers. I've never eaten so much stickum in my life."

He then launched a 29-yard touchdown throw to Golden Richards for the clinching score in a 27–10 Dallas win. (After which he no doubt hustled to the sideline and washed the Stickum down with a few gulps of Gatorade.)

It's Up and Good!

Jim Turner was a kicking machine for the 1968 Jets. It wasn't just the thirty-four field goals he booted in the regular season—a pro record at the time—it was all the *other* three-pointers he made.

Turner had nine field goals, for instance, in the preseason. He also had two in the AFL title game, three in the Super Bowl upset of the Colts, and six more in the All-Star Game.

Grand total: fifty-four.

It's a mark that still stands all these years later—not that you'll ever find it in the record book. (Just *this* book.)

Next closest: fifty-two by the Rams' Jeff Wilkins in 2003 (six preseason, thirty-nine regular season, five playoffs, two Pro Bowl) and the 49ers' David Akers in 2011 (four preseason, forty-four regular season, four playoffs).

• • •

AstroTurf was invented when the first pop flies started disappearing into the glare of the original Astrodome roof. So the fielders on the Houston Astros baseball team could see the ball, the glass roof was painted over. Because the glass was painted over, the grass died. Because the grass died, Monsanto invented AstroTurf. The Astrodome, along with the huge expenditure it represented, was saved. Because baseballs started to disappear, a good deal of professional football today is played on artificial turf. — From *Razzle Dazzle*, Phil Patton's 1984 book about the marriage between pro football and television

• • •

Number of the Decade: 28

After blowing out his knee in 1968, Bears great Gale Sayers managed one more 1,000-yard season but never had a run from scrimmage longer than 28 yards. (Longest reception: 25.)

If only there had been arthroscopy.

We Shall Overcome

I don't know how else to put this, so I'll just come out and say it: It's strange how many famous kickers in the NFL have had something wrong with their kicking foot.

Ben Agajanian, whose career spanned from 1945 (Eagles/Steelers) to '64 (Chargers), had four toes amputated in college after they were crushed in an elevator accident. As a result, he wore one shoe that was three-and-a-half sizes smaller than the other (7½ vs. 11).

Before the operation, he said, the surgeon told him, "'Don't worry, Aggie, I'll square off the stumps, and you'll kick better than ever!' What I didn't know was that [he'd] told [Ted] Shipkey"—Agajanian's coach at New Mexico—"that I would never play again, and that I would always walk with a limp."

Then there's Pat Summerall, who booted the Giants into two title games in the late '50s (and another in 1961). Pat was born with a club foot; that is, it was facing the wrong way.

"At that time," he said in Richard Whittingham's oral history, *Giants In Their Own Words*, "the way they treated it was by breaking both bones in the bottom of the leg and just turning the foot around. The doctor told my mother afterwards that I would be able to walk but I would probably never be able to run and play with other kids."

And let's not forget Tom Dempsey, whose 63-yard field goal for the Saints in 1970 is still the record (though it has been tied twice). Dempsey was born with a toeless, truncated foot and had to wear a special shoe for kicking.

Yet all three were among the most celebrated kickers of their eras. (Indeed, Agajanian might have had more nicknames than any player in pro football history. Besides Aggie, he was known as "The Toeless Wonder," "Bootin' Ben," and "The Automatic Armenian.")

Nothing stopped these guys. Agajanian, for instance, fractured his right arm as a rookie and had to wear a sling. But that didn't keep him from kicking a field goal the next week to help the Steelers beat the Cardinals. He'd dealt, after all, with far worse.

The Price of Specialization

In April 1969 the Rams' George Allen hired a little-known Stanford assistant, Dick Vermeil, to be the NFL's first special teams coach. The impact of this move — on the return game in particular — has been rather dramatic. Check out the top ten seasons for kickoff-return and punt-return average . . . and note that only two came after 1969 (and neither later than '74):

HIGHEST KICKOFF RETURN AVERAGE (SINGLE-SEASON)

Year, returner, team	Avg.
1967 Travis Williams, Packers	41.1
1967 Gale Sayers, Bears	37.7
1958 Ollie Matson, Cardinals	35.5
1970 Jim Duncan, Colts	35.4
1952 Lynn Chandnois, Steelers	35.2
1968 Preston Pearson, Colts	35.1
1953 Joe Arenas, 49ers	34.4
1965 Tom Watkins, Lions	34.4
1950 Vitamin Smith, Rams	33.7
1969 Bobby Williams, Lions	33.1

HIGHEST PUNT RETURN AVERAGE (SINGLE-SEASON)

Year, returner, team	Avg.
1952 Jack Christiansen, Lions	21.5
1961 Dick Christy, New York Titans	21.3
1948 Rex Bumgardner, Buffalo Bills*	21.0
1948 Jerry Davis, Cardinals	20.9

1949 Red Cochran, Cardinals	20.9
1968 Bob Hayes, Cowboys	20.8
1950 Billy Grimes, Packers	19.1
1951 Jack Christiansen, Lions	19.1
1974 Lemar Parrish, Bengals	18.8
1946 Chuck Fenenbock, LA Dons*	18.7

*All-America Conference

Interesting, isn't it? Not even Devin Hester, who ran back eleven punts and kickoffs for touchdowns in his first two seasons with the Bears, was able to crack the top ten. Hester's highest kickoff-return average is 26.4 (2006), and his highest punt-return average is 17.1 (2010).

Once the NFL started giving special teams the attention they deserved, you stopped seeing kickoff-return averages in the midthirties and punt-return averages up around twenty. Of course, that wasn't the only factor involved. After 1970 you didn't often have future Hall of Famers like Gale Sayers, Ollie Matson, and Bob Hayes running back kicks. And the expansion of rosters from forty in 1969 to fifty-three today has enabled clubs to use actual specialists on their kicking units rather than stocking them with starters, who already have enough to do. Punters and kickers have improved, too.

But there's no question special teams coaches have helped professionalize — to a far greater degree than before — this area of the game. Until Vermeil came along, special teams tended to be a shared responsibility on coaching staffs, and there wasn't much time spent on them. But that changed in a hurry. The next year the 49ers brought in Doug Scovil to oversee their kicking units, and it just mushroomed from there.

(Vermeil held the job for only a year, but it sounds like he did some real experimenting. In a 9–7 win over Chicago, for instance, one of the Rams' field goals was set up by a bad snap that punter Bobby Joe Green couldn't catch. What caused it, Vermeil said, was lining up Hall of Fame defensive end Deacon Jones "right over their center. The Bear coaches started yelling 'Jones is in the game' [and] . . .

'Jones is over your nose.' This apparently upset [center Mike] Pyle. It caused the high snap. We've used [Deacon] three times on punts this year where he has been placed over the center. And twice the ball has been snapped over the punter's head.")

The last straw for Allen — what made him finally see the light — was when his Rams got knocked out of playoff contention in the next-to-last game of 1968. One of the key plays in the 17–16 loss was an 88-yard kickoff return by the Bears' Clarence Childs. In a book he later collaborated on, *George Allen's Guide to Special Teams*, Allen blamed the return on a missed tackle by reserve running back Vilnis Ezerins, an error George attributed to Ezerins's "lack of tackling fundamentals."

"We never should have placed him in that position; he was not the right man for the job," Allen wrote. "It was then that I decided a special teams coordinator was needed!"

That was Ezerins's only NFL season. Career statistics: two rushes for 2 yards. But he left a mark on the game nonetheless. He helped spark a special teams revolution.

• • •

The *human* body isn't meant to play football at *any* level. — Don Meredith, former Cowboys quarterback (as quoted by sportscaster Jim Lampley in Curt Smith's *Of Mikes and Men*)

• • •

Johnny B. Bad

Grudges in pro football can linger longer than a bad case of jock itch. Exhibit A: Johnny Sample, the Jets' motormouthed cornerback, who waited *eleven years* to get even with Otto Graham for hardly playing him in the 1958 College All-Star Game.

Lots of players, of course, didn't see much action in the annual game against the NFL champions (such as future president Jerry Ford — then *Michigan center* Jerry Ford). But that wasn't the only problem Sample had with the All-Stars' coach. He also was upset that, after the game, Graham had written a letter to the Colts, who had drafted Johnny, and given him a less-than-glowing recommendation.

There was such antipathy between the two that when Otto took over the Redskins in 1966, one of the first things he did was trade the high-strung Sample, even though Johnny was the club's best corner. Soon enough, Sample was being drummed out of the NFL—and into the arms of the AFL's Jets.

Wonder of wonders, the Jets upset the Colts in Super Bowl III, which meant *they* got to play against the College All-Stars the following August. And who should be back coaching the All-Stars—after a failed stint with the Redskins—but Otto Graham?

Talk about an accident waiting to happen. In this case, it waited until the last minute of the game, when Sample cracked the All-Stars' Gene Washington with a forearm that left a welt under the receiver's right eye. Graham charged onto the field demanding a penalty. Johnny told Otto to butt out and, for good measure, bashed his facemask into the bridge of Otto's nose. Blood flowed. Somewhere in there, the coach threw some punches that caromed harmlessly off the cornerback's helmet.

After they were separated, Graham was hit with a 15-yard penalty for leaving the bench area. But that wasn't quite the end of it. There were reports that Otto's *son*, David, went after Sample—not once but twice—and landed a couple of blows.

Sample never played another game. He hurt his back against the All-Stars, was put in traction upon returning to New York, and decided to retire when the condition didn't improve. Which was just was as well, Joe Namath said. If Johnny had kept it up much longer, the Jets' quarterback joked, he would have been "the first man to be blackballed from both leagues."

What I've Learned: Johnny Sample

Trash-talking cornerback with the Colts, Steelers, Redskins, and Jets, 1958–68

"I try to see through the receiver and anticipate him. I play him as close as possible, but when the quarterback releases the ball, I figure it belongs as much to me as to anyone else."

"The more I can irritate a player, the better it is for me. If I make him mad enough so he wants to try and get back at me, it'll hurt him. He'll run a different play from what he should."

"You have to be violent to be a good defensive back. You have to want to hurt the other guy."

"I'll break them in half when they're trying to catch a pass. The man on the field has to be better than the man on the bench. So if I can stun the man on the field, the man on the bench has to come in."

"I know I have the reputation of trying to intimidate the receiver. [Coach Weeb] Ewbank told me a long time ago when I was with the Colts that if I kept it up, I'd become unpopular. I decided to make my bed. It's my way of life."

"Lance Alworth is a much better receiver than [Homer] Jones or Bob Hayes. Homer doesn't make any moves on you, he just tries to outrun you. Hayes doesn't like to get hit. He'll catch passes against a team like New Orleans, but he never does anything against a tough team like the Packers."

"I think [Fred Biletnikoff] is an average receiver. I don't think he will ever be a great receiver because he hasn't got blazing speed."

"[Steelers coach Buddy Parker once told him during contract talks] that black ballplayers don't deserve as much money as white ballplayers."

"One of the most satisfying moments in the 1964 season came

in our first game with the Steelers. I intercepted a pass that game and took it all the way back for a touchdown. After hitting the end zone I ran straight over to the Steeler bench and threw the ball at Buddy Parker's face."

"I told [Redskins owner Edward Bennett] Williams that if a top pass receiver gets forty thousand dollars and I can hold the guy down, why shouldn't I get as much money as him?"

"Most of the guys in the NFL feel their league is superior [to the AFL]. I'll admit I felt the same way. But after I got here I realized there wasn't that much difference. I was really surprised by the caliber of play. I had to work as hard as I ever did."

"Every pro wants to get to the Super Bowl. But, for me, it means more than money or glory. I'm bitter, I admit it. I want to be on the first AFL team to beat the best in the NFL."

"[Super Bowl III vs. the Colts] means more to me than any game I've ever played in my life, more to me than anything I've ever done. If we don't win the game, to me the whole season, my whole career will be for nothing. That's what this game means to me."

"[Pete] Rozelle has too much power. He's biased against the AFL, because it was the NFL which gave him his job."

"The option clause doesn't mean anything anymore. They've got you by the throat. Rozelle and the owners, if they want to get you, they get you.

"Every black player who has ever spoken out has been dealt with one way or the other."

"I got into plenty of trouble. But I stood up for what I believed in.

1960s

375

I didn't kiss a white man's ass or snitch on my black brother to get where I did. I made it on my ability."

"Football is valuable. It teaches you something about the competitive system of America. You learn you've got to fight to survive, work harder than the next guy, hit harder if you want to get to the top. And try to take a little advantage if you can, if you don't get caught."

Afterword

This is as good a place to stop as any. Think about it: The book began with the Silent '20s—so quiet you could hear the wind whip-
ping through the stadium—and it ends with Johnny Sample running his mouth (often for the pure sport of it). Pro football had
finally found its volume dial . . . and now, forty years later, everybody is Mic'd Up. Thanks to TV, radio, and the Internet, the NFL
doesn't have a single unexpressed thought anymore.

Besides, everything after 1969 has been epilogue. The NFL hasn't
had to deal with a serious threat since it merged with the AFL—only
with mosquitoes like the World Football League, the United States
Football League, and the XFL. The past four decades have basically
been spent fine-tuning the product, maximizing profits, fending
off lawsuits, and tending to labor matters. I'll let *you* write the book
about *those* years.

To me, the first fifty years were the best fifty years. They were the
years of struggle. They were the years of creation. They were the
years of "We interrupt this program to bring you the Second World
War." They were the rough-around-the-edges years when people
said what was on their mind—without parsing words or worrying
too much about the consequences.

Don't get me wrong, pro football is still a joy to watch. But the
enterprise itself has become exceedingly corporate. Jerry Richard-
son of the Carolina Panthers is the only owner—and probably the

last—to have gotten his uniform dirty on the fields of the NFL. And Al Davis went from being the AFL's lovable renegade to the NFL Owner Most Likely to Sue the League. (Assuming, that is, he could decide whether to file in Oakland or Los Angeles.)

Everything about the game these days is neater. But maybe it wasn't meant to be so neat. Maybe it was meant to be more unpredictable, to have more twists and turns.

Allow me to illustrate. In 1950 NFL teams committed 582 turnovers and missed 99 field goals and 29 extra points. Total number of hiccups: 710, or 9.1 per game. At least once a quarter, in other words, each club would either lose the ball or miss a kick. You don't think it made those games absolutely wild? (And we haven't even talked about dropped passes, which I'm guessing were more prevalent because gloves hadn't come into fashion yet.)

Now let's look at the recently completed 2010 season. The turnovers/missed field goals/missed PATs total was 1,044—4.1 per game. That's *five* fewer momentum-turning, blood-pressure-elevating plays a game. You can't tell me that doesn't change the viewing experience.

Bert Bell, the longtime commissioner, dropped dead at an NFL game in the '50s. So did 49ers owner Tony Morabito. So did two spectators, including George Halas's sister-in-law, at a Bears-Packers matchup in 1941. Something tells me it wasn't a coincidence. There was a topsy-turvy aspect to pro football in those years that's missing now.

NFL football in the new millennium is more like a video game. You have quarterbacks completing twenty-two, twenty-three, twenty-four consecutive passes (many of them barely crossing the line of scrimmage). You have running backs carrying the ball five hundred or more times without a fumble. You have kickers going an entire season without misfiring.

Yet, for all this exactness, teams are scoring fewer points than they did in 1950. (And they'd be scoring *many* fewer points if kickers hadn't gotten so darn good.)

OK, I'm done pontificating. Maybe you agree with me, maybe you don't. Just thought the first fifty years of pro football deserved a book of their own.

FIFTY REASONS WHY THE FIRST FIFTY YEARS OF PRO FOOTBALL ARE BETTER THAN THE SECOND FIFTY

1. The personal seat license hadn't been invented yet.
2. Neither had the organized team activity.
3. Or Twitter—and all its opportunities for embarrassment—for that matter.
4. Fans didn't spend the day after the Super Bowl talking about the commercials.
5. In the early days it was more than just a big-city game. The NFL also had clubs in Pottsville, Pennsylvania; Staten Island, New York; and Marion, Ohio.
6. If so inclined, a player (e.g., Gus Sonnenberg) could spend the off-season becoming the heavyweight wrestling champion of the world.
7. To this day, no one has matched the forty points scored by the Cardinals' Ernie Nevers against the Bears in 1929.
8. Ask any old-timer and he'll tell you: It was more of a players' game. Translation: Quarterbacks called their own plays. Coaches didn't micromanage as much.
9. Sixty-minute men.
10. The dropkick.
11. Bronko Nagurski. Red Grange said trying to tackle the Bears legend was "almost like getting an electric shock." A trainer for another team said, "Nagurski was responsible for more mysterious ailments than an unknown germ from the Orient." Tuffy Thompson, who graduated from Minnesota several years after Nagurski, told me, "One day during winter practice in the field house, he came in with a coat on and a hat, and I got behind him and you couldn't even see me. And I had my pads on! His arms were as big as my legs." Grown men, the toughest of tough guys, talked about Bronko with absolute awe. There'll never be another like him.

12. What could be better than a Wednesday night game in Portsmouth, Ohio?

13. With a white football, no less.

14. There were no uniform police. Heck, you weren't even required to wear socks until 1945.

15. More touchdowns, fewer field goals.

16. Before face masks, when a player had a nose for the ball, he *really* had a nose for the ball.

17. There's something romantic about train travel — marathon card games, swapping stories, Pullman cars . . . and watching America go by.

18. The Bears-Cardinals rivalry — with Chicago bragging rights at stake.

19. The defense had more of a fighting chance. Holding by offensive linemen hadn't been legalized yet. Neither had intentional grounding. The one-bump rule, meanwhile, was still a few years off.

20. Pro football was one big laboratory in its first half century. In the mid-'40s, for example, the Packers' Curly Lambeau coached several games from the press box, just to see if it might give him an edge. He eventually abandoned the experiment, but hey, at least he gave it a shot.

21. The goalposts were on the goal line, creating all kinds of possibilities. Don Hutson, the Packers Hall of Fame receiver, once swung around one of the posts, left his defender in the dust, and caught a touchdown pass in the corner of the end zone — his own version of the post-corner route.

22. You could buy a ticket on the day of the game.

23. Smaller rosters — and more limited substitution — forced players to multitask. In 1946 the Rams' Bob Waterfield led the NFL in touchdown passes (seventeen), converted six of nine field goal tries, averaged 44.7 yards a punt, and intercepted five passes.

24. The rules allowed for more trickery. It wasn't until 1951, for instance, that the tackle-eligible play was outlawed.

25. Also, the Statue of Liberty play was run the way it's *supposed* to be

run. As Cardinals Hall of Famer Charley Trippi described it, "A back fades back as if to pass, cocks his arm back, and then another back or end runs behind him and takes the ball out of his hand to run with it."

26. On top of that, the halfback pass — always a crowd-pleaser — was more common because halfbacks could actually pass proficiently. Players simply were more well-rounded back then.

27. Nobody got too bent out of shape when a game ended in a tie.

28. What's wrong with having a little thrill in the extra point (never mind the field goal)?

29. Owners had much more interesting personal lives. The Redskins' George Preston Marshall and the Dodgers' Dan Topping were married to movie stars. The Eagles' Lex Thompson competed in the 1939 world bobsledding championships (and once broke his ankle in a crash at Lake Placid). The Steelers' Art Rooney was a legendary horse player. I could go on, but you get the idea.

30. A 1,000-yard season in a twelve- or fourteen-game schedule really meant something.

31. Coaches didn't agonize much about running up the score. Indeed, the seven highest point totals in NFL history — 73, 72, 70, 65 (twice), 64, and 63 — all came in the first fifty years. After laying 70 on the Colts in an *exhibition* game in 1950, Rams coach Joe Stydahar said, "Sure we poured it on. I wish we could have beaten them by a hundred points."

32. The NFL draft was dispensed with in a day.

33. There was no *Dancing with the Stars*.

34. Jack Kemp. After quarterbacking the Bills to two AFL titles, he went into politics and became the Republican nominee for vice president. Don't count on anybody doing *that* again.

35. A player never injured himself while celebrating.

36. The greatest team name in pro football history, hands down, is the Providence Steam Roller.

37. Quirky stadiums. At the Cycledrome in Providence the field was

surrounded by a bicycle track that chopped five yards off the corners of one end zone. At Wrigley Field in Chicago the ivy-covered wall and one of the baseball dugouts both could get in the way. At Yankee Stadium in New York the field sloped decidedly downhill (or uphill, depending on which direction you were going). It just added to the unpredictability of the games.

38. No strike seasons, no replacement players.

39. Quarterbacks took ball faking more seriously.

40. Dynasties could run their natural course. They weren't cannibalized by free agency.

41. Nicknames weren't just more numerous, they were more imaginative. Such as: Walter "Sneeze" Achui (Dayton Triangles back, 1927–28). And: Edgar "Eggs" Manske (Bears, Eagles, and Pittsburgh Pirates end, 1935–40). Manske got stuck with the moniker, he once explained, because "I love eggs. Always did. As a kid, reared on a farm, I could have as many eggs as I wanted to. Fact is, I was so fond of [them] I'd eat 'em raw. Sometimes I eat them three times a day. Any style — fried, scrambled, poached, soft-boiled, baked, hard-boiled. . . . I don't know anyone else named Eggs. I much prefer it to my given name."

42. When Kate Smith sang the national anthem before the Yanks' first game in Boston in 1944, she didn't lip-synch it.

43. The College All-Star Game, which pitted a team of All-Americans against the defending NFL champs, was a much better way to kick off the season than the Hall of Fame Game. (For one thing, starters actually *played* in the College All-Star Game.)

44. The voice — authoritative, understated — of CBS's Ray Scott. ("And we're underway at Lambeau Field!") For Ray, less was always more.

45. There's never been a rival league like the AFL.

46. Until the Super Bowl era, title games were more subject to the elements. (In fact, the weather was often the twelfth man on the field.)

47. Players didn't live in gated communities or dine in cordoned-off sections of restaurants.

48. Nobody ever got arrested for solicitation on the eve of the championship game.
49. Vince Lombardi's last day on earth was September 3, 1970.
50. Howard Cosell—the sportscaster who made "the world of fun and games sound like the Nuremberg trials," as Larry Merchant once put it—debuted on *Monday Night Football* eighteen days later.

Appendix

Bests, 1930–39

Note: All statistics except for scoring are for the 1932–39 period. League stats didn't become official until 1932.

Quarterbacks

Passing yards

DECADE: 6,189, Arnie Herber, Packers

SEASON: 1,324, Davey O'Brien, Eagles, 1939

GAME: 335, Sammy Baugh, Redskins vs. Bears, December 12, 1937 (title game)

Touchdown passes

DECADE: 60, Herber

SEASON: 11, Harry Newman, Giants, 1933; Herber, 1936; Frank Filchock, Redskins, 1939

GAME: 5, Ray Buivid, Bears vs. Cardinals, December 5, 1937

Percent completions

DECADE: (350 or more attempts): 49.9, Baugh

SEASON: 61.8, Filchock, 1939

Running Backs

Rushing yards

DECADE: 3,511, Cliff Battles, Redskins

SEASON: 1,004, Beattie Feathers, Bears, 1934

GAME: 215, Battles vs. Giants, October 8, 1933

Rushing touchdowns

DECADE: 36, Dutch Clark, Portsmouth Spartans/Lions

SEASON: 9, Johnny Drake, Rams, 1939

GAME: 3, Andy Farkas, Redskins vs. Rams, September 25, 1938

Yards from scrimmage

DECADE: 4,057, Battles

SEASON: 1,178, Feathers, 1934

GAME: 215, Battles vs. Giants, October 8, 1933

LONGEST RUN: 97, Andy Uram, Packers vs. Cardinals, October 8, 1939

Receivers

Receptions

DECADE: 159, Don Hutson, Packers

SEASON: 41, Hutson, 1937; Gus Tinsley, Cardinals, 1938

GAME: 8, by several (last to do it: Red Ramsey, Eagles vs. Bears, November 19, 1939)

Receiving yards

DECADE: 2,902, Hutson

SEASON: 846, Hutson, 1939

GAME: 167, Tinsley (twice), vs. Redskins, September 24, 1937, vs. Rams November 27, 1938

Touchdown catches

DECADE: 36, Hutson

SEASON: 11, Johnny (Blood) McNally, Packers, 1931

GAME: 3, by many (Hutson did it three times, the last vs. Rams, October 30, 1938)

LONGEST RECEPTION: 99, Farkas, Redskins vs. Pittsburgh Pirates, October 15, 1939

Scoring

Points

DECADE: 369, Dutch Clark, Portsmouth Spartans/Lions

SEASON: 84, McNally, 1931

GAME: 22, Hank Bruder, Packers vs. Cincinnati, October 14, 1934

Touchdowns

DECADE: 42, Clark

SEASON: 14, McNally, 1931

GAME: 3, by many (last to do it: Farkas, Redskins vs. Brooklyn Dodgers, November 12, 1939)

Field goals

DECADE: 38, Jack Manders, Bears

SEASON: 10, Manders, 1934

GAME: 3, Phil Martinovich, Lions vs. Giants, November 5, 1939

LONGEST FIELD GOAL: 54, Glenn Presnell, Lions vs. Packers, October 7, 1934

Miscellaneous

LONGEST WINNING STREAK: 18, 1933–34 Bears

LONGEST UNBEATEN STREAK: 23, 1928–30 Packers (21-0-2)

Bests, 1940–49

Quarterbacks

Passing yards

DECADE: 17,002, Sammy Baugh, Redskins

SEASON: 2,938, Baugh, 1947

GAME: 468, Johnny Lujack, Bears vs. Cardinals, December 11, 1949

Touchdown passes

DECADE: 149, Baugh

SEASON: 29, Frankie Albert, 49ers (AAC), 1948

GAME: 7, Sid Luckman, Bears vs. Giants, November 14, 1943

Percent completions

DECADE: (800 or more attempts): 58.7, Baugh

SEASON: 70.3, Baugh, 1945

Running Backs

Rushing yards

DECADE: 4,904, Steve Van Buren, Eagles

SEASON: 1,432, Spec Sanders, New York Yankees (AAC), 1947

GAME: 250, Sanders, vs. Chicago Rockets, October 24, 1947

Rushing touchdowns

DECADE: 59, Van Buren

SEASON: 18, Sanders, 1947

GAME: 3, by many (last to do it: Joe Perry of the AAC's 49ers vs. Buffalo Bills, October 16, 1949)

Yards from scrimmage

DECADE: 5,365, Van Buren

SEASON: 1,617, Chet Mutryn, Buffalo Bills (AAC), 1948

GAME: 250, Sanders, vs. Chicago Rockets, October 24, 1947

LONGEST RUN: 97, Bob Gage, Steelers vs. Bears, December 4, 1949

Receivers

Receptions

    DECADE: 329, Don Hutson, Packers

    SEASON: 77, Tom Fears, Rams, 1949

    GAME: 14, by several (last to do it: Ralph Heywood, New York Bulldogs vs. Lions, December 4, 1949)

Receiving yards

    DECADE: 5,089, Hutson

    SEASON: 1,211, Hutson, 1942

    GAME: 303, Jim Benton, Rams vs. Lions, November 22, 1945

Touchdown catches

    DECADE: 63, Hutson

    SEASON: 17, Hutson, 1942

    GAME: 4, by several (last to do it: Bob Shaw, Rams vs. Redskins, December 11, 1949)

    LONGEST RECEPTION: 99, Mac Speedie, Browns vs. Buffalo (AAC), November 2, 1947

Scoring

Points

    DECADE: 589, Hutson

    SEASON: 138, Hutson, 1942

    GAME: 31, Hutson, vs. Lions, October 7, 1945

Touchdowns

    DECADE: 67, Hutson

    SEASON: 19, Sanders, 1947

    GAME: 4, by several (last to do it: Bob Shaw, Rams vs. Redskins, December 11, 1949)

Field goals

    DECADE: 33, Ted Fritsch, Packers

    SEASON: 15, Ben Agajanian, Los Angeles Dons (AAC), 1947

    GAME: 3, Lou Groza, Browns vs. Miami Seahawks (AAC), September 6, 1946; Agajanian, vs. Brooklyn Dodgers (AAC), November 23, 1947

    LONGEST FIELD GOAL: 53, Agajanian, vs. Baltimore Colts (AAC), October 19, 1947; Groza, vs. Brooklyn Dodgers (AAC), October 10, 1948

Miscellaneous

Interceptions

    DECADE: 34, Irv Comp, Packers

SEASON: 13, Dan Sandifer, Redskins, 1948

GAME: 4, by several (last to do it: Bob Nussbaumer, Cardinals vs. New York Bulldogs, November 13, 1949)

LONGEST INTERCEPTION RETURN: 102, Bob Smith, Lions vs. Bears, November 24, 1949

Punting average

DECADE: (150 or more punts): 46.4, Glenn Dobbs, Brooklyn Dodgers/Los Angeles Dons (AAC)

SEASON: 51.4, Baugh, 1940

LONGEST PUNT: 88, Bob Waterfield, Rams vs. Packers, October 17, 1948

PUNT RETURN TOUCHDOWNS, DECADE: 3, Scooter McLean, Bears

LONGEST PUNT RETURN: 94, Tom Casey, New York Yankees vs. Brooklyn Dodgers (AAC), August 27, 1948

KICKOFF RETURN TOUCHDOWNS: 3, Van Buren

LONGEST KICKOFF RETURN: 105, Frank Seno, Cardinals vs. Giants, October 20, 1946

LONGEST WINNING STREAK: 18, 1941–42 Bears (including 1941 title game); 1947–48 Browns (including 1947 and 1948 AAC title games)

LONGEST UNBEATEN STREAK: 29, 1947–49 Browns (27-0-2, including 1947 and 1948 AAC title games)

Bests, 1950–59

Quarterbacks

Passing yards

DECADE: 20,539, Norm Van Brocklin, Rams/Eagles

SEASON: 2,899, Johnny Unitas, Colts, 1959

GAME: 554, Van Brocklin, Rams vs. New York Yanks, September 28, 1951

Touchdown passes

DECADE: 151, Bobby Layne, Lions/Steelers

SEASON: 32, Unitas, 1959

GAME: 7, Adrian Burk, Eagles vs. Redskins, October 17, 1954

Percent completions

DECADE: (1,000 or more passes): 55.7, Otto Graham, Browns

SEASON: 64.7, Graham, 1953

Running Backs

Rushing yards

DECADE: 7,151, Joe Perry, 49ers

SEASON: 1,527, Jim Brown, Browns, 1958

GAME: 237, Brown, vs. Rams, November 24, 1957

Rushing touchdowns

DECADE: 49, Perry

SEASON: 17, Brown, 1958

GAME: 5, Brown, vs. Colts, November 1, 1959

Yards from scrimmage

DECADE: 8,422, Perry

SEASON: 1,665, Brown, 1958

GAME: 276, Ollie Matson, Cardinals vs. Steelers, November 28, 1954

LONGEST RUN: 96, Jim Spavital, Colts vs. Packers, November 5, 1950; Bob Hoernschemeyer, Lions vs. New York Yanks, November 23, 1950

Receivers

Receptions

DECADE: 404, Billy Wilson, 49ers

SEASON: 84, Tom Fears, Rams, 1950

GAME: 18, Fears, vs. Packers, December 3, 1950

Receiving yards

DECADE: 6,091, Billy Howton, Packers/Browns

SEASON: 1,495, Elroy "Crazylegs" Hirsch, Rams, 1951

GAME: 302, Cloyce Box, Lions vs. Colts, December 3, 1950

Touchdown catches

DECADE: 49, Hirsch

SEASON: 17, Hirsch, 1951

GAME: 5, Bob Shaw, Cardinals vs. Colts, October 2, 1950

LONGEST RECEPTION: 98, Night Train Lane, Cardinals vs. Packers, November 13, 1955

Scoring

Points

DECADE: 742, Lou Groza, Browns

SEASON: 128, Doak Walker, Lions, 1950

GAME: 36, Dub Jones, Browns vs. Bears, November 25, 1951

Touchdowns

DECADE: 56, Perry; Matson, Cardinals/Rams

SEASON: 18, Brown, 1958

GAME: 6, Jones, vs. Bears, November 25, 1951

Field goals

DECADE: 131, Groza

SEASON: 23, Groza, 1953

GAME: 5, Bob Waterfield, Rams vs. Lions, December 9, 1951

LONGEST FIELD GOAL: 56, Bert Rechichar, Colts vs. Bears, September 27, 1953

Miscellaneous

Interceptions

DECADE: 59, Emlen Tunnell, Giants

SEASON: 14, Lane, Rams, 1952

GAME: 4, by several (last to do it: Jack Butler, Steelers vs. Redskins, December 13, 1953)

LONGEST INTERCEPTION RETURN: 99, Jerry Norton, Eagles vs. Giants, October 5, 1957

Punting average

DECADE: (200 or more punts): 44.5, Pat Brady, Steelers

SEASON: 47.13, Yale Lary, Lions, 1959

LONGEST PUNT: 86, Larry Barnes, 49ers vs. Cardinals, September 29, 1957

PUNT RETURN TOUCHDOWNS, DECADE: 8, Jack Christiansen, Lions

LONGEST PUNT RETURN: 96, Bill Dudley, Redskins vs. Steelers, December 3, 1950

KICKOFF RETURN TOUCHDOWNS: 6, Matson, Cardinals

LONGEST KICKOFF RETURN: 106, Al Carmichael, Packers vs. Bears, October 7, 1956

LONGEST WINNING STREAK: 11, Browns, 1951 and 1953

Bests, 1960–69

Quarterbacks

Passing yards

DECADE: 26,548, Johnny Unitas, Colts

SEASON: 4,007, Joe Namath, Jets, 1967

GAME: 505, Y. A. Tittle, Giants vs. Redskins, October 28, 1962

Touchdown passes

DECADE: 207, Sonny Jurgensen, Eagles/Redskins

SEASON: 36, George Blanda, Oilers, 1961; Tittle, 1963

GAME: 7, Blanda, vs. New York Titans, November 19, 1961; Tittle, vs. Redskins, October 28, 1962; Joe Kapp, Vikings vs. Colts, September 28, 1969

Percent completions

DECADE: (1,000 or more passes): 58.9, Bart Starr, Packers

SEASON: 63.7, Starr, 1968

Running Backs

Rushing yards
    DECADE: 8,514, Jim Brown, Browns
    SEASON: 1,863, Brown, 1963
    GAME: 243, Cookie Gilchrist, Bills vs. Jets, December 8, 1963
Rushing touchdowns
    DECADE: 76, Jim Taylor, Packers/Saints
    SEASON: 19, Taylor, Packers, 1962
    GAME: 5, Gilchrist, vs. Jets, December 8, 1963
Yards from scrimmage
    DECADE: 10,630, Brown
    SEASON: 2,131, Brown, 1963
    GAME: 330, Billy Cannon, Oilers vs. New York Titans, December 10, 1961
    LONGEST RUN: 91, Sid Blanks, Oilers vs. Jets, December 13, 1964

Receivers

Receptions
    DECADE: 567, Lionel Taylor, Broncos/Oilers
    SEASON: 101, Charley Hennigan, Oilers, 1964
    GAME: 16, Sonny Randle, Cardinals vs. Giants, November 4, 1962
Receiving yards
    DECADE: 10,289, Don Maynard, New York Titans/Jets
    SEASON: 1,746, Hennigan, 1961
    GAME: 272, Hennigan, vs. Patriots, October 13, 1961
Touchdown catches
    DECADE: 84, Maynard
    SEASON: 17, Bill Groman, Oilers, 1961
    GAME: 4, by several (last to do it: Dave Williams, Cardinals vs. Saints, November 2, 1969)
    LONGEST RECEPTION: 99, Bobby Mitchell, Redskins vs. Browns, September 15, 1963; Pat Studstill, Lions vs. Colts, October 16, 1966; Gerry Allen, Redskins vs. Bears, September 15, 1968

Scoring

Points
    DECADE: 1,100, Gino Cappelletti, Patriots
    SEASON: 176, Paul Hornung, Packers, 1960
    GAME: 36, Gale Sayers, Bears vs. 49ers, December 12, 1965
Touchdowns
    DECADE: 84, Brown; Maynard, Jets

SEASON: 22, Sayers, 1965

GAME: 6, Sayers, vs. 49ers, December 12, 1965

Field goals

DECADE: 171, Lou Michaels, Rams/Steelers/Colts

SEASON: 34, Jim Turner, Jets, 1968

GAME: 7, Jim Bakken, Cardinals vs. Steelers, September 24, 1967

LONGEST FIELD GOAL: 55, Blanda, Oilers vs. Chargers, December 3, 1961; Tom Dempsey, Saints vs. Rams, October 5, 1969

Miscellaneous

Interceptions

DECADE: 57, Bobby Boyd, Colts

SEASON: 12, Fred Glick, Oilers, 1963; Paul Krause, Redskins, 1964; Dainard Paulson, Jets, 1964

GAME: 4, by many (Jerry Norton, Cardinals, did it twice, vs. Redskins, November 20, 1960, and vs. Steelers, November 26, 1961)

LONGEST INTERCEPTION RETURN: 102, Erich Barnes, Giants vs. Cowboys, October 15, 1961

Punting average

DECADE: (200 or more punts): 46.2, Yale Lary, Lions

SEASON: 48.9, Lary, 1963

LONGEST PUNT: 98, Steve O'Neal, Jets vs. Broncos, September 21, 1969

PUNT RETURN TOUCHDOWNS, DECADE: 4, Dick Christy, New York Titans; Speedy Duncan, Chargers

LONGEST PUNT RETURN: 98, Charlie West, Vikings vs. Redskins, November 3, 1968

KICKOFF RETURN TOUCHDOWNS: 6, Gale Sayers, Bears

LONGEST KICKOFF RETURN: 106, Noland Smith, Chiefs vs. Broncos, December 17, 1967

LONGEST WINNING STREAK: 12, 1961–62 Packers (1961 title game included); 1969 Vikings

LONGEST UNBEATEN STREAK: 15, 1966–67 Colts (13-0-2, including Playoff Bowl after 1966 season)

A Note about Sources

Out of necessity, not choice, much of this work relies on second-ary sources. Let's face it, a séance would be required to interview a player from the '20s or '30s these days, and those from the '40s and '50s are going fast. That leaves the '60s, and who remembers much of *anything* from those smoke-filled years? (Just kidding.)

Not that I didn't track down a fair number of pro football pio-neers and get their recollections on tape. I drove five hundred miles one weekend when the Redskins were in Dallas to talk to Slingin' Sammy Baugh on his ranch in Rotan, Texas. I drove from Pitts-burgh to Ashtabula, Ohio, after a Penguins-Capitals playoff series to reminisce with Ray Kemp, one of the early black players. I looked up Sid Luckman in Florida, spent several nights with Joe Perry in Arizona, called Hal Van Every (the World War II prisoner of war) on the phone, and exchanged e-mails with Ede Prendergast (grand-daughter of the great — and forgotten — Harry March, the Giants' first general manager). I did, in other words, what I could.

But when you reach as far back into the past as I'm reaching, you have to be willing to settle for less than the horse's mouth. You have to read voluminously — old books, newspapers, magazines, scrapbooks, anything that will give you a glimpse into this van-ishing era. You have to spend time looking at vintage game tapes at the Pro Football Hall of Fame. You have to block off days just for browsing, for throwing names and words (like "ran into the goalpost") into search engines and seeing what turns up. Some of my favorite items in the book are ones I stumbled across while researching other items. So it goes in the history racket.

Fortunately, having explored this turf before, I knew what I was getting into. I knew that even good *secondary*-source material could be hard to come by, knew that many stories would have to be built almost like a mosaic — with snippets from newspapers (often several), sound bites from interviews (ditto), brief passages from books (ditto again), and whatever kitchen sink I might throw in.

In many places the source of the material is cited in the text. The extensive bibliography that follows should answer any other questions you might have about where I got my information. My goal, as much anything, was to hack away at the mythology that, like a poison vine, has grown up around the early days of the game. Remember that famous line from *The Man Who Shot Liberty Valance*: "When the legend becomes fact, print the legend"? Well, there's none of that nonsense going on here.

Anything that didn't pass the smell test — or couldn't be verified by multiple sources — was quickly cast aside. And for what it's worth, my olfactory attributes are the product of thirty-five years in the sportswriting profession (and almost that many nosing around in pro football's dusty archives). Hope you enjoy the final product.

Bibliography

Books

All-America Conference team media guides. All-America Conference, 1946–49.

Allen, George, and Joseph G. Pacelli. *George Allen's Guide to Special Teams*. Champaign IL: Leisure Press, 1990.

American Football League Official Guide. St. Louis: Sporting News, 1962–69.

American Football League Official History. St. Louis: Sporting News, 1970.

Bagli, Vince, and Norman L. Macht. *Sundays at 2:00 with the Baltimore Colts*. Centreville MD: Tidewater, 1995.

Becker, Carl M. *Home and Away*. Athens: Ohio University Press, 1998.

Bisheff, Steve. *Los Angeles Rams*. New York: Macmillan, 1973.

Canadian Football League Statistics. Canadian Football League, 1950–66.

Carroll, Bob, Pete Palmer, and John Thorn. *The Hidden Game of Football*. New York: Warner, 1988.

Carroll, Bob, et al. *Total Football*. New York: HarperCollins, 1997.

Carroll, John M. *Fritz Pollard*. Urbana: University of Illinois Press, 1992.

———. *Red Grange and the Rise of Modern Football*. Urbana: University of Illinois Press, 1999.

Christman, Paul. *Tricks in Passing*. Chicago: Ziff-Davis, 1948.

Clark, Potsy. *Football*. New York: A. G. Spalding and Brothers, 1935.

Clary, Jack. *Cleveland Browns*. New York: Macmillan, 1973.

———. *Washington Redskins*. New York: Macmillan, 1974.

Cohen, Rich. *Tough Jews*. New York: Simon and Schuster, 1998.

Complete Pro Football Draft Encyclopedia. St. Louis: Sporting News, 2005.

Conerly, Perian. *Backseat Quarterback*. Garden City NY: Doubleday, 1963.

Cope, Myron. *Broken Cigars*. Englewood Cliffs NJ: Prentice Hall, 1968.

————. *The Game That Was.* New York: World Publishing, 1970.

Curran, Bob. *The $400,000 Quarterback.* New York: Macmillan, 1965.

————. *Pro Football's Rag Days.* Englewood Cliffs NJ: Prentice Hall, 1969.

D'Amato, Gary, and Cliff Christl. *Mudbaths and Bloodbaths.* Madison WI: Prairie Oaks Press, 1997.

Davis, Jeff. *Papa Bear.* New York: McGraw-Hill, 2005.

Dickey, Glenn. *The San Francisco 49ers: The First Fifty Years.* Atlanta: Turner Publishing, 1995.

Didinger, Ray. *Pittsburgh Steelers.* New York: Macmillan, 1974.

Didinger, Ray, and Robert S. Lyons. *The Eagles Encyclopedia.* Philadelphia: Temple University Press, 2005.

Donovan, Art, and Bob Drury. *Fatso.* New York: Morrow, 1987.

Eisenberg, John. *Cotton Bowl Days.* New York: Simon and Schuster, 1997.

Eskenazi, Gerald. *There Were Giants in Those Days.* New York: Grosset and Dunlap, 1976.

Evans, Lon. *The Purple Lawman: From Horned Frog to High Sheriff.* Fort Worth TX: Summit Group, 1990.

Fitzgerald, Ed, ed. *Kick-Off!* New York: Bantam, 1948.

Football Guide. St. Louis: Sporting News. 1970–2006.

Football Register. St. Louis. Sporting News. 1966–2006.

Foss, Joe, with Donna Wild Foss. *A Proud American: The Autobiography of Joe Foss.* New York: Pocket Books, 1992.

Fried, Albert. *The Rise and Fall of the Jewish Gangster in America.* New York: Columbia University Press, 1993.

Gildea, William. *When the Colts Belonged to Baltimore.* New York: Ticknor and Fields, 1994.

Gottehrer, Barry. *The Giants of New York.* New York: Putnam, 1963.

Graffis, Herbert, ed. *Esquire's First Sports Reader.* New York: Barnes, 1945.

Grange, Red, as told to Ira Morton. *The Red Grange Story.* New York: Putnam, 1953.

Green, Jerry. *Detroit Lions.* New York: Macmillan, 1973.

Griffith, Corinne. *My Life with the Redskins.* New York: Barnes, 1947.

Halas, George, with Gwen Morgan and Arthur Veysey. *Halas by Halas.* New York: McGraw-Hill, 1979.

Johnson, Chuck. *The Green Bay Packers.* New York: Thomas Nelson and Sons, 1961.

Johnson, Harold. *Who's Who in Major League Football.* National Football League, 1936.

Johnson, Harold, and Wilfrid Smith. *Who's Who in Major League Football*. National Football League, 1935.

Johnson, Pearce B., ed. *Professional Football's National Growth*. 2 vols. Providence RI: Pearce B. Johnson, n.d.

King, Joe. *Inside Pro Football*. Englewood Cliffs NJ: Prentice Hall, 1958.

Lawes, Lewis E. *Life and Death in Sing Sing*. Garden City NY: Sun Dial Press, 1937.

————. *Meet the Murderer!* New York: Harper, 1940.

————. *20,000 Years in Sing Sing*. New York: New Home Library, 1944.

Layden, Elmer, with Ed Snyder. *It Was a Different Game*. Englewood Cliffs NJ: Prentice Hall, 1969.

Levy, Bill. *Return to Glory: The Story of the Cleveland Browns*. Cleveland: World Publishing, 1965.

Lowry, Philip J. *Green Gridirons*. Professional Football Researchers Association, 1990.

Luckman, Sid. *Luckman at Quarterback*. Chicago: Ziff-Davis, 1949.

————. *Passing for Touchdowns*. Chicago: Ziff-Davis, 1948.

Lynch, Etta. *Tender Tyrant*. Canyon TX: Staked Plains Press, 1976.

March, Dr. Harry A. *Pro Football: Its Ups and Downs*. 1st and 2nd eds. Albany NY: J. B. Lyon, 1934, 1939.

McGuire, Dan. *San Francisco 49ers*. New York: Coward-McCann, 1960.

Miller, Jeff. *Going Long*. New York: Contemporary Books, 2003.

Morris, James McGrath. *The Rose Man of Sing Sing*. New York: Fordham University Press, 2003.

Names, Larry. *The History of the Green Bay Packers*. 4 vols. Wautoma WI: Angel Press, 1987, 1989, 1990, 1995.

National Football League Record and Roster Manual. National Football League, 1941–43.

National Football League, Record and Rules Manual. National Football League, 1944–61.

National Football League Record Manual. National Football League, 1962–69.

National Football League team media guides. National Football League, 1934–65.

Neft, David, and Richard Cohen. *The Sports Encyclopedia: Pro Football (The Modern Era)*. New York: St. Martin's Press, 1989.

Neft, David, Richard Cohen, et al. *The Sports Encyclopedia: Pro Football (The Early Years)*. Ridgefield CT: Sports Products, 1987.

Nelson, David M. *The Anatomy of a Game*. Newark: University of Delaware Press, 1994.

Oates, Bob. *The Los Angeles Rams*. Culver City CA: Murray and Gee, 1955.

Official Guide of the National Football League. National Football League, 1935–40.

Owen, Steve, with Joe King. *My Kind of Football*. New York: David McKay, 1952.

Palmer, Pete, et al., eds. *The ESPN Pro Football Encyclopedia*. New York: Sterling, 2006.

Patton, Phil. *Razzle Dazzle*. Garden City NY: Dial Press, 1984.

Petritz, Joe, ed. *The All-America Football Conference 1946 Information Booklet*. All-America Conference, 1946.

———. *The All-America Football Conference Record Manual*. All-America Conference, 1946–49.

———. *The All-America Football Conference Supplement to the 1949 Record Manual*. All-America Conference, 1950.

Pluto, Terry. *When All the World Was Browns Town*. New York: Simon and Schuster, 1997.

Pollack, Channing. *Harvest of My Years*. New York: Bobbs-Merrill, 1943.

Porter, David L., ed. *Biographical Dictionary of American Sports: Football*. New York: Greenwood Press, 1987.

Prochnow, Herbert V. *The Toastmaster's Handbook*. New York: Prentice Hall, 1949.

Ratterman, George, with Robert G. Deindorfer. *Confessions of a Gypsy Quarterback*. New York: Coward-McCann, 1962.

Riffenburgh, Beau. *The Official NFL Encyclopedia*. New York: New American Library, 1986.

Roberts, Howard. *The Chicago Bears*. New York: Putnam, 1947.

Robinson, Ray. *Rockne of Notre Dame*. New York: Oxford, 1999.

Sample, Johnny, with Fred J. Hamilton and Sonny Schwartz. *Confessions of a Dirty Ballplayer*. New York: Dial Press, 1970.

Shaughnessy, Clark, Ralph Jones and George Halas. *The Modern "T" Formation with Man-in-Motion*. 3rd ed. Self-published, 1946.

Shropshire, Mike. *The Ice Bowl*. New York: Penguin Putnam, 1997.

Smith, Curt. *Of Mikes and Men*. South Bend IN: Diamond, 1998.

Smith, Don. *New York Giants*. New York: Coward-McCann, 1960.

Smith, Myron. *Pro Football Bio-Bibliography*. West Cornwall CT: Locust Hill Press, 1989.

Squire, Amos O. *Sing Sing Doctor*. Garden City NY: Doubleday, 1935.

Steadman, John F. *Football's Miracle Men*. Cleveland: Pennington Press, 1959.

Stockton, J. Roy. *The Gashouse Gang and a Couple of Other Guys*. New York: Barnes, 1945.

Stram, Hank, with Lou Sahadi. *They're Playing My Game*. New York: Morrow, 1986.

Strode, Woody, and Sam Young. *Goal Dust*. Lanham MD: Madison Books, 1990.

Swain, Glenn. *Packers vs. Bears*. Oceanside CA: Charles Publishing, 1996.

Terzian, Jim. *New York Giants*. New York: Macmillan, 1973.

Thornton, Patrick K. *Sports Law*. Sudbury MA: Jones and Bartlett, 2010.

Torinus, John. *The Packer Legend*. Neshkoro WI: Laranmark Press, 1982.

Treat, Roger. *The Official National Football League Football Encyclopedia*. New York: Barnes, 1952.

Trippi, Charles. *Backfield Play*. Chicago: Ziff-Davis, 1948.

Tunnell, Emlen, and William Gleason. *Footsteps of a Giant*. Garden City NY: Doubleday, 1966.

Turner, Clyde "Bulldog." *Playing the Line*. Chicago: Ziff-Davis, 1948.

Vass, George. *George Halas and the Chicago Bears*. Chicago: Regnery, 1971.

Ward, Arch. *The Green Bay Packers*. New York: Putnam, 1946.

Whittingham, Richard. *Bears in Their Own Words*. Chicago: Contemporary Books, 1984.

———. *Giants in Their Own Words*. Chicago: Contemporary Books, 1992.

———. *What a Game They Played*. New York: Harper and Row, 1984.

Wismer, Harry. *The Public Calls It Sport*. Englewood Cliffs NJ: Prentice Hall, 1965.

Ziemba, Joe. *When Football Was Football*. Chicago: Triumph, 1999.

Other Materials

Conzelman, James G. "The Young Man's Physical and Mental Approach to War." (Address given at University of Dayton commencement, May 10, 1942.)

A Documentary Scrapbook of Football in Frankford. Frankford PA: Historical Society, 1985.

National Football League Constitution and Bylaws. National Football League, 1926.

Touchback. (National Football League newsletter sent to players in the service during World War II.)

1930 United States Census. (Via Ancestry.com.)

Newspapers and Wire Services

Associated Press

Canadian Press

News (later Newspaper) Enterprise Association

Parade Magazine

United Press/United Press International

Baltimore MD, *News and Post, Sun*

Bangor ME, *Daily News*

Boston MA, *Evening Globe, Globe, Traveler*

Canton OH, *Repository*

Chicago IL, *Daily News, Defender, Herald and Examiner, Southtown Economist, Tribune*

Cincinnati OH, *Enquirer*

Cleveland OH, *Plain Dealer, Press*

Colorado Springs CO, *Gazette*

Columbus OH, *Ohio State Journal*

Corpus Christi TX, *Times*

Dallas TX, *Morning News, Times Herald*

Decatur IL, *Daily Review*

Detroit MI, *Free Press, News*

Emporia KS, *Weekly Gazette*

Fort Worth TX, *Star-Telegram*

Gilmer TX, *Mirror*

Green Bay WI, *Press-Gazette*

Hammond IN, *Times*

Honolulu HI, *Advertiser, Star-Bulletin*

Houston TX, *Post*

Kansas City MO, *Journal*

Long Beach CA, *Press-Telegram, Independent*

Longview TX, *Daily News, Morning Journal*

Los Angeles CA, *Herald-Express, Times*

Massillon OH, *Evening Independent*

Memphis TN, *Commercial Appeal*

Miami FL, *Herald*

Milwaukee WI, *Journal, Sentinel*

Nashville TN, *Tennessean*

New Orleans LA, *Times-Picayune*

New York NY, *Brooklyn Eagle, Daily Mirror, Daily News, Evening Journal, Herald Tribune, Times, World-Telegram*

Oakland CA, *Tribune*

Ogden UT, *Standard-Examiner*

Oshkosh WI, *Daily Northwestern*
Philadelphia PA, *Bulletin, Inquirer*
Pittsburgh PA, *Post-Gazette, Press*
Portland ME, *Press Herald*
Portsmouth OH, *Times*
Providence RI, *Journal*
Reno NV, *Nevada State Journal*
San Diego CA, *Union*
San Francisco CA, *Chronicle, Examiner*
San Mateo CA, *Times*
Sheboygan WI, *Press*
Stevens Point WI, *Daily Journal*
St. Louis MO, *Post-Dispatch*
Syracuse NY, *Herald*
Toledo OH, *News-Bee*
Tulsa OK, *World*
Washington DC, *Daily News, Post, Star, Times, Times-Herald*
Wilmington DE, *Journal*
Winnipeg MT, *Free Press*

Magazines

Collier's
Football Digest
Life
Literary Digest
Look
New Yorker
Pro Football Guide
Pro Football Illustrated
Saturday Evening Post
Sport
Sporting News
Sports Illustrated
Time

Internet Sites

Pro-Football-Reference.com
Internet Movie Database (imdb.com)

Interviews

Al Baisi (Bears, 1940–41, 1946; Eagles, 1947)

Sammy Baugh (Redskins, 1937–52)

Fred Bednarski (soccer-style kicking pioneer)

Steve Belichick (Lions, 1941)

Jim Black (Staten Island Stapletons clubhouse boy)

Red Corzine (Cincinnati Reds, 1933–34; St. Louis Gunners, 1934; Giants, 1935–37)

Glenn Dobbs (Brooklyn Dodgers, AAC, 1946–47; Los Angeles Dons, AAC, 1947–49)

Walt Doleschal (soccer-style kicking pioneer)

Bob Dove (Chicago Rockets, AAC, 1946–47; Cardinals, 1948–53; Lions, 1953–54)

Sam Francis (Bears, 1937–38; Pittsburgh Pirates, 1939; Brooklyn Dodgers, 1939–40)

Bill Hoffman (Frankford Yellow Jackets, 1924–26)

Pearce Johnson (Providence Steam Roller executive)

Tom Keane (Rams, 1948–51; Dallas Texans, 1952; Colts, 1953–54; Cardinals, 1955)

Ray Kemp (Pirates, 1933)

Jim Long (retired coach, Huron College)

Blanche Luckman (Sid Luckman's sister)

Sid Luckman (Bears, 1939–50)

Gil Mains (Lions, 1953–61)

Joe Maniaci (Dodgers, 1936–38; Bears, 1938–41)

Ookie Miller (Bears, 1932–36; Rams, 1937; Packers, 1939)

Emmett Mortell (Eagles, 1937–39)

Ray Nolting (Bears, 1936–43)

Derrell Palmer (New York Yankees, AAC, 1946–48; Browns, AAC/NFL, 1949–53)

Evan Paoletti (soccer-style kicking pioneer)

Joe Perry (49ers, AAC/NFL, 1948–60, 1963; Colts, 1961–62)

Ede Prendergast (Harry March's granddaughter)

Glenn Presnell (Portsmouth Spartans/Detroit Lions, 1931–36)

Buster Ramsey (Cardinals, 1946–51)

Jack Russell (Yankees/Yanks, AAC/NFL, 1946–50)

Johnny Siegal (Bears, 1939–43)

Hank Soar (Giants, 1937–44, 1946)

George Squires (soccer-style kicking pioneer)

Russ Thompson (Bears, 1936–39; Eagles, 1940)
Tuffy Thompson (Pirates, 1937–38; Packers, 1939)
Hal Van Every (Packers, 1940–41)
Lowell Wagner (Yankees, AAC, 1946–48; 49ers, AAC/NFL, 1949–53, 1955)
Dick Weiss (Sid Luckman's son-in-law)
Johnny Wilson (Rams, 1939–42)